ITALIAN ASSAULT CRAFT

1940–1945

ITALIAN ASSAULT CRAFT
1940–1945

Human Torpedoes and other Special Attack Weapons

Erminio Bagnasco

Seaforth
PUBLISHING

Frontispiece: Upper: MTM explosive motorboats commissioned by the Israelis in 1948.
Lower: A Mk 1 'Chariot' exercising in the Mar Grande at Taranto during 1944. The craft, loaned to Mariassalto by the Royal Navy, is piloted by operators wearing Italian suits and breathing apparatus. *(Courtesy of S Battaglia)*

English translation by Alessandro Nati Fornetti

First published in Great Britain in 2023 by
Seaforth Publishing
An imprint of Pen & Sword Books Ltd
George House, Unit 12 & 13, Beevor Street,
Off Pontefract Road,
Barnsley, South Yorkshire S71 1HN

www.seaforthpublishing.com
Email info@seaforthpublishing.com

British Library Cataloguing in Publication Data
A CIP data record for this book is available from the British Library

978-1-3990-5608-3 (Hardback)
978-1-3990-5609-0 (ePub)
978-1-3990-5610-6 (Kindle)

Pen & Sword Books Limited incorporates the imprints of Atlas, Archaeology, Aviation, Discovery, Family History, Fiction, History, Maritime, Military, Military Classics, Politics, Select, Transport, True Crime, Air World, Frontline Publishing, Leo Cooper, Remember When, Seaforth Publishing, The Praetorian Press, Wharncliffe Local History, Wharncliffe Transport, Wharncliffe True Crime and White Owl.

Typeset and designed by Stephen Dent
Printed and bound in India by Replika Press Pvt. Ltd.

FSC www.fsc.org MIX Paper from responsible sources FSC® C016779

CONTENTS

INTRODUCTION AND ACKNOWLEDGEMENTS

This edition of *Italian Assault Craft 1940–1945* is inspired by the volume that I prepared with my friend Marco Spertini – who unfortunately passed away several years back – in the now distant 1991. It was the first – and is still the only – work dedicated to this typically Italian naval speciality whose content is oriented above all to the technical-historical aspects of the conception, realisation and development of our assault craft. Obviously, there is no lack of extensive references to their operational activity – a topic closely linked to the refinement of technical characteristics – which has been discussed in detail in many other works. The extraordinary endeavours that have been carried out by Italian assault operators since the Great War have in fact prompted many authors, including some of the protagonists, to produce works expressly dedicated to them, among which the most famous is undoubtedly the fundamental *Decima Flottiglia Mas. Dalle origini all'armistizio* that Commander Junio Valerio Borghese published in 1950. Following the general lines masterfully traced by Borghese, together with Marco Spertini – who had been a very young pilot of X^{a} Mas explosive motorboats – we revisited the whole subject: he mainly carried out archival research and interviews, I devoted myself to the organisation of the material collected, and definitive draft of

A 'slow-running torpedo' (or SLC, nicknamed 'pig') in Venice-S Andrea in summer 1945. *(Imperial War Museum)*

MT explosive motorboats on exercise in spring 1941.

the text, as well as taking care of the illustration of the volume.

Making use of the rare documents that could be traced – records were always considered highly confidential and often immediately destroyed – and the memories of some of the technicians and operators of the time, the book concentrated on the design and implementation aspects of the different models of assault craft which until then had almost always been hastily dealt with in literature. Much more space had in fact been given to illustrating the extraordinary actions carried out by their operators, and the remarkable successes achieved. The result was a work with many unique aspects – among which, for example, was a quantitative analysis of the production of the different types of craft (a veritable secret within a secret) which garnered considerable interest. We also paid particular attention to the designs of new models, but limited the description to the prototypes actually built, even if they were not completed, leaving out all those very numerous projects whose realisation, for a great variety of reasons, was never started either before or during the Second World War.

It is a practical impossibility to cite all those who enthusiastically contributed to the completion of this work with letters, documents, interviews and illustrative material, but at least I want to remember the agencies and people who provided the greatest collaboration, not forgetting however that many of these, by the unstoppable passage of time, have now unfortunately disappeared. First of all I want to thank the Historical Office of the Italian Navy and its pro-tempore directors; the CABI-Cattaneo Company of Milan, in the persons of the late president Bruno Orlando and the current Alberto Villa, engineer Lino Mancini and technicians Ernesto Gini and Arnaldo Pinti; the Italian Navy 'Comando Subacquei e Incursori' (COMSUBIN); the Baglietto yards of Varazze; the Officine Panerai of Florence; the Imperial War Museum in London; the Naval Historical Center of the US Navy; the 'Associazione Navimodellisti Bolognesi' and 'Gruppo di cultura navale' in the person of its president Gino Chesi; the Gold Medal holders of submarines and assault craft Mario Arillo, Gino Birindelli, Luigi Durand De La Penne, Luigi Faggioni, Luigi Ferraro, Emilio Bianchi and Evelino Marcolini; Antonio Ramognino, patron of Villa Carmela in Algeciras; Admirals Antonio Scialdone,

Securing explosive charges to a hull during assault diver training, probably in the 1950s.

Aldo Massarini, Mario De Feo, Nicola Sarto, Vezio Vascotto, Vincenzo Pellegrino, Franco Prosperini and Tiberio Moro; commanders Eugenio Massano, Sergio Nesi, Giancarlo Garello, Flavio Serafini and Giorgio Pitacco; the X^{a} Mas operators and 'Gamma' Sergio Denti, Franco Fracassini, Giuseppe Guglielmo, Armando Memoli and Mario Nardin; engineer Sebastiano Battaglia, head of Mariassalto technical department in 1944–1945; architect Franco Harrauer, a skilled and imaginative designer, engineer Licio Sassaroli; Antonio Fulvi, who provided me with copies of precious unpublished notes by Admiral Ernesto Forza; my friends Lorenzo Bovi, Luigi Carretta, Joseph Caruana, Enrico Cernuschi, Marco Gemignani, Giorgio Giorgerini, Mark Grossman, Paul Kemp, Tullio Marcon, Giorgio Martini, Decio Romano, Guido Ronconi and Alberto Santoni.

Finally, special thanks go to the collectors and profound connoisseurs of naval images Guido Alfano, Giorgio Arra, Franco Bargoni, Maurizio Brescia, Aldo Fraccaroli, Aureliano Molinari, Fulvio Petronio and Achille Rastelli, holders of important photographic collections, whose names often appear as credit in many of this volume's captions.

Milan, November 2019
E Bagnasco

Erminio Bagnasco co-founded *STORIA Militare* monthly with Ermanno Albertelli in 1993, and was its editor for many years. Formerly a senior officer of the Italian Navy and later an industrial manager, he was the author of numerous books on the history of contemporary warships published both in Italy and abroad. He died in Milan on 13 January 2022.

Part 1

ORIGINS, DEVELOPMENT AND USE OF ASSAULT CRAFT

In the naval field an assault craft is generally a small boat with special features or unusual purpose. It is capable of inflicting damage upon a much bigger and heavily armed enemy, mainly through surprise. It may even consist in a single man with unique equipment, as in the case of frogmen.

The first assault craft in naval history were the infamous fireships of the sail and oar era. These generally small, low-value craft were loaded with flammable materials; set on fire at the last moment, they were left to drift on wind and current towards a fleet at anchor or unable to manoeuvre quickly, starting awful fires aboard the wooden vessels of that time. During the American Civil War (1861–1865) fireships were supplemented by the first, pioneering underwater or semi-submersible craft. Conceived to attack Unionist ships blockading Confederate harbours at anchor, they obtained a few unforeseen successes, though at a high price.

Nevertheless, with the rapid establishment of mechanical propulsion and the spread of iron shipbuilding, fireships and small, pioneering, often hand-powered submarines lost their efficacy: it was not until the second decade of the twentieth century that new, hard-hitting assault craft were to see action.

The Great War and the birth of assault craft in Italy

During the First World War the unique geostrategic situation of the Adriatic Sea pushed the Italian Admiralty Board towards the development of new weapons with a specific purpose, allowing attacks on the Austro-Hungarian battlefleet which sheltered in well-defended bases, as it had no realistic opportunity to engage the larger and more powerful Allied battlefleets at sea.

The first and most important of these craft was definitely the Mas (M.A.S.= Motobarca Armata Silurante

Venice, spring 1918. Admiral Paolo Tahon de Revel, in the grey-green coat, aboard a 'jumping' boat ready for an exercise in the Lagoon. The first unit to the left is *Pulce*. *(Courtesy of* STORIA Militare*)*

Venice Shipyards, 1917. Two close-ups of the 'jumping' boat prototype. In the top picture the early hook and its driving cables are clearly visible under the bow; later these would be replaced by two chain tracks with crampons running around the wales, allowing the boat to overcome the floating obstructions in Pola harbour. *(A Molinari collection)*

or Motobarca Armata SVAN, from the name of the first builder's yard): a motor torpedo boat, later converted to an anti-submarine motorboat (still named MAS, though with a different meaning: Motobarca o Motoscafo Anti Sommergibili), reverting to anti-ship torpedo tasks, where it achieved the greatest successes. The first war actions of the torpedo-armed Mas – boats about 12 metres long with a maximum speed of just over 23 knots – followed the standard tactics of assault craft: stealthy penetration of enemy harbours and bases unprepared to defend against this new form of attack.[1] Overcoming the initial surprise, albeit slowly, the Hapsburg Navy prepared such defences for its anchorages that the Mas were no longer effective, even though by then they had been fitted with electric motors for silent approach, and cutting or lowering equipment to deal with boom defences. As a result, torpedo boats began switching their attention to ships at sea in coastal waters; however, at the same time, investigations began into new technology specifically designed for the stealthy forcing of enemy bases.

1. On 7 June 1916, *MAS 5* (tv Berardinelli) and *7* (tv Pagano di Melito) obtained the first success with the new torpedo craft, penetrating into Durazzo harbour (Albania) and sinking the Austrian steamer *Lokrum*. There were many more similar actions by the Mas – which again attacked Durazzo, in addition to the Fažana Channel and the port of Buccari – achieving their greatest success on 10 December 1917, when *MAS 9* and *13* (under the command of tv Luigi Rizzo) forced the port of Trieste, sinking the coastal battleship *Wien* and retiring unharmed. From late 1917, however, the torpedo Mas were also used against moving targets, and on 10 June 1918, *MAS 15*, commanded by Luigi Rizzo, achieved the greatest Italian naval success of the entire conflict, sinking the modern dreadnought *Stzent Istvan* off the islet of Premuda, in Dalmatia, with two torpedoes.

GRILLO TYPE 'JUMPING' BOATS

In June 1917 engineer Attilio Bisio of the SVAN shipyards of Venice presented the project of a light motorboat, armed with a torpedo and crewed by a single operator, equipped to overcome the obstructions of an enemy port in a similar way to that used by Mas for forcing the Fasana Channel anchorage (2 November 1916), or through the submerging of floating obstructions by the application of large weights.

The Regia Marina Chief of Staff, ammiraglio Paolo Tahon di Revel, appointed a commission composed of capitano di vascello Pignatti di Morano and capitano di fregata Costanzo Ciano, with the task of evaluating the actual capabilities of the craft proposed and, if necessary, to suggest the most suitable features for a possible forcing of Pola harbour whose floating defences, at the narrow entrance, could not be overcome by the use of weights. A craft capable of quickly climbing the booms appeared necessary, and so the subsequent studies were directed to that end.

A prototype experimental craft was quickly and secretly built by the royal dockyard of Venice. The craft was intended to 'jump' the obstructions with rapid changes in its longitudinal balance: initially, by lowering the stern first, and the bow immediately after, but the results achieved were not satisfactory. A later idea was to fit the sides of the craft (which was raft-like in form) with two gunwale chains, equipped with crampons and held in tension by three pairs of pulleys, sliding within two guides like the tracks of a tank. The movement of the two chains, driven by an electric motor, allowed the boat to cling to the floating obstruction, then clamber over it until jumping past.

A series of tests with a prototype was successfully completed by the end of 1917 and the construction of a series of four units was begun in the same dockyard. They were nicknamed 'marine tanks' for their similarity to the British armoured vehicles of the time, or most commonly 'jumping boats', hence their naming after jumping insects: *Grillo, Cavalletta, Locusta* and *Pulce*. The building of the four small boats proceeded fairly quickly, and by February 1918 they were ready for trials. These units had a weight of about 8 tons, with a 16m long, 3.10m wide flat wooden hull, and about 70cm maximum draught.

Propulsion was by two battery-powered 5hp electric motors. These engines drove a propeller placed in a

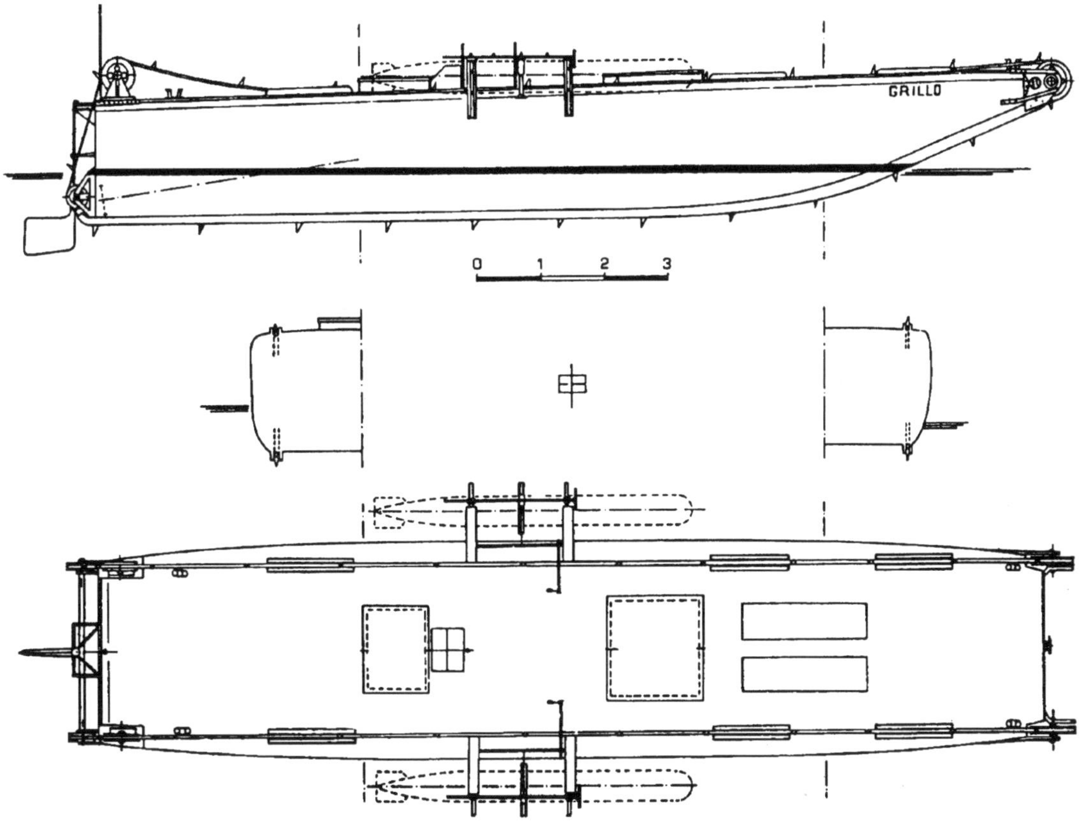

Some pictures taken inside the Venice Shipyards in spring 1918, showing the four newly completed 'jumping' boats. *(USMM)*

recess in the stern area in order to protect it from damage while climbing the obstructions. The rudder was immediately aft of the propeller, protruding about 50cm below the keel and fitted with a lifting system. The two motors could be separated mechanically from the propeller shaft and linked to the 'track' system which they drove through the axles of the two lower stern toothed pulleys.

The movement of the tracks, and an appropriate

change of longitudinal balance of the craft obtained by moving weights from stern to bow, made it possible to climb over obstructions of considerable size: some trials carried out in Venice proved that a 5m wide obstruction could be crossed in 2 minutes and 40 seconds. Due to the particular hull shape, seaworthiness of these boats was definitely mediocre and their maximum speed over calm water was just about 4 knots, with range of about 30 miles, corresponding to little more than seven hours while on the move.

Armament comprised two racks for 450mm torpedoes fitted with cutters to pierce common torpedo nets. The four-man crew could access the interior of the hull through a watertight door on the deck but – with the exception of the commander who stood at the helm in the stern cockpit – during attacks the crew were kept lying on the deck in order to operate the rudder lifting device and torpedo launchers.

All phases of construction and trials of the 'jumpers' were carried out in maximum secret, an element that constituted one of the fundamental reasons for their success. To prevent their capture by the enemy if discovered during an action or after the launch of torpedoes, they were equipped with a self-destruction system composed of small explosive charges connected to each other which, together with the opening of some valves in the hull, was to ensure their quick sinking. Being exclusively equipped with electric motors suitable for low-speed silent movement, the 'jumpers' needed assistance from what the Italians termed an 'approacher' which brought them near the enemy target base; then, inside the limits of their short range, they would proceed on their own power. Small torpedo boats were chosen for this task; these would tow them for the longer journeys, then pass the tow to Mas equipped with electric motors for the last part of the approach. However, in May 1918 a special timber slide was fitted on the stern of the 'Pilo' class destroyer *Abba* to transport and launch the 'jumper' at a point close to its target. The inspiration for this arrangement was the failure of the first attempts at forcing Pola, mainly due to delays occurred during the long voyages of the craft under tow by torpedo boats in unfavourable sea conditions. However, the facilities of the *Abba* were never used, and the unfortunate 13 May 1918 operation of the *Grillo* employed the usual towing procedures, albeit in good weather conditions.

After its scuttling on 13 May, the wreck of the *Grillo* was recovered by the Austro-Hungarian navy; summarily repaired, it was found in Pola at the end of the conflict. Today, some fragments of the unit's bow are preserved like heirlooms in Italian naval museums.

Cavalletta and *Pulce* were scuttled off Pola on 13 April 1918 to avoid holding up the return journey of the support units after it was decided to abandon the action because of accumulated delays. *Locusta*, the only 'jumper' to survive the conflict, remained decommissioned for some time, and was finally broken up shortly after 1921. All the light boats of this type are registered in the 'Quadro del Naviglio Militare' (Register of Military Ships) as 'motoscafo speciale d'assalto' (special assault motorboat).

The birth of the first real naval assault craft dates back to the beginning of 1917 when engineer Attilio Bisio – director of the aforementioned SVAN (Società Veneziana Automobili Navali) shipyard, which was the first Mas builder – was given charge of a project for a new torpedo-armed craft able to climb over the fixed obstructions defending the main enemy naval bases, and notably that of Pola, which consisted in large and robust floating booms supporting steel nets that extended down to the seabed.

Following tests and experiments carried out with a prototype throughout 1917, the features of the type of craft considered most suitable for this purpose were finally defined: it became known as a 'jumping boat', from its ability to silently cross the sturdy floating obstructions of the type used in the fortified Istrian base. Four examples were immediately and secretly constructed in Venice, being ready for use by March 1918 – they were assigned the names *Grillo*, *Cavalletta*, *Locusta* and *Pulce* after species of 'jumping' insects.

Fitted with electric motors powered by accumulators, they employed chains with crampons – similar to caterpillar tracks – to climb over the floating obstructions. Carrying two torpedoes and a crew of four, these craft – sometimes called 'marine tanks' because of their tracks – attempted four missions against Pola between April and May 1918; all had to be called off because of delays and accidents during towing towards the target.

Finally on 13 May 1918 the *Grillo* alone succeeded in reaching Pola's harbour booms: it was immediately discovered but, despite intense fire from the defences, it quickly managed to get over four of the five lines of obstructions that blocked the mouth of the port. Then, with the craft badly damaged by fire and the entire

Major (engineer) Raffaele Rossetti in 1918.

Captain (medical corps) Raffaele Paolucci towards the end of 1918.

base now alert, the motorboat commanding officer, tenente di vascello Mario Pellegrini, was forced to order its scuttling.

The substantial failure of the action showed that, despite the undoubted ingenuity of the craft, the defences of a large naval base such as that of Pola were not easily bypassed on the surface and that recourse should be made, as we shall see, to something much less visible. The end of hostilities in early November 1918, however, halted the preparations for an attempt to force the port of Fiume to be carried out later that month with the *Locusta*. Some changes had been made to this craft, which carried out numerous trials in October 1918; it would have also carried some swimmers, with the task of applying magnetic charges equipped with clockwork activation devices to the hulls of enemy ships. It is interesting to underline this particular use of operators, who did not yet have diving skills, but nevertheless constitutes an anticipation of what, a little over twenty years later, would be successfully entrusted to the assault divers called 'Gamma'.

Also with the aim of infiltrating enemy naval bases, at the end of 1917 some studies and experiments began in Venice by modifying some 'A' and 'B' type mini-submarines, together with the standard type submarine *Galileo Ferraris*. These boats were equipped with special devices to silently overcome the enemy obstructions, and with 'decompression chambers' (or 'Belloni tanks') to allow the exit of a small group of 'autonomous divers', equipped with special diving suits and explosive charges to be applied to enemy hulls.

Both the conception and construction of the aforementioned equipment, in addition to that of the special autonomous diving suits, were the work of (by then) tenente di vascello Angelo Belloni, an ingenious inventor who remained intimately linked to the development of Italian underwater assault craft right down until the end of the Second World War. Despite the trust Admiral Tahon di Revel placed in Belloni, his experiments conducted during the Great War did not lead to tangible results, probably because, despite his genius, times and techniques were not yet ripe. However, although abandoned with the end of the conflict, those same studies would constitute the starting point for their resurrection towards the end of the 1920s.

Overcoming the unbreachable obstructions of Pola, and above all avoiding the strict vigilance with which they were protected, required something really unusual. This realisation turned attention to other types of proposals that had not aroused any interest previously. In particular, there were the projects of capitano (engineer corps) Raffaele Rossetti and tenente (medical corps) Raffaele Paolucci, who separately studied two different systems for breaking into a large naval base and sinking the ships at anchor. The first, through a self-propelled semi-submersible device of his own invention, very similar to a torpedo, equipped with explosive charges and conducted by one or two operators; the second, by simply towing a large explosive charge.

Engineer Rossetti had started working on his project in September 1915 while following the preparation and trials between Genoa and La Spezia of some new scouts built by Ansaldo. The idea was suggested to him by petty officer Luigi Martignani, 'engine accountant' aboard the scout *Poerio*, who proposed to use a suitably modified normal torpedo, ridden by an operator. Discarding this idea initially for the obvious reason of transverse stability, Rossetti first envisaged a torpedo with enlarged propellers, running on the surface at low speed, with an operator lying on top and towing a normal torpedo to be aimed at the target once it had reached a suitable distance; this later became a similar device, but with two operators, and equipped with detachable explosive charges. These two proposals were supported by some trials carried out secretly and with various expedients, including 'stealing' an old 'B.57' torpedo from the Mas boats. He had informed some of his superiors about his activities, but until early 1918 he had obtained no official (or even unofficial) authorisation to carry out his project.

Doctor Paolucci was embarked on the old battleship *Emanuele Filiberto*, often at anchor in the Venice lagoon in those days. A strong and enthusiastic swimmer, he was convinced he could tow a large explosive charge for a voyage of about three kilometres, which was the distance he calculated between the external obstructions of Pola and the moorings of large ships in the roadstead, with time to complete the attack during the hours of darkness in the winter months. With this in mind, he had secretly started training in the cold waters of the lagoon from February 1917, reaching in a reasonable time distances of about 4 kilometres (Malamocco-Pomeglia) at first, and finally almost 8, dragging a barrel ballasted to simulate a charge of about 150kg with a slight positive buoyancy. Actually, the routes that would have had to be completed within the Pola roadstead to reach the targets were significantly longer, but these were good performances, also considering the lack of suitable clothing.

The (then) capitano di vascello Costanzo Ciano, leader of Mas flotillas, who was in charge of all projects for attacks on enemy bases, was made aware of the activities of these two officers in the first months of 1918. He came up with the idea of unifying their approaches: that is, two skilled and capable swimmers who would have used the 'self-propelled Rossetti torpedo' to carry charges to be dragged under the target.

The dockyard of Venice was commissioned to build two devices as soon as possible, designated *S.1* and *S.2*,[2] following the technical specification provided by engineer Rossetti. After making various improvements and changes to the original concept, the first of the two self-propelled craft was ready to begin the working-up phase and the operators' training sessions at the end of May 1918. To carry out the planned action Rossetti, now promoted to maggiore, had requested as his 'second' Giuseppe Sanna, who had worked with him since the unofficial first experiments conducted with a 'B.57' type torpedo; but Captain Ciano chose doctor Paolucci both because he was a better swimmer, and because it was preferable to entrust a frontline operation to a soldier.

Training and tests – including swimming over obstructions of various types in almost complete silence – lasted all summer in the waters of the Venice lagoon, especially at night, while continuous modifications were made to the craft; only by the end of September 1918 could men and equipment be considered ready for deployment. On 19 October, Admiral Tahon di Revel gave the order to attack Pola during the period of new moon in the early part of November and in the following days exercises were intensified under particularly realistic conditions: these included the attack on a sailing ship at anchor off Punta della Salute, starting from inside the Dockyard and covering all the San Marco basin, which was completed successfully on 25 October, and a long distance trial conducted two days later in the San Clemente channel.

Finally, in a thick fog on the afternoon of

2. In the Italian Navy, 'caratteristica' (characteristic) is the numeric or alphanumeric abbreviation which replaces the name for small units or vessels, generally for local use.

The Austro-Hungarian battleship *Viribus Unitis* sank in Pola on the morning of 1 November 1918 at the end of the action by Rossetti and Paolucci with the *S.2* 'mignatta'. The *Viribus Unitis* was the first important victim of the Italian assault craft.

31 October, the mission set out from Venice with the *S.2* device, meanwhile unofficially nicknamed *Mignatta*, which had been hoisted on board the steam torpedo boat *65 PN* the previous evening. After completing the last miles of the long approach to the enemy base of Pola in tow of the *MAS 95*, at 22.31 of the same day the craft set off on its own electric motors, and its operators were left alone to move towards the external obstructions of the harbour. By 03.00 Rossetti and Paolucci had managed to overcome the various orders of obstructions without being discovered, by using the small spaces existing between the floats of the boom defences themselves; they then began the final approach to the target, the nearest of a long line of big ships at anchor, designated as the main objective of the action. It was the modern dreadnought *Viribus Unitis* of 21,370 tons, sister-ship of the *Szent Istvan* sunk by Luigi Rizzo's Mas off Premuda on the previous 10 June.

At 05.30, after 'reveille' had already sounded on board the battleship, the first charge of the *Mignatta* was attached to the hull of the target, under the engine room area; the time fuse was immediately initiated. Dawn was now approaching and, having been discovered in the meantime, the two operators also activated the second charge of the craft. While they were being hoisted aboard, a surveillance motorboat directed the device with the propellers in motion towards the inside of the harbour. The craft travelled about 500 metres and ended up under the stern of the big steam liner *Wien* moored in the Vergarola basin: the subsequent explosion caused the sinking of the steamer as well as the complete destruction of the *Mignatta*. Shortly after, the first charge also exploded, opening a large hole in the hull of the *Viribus Unitis* that caused its loss in a few hours.

Taken aboard the battleship they had attacked, Rossetti and Paolucci acted out a drama very similar to the well known story of tenente di vascello Luigi Durand de La Penne twenty-two years later in Alexandria on board the battleship HMS *Valiant* that he had placed in similar jeopardy. They warned the ship command of the danger that the ship was in, advising immediate evacuation of the crew to avoid

ROSSETTI SELF-PROPELLED TORPEDO ('MIGNATTA')

Two of these semi-submersible craft were built (*S.1* and *S.2*) at the workshops of the royal dockyard of Venice between spring and summer of 1918 to a design by (then) capitano (engineer) Raffaele Rossetti. Several modifications were made to his plans during construction and after tests carried out in the Venice lagoon between June and October 1918.

Generally similar to a torpedo in appearance, the craft was little less than 8m long, and the cylindrical body had a diameter of 600mm. The propulsion was by the unheated compressed air-powered machinery from an A 115 x 5.230 'Schneider' built torpedo, fitted with two big four-blade coaxial propellers already successfully tested on the 'B.57' torpedo in the first experiments by Rossetti. The compressed air contained in the high-strength steel

Gold Medal General (medical corps) Raffaele Paolucci on the quarterdeck of a torpedo boat in 1938. *(USMM)*

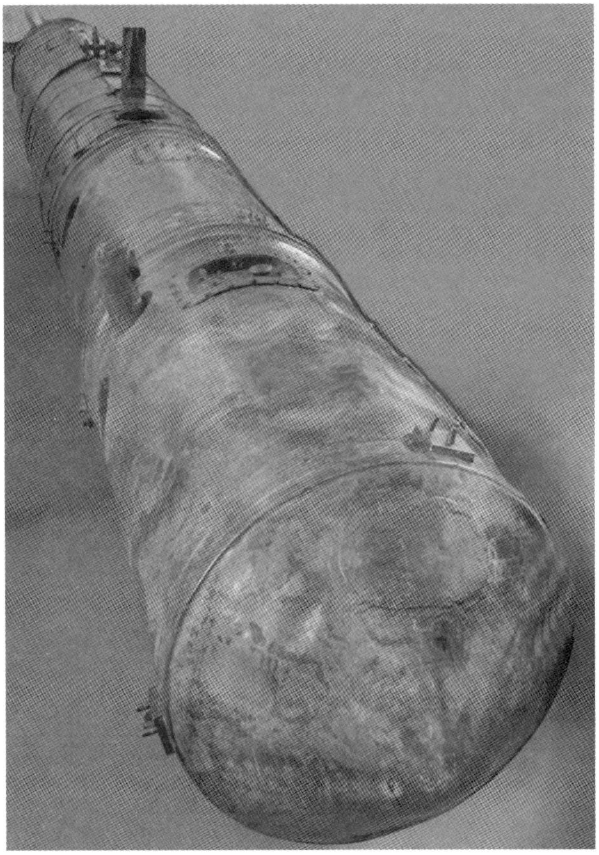

Close-up of the *S.1* 'mignatta' now on display in the Naval Technical Museum in La Spezia.

tank, located close to the centre of the weapon at a pressure of 205kg/cm^2, was brought to the operating pressure of 130-150kg/cm^2 and allowed a range of about 10 miles at the maximum speed of about 2 knots.

The device had two steel sheet cylindrical explosive charges containing 175kg of TNT each and fitted with a clockwork fuse with a maximum setting of six hours. The charges were placed one after the other forward of the compressed air tank, and the front one was equipped with a truncated-cone fore section to reduce resistance. The central body, clad in wooden staves held by several copper hoops, contained the big compressed air tank and, at the centre of gravity of the weapon, was a metal frame equipped with an eyebolt for lifting the craft during launch and recovery operations. A truncated-cone section, also covered with wood, was connected to the stern of the cylindrical body centre; it contained the engine and a tank which could be emptied by compressed air to control the longitudinal balance of the craft. The crew could ride the craft, one behind the other but, when advancing in such configuration, the craft took such a stern-down attitude that the rear man (Paolucci) was immersed almost to his neck. To escape being frequently plunged underwater, also to avoid the effects of small waves, the crew generally preferred being carried along the sides of the craft, hanging on to special handles on the centre body. A most important precaution for the

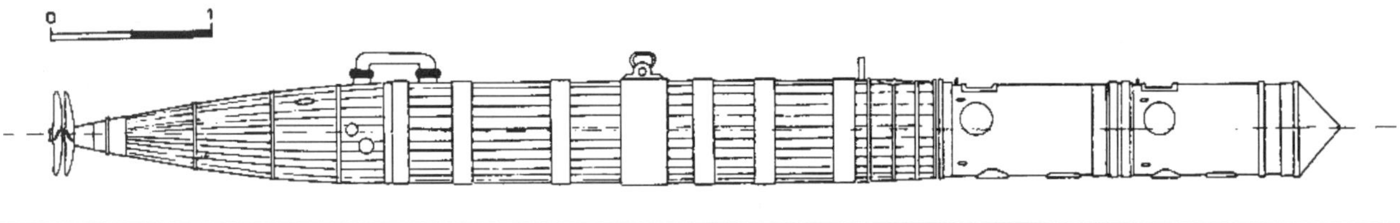

crew was always keeping forward of the propellers – which were not surrounded by any guard – to avoid injury.

The self-propelled craft was not equipped with a rudder: in order to change the direction of travel, the two operators had to increase the craft's resistance on the side towards which they intended to turn, by stretching out arms and legs. The only propulsion control was the key of the valve that opened, closed and adjusted the flow of compressed air from the tank to the engine. Other valves controlled the filling and emptying of the aforementioned small aft trim tank. A self-destruct device, probably made up of a small explosive charge with a clockwork fuse, was placed in the aft section. A magnetic or electromagnetic system – from which the unofficial nickname of *Mignatta* (leech) probably derived – was initially envisaged to secure the charges to the metallic hulls of the target; but it seems that during of the attack on the *Viribus Unitis* the charge was secured (also or only) with rope sections.

The two operators were equipped, in addition to 'wools' like those of the divers, with a drysuit in waterproof cloth with upturned collar, closed at the front by metal clasps and with rubber wrist rings, complete with a unproofed hood which left face and ears free.

The self-propelled Rossetti torpedo was designed to have a positive buoyancy of just a few kilograms and navigate semi-surfaced; the two coaxial and counter-rotating propellers guaranteed a certain course stability, but the two operators, riding in the water, could correct the course when necessary. In order to overcome obstructions, the operators generally stopped the propellers, and swam pushing the craft through any narrow passages which they could find, taking the utmost care not to produce any kind of unusual noise.

Notwithstanding the genius and originality of its concept as a genuine assault craft, the *Mignatta* was essentially a rather primitive semi-submersible device, whose employment required truly exceptional efforts and performance by the operators. Its chances of success depended most of all on the surprise factor as was indeed achieved. To this we must certainly add a good dose of luck and, it must be admitted, a certain relaxation of enemy vigilance in those abnormal days just before the armistice and the end of conflict.

With the hostilities over, the only self-propelled Rossetti torpedo left available, *S.1*, was retained for some time probably in Venice, locked in a shed of the dockyard, to be entrusted to the Naval Museum of La Spezia some time before 1924. It is still preserved there today, and exhibited next to a specimen of an SLC (slow running torpedo) or 'pig', an underwater assault craft of the Second World War of which the *Mignatta* was certainly the precursor.

The *S.1* 'mignatta' as displayed in the 1920s. Compared to its present preserved condition, several more small fittings can be seen.

unnecessary human loss. But once aboard, Rossetti and Paolucci also had a surprise: *Viribus Unitis* was no longer the flagship of the Imperial Royal Austro-Hungarian navy, having been transferred to the newly-established Yugoslav state a few days previously. Along with all the other units of the fleet, it had been ceded in an attempt, ultimately proved useless, to avoid its capture by the forces of the Entente, whose complete victory was now imminent.

Rossetti and Paolucci were in fact released a few days later with the entry into Pola of the first Italian warships following the armistice, and both were decorated with the Gold Medal for Military Valour for their exceptional achievement.[3]

During the Great War the Italian Navy was the only one among the belligerents to conceive and implement genuine assault craft. As will be seen, this was a speciality that would be consolidated with the coming of the Second World War.

From 1916 the Royal Navy commissioned torpedo boats known as CMBs (Coastal Motor Boats) that were similar to Italian Mas boats but faster, although of much lighter construction and much less seaworthy. However, it was only after the end of the war that these craft achieved significant operational successes in forcing enemy harbours, and even then in very particular situations like those of the attacks conducted in the Baltic anchorages against ex-Russian Navy ships commissioned by the Soviets in 1919.

The Germans planned and employed, mainly for defensive purpose, a particular type of 'explosive motorboat' which in concept was an updating of the 'coast-saver' idea, created by the Austrian Giovanni Luppis around 1860. This autonomous explosive craft was not a practical weapon but is best remembered for inspiring the subsequent development of the torpedo by Robert Whitehead. The FL ('Fern Lenk-Boote') were unmanned boats, 13 metres long, containing a charge of 700kg of TNT, which were guided towards enemy ships by coastal stations – sometimes assisted by seaplanes – by electrical pulses transmitted through a thin insulated copper cable that paid out from a drum placed on the stern of the motorboat itself. Designed around 1906, about fifteen were built in 1915. The only success of any importance achieved by the 'FL' was the damaging of the monitor HMS *Erebus* of about 8450 tons off the coast of Ostend on 28 October 1917. Despite the really remarkable weight and power of the warhead, its explosion did not prove enough to sink the British ship: it went off at sea level at the moment of impact of *FL 12* against the target, discharging most of its energy into the air. Therefore, only the large anti-torpedo bulge of the *Erebus* was damaged, and later repaired in 30 days of drydock work. Much more damage would have resulted had the

3. The bold sinking of the *Viribus Unitis* had some little-known ramifications that are worth recording for completeness. The High Council of the Italian Royal Navy established a suitable cash prize for the destruction of the enemy unit, to be divided equally between the two operators and capitano di vascello Costanzo Ciano, organiser of the endeavour, in which he had participated aboard *MAS 95*. The honour, however, did not recognise engineer Rossetti, in the meantime promoted to tenente colonnello of the Genio Navale, who was the sole 'father' of the self-propelled craft that bore his name: instead, it credited its invention partly to Ciano. This was a source of bitter controversy between Rossetti and the Ministry of the Navy; although Ciano declared himself in support of Rossetti, the dispute caused the latter to resign from the Navy, and take political positions that later pushed him to travel to Paris and join the anti-fascist exiles of the Rosselli brothers circle.

system been set up to blow the main charge of these speedboats at depth, as was to be implemented on the Italian 'explosive motorboats' of the Second World War.

Projects and experiments in the 1920s and 1930s

The brilliant actions carried out by Italian assault craft – and in particular the destruction of the *Viribus Unitis* which had huge potential significance – demonstrated both the validity of the concept and the effectiveness of the execution. Nevertheless, after the war this type of operation was not the subject of particular attention in the naval world, absorbed above all in those years by the search for new technical features for large ships in the light of recent war experiences, by analysis of the submarine war, and developments in embarked aviation. It was only necessity that re-awakened interest in methods of special assault: and it happened once more in Italy, as will be seen, at the time of the Ethiopian campaign.

Even earlier however, in August 1929, a new series of underwater experiments had started, aimed at proving the effectiveness of the improvements made to the 'Belloni tank' [a submarine escape chamber for divers] and to the self-contained breathing apparatus of divers, now equipped with the new, simple 'Belloni hood' (*cappuccio Belloni*). Some submarines took part (*F 17, N 5* and the modern *Toti*), with good results in the exit and recovery of the divers, and in the precision underwater navigation tests, using compensating chain

Mini-submarine *B.3* in drydock in Venice, fitted with special tracks to ease movements along the bottom. It is one of the few known pictures of a series of experiments, probably caried out at the end of the Great War, with the aim of forcing enemy bases with submarines. *(A Curami collection)*

Left and below: Two pictures of a German FL type remote-control explosive motorboat of the First World War.

sections hanging outboard whose presence allowed the submarine to proceed fairly easily just a few metres above the bottom. The goal was always to infiltrate enemy bases and to facilitate the 'approach' to the targets by autonomous divers, thereafter followed by a hard march across the sea bottom, carrying their offensive charges on their shoulders. This was a very difficult procedure to implement, and also restricted by the still rather limited range of the breathing apparatus of the time.

The Italian campaign to conquer Ethiopia started in October 1935, and immediately provoked a serious crisis in foreign relations, especially with Great Britain, and later led to economic sanctions applied against the Kingdom of Italy by the League of Nations. The deployment of large parts of the British Home Fleet to the Mediterranean, in addition to the considerable number of Royal Navy warships already located in this area, had significantly altered the ratio of forces with the Italian Navy, despite its current expansionary phase. Only the mass use of new weapons against the British fleet could reduce this disparity, re-establishing a more acceptable balance.

It was within this context that the use of assault craft returned to the top of the Regia Marina's agenda, but with completely new equipment and procedures. Two young engineer corps officers, Teseo Tesei and Elios Toschi, proposed the building of a 'submarine self-propelled craft', which consisted in a submarine version of the original *Mignatta* by Rossetti; and Admiral Aimone di Savoia-Aosta that of an 'explosive motorboat' transported close the targets to be attacked by SM.55 flying boats, as suggested by his brother Amedeo, Duke of Aosta and Regia Aeronautica general. From these two embryonic proposals, and from the experiments that were immediately authorised by the Regia Marina Chief of Naval Operations ammiraglio Domenico Cavagnari, were born the two main types of assault craft that Italian sailors would later employ, with noted success, during the Second World War: the *Siluro a Lenta Corsa*, abbreviated 'SLC', a slow-running torpedo, nicknamed the *Maiale* or 'pig', and the 'explosive motorboat', conventionally 'MT' (Motoscafo Turismo, touring boat).

The prototypes of the two craft were prepared quite quickly and, despite the technical difficulties encountered in their construction, they demonstrated the possibility of extensive improvements, also giving some flattering indications of their potential success – always assuming that the most rigorous secrecy was maintained around them, and their operating modes.

The intention was to make mass use of them in the first few nights of a possible conflict, taking full advantage of the element of surprise. This was a rather optimistic evaluation, given that maintaining absolute confidentiality would inevitably have been compro-

A twin-hull S.55 flying boat in the 1930s. The original 'explosive motorboats' project envisaged the use of this model for target 'approaching'.

One of the 'self-propelled mine' prototypes, later to become the 'slow-running torpedo' (SLC), brainchild of Teseo Tesei and Elios Toschi. *(USMM)*

mised with the expansion of the organisation in charge of the building of the craft, and the recruitment and training of crews which would have been made necessary by the planned simultaneous use of many craft at the start of hostilities. It is true that the units in charge of the later development and use of assault craft in the Regia Marina (Flottiglia Mas Speciale and later Xª Flottiglia Mas) generally managed to keep the secret of their actions during the course of the Second World War, but this was only possible because the people directly involved in the activity did not exceed a few dozen, at least initially.

The favourable conclusion of the Ethiopian campaign in the late spring of 1936 and the relative relaxation in international tension that followed, also resulted in a loss of interest in assault craft by the Stato Maggiore of the Regia Marina. In a decision that subsequent events would reveal as very short-sighted, the prototypes of the submarine self-propelled craft were almost immediately consigned to storage, followed by the explosive motorboats shortly afterwards, while the technicians and operators who had carried out the first tests were assigned to other tasks and different service appointments.

At the same time as the initial development of the 'self-propelled Tesei craft' which led to the building of the first prototypes, it had been recognised that their 'approach' to the targets was a problem, given the rather modest endurance of both the craft and the breathing apparatus of the operators, consisting at that time of modified 'Davis' oxygen models. Using a submarine appeared the most obvious way: a pair of self-propelled craft could easily be placed on deck saddles; after secretly overcoming the obstructions of the enemy base, they would be released directly into the harbour. A second penetration of the obstructions in order to leave the port was considered problematic so the submarine, once it had released its self-propelled

Submarine *H 6*, fitted with the special device to overcome harbour defence barriers while submerged, pictured at La Spezia in 1936 *(USMM)*.

Three telling images of the equipment used by 'bottom walkers' in 'heavy' trim, brainchild of Angelo Belloni, from which Eugenio Wolk would later develop the 'Gamma'. *(USMM)*

craft, was intended to act autonomously with its own torpedoes, and finally to be scuttled at the end of the action.

Following this operational plan, two of the small and handy 'H' class boats (*H 6* and *H 8*) were assigned to the relevant experiments. In January 1936 the first of the two submarines, the *H 6*, was fitted in the La Spezia dockyard with a special piece of equipment called the 'mobile runner' which, with the help of a couple of autonomous divers exiting the submarine, should allow the passage of the boat under a suitably raised floating anti-submarine net. Transferred in Porto Santo Stefano at the end of the following month, the *H 6* successfully completed a first test of passing an obstruction. The proof was to be repeated in April in La Spezia under hydrophone control, since maximum silence was required for the operation. The test carried out on 15 April 1936 was a complete failure due to the

An SLC being launched for a drill at the Bocca di Serchio base, probably in 1941.

malfunctioning of the 'mobile runner'; the second, held in May, did not go much better and it was decided to make substantial changes to the equipment which finally allowed easy overcoming of underwater obstacles in July and August 1937, even though it created significant noise.

Meanwhile, given the normalisation of international politics, the interest in assault craft was somewhat diminished. Furthermore, the improvement in the performance of self-propelled craft and the increase in the range of the new self-contained breathing apparatus persuaded the Regia Marina that the SLCs could be released by the 'approacher' submarine just outside the enemy harbour, and would then be able to overcome the obstructions on their own. For these reasons the trials with the *H 6* were suspended: having disembarked the special equipment, it returned to its normal duties.

Development and use of Italian assault craft 1940–1943

It was only towards the end of 1938 that Italy resumed studies and experiments related to naval assault craft, in anticipation of a likely short-term deterioration in international relations, However, despite the renewed commitment, the two years lost in the interim would no longer allow such mass use of sufficiently tested equipment that had been foreseen by the creators for the first days of war.

The new European conflict, soon destined to become world-wide, had broken out for the Italians earlier than expected in June 1940. It would find the Regia Marina still with few – and not yet fully developed – assault craft and relevant underwater and surface 'approachers'.

A first action with self-propelled type SLCs against the fleet at moorings in the British base of Alexandria in Egypt had been planned since July 1939, but would be cancelled in the summer of the following year with the loss of two 'approacher' submarines (*Iride* and *Gondar*) and of valuable materials and trained operators. A little less unfortunate, but again with no results, were the first, similar missions against Gibraltar. As was unfortunately predictable, all these attempts began to alert the British to the possibility, not yet well defined, of attacks with unconventional submarine craft against the fleet within their bases.

The first success was obtained by the 'explosive motorboats' in Suda Bay, on the island of Crete, on 25 March 1941 with the immobilisation and subsequent loss of the heavy cruiser HMS *York*. However, the capture, on the same occasion, of one of the small motorboats left unexploded revealed to the British the performance and operating method of Italian surface assault craft.

From then on it was only possible to achieve a few tactical surprises – and this happened more than once with good results – but the strategic surprise, which had been hypothesised by the creators of the craft, had now vanished. All successes obtained subsequently would be achieved with much more effort and at the

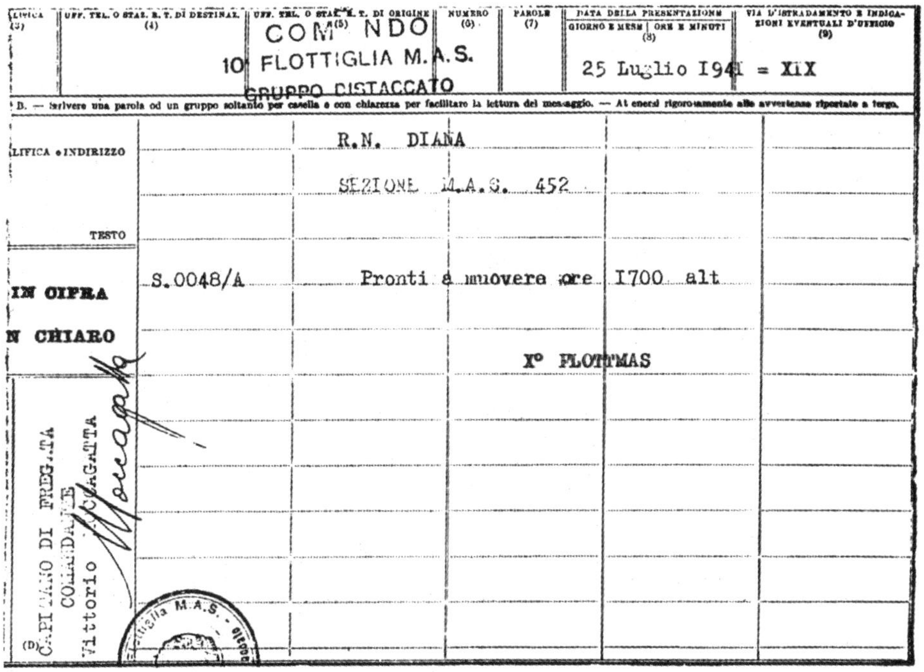
UFF. TEL. O STAZ. R. T. DI DESTINAZ. (4) | UFF. TEL. O STAZ. R. T. DI ORIGINE (5) | NUMERO (6) | PAROLE (7) | DATA DELLA PRESENTAZIONE GIORNO E MESE / ORE E MINUTI (8) | VIA D'ISTRADAMENTO E INDICAZIONI EVENTUALI D'UFFICIO (9)

COMANDO 10ª FLOTTIGLIA M.A.S. GRUPPO DISTACCATO

25 Luglio 1941 = XIX

QUALIFICA e INDIRIZZO: R.N. DIANA SEZIONE M.A.S. 452

TESTO IN CIFRA / IN CHIARO: S.0048/A Pronti a muovere ore 1700 alt

Xº FLOTTMAS

CAPITANO DI FREGATA COMANDANTE Vittorio Moccagatta

The 'ready to move' order for the units taking part in the action against Malta on 26 July 1941. Note that this document shows the flotilla number both in Arabic (10, in the stamp) and Roman numerals (Xº, in the sender's telegraphic address). *(Courtesy of P Morzone)*

Commander Ernesto Forza (right), X Flotilla Mas leader since summer 1941, and Lieutenant Commander Junio Valerio Borghese, then commanding officer of the flotilla underwater group and of the submarine *Sciré*.

price of greater losses. This obviously redounds to the greater credit of those skilled, determined and courageous operators to whom the Italian Navy owes a large part of its reputation, but it is beyond doubt that it reduced the extent of the successes.

From the 'Sezione Armi Speciali' to the '10a Flottiglia Mas'

Experimentation and development of assault craft in the Regia Marina was initially entrusted to the Command of the 1° Gruppo Sommergibili in La Spezia; then, in 1938, these responsibilities were passed to the 1ª Flottiglia Mas, always based in La Spezia. The following year a 'Sezione Armi Speciali' ('Special Weapons Section') was formed, still under the auspices of that flotilla, and later it became autonomous as the 'Flottiglia Mas Speciale', a name it kept for only a short time. Finally, in March 1941 it assumed the definitive and famous denomination of 10ª Flottiglia Mas (Xª Flotmas), widely known simply as Decima ['Tenth'].[4]

In summary, the tasks assigned by the Stato Maggiore of the Regia Marina to the unit were: 'Sinking/damaging enemy war and merchant ships in order to make the ratio of naval forces contributing to fighting enemy shipping evolve favourably'.[5] Consequently, the main targets assigned were, in order: 'Aircraft carriers, battleships, submarines, merchant ships'.

The craft available were few and, above all, as yet the underwater ones did not work perfectly. Self-contained breathing apparatuses were not as easy and safe to use as desirable, and self-propelled SLC craft suffered from all too frequent failures, which severely limited their operation. However, thanks to feedback from those involved in the Gibraltar operations – who were almost always able to escape after the actions – continuous improvements could be made to the devices, that augured well for the future.

In the wake of the brilliant success achieved by the explosive boats at Suda, the command of the flotilla began to think seriously about Malta: 'Assaulting Malta …' was, in the words of Admiral Antonio Scialdone, 'The secret dream of every soldier!'

This is an operation that is all too well known to describe it here once again: it is also well known that it

4. In the Italian language the Roman numerals do not usually need any suffix (eg: °, ª etc.), as they represent an ordinal (*eg* V Section, IV Battalion, III Squadron, XIII Wing etc); in the case of the Decima Flottiglia MAS the corresponding figure in Roman numerals was instead accompanied, on many official documents by the superscript ° suffix (*ie* X° Flotmas) and, during the 1943–1945 Republican Navy, with the ª suffix (*ie* Xª MAS) also repeated on the well-known unit badge.

5. This, like other references that follow indicated 'in quotation marks', are taken from unpublished notes by Admiral Ernesto Forza M dO [Medaglia d'oro al Valor militare], former commander of Decima Flotmas and later of Mariassalto, written as not-always-benevolent commentary to the publication of *Cento uomini contro due flotte* (listed in the bibliography) by Admiral Virgilio Spigai in 1954.

Bocca di Serchio, late summer 1940. Visit by Admiral Aimone of Savoia-Aosta, duke of Spoleto, to assault craft operators under training. The duke is sixth from right in the second row, with eng Guido Cattaneo of CABI to his right; also in the standing row, second from right is Lt Gino Birindelli and, first on the left, Capt eng Teseo Tesei.

was a complete, albeit heroic failure. 'No naval action was more glorious in the whole war as, perhaps, no raid was worse planned and conducted'.[6]

Factors contributing to the disaster included: a heterogeneous force that approached within a few miles of Grand Harbour on the night of 26 July 1941 under the pious illusion that no one had noticed it; the use of craft with very different characteristics following a rigid 'interlocking' plan for a variety of tactical phases; the support units waiting beyond the allowed time for the return of the operators – something that, given the disastrous outcome of the attack, was unlikely – until they were surprised at dawn by British aircraft, etc. The number of personnel killed was particularly high during the operation and with the deaths of the commanders Moccagatta and Giobbe, the flotilla lost its leader and the head of the surface department respectively.

The then capitano di fregata Ernesto Forza was called to replace the former; despite having received a well-deserved Gold Medal just a few days before for a bold Mas action, he was anything but a hothead. Those who knew him remember him above all as a very intelligent officer, perhaps with a 'difficult' character, but extremely rational. Arriving at the Decima flotilla, he quickly took control, leaning particularly on the wide experience now possessed by the submarine department chief, capitano di corvetta Junio Valerio Borghese, who was also the skilled commander of the *Sciré*, the 'approacher' submarine which had already penetrated Gibraltar's defences twice with SLC embarked.

And SLC craft transported by this boat achieved the first successes after the setback of Malta: in Gibraltar in September 1941, then at Alexandria in Egypt in the following December, when they put out of action for many months the only two battleships of the Mediterranean Fleet, HMS *Valiant* and *Queen Elizabeth*. This was the great exploit that the assault craft were waiting for: the task for which they had been created finally bore fruit. But the favourable modification of the ratio of forces thus obtained – a sort of reply to the British torpedo attack on Taranto in 1940, as it was often seen – could not be translated into an actual advantage, as the balance of the naval war in the Mediterranean no longer depended on battleships alone, but on light ships to attack and defend convoys, together with the ever growing presence and effectiveness of maritime air power.

'At the beginning of 1942', again quoting Admiral Forza,

> the assault craft no longer constituted a proper secret to the enemy. He was aware of their technical characteristics (being in possession of examples or parts of them) and already had experience of the operational plans adopted by us.[7] But he didn't know about the 'MTSM' [light motor torpedo boats], the 'Gamma' [assault divers] and the 'CA' [small 'Gamma' carrier submarines]. However, underwater assault craft (SLC or 'pigs') retained their efficacy and chance of success because devising and implementing suitable countermeasures would take time and above all a great expenditure of resources [beyond] restraining his freedom of action … The X^{a} Flottiglia Mas had fulfilled its institutional task in a very satisfactory fashion, but this last, eye-catching tactical success (two battleships out of action) could not be exploited fully on the

6. These are heavy judgements, filled with the disenchanted realism which permeated all the writings and thoughts of Antonio Scialdone M d'O. (a decoration earned in 1943 as a young MTB commander), who in the 1970s was the chief of Comsubin (the Italian Navy assault divers unit), heir of the tasks and traditions of the Decima Flottiglia Mas. The writer still remembers with regret when, as an officer of the watch, he did not think of taking notes during the interesting talks about assault craft that took place during certain night passages on the bridge of the old cruiser *Garibaldi*, of which the (then) capitano di vascello Scialdone, great sailor and fighter, was the commanding officer.

7. To get an idea of the type and quantity of materials related to the Italian assault craft that ended up in British hands, and their use, the box on page 29 summarises a long, specific study published on the subject (see E Bagnasco, 'Gli inglesi sapevano...' in *STORIA militare* 120, September 2003).

> strategic level because our diminished naval superiority did not have the weight that it was thought to have beyond 100 miles off our coast. We had to come to terms with naval air power that effectively pressured our communications ... despite the lack of battleships. This was understood very well by the enemy who refrained from sending other [large] ships to Alexandria, strengthened Malta [as much as possible] and took the best practical steps for defence: he took the *pure* objectives away from us...

'However, the Xª Flottiglia Mas continued his own tasks...' and, consequently, the objectives could be achieved 'by intensifying the underwater pressure against Gibraltar (aircraft carriers, battleships and transport) ... and devising new forms of action that made surprises possible again'. For this purpose the command of the Decima addressed its efforts towards: strengthening the clandestine bases in Spanish territory near Gibraltar (tanker *Olterra*–Villa Carmela system) and elsewhere; the organisation and the improvement of materials and training of the 'Gamma' force; increase in the number of 'approacher' submarines for underwater assault craft; development of 'SSB', a new and more effective model of 'pig', and the aforementioned 'CA' type mini-submarines. For surface craft, the interest in the development and improvement of light motor torpedo boats persisted, while no significant use of explosive boats was expected, except for the testing of a similar, smaller craft ('MTR'), which could be transported in the waterproof cylinders of 'approacher' submarines.

In this situation the Stato Maggiore ordered the Flottiglia to prepare a land convoy for the transportation and support of a task force of explosive motorboats and light motor torpedo boats to be transferred to the Black Sea for operations against Soviet naval forces. The news of this overseas expedition was welcome to the Decima since 'Not minimally distracting ...' the organisation of the unit from its main tasks 'satisfied the desire of the surface personnel ... employing elsewhere a craft that had had its day in the Mediterranean.' Together with the assault craft, the Regia Marina also designated to Black Sea operations a squadron of CB type mini-submarines and three squadrons of modern Mas boats that achieved good results.

If the successes of the Decima in the Black Sea were not, as was easily predictable, exciting, its presence on that front had a certain propaganda value for their German ally and in the summer of 1942 contributed, with disruptive actions, to the favourable trend of operations around Sevastopol. The Decima convoy returned to Italy almost completely at the beginning of 1943.

The use of assault craft in the second half of 1942 was characterised by the continuation and intensification of attacks with the SLC against merchant shipping moored in Gibraltar bay, by now operating from *Olterra*, an old Italian tanker interned in Algeciras and moored in view of the Rock, which had been turned into an advanced base of the Decima.

In September, assault divers or 'Gamma' [from the initial letter of 'guastatori' ('sappers')] were successfully employed for the first time from their base at Villa Carmela in Spanish territory. This speciality above all was born out of the need to act against targets, such as merchant ships, requiring a smaller charge than that carried by the 'pigs'. For the same purpose charges divided into two sections, each more than enough to sink a ship not equipped with underwater protection, were devised for the SLC. From their first actions the 'Gamma' – which only needed light and inconspicuous

An MTSM light motor torpedo boat on transfer along the Crimean coast of the Black Sea.

The tanker *Olterra* waiting to be scrapped in Vado Ligure (Savona) in early 1961.

WHAT THE BRITISH KNEW

Regardless of possible general information they could derive from intelligence sources – about which, however, there is not much evidence – the first news about the existence of new, probably submarine weapons, intended to attack ships in ports, were obtained by the Royal Navy directly 'in the field', as early as the third month of war. The clear aerial photos of 'approacher' submarine *Gondar* sinking off the coast of Alexandria in Egypt on 30 September 1940 clearly showed three previously unseen large cylinders on the deck, evidently designed to transport 'something'; moreover, besides the approximately 45 people who normally made up the crew of a submarine of that type under the command of a Lieutenant, British ships rescued a further nine castaways including a Commander, four more officers, and four petty officers of which three were in the 'diver' category. They were capitano di fregata Mario Giorgini – chief of the assault craft (then Sezione Armi Speciali) of 1ª Flottiglia Mas – and the six operators, in addition to two reserves, for the three 'pigs'. This certainly did not go unnoticed, raising many questions among the British.

Further information was acquired by the British Navy from the first (failed) action by SLCs launched from the *Sciré* in Gibraltar harbour on 29 October 1940. The likelihood of the enemy finding wrecks of submarine self-propelled craft, or part of them, at the end of actions was a risk well known to the Italian assault craft commands from the beginning. On the other hand, despite the self-destruct systems (small explosive charges) and the official procedures for the scuttling of the 'pigs', it was inevitable that not everything would be totally destroyed. Of three SLCs on that unfortunate mission, all of which suffered mechanical failures,[8] one was recovered almost intact by the Spaniards, while the heavily damaged wreck of a second was found at the bottom of the harbour by British divers. Furthermore, a pair of operators were captured inside the base after activating the charge on their craft, which irreparably sank to the bottom. Despite the failure of British pressure on the Spaniards to obtain the self-propelled craft in their possession, it is quite likely that they managed to photograph many details.

Those images, compared with the recovered wreck and the equipment of the captured operators, gave the British specialists a first insight, even if approximate, into the characteristics and operating methods of the 'pigs'. Some information obtained from interrogation of the captured operators also contributed to a better

Submarine *Gondar* under aerial attack in a picture taken by a British aircraft on 30 September 1940. The assault craft transport cylinders fitted on the deck are plainly visible. *(Imperial War Museum)*

8. See the 'Chronology and summary of the main actions conducted by the Italian assault craft (1918 and 1940-1945)' section on page 52.

The wreck of an SLC that took part in the action against Gibraltar on 29 October 1940 recovered by British divers. *(Imperial War Museum)*

The slightly damaged SLC of Teseo Tesei/Alcide Pedretti recovered in October 1940 by the Spaniards, who tested it for a long time. The craft is pictured on display in Cartagena in the early 1970s, after many modifications. It would be later given back to the Italian Navy.

understanding of the whole weapon system, though the prisoners deliberately distorted them.[9] The full characteristics of this craft, and also of the equipment of its operators, became clearer in July 1941, when the British acquired the wreck of one of the two SLCs that had participated in the attack on Malta. Although the craft had been sabotaged and was found broken into three sections, it was substantially intact, and very detailed reports and drawings could be gathered from its study.

However, it was only after the resounding success at Alexandria that the Royal Navy, pushed by the Prime Minister Winston Churchill himself, began the development of a similar craft, the Chariot Mk I, which became operational in September 1942 (see the detailed description on page 41) and had a brief operational career, though not without success.

It should also be borne in mind that the confirmed existence of Italian self-propelled submarine craft and the general knowledge of their attack procedures did not prevent their use (and success) as the defensive infrastructure could not be set up rapidly. Furthermore, these countermeasures formed a considerable logistical and economic burden for the enemy, even if it was not decisive. This alone constituted a far-reaching strategic success for the assault craft.

9. See A Santoni, 'L'intelligence e la "Decima"' in *STORIA Militare* 120, September 2003.

The *MT 16* explosive motorboat found nearly intact but broken down by the British following the disastrous attack on Malta in July, 1941, being inspected and partly dismantled.

MT 16 repaired by the British, during a series of trials in Grand Harbour in late summer 1941.

As for the surface assault craft, the first 'explosive motorboat' fell into British hands during the debut of the 'MT' with the attack on the cruiser HMS *York* anchored in the deep Cretan bay of Suda on 26 March 1941. One of the craft, afloat and undetonated, was found by the British, and was summarily examined before its accidental explosion. A second boat – abandoned because of mechanical failure but intact – was recovered by the Royal Navy after the Malta action of 26–27 July 1941. This craft was easily repaired, tested and then transferred to Great Britain to serve as a model for the development of a similar parachutable small boat whose prototype was tested successfully in 1944, but was never followed-up.

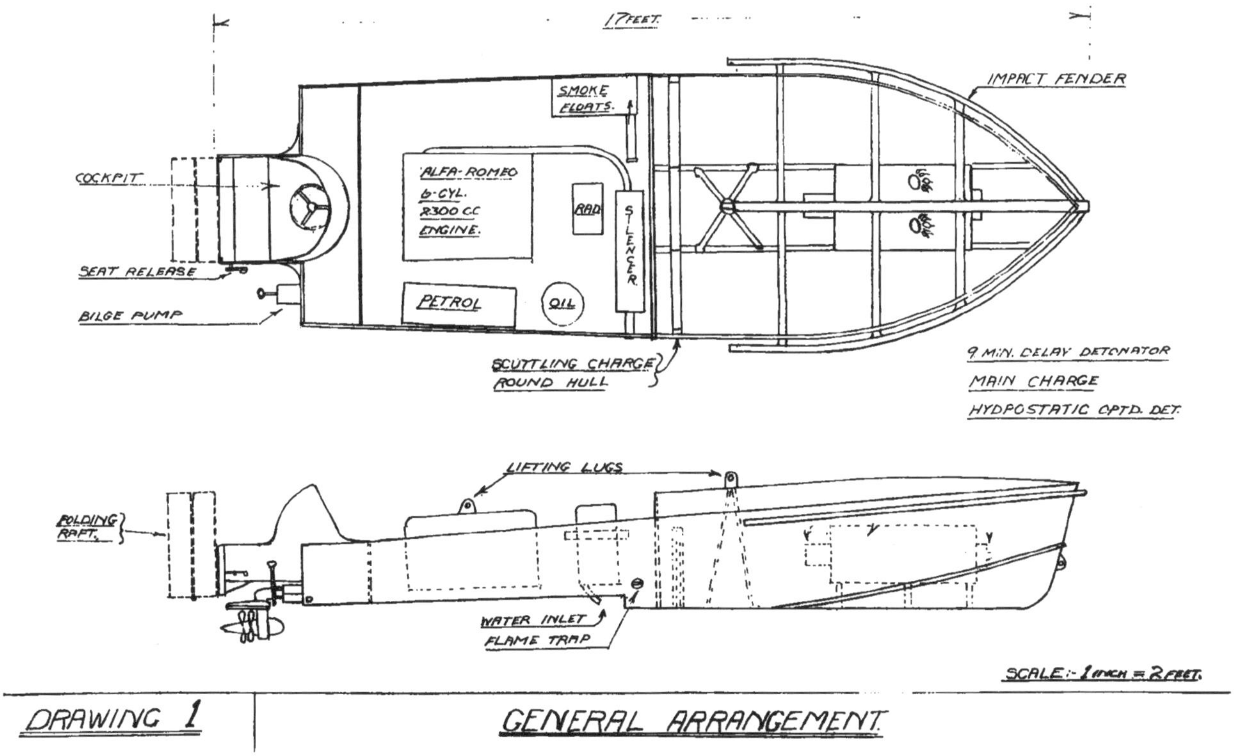

General arrangement of *MT 16* as surveyed by the British in Malta. The drawing has several inaccuracies, especially in the stern hull lines.

equipment – showed a remarkable flexibility of use: they could act practically anywhere and, with some limits, raised a 'never safe' psychology in the enemy, forcing him to create extensive and expensive defence arrangements.

The only serious problem for the Decima was the modest number of properly trained 'Gamma' operators available for operational use. Not all the divers passing out from the Livorno School, organised using equipment from the Naval Academy, were 'Gamma'. The exceptional physical and mental qualities essential for such service could only be found in a small percentage of the divers, whose training was divided into three stages: the first enabled them to 'go underwater', and the second to perform underwater work; only after the 3rd, and a very stiff selection procedure, were they considered ready to carry out war missions. Despite this, the few available 'Gamma' achieved exceptional results, not just in terms of courage and resolution, but, from the military point of view, at the highest levels of cost-effectiveness.

An interesting operational combination was that of joint actions between submarine self-propelled craft and 'Gamma'. The first, which is very little known, was to be performed with three 'pigs' transported by the submarine *Ambra* (capitano di corvetta M Arillo) and about twenty 'Gamma' from the land. It was planned for the autumn of 1942 against the French fleet, gathered in Toulon under armistice terms, to prevent it leaving that base and joining the Allies who were about to land in French North Africa; only the rapid change in the strategic situation and the German attack on the Toulon naval base led to the cancellation of this operation. The second was carried out by the same *Ambra* (with 3 SLC and 10 'Gamma') in the following December against Algiers, obtaining a moderate success.

As for the surface craft, for a brief African period they were used against light enemy shipping from aboard large fishing boats or special land convoys, achieving some success. With the fall of Tunisia imminent, the Decima's light motor torpedo boats were among the last Italian naval units to operate offensively against the now overwhelming superiority of enemy air and naval forces. Following the abandonment of the last African bastion in May 1943, torpedo and explosive motorboats were withdrawn to Sicily and Sardinia, and tasked with opposing the invasion which, given the general trend of operations in the Mediterranean, did not seem far off. When this occurred in the following July, the sea/air situation was so compromised that their use proved impracticable.

The armistice of 8 September 1943 surprised the X^a Flottiglia Mas, commanded since May 1943 by capitano di fregata Junio Valerio Borghese. At the time it was very active, with many projects about to materialise and some important near-future actions even firmly scheduled, such as, for example, an action with 'SSB' (the new model of submarine self-propelled craft) and MT against Gibraltar. Experiments with the CA type boats continued, and they were expected to be used in the medium term against the Atlantic harbours of the United States and in North Africa. This was an ambitious programme that, had it been completed, would have forced the Allies at enormous expense to defend naval bases and vast commercial and industrial areas that, until then, had not known this kind of threat.

'200' series SLC in a Decima workshop probably in 1943. The craft in the foreground is fitted with a double explosive charge.

Two stages of Decima divers initial and advanced training in use of the self-contained oxygen breathing apparatus.

From 10 June 1940 to September 1943, when the Regia Marina ceased hostilities against the Anglo-Americans as a result of the armistice, the activity of the assault craft had caused the Allies direct losses of more than 72,000 tons of naval vessels and about 135,000 gross tons of sunken or severely damaged merchant ships, amounting to 5 and 23 units respectively, with 60% of the military and 95% of the merchant losses due to underwater craft, 'Gamma' included, and the rest to surface craft. Furthermore, indirect damage of important, though not easily quantifiable value, was derived by the enemy need to create, organise and maintain the defence infrastructure of the harbours and naval bases of the whole Mediterranean and surrounding areas.

Therefore, even at the cost of sacrifices and painful losses, the Italian assault craft had caused significant damage to enemy potential, while employing extremely limited material resources, and the use of an of operational force which did not exceed an average of 100 men. It affected the freedom of movement of enemy fleets and subjected senior officers and crews to a form of continuing tension after returning from long and risky war missions deriving from the insecurity of even the best equipped naval bases.

A close-up of submarine *Ambra* fitted as assault craft 'approacher' (like the similar *Sciré*) in a picture taken in La Spezia on 2 April 1942 during an Italo-German ceremony.

Wreck of US merchant ship *Pat Harrison* pictured at Gibraltar in summer 1943 by a Regia Marina Information Service agent. It was a 'Liberty' type cargo ship attacked by SLC from the *Olterra* the previous May.

Armistice and Italian co-belligerencies 1943–1945 (Xª Mas; Mariassalto)

Marshal Badoglio's announcement on the evening of 8 September 1943 released by the national radio to inform Italians of the signature of an armistice with the Allies, took the assault craft organisation by complete surprise, like all the units of the Regia Marina and other Italian armed forces. Headquarters of the Comando Flottiglia and the greatest concentration of men and the craft that were part of it was in the North: in La Spezia, Bocca di Magra, Livorno or near the Ligurian and Lombard industries which were entrusted with the construction and development of 'barchini' and submarine self-propelled craft. In the south and in Sardinia a total of twenty surface craft was located, designated above all to defend the coasts.

In the Muggiano headquarters of Xª Mas, in La Spezia, Commander Borghese faced the general disintegration of the shore structures of the Navy that followed the departure of the ships of the battle forces from the Ligurian base, and the scuttling of the few remaining units that were unable to move because of dockyard work. He managed initial clashes with the Germans, keeping his unit firmly together; indeed, at that time he concluded a sort of 'alliance agreement' between the Xª Mas and the German Commands.

The Italian Social Republic (RSI) was established after the liberation of Mussolini from the Gran Sasso, where he had been held formally a prisoner of the pro-Armistice regime. The 'Xª' gave its loyalty to the RSI and became part – albeit a distinctive one – of the Marina Nazionale Repubblicana, preserving however a vast operational autonomy and privileged relationship with the German Navy.

Italian and German craft during training in Sesto Calende, on Lake Maggiore, in 1944.

A large mass of young volunteers soon flocked to the base of the flotilla, which enjoyed not only a wide and deserved reputation, but also the favour of those who wanted to continue to fight the Anglo-Americans. To employ these men, the core of 'traditional' submarine and surface assault craft was supplemented by setting up naval infantry and raider (NP = parachutist swimmers) units, which became to all intents and purposes part of the 'Xª', being used alongside German troops until the end of hostilities.

As for the assault craft, now under the direct command of capitano di corvetta (Gold Medal) Mario Arillo, the Xª Mas commissioned mainly explosive and light torpedo motorboats of various types, some already existing on 8 September 1943 and others built later by several companies and yards in Northern Italy (SIAI, Baglietto, Caproni, CABI-Cattaneo etc). It is interesting to remember that the 'Xª' also incorporated some Mas and motor torpedo boats ceded by the German Navy, which had taken them over in the

MTM explosive motorboats lashed down on the deck of the aircraft transport *Giuseppe Miraglia* in the first months of 1944. This is probably a transfer passage of the surface assault craft based in Sardinia at the time of the armistice.

Mariassalto craft exercising in the Gulf of Taranto in 1944. Two MSTM – one showing the number *230* – are in the foreground, with the motor torpedo boat *MS 74* behind.

AVAILABILITY AND NUMBERING: Xª MAS AND MARIASSALTO (RM) SURFACE ASSAULT CRAFT 1943–1945

MTM type

(Xª)	(RM)
2b	
3b	
4b	
15b	
16b	
17b	
26b	
28b	
30b	
33b	
63b	
75b	
42	
48	
50	
	52
	68
	70
	72
	74
	78
	82
	90
98	
	102
104	
	106
	108
110	
112	
114	
	116
	120
517	
536	
545	
549	
552	
553	
554	
555	
558	

MTR type

(Xª)	(RM)
02	
04	
014	
020	

MTL type

(Xª)	(RM)
442	
476	
571	

MTSM type

(Xª)	(RM)
204	
206	
208	
	210
	212
216	
	218
	220
226	
230	
230 (ii)	
234	
236	
	244
	246
	248
	250
	256
	262
264	
268	

MTSMA (or 'SMA) type

(Xª)	(RM)
302	
304	
308	
310	
312	
314	
316	
318	
320	
324	
326	
328	
334/8	
336/3	
349/9	
358/14	
362/16	
366/18	
380/25	
404/39	
405/40	
50	
1B.1	

Units by type

Type	(Xª)	(RM)
MTM	**29**	**13**
MTSM	**10**	**10**
'SMA	**23**	–
MTR	**4**	–
MTL	**3**	–
Totals	**69**	**23**

confused days of the armistice, mostly seizing them in the yards where they were under construction. They were largely modern Mas boats from the different series of the '500' class (*MAS 505, 525, 553, 556, 561* etc) and a couple of 60-ton motor torpedo boats. They were not proper assault craft, but traditional naval units in all respects, whose description is beyond the scope of this work – except for the *MS 74* and *75*, modified to operate as fast 'approachers' for explosive motorboats and SLC and therefore included among the surface approachers.

The surface assault craft of the republican 'Xª', which did not exceed seventy units in total,[10] operated almost exclusively in the Tyrrhenian Sea, first in the Anzio-Nettuno area, then off the West Ligurian coast, while in the Adriatic they were limited to some activities conducted with craft transferred by the Germans for that specific theatre, and operating from the bases of Istria. Their task was no longer what they were created for (the forcing of enemy bases), but the stealth role implemented in the Black Sea and on the African coasts: surprise night attacks on small-medium sized ships sailing in coastal waters. Therefore, the technical-nautical limitations specific to these small craft meant that successes – though not lacking – could never be significant, while the losses were quite high.

Only courage and the spirit of sacrifice were never in short supply: for the rest almost everything was always scarce, from fuel to spare parts and so on, even if the organisation of the flotilla managed to provide the

10. According to a list kindly provided to me by the late Commander Nesi, and compiled on the basis of official Republican Navy documents in the spring of 1945 (see table above), the surface assault craft officially armed by the Xª MAS between 1943 and the end of the conflict were 69 in total: 29 MTM, 4 MTR, 10 MTSM, 23 MTSMA (or 'SMA) and 3 MTL.

An MTM assigned to the republican Decima Pilot School in Sesto Calende during a drill on Lake Maggiore. The picture – taken as the pilot abandons ship after pointing the craft towards the target – shows *MTM 98*, recognisable, amongst other things, by the missing 'palmola'. *(M Spertini collection)*

basic necessities most of the times. The diver department comprised some run-down SLCs and a few new SSBs still in the development phase, concentrated in Venice and La Spezia, and a group of 'Gamma'. It was necessarily rather limited in its activity, principally restricted by the unavailability of 'approacher' submarines and delays in introducing the new CAs, so obtained no significant results.

The republican Decima *MTSMA 312* during an exercise in the Gulf of La Spezia in 1944. The ship in the background is the cruiser *Gorizia*, by then a wreck stranded on a shoal; the officer with binocular is Lt Sergio Nesi.

In Southern Italy things were quite different. The Regia Marina tracked down a few craft in southern Italy and Sardinia – a total of 22 motorboats, of which 13 were MTM and 9 MTSM, but no SLC underwater craft – and with this small force established a new assault craft unit in Taranto San Vito, calling it Mariassalto , whose command was again entrusted to Gold Medal Ernesto Forza, promoted capitano di vascello in the meantime.

Maintaining the efficiency of the craft and those few special materials available was really difficult, as all the supplier companies were in the north, and therefore in an area occupied by the Germans. The problem of finding spare parts, especially for engines, seemed insoluble; this situation was rectified by the dockyard of Taranto, but only with difficulty and inevitable delays partly due to the total lack of technical documentation, construction drawings etc. Another problem was represented by the few trained staff available, who largely remained in the north: a solution was found by requesting the Allies – with whom the Kingdom of Italy was now formally a co-belligerent – to release all those assault craft operators captured after the actions undertaken since 1940 and held as prisoners of war. The request was largely accepted fairly quickly, given that the Anglo-American commanders were extremely keen to restart the activities of the assault craft teams, as they were very interested in absorbing their ideas and experience, which given the Allies' remarkable industrial potential, might be applied on a large scale in the rest of the conflict.

A republican Decima MTM explosive motorboat undergoing maintenance at San Remo 'West' base, probably in the autumn of 1944.

In the field of co-belligerency, the few available motor torpedo boats carried out reconnaissance missions and landing/recovery of informants behind the lines in the Adriatic and Tyrrhenian; an attack on a German ship inside Suda Bay (Crete) with explosive motorboats was planned, but was cancelled due to persistent adverse weather conditions. Mariassalto also conducted two intruder actions in Italian harbours occupied by the Germans, in collaboration with the Royal Navy: La Spezia (with Italian 'approachers', British Chariot type underwater self-propelled craft and some Italian 'Gamma' frogmen) where the abandoned hull of the cruiser *Bolzano* was sunk; and Genoa (Italian 'approachers', Italian divers with loaned Chariot Mk I British underwater self-propelled craft), where the immobilisation of the big hull of the unfinished aircraft carrier *Aquila* (formerly the liner *Roma*) was attempted, to prevent its scuttling to block the entrance to the harbour.

A Mk 1 'Chariot' – a British copy of the Italian SLC – is launched while its operators wait in the water. It is often claimed that the source of this picture is Italian not British, which if true might make it one of the Mariassalto 'Chariots'. *(USMM)*

At the end of the conflict most of the efficient assault craft in Decima service were either destroyed or scuttled. The interest of the Anglo-Americans, who by now

The ramp of the former Muggiano seaplane base at La Spezia, 1944. Republican Decima light motor torpedo boats on their trailers are made ready to be transferred to their operational bases.

knew the characteristics of the surface craft well, focused on the underwater weapons: apart from the now outdated SLC, the new SSB attracted the attention of their technicians. In Venice four examples of the republican Xª Mas were recovered in different states of efficiency, and a series of comparative tests was immediately conducted between an SLC and an SSB with the aid of Mariassalto staff and former Xª operators, held in a particular, very mild, form of war captivity. The trials were carried out in the waters of the former seaplane base of San Andrea and when they were over two SSB were transferred to Great Britain to undergo further trials and the other two, with an SLC, to the United States together with some of their most experienced operators. The latter returned after a few months, during which they had carried out an intense experimental programme in a US Navy base. Documents recently declassified from the US archives, as well as memoirs of some of those operators, indicate some short-lived interest by the Americans in a possible employment in the Pacific (where the conflict with Japan went on until August) of submarine self-propelled craft and assault divers inspired by Italian 'Gamma' units.

In the immediate post-war years the divers of Mariassalto were assigned to the difficult task of demining national harbours. This allowed the Italian Navy to keep the unit together, without losing the precious experiences gained in an activity that the punitive 1947 peace treaty would later expressly forbid in Italy, but which in reality never ceased. Those same men who had participated in the actions of the assault craft in the Second World War finally created the 'Raggruppamento Subacquei e Incursori' ('Divers and Raiders Group') [Comsubin] named 'Teseo Tesei' in honour of the underwater pioneer and based at the Forte del Varignano in the Gulf of La Spezia, which has been one of the leading units of Italian Navy for many years.

Explosive motorboats in the Middle East in 1948

For completeness, however, this book should also mention the successful use of a small group of MTM by the newly formed Israeli Navy during the first of the long series of Arab-Israeli conflicts and, in particular, during that phase generally called the Israeli War of Independence (1948–1949).

The State of Israel concluded that an armed confrontation with the surrounding Arab states was inevitable, and especially with Egypt, the only one to

Venice-S Andrea, summer 1945. An SSB (foreground) and an SLC during a series of comparative trials carried out for the benefit of the Allies by Italian and Anglo-American operators in the waters of the former seaplane base. *(Imperial War Museum)*

A long-decommissioned Israeli MTM transferred by helicopter in the 1960s.

have some naval forces. Israel decided to investigate the possibility of acquiring assault craft to counter the naval superiority of its enemies. In May 1948 it concluded confidential negotiations begun the previous February, and with the benevolent endorsement of the Italian military authorities and the collaboration of CABI-Cattaneo of Milan, a group of six MTM was taken secretly to the Middle East by road. These were among the many motorboats of this type built during the war but left unfinished, and were delivered after being been overhauled and fitted out. With the small boats went Fiorenzo Caprotti as an instructor and adviser; formerly a Decima Mas pilot of explosive motorboats, he had been recently released from a captivity began in July 1941, after the unfortunate attack on Malta (of which he was one of the protagonists) and for which he was awarded the Silver Medal of Valour.[11] With tight training activities in progress, a logistics unit similar to those of Decima Flottiglia Mas was set up, as well as the adaptation of the armed yacht *Ma'oz* (an old American-built ship of 1700grt from 1896) as 'approacher' for a total of four explosive motorboats. Leaving Jaffa on 22 October 1948, *Ma'oz* put the small boats into the water that same evening: three had an explosive charge and one equipped for the immediate recovery of pilots off the port of Gaza. The small expedition overcame the obstructions easily, and the precise targeting of the MTM led to the destruction of two old Egyptian escorts (the *El Amir Farouq* and, probably, the *Fowey*) of a thousand tons each; all the operators returned safely to the 'approacher' after the operation. Israeli propaganda, with much exaggeration, celebrated the Gaza action as a great naval victory, so much so that the date of 22 October was chosen to celebrate the annual 'Navy Day' and a surviving 1948 explosive motorboat is still preserved today as an exhibit at the Israeli War Museum in Tel Aviv.

11. Almost in parallel with the interest in Italian surface assault craft, the newly formed Israeli Navy laid the foundations for the training of assault divers, under the supervision of another Italian Royal Navy veteran, tenente di vascello Nicola Conte, Gold Medal for Valour for forcing Genoa harbour on 19 April 1945.

Assault craft used by other navies during the Second World War

It seems that other navies only began to study and test assault craft following the news of their use by the Italians. Excluding the torpedo-armed mini-submarines similar to the Italian CB built in Japan and Germany, the only navies that built and employed proper assault craft during the Second World War were the British, German and Japanese ones.

Royal Navy

The two main assault craft employed operationally by the British Navy in the Second World War were the 'X' type midget submarines and the underwater self-propelled craft called 'Chariots'. The X-craft, which began to enter service in 1942, were midget submarines a little more than 15 metres long and had a crew of 4 men. Designed for attacking major warships moored within their bases, they had two big charges each of about 1.5 tons arranged on the sides of the boat and detachable from inside. These charges had to be released on the seabed near the target or, if the possibility arose, attached to the latter by two divers whose exit and subsequent return was through a special floodable compartment like those in a submarine escape system. Their employment was quite similar to that foreseen for Italian CA craft after their conversion into assault submarines which, however, did not become operational in the time available.

The main actions carried out by the X-craft were those that seriously damaged the German battleship *Tirpitz* moored in the Alten Fjord in Norway, and the sinking of the Japanese heavy cruiser *Takao* at anchor off Singapore. The first took place on 22 September 1943 by two of the five X-craft that had been towed to the area by the same numbers of fleet submarines, and was a tactical success of considerable importance. The second was carried out on one of the last days of the conflict, 31 July 1945. Overall, including prototypes, training and operational units, the Royal Navy commissioned thirty of these midget submarines in different versions.

The Chariot Mk I was a direct derivative of the Italian SLC, both as a design and in its methods of use.

A British 'X' type midget submarine during exercises.

More than seventy were built from 1942, and were employed in northern European waters, in the Mediterranean and (the Mk II version) in the Far East. Two Mk I Chariots, lent by the Royal Navy to the Italian co-belligerent navy, were used by Italian Mariassalto operators for forcing Genoa harbour on 19 April 1945.

Among other British underwater assault craft, mention must be made of the unsuccessful 'Welman' type, more than 100 of which were built from 1942 but, plagued by irreparable design flaws, it had been taken out of service by 1944. It was a squat mini-submarine about 6 metres long, crewed by a single man, equipped with a 540kg charge of high explosive placed at the extreme bow which was detachable near the target. A few 'Welman' carried out an unsuccessful action against Bergen, in Norway, in November 1943.

Another interesting British assault craft, which never became operational, was the 'parachutable explosive motorboat' derived from captured Italian MTs found unexploded in Suda and off Malta in 1941. About 5.40 metres (18ft) long, it retained the general characteristics and even the peculiar stern drive of the Italian explosive motorboat; the charge was about 225kg and the petrol engine could develop about 120 HP for a maximum speed in the order of the 30 knots. The organisation in charge of development and employment of British explosive motorboats was not the Royal Navy proper but the Royal Marines, which had given them the cover designation 'Boom Patrol Boats'.

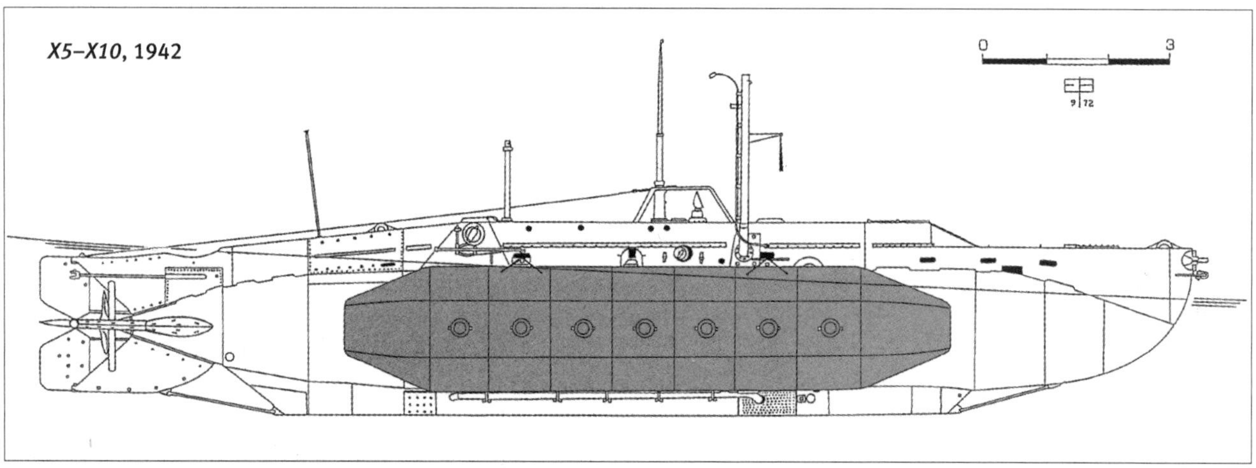

BRITISH CHARIOT TYPE UNDERWATER SELF-PROPELLED CRAFT

The Royal Navy began the development of this assault craft in January 1942 when, following the famous action of the Italian 'pigs' in Alexandria against the only two battleships of the Mediterranean Fleet, First Minister Winston Churchill sent a message addressed to General Hasting Ismay, secretary of the British Chiefs of Staff Committee on the 18th of the same month:

> 'Please report on what has been done to emulate the successes of the Italians in the port of Alexandria through similar methods [...]. Is there some reason why we are incapable of the same kind of scientific aggressive action as demonstrated by the Italians?'

Following this explicit intervention, the task of overseeing development was quickly assigned to the Submarine Service. Working from the now abundant technical data about Italian SLCs that British specialists have been gathering since the middle of 1940, a self-propelled model very similar to the Italian design was built at the Gosport submarine base.

Operator training began while the construction of the first craft was in progress, using a wooden unpowered mock-up towed semi-submerged by a speedboat. The operators used a modified 'Davis' type self-contained breathing apparatus. This mock-up went through a succession of different unofficial names: *Kerry Mark II* first, then *Cassidy*, and finally the definitive *Chariot*. As for the breathing apparatus, it was a modified version of the closed-circuit oxygen devices, with a 'lung' bag on the chest and a tank underneath (later carried on the back), which the Royal Navy used for rescue operations from damaged submarines. Moreover, the operators wore a particular type of watertight rubber outfit called a 'Sladen suit' from the name of its inventor. It was characterised by a purge valve placed on the top of the cap, with a facemask equipped with a single glass that could be lifted and fixed by 'wing nut' screws.

A Mk I 'Chariot' lifted by a support ship sling.

Close-up of a Mk I 'Chariot' under way on the surface. Note the typical arrangement of the British 'Sladen' type diving suit hood with the air purge valve on top. *(Imperial War Museum)*

The first prototype self-propelled craft, nicknamed *The real one*, was ready to be tested at sea in June 1942, followed at short intervals by many other units whose official designation was now 'Chariot'. The setup was not easy and was never definitively finalised: the Mark I Chariots remained none too reliable craft, just like the first series SLCs of which the British craft was practically a copy. Nevertheless, training intensified and in about three months a few dozen operators could be declared combat ready.

After the first trials in Portsmouth, the main Chariot training base was moved to the north of Scotland, first to

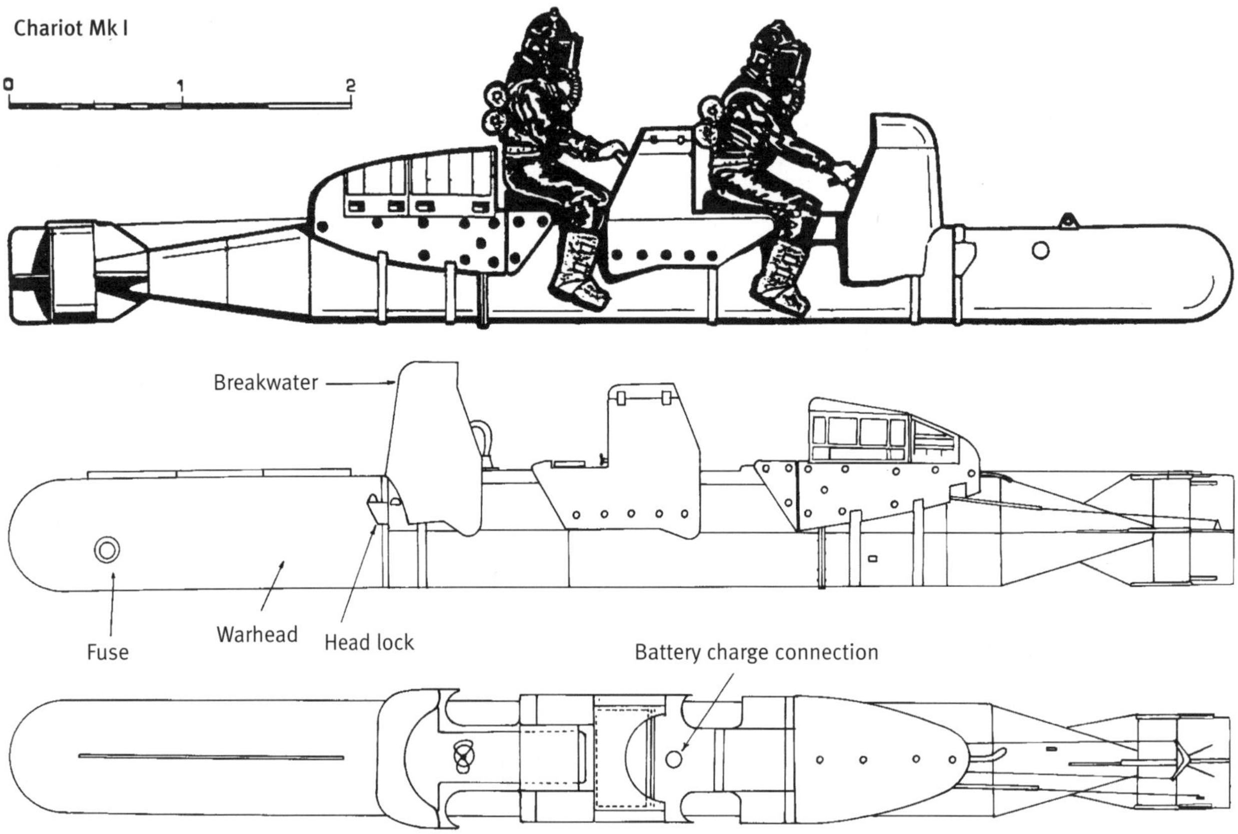

Erisart, which proved unsuitable, and then to Loch Cairnbawn where the old depot and submarine support ship HMS *Titania* was also relocated. Besides frequent craft failures, the waterproof suits and breathing apparatus also gave problems which could never be completely solved.

The main technical data and performance of the Mk I Chariots, that did not differ much from those of the initial production Italian SLCs ('100' series), were as follows:

- Total weight: about 1500kg
- Length overall: 6.80m (about 20ft), though some sources give 7.20–7.65m
- Main body diameter: 533mm (21in);
- Propulsion system: one 2 HP 60V dc electric motor
- Maximum speed: 2.9 knots
- Range: about 6 hours at 2.9 knots = 17.4 miles
- Detachable 245kg TNT warhead charge.

The engine was powered by a battery series and had four forward and two rear speed settings. The general arrangement, positions of the dive tanks etc were similar to those of the Italian 'pigs', which Mk I Chariots closely resembled. Their colouring was dark green, and progressive numbering of the craft was in Roman numerals, for a total of about eighty units excluding prototypes.

The control of the British craft was quite similar to that of the Italian 'pig' but, unlike the latter, the operation of the steering and depth rudders occurred in combined mode, like on aircraft, by means of a small joystick, instead of independent actions by wheel and stick. According to Italian operators who, besides training, also used them in action (Genoa, April 1945), the Chariots were inferior in performance, generally speaking, compared to SLCs of the last series produced, and suffered from frequent failures, especially of the electric (propulsion) system. As for British breathing apparatus and wetsuits, these were less efficient and safe than the Italian equivalents: it is significant that the aforementioned 'Sladen' suit was nicknamed 'Clammy Death' by Royal Navy Charioteers.

The first use of Mk I Chariots occurred in October 1942 against the battleship *Tirpitz* moored in a Norwegian

Opposite, top: A Mk I 'Chariot' without its explosive head. *(Imperial War Museum)*

Opposite, bottom: Close-up of the forward operator's seat in a Mk I 'Chariot'. *(Imperial War Museum)*

Portrait of a 'Chariot' operator. The self-contained breathing apparatus is a closed-circuit oxygen 'Davis' type with lung bag and back-mounted cylinders. Note the moveable mask glass and its closing wing screws *(Imperial War Museum)*.

fjord. It was a complete failure since the craft, 'approached' using a fishing boat, were lost before arriving near target because of the unsafe transport conditions. Solutions inspired by the Italians were therefore studied: using towing submarines to approach targets, or transporting the Chariots in waterproof cylinders secured to the deck of big 'T' class submarines.

As soon as these became available, a complex operation employing numerous Chariots was organised in the Mediterranean for January 1943. Named 'Principal' it foresaw the almost simultaneous attack on naval moorings in the Maddalena islands (the heavy cruisers *Trieste* and *Gorizia* were the targets) and the forcing of Palermo harbour to sink part of the large fleet normally present. The action in the Sardinian waters failed due to the loss of the submarine *P.311* with the Chariots *X* and *XVIII* and no survivors, probably due to hitting a mine in the Italian defensive barrier. The attack on Palermo therefore constituted the first and most important success of the British underwater assault craft: transported by the submarines HMS *Trooper* and *Thunderbolt*, with the smaller *Unruffled* in support, the five Chariots *XV, XVI, XIX, XXII* and *XXIII*, were released near the harbour entrance on the night of 2/3 January 1943. Mechanical failures of the craft and in the breathing apparatus of the operators forced three to be scuttled but the other two managed to overcome the obstructions undiscovered. The crew of the *XXII* (Lieutnant R T G Greenland and Petty Officer A Ferrier) managed to attach the main charge to the hull of the light cruiser *Ulpio Traiano* (only launched a little over one month earlier) at the beginning of the operation, and small additional charges (limpet mines) to the destroyer *Grecale*, destroyer-escort *Cyclone* and steamer *Gimma*. Chariot *XVI* (Sub-lieutenant R G Dove and Petty Officer J Freel) placed its main charge under the motor vessel *Viminale*. The hull of the *Traiano* sank with only the

British submarine *Trooper*, a big 'T' class boat, fitted with waterproof cylinders for 'Chariot' transport. Its arrangement is similar to that of the first Italian 'approacher' submarines.

One of the 'Chariots' that took part in the attack against Italian ships anchored in Palermo in January 1943 recovered by Regia Marina divers after the action.

extreme end of the bow visible, while the motor vessel was seriously damaged; on the other hand, the small charges applied to the two aforementioned destroyers and to the *Gimma*, did not explode as the safety pins were not removed. Most of the British raiders were captured shortly after the action and one of the Chariots was immediately recovered, almost intact, by Italian divers. Completing this operational cycle, Chariots *XII* and *XIII*, carried by the submarine HMS *Thunderbolt* attempted to force Tripoli harbour (Operation 'Welcome') on the night of 18/19 January 1943, but the action failed and the two craft were lost.

With the invasion of Sicily imminent some Chariots, using small 'U' class submarines as 'approachers', carried out some hydrographic surveys of the planned landing beaches on the southern coast of the island. Finally, during 1943 operations were planned against the main bases of the Italian fleet, but the armistice ended these projects.

During the period of Italian co-belligerency with the Allies, Chariots *LVIII* and *LX* participated in the forcing of La Spezia naval base (in German hands) on 22 June 1944 together with Italian 'approachers' and 'Gamma' divers, sank of the hull of the now abandoned cruiser *Bolzano*, severely damaged two years before and never repaired. Two more self-propelled craft of the same type, but crewed by Mariassalto operators to whom the craft had been 'loaned', were the protagonists of the 19 April 1945 attack on the unfinished aircraft carrier *Aquila* (formerly the liner *Roma*) moored in Genoa: only one of the two Chariots completed the action (Operation 'Toast', with the aim of preventing the big hull from being used by the Germans to

Another portrait of a British 'charioteer' showing many details of the suit and self-contained breathing apparatus. *(Imperial War Museum)*

Chariot Mk II General arrangement

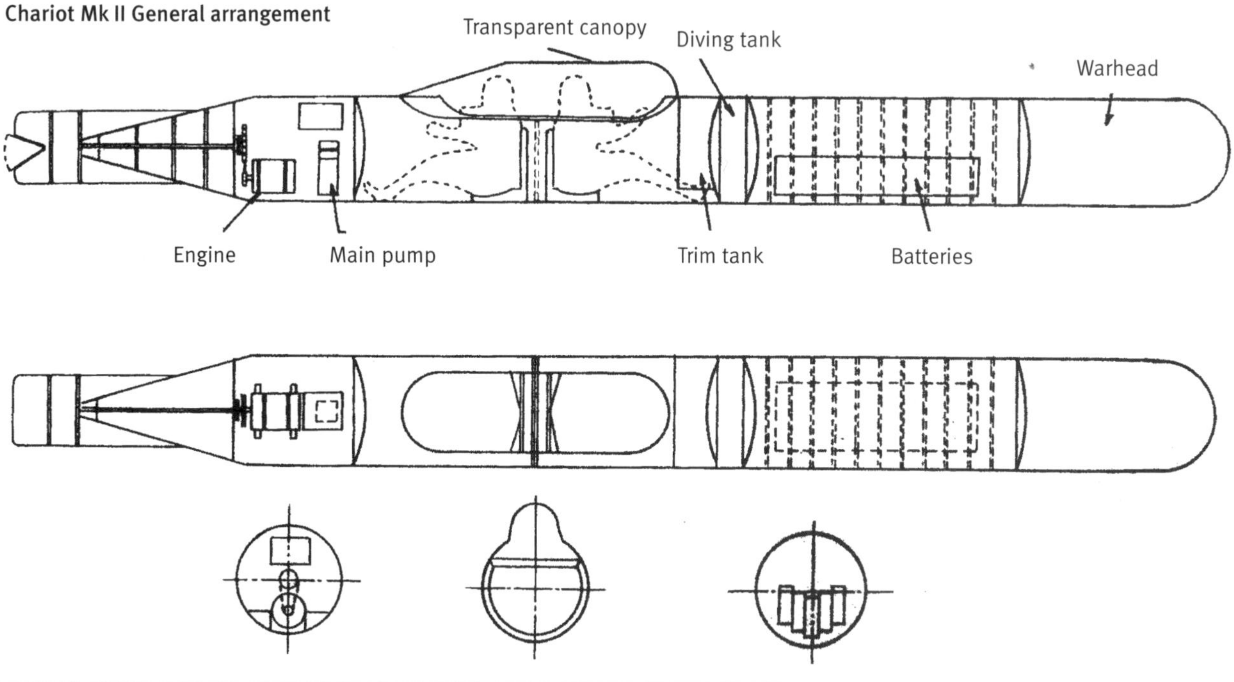

A group of 'charioteers' introduced to King George VI during a visit to a Royal Navy divers unit in spring 1944. *(Imperial War Museum)*

block the harbour entrance) but, for a complex of reasons, the target was found still afloat at the occupation of the Ligurian capital by the Allies a few days later.

Towards the end of the conflict the Royal Navy built an improved and enlarged version of the Mk I: the Mk II, also called the 'Terry Chariot'. In this model the two operators sat back-to-back, protected by a Perspex transparent dome somewhat resembling the SSB version of the original Italian 'pig'. Few were built, with numbers following that of Mk I. The Terry Chariot' saw action just once, in the far East, where two craft (*LXXIX* and *LXXX*) sank two merchant ships in Phuken, just north of Penang, in October 1944. These were the former Italian motorships *Sumatra* and *Volpi*, captured by the Japanese. Having returned aboard the 'approacher' submarine HMS *Trenchant* after the action, the self-propelled craft crews had the satisfaction to observe the ships sinking, through the periscope.

The first actual dropping of an explosive motorboat and its pilot took place on 10 June 1944 off the coast off Harwich from an altitude of 1500 metres (5000ft) from a four-engine Avro Lancaster bomber modified to carry a craft of this type under the fuselage. Suspended by a set of three parachutes, the motorboat touched the water with no damage, and ready to move. Despite the success of this test and the immediate availability of a few dozen craft, the British explosive motorboats had no opportunity for attacks on ships moored in enemy bases, as the famous canoes of the 'Special Boat Squadron', whose employment was a lot less expensive, simpler and less showy, were preferred. In fact, different models of small canoes (mostly paddle-powered) were built in Great Britain, and were successfully used as very quiet final 'approachers' for Commandos and assault swimmers for attacks on coastal installations and medium/small naval targets, with charges similar to those of the Italian 'Gamma' divers.

We must also remember the activity of the British

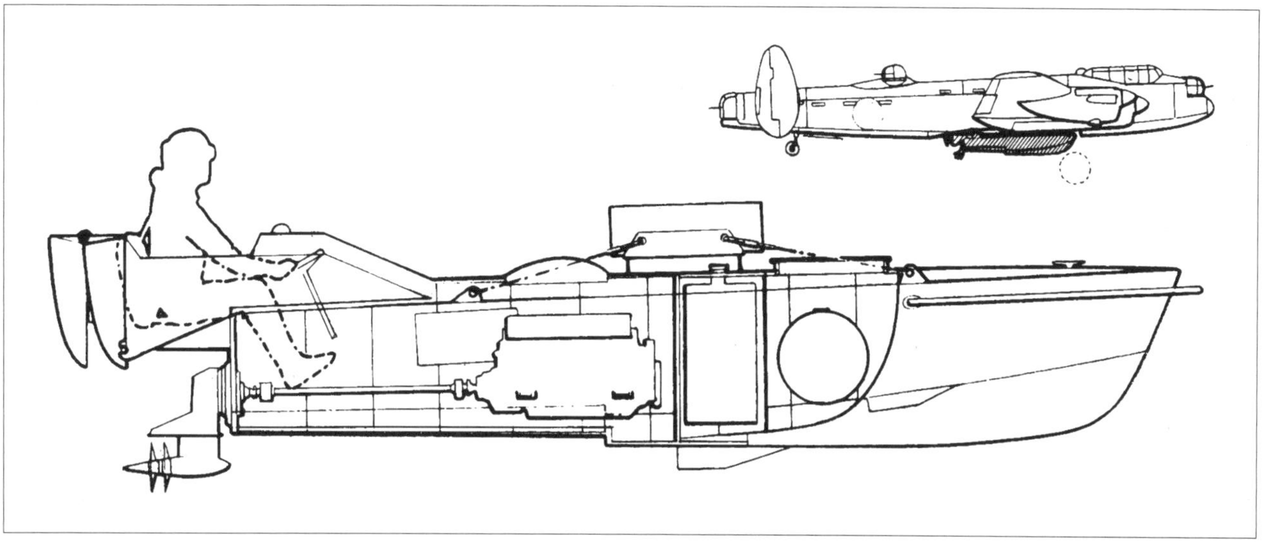

Parachutable British explosive motorboat 1944 –1945. The inset drawing shows the boat being carried beneath a Lancaster bomber. *(F Harrauer drawing)*

'Frogmen', originally intended for defence against the attacks of Italian divers, but later developed into the classic assault swimmers. Patron of this activity was the well-known Commander Lionel Crabb who worked for a long time with the 'Bombs and Mines Disposal Group' of Gibraltar. Crabb was to literally 'disappear' in mysterious circumstances in the waters off Portsmouth during the visit of the Soviet cruiser *Ordzhonikidze* in 1956 during the depth of the Cold War; but after the Italian armistice of September 1943 he had managed to rebuild an SLC with spare parts found aboard the *Olterra* when the British boarded the old tanker moored in Algeciras, having finally discovered its role as an advanced base. Named *Emily*, the British 'pig' was tried at sea by Crabb, but on 7 January 1944 it was lost in deep waters due to a sudden and uncontrollable shift in weight. In the immediate post-war period Crabb was also present, especially in Venice, for the tests led by the Allies with those 'Xa MAS' submarine assault craft which had come into their possession.

Kriegsmarine

In Germany, the drive to build naval assault craft was an initiative not by the Navy but by the Army, that had a special unit (Regiment Brandenburg), which included groups of sappers with various specialisations, including that of the Küstenjäger (Coastal hunters). At the beginning of 1944, however, the

Commander Lionel Crabb pictured in Venice in spring 1945.

A German 'Linse' type explosive motorboat, a direct descendant of Italian MTM explosive motorboats, but fitted with radio-control for the final run against the target.

Close-up of a 'Linse' undergoing maintenance.

A group of 'Linsen' being prepared for an exercise.

responsibility for designing and using assault craft – both surface and underwater – was transferred to the Kriegsmarine, that established a special task force (Kommando der Kleinkampfverbände) conventionally referred to as 'Unit K'.

A model of an explosive motorboat was developed based on First World War experience and on the boats studied by the Army (Sprengboote). Known as the 'Linse', its characteristics were similar to the Italian MTM, with the peculiarity, however, that after the pilot had taken to his life-raft, the craft was radio-controlled by a guide motorboat to the target. 'Linsen' had a burst charge of about 300kg placed in the centre section of the hull. One radio guide motorboat (Fuhurungboot) for every two 'Linsen' was planned; three units formed an attack group (Rotte). From March 1944 to the end of the conflict, little more than a year later, more than 1500 'Linsen' were built: their main task should have been opposing the Allied landing attempts along the coasts of 'Fortress Europe' from Norway to the Mediterranean.

After the Italian armistice many dozens of explosive

MTM 8B outfitted by CABI for the Kriegsmarine ('D' type MTM). This explosive motorboat was captured off Provence by the destroyer USS *Gleaves* on 2 October 1944 and is shown aboard the cruiser USS *Philadelphia* which is transporting it to the United States. *(US Navy)*

German officers aboard an 'MT-Gamma' type motorboat used in the Adriatic for transporting assault divers.

motorboats (MTM type) and torpedo boats (MTSMA) built by the CABI and SIAI companies on German orders, were armed in the Mediterranean by the Kriegsmarine with tasks similar to those of the 'Linsen'. Despite the high number of boats available, the results obtained by the Germans were rather modest.

In the field of underwater assault craft the German Navy turned its attention to the so-called 'piloted torpedoes': large electric torpedoes that housed an operator, and carried another torpedo hung below as armament. The first Kriegsmarine piloted torpedo was the 'Neger', over 7 metres long and derived from the 'Ge7' electric torpedo: about 200 were built. These were followed by about 300 of the 'Marder' type, with slightly improved features. Other models were the 'Delphin' and the 'Hai', of similar performance, which did not go beyond the experimental phase. Generally, all these craft had torpedo hulls, travelling almost at sea level at modest speed, and

Close-up of a German 'Neger' type piloted torpedo.

A Kriegsmarine assault diver with modified 'Dräger' oxygen self-contained breathing apparatus.

piloted by a single operator equipped with a 'Dräger' oxygen breathing apparatus.

Halfway between the assault craft and the mini-submarine were the 'Biber' and 'Molch', armed with two torpedoes, over 700 of which were built between 1944 and 1945.

The large-scale building of underwater assault craft and small 'pocket' submarines (types 'Hecht', 'Seehund' etc) began in Germany only in March 1944. In July of the same year the construction of these units even took precedence over all other types of submarines – with the exception of the XXI and XXIII type Elektroboote – with the intention of using them for a mass last-ditch defence of the coasts. The considerable industrial and training effort expended, in desperate times for Germany, did not pay a significant dividend when their time came: these craft succeeded in sinking only some transport vessel of the Allied invasion fleets and a few minor units at the price of very heavy losses, especially among the piloted torpedoes.

Imperial Japanese Navy

Although Japan had been building torpedo-armed mini-submarines with crews of 2, 3 and 5 people since 1936, the design and construction of underwater and surface assault craft only began in early 1944. The surface craft, developed collaboratively by the Army and Navy, were explosive motorboats inspired by similar Italian craft, though a little less elaborate, and conceived essentially for coastal defence. At first known as 'Maru Yon' and later 'Shynyo' (literally 'Ocean Agitator'), several variants of these boats were built (from 'Nº 1' to 'Nº 5'), totalling 6200 units by the Navy and about 3000 by the Army.

The 'Shynyo' attack technique was usual for the explosive motorboats, inspired by the Italian use of this type of craft. The pilot was expected to abandon the motorboat by jumping into water just before impact with the target, but it was quite common amongst Japanese operators to sacrifice themselves by driving their boats until the end, or perishing from the effects of the explosion after bailing out too late. This was a peculiarity of the 'Shynyo', which effectively became suicide boats, unlike similar Italian, German and British craft where the pilot's survival was central to the operational concept.

The first mass use of the 'Shynyo' occurred in January 1945, against the US invasion fleet in the Gulf of Lingayen in the Philippines. The action took the US Navy by complete surprise, and many landing and transport ships and craft were sunk or suffered considerable damage as a consequence, even though the

Some of the many 'Shynyo' found on Okinawa at the end of the US conquest in spring 1945.

amphibious operations suffered no significant slowdowns. However, having recovered from the initial surprise, the Americans organised appropriate defences using mainly small units (PC, PCE and PT Boats), but above all the well-armed escort gunships of the LCS(L) type. In subsequent amphibious operations, the attacks by 'Shynyo' were almost completely neutralised, despite the high number of boats available to the Japanese defence forces. To get an idea of the quantities involved, it should be remembered that at the time of the occupation of the small island of Kerama Retto about 390 'Shynyos' were found, ready to attack the US naval forces if they attempted a landing on Okinawa. The plan failed because Kerama Retto was occupied before Okinawa, completely surprising the Japanese. On Okinawa, the Japanese were forced to sabotage more than 700 explosive motorboats that could not be employed.

In anticipation of the invasion of the Japanese home territory a total of about 2000 'Shynyo' were ready for the last-ditch defence, as early as the late spring of 1945. It was estimated that this mass of light motorboats could have attacked the Allied invasion fleet for ten consecutive days.

A Japanese mod 1/1 'Shynyo' suicide attack explosive motorboat on trials in 1944.

'Kaiten' launch test from one of the stern slides on the Japanese light cruiser *Kitakami*.

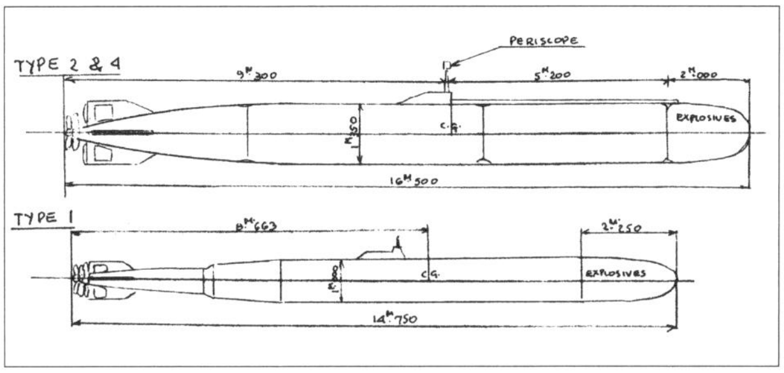

General sketch of the two main 'Kaiten' types. *(S Fukui drawing)*

The main underwater assault craft employed by the Japanese was the 'Kaiten' (literally 'turn towards the sky'), described as a 'guided torpedo', whose production began towards the middle of 1944. They were small torpedo-shaped submarines, 14 to 16 metres long depending on the model, built around a 'Type 93' (the famous 'Long Lance') oxygen torpedo engine. Fitted with a 1560–1800kg explosive charge in the nose and crewed by only one man, their range was around 40 miles at 12 knots continuous speed, while the maximum attack speed reached 30 knots. Three main 'Kaiten' models were built: the second, produced in very few units, was propelled by a closed-cycle turbine of the German 'Walter' type, and could reach 40 knots.

The idea of using guided torpedoes crewed by pilots consciously devoted to sacrifice had been cherished for some time in the Japanese naval circles, that had followed with interest and admiration the successes achieved in two world wars by the Italians – even if the Italians did not expect the voluntary sacrifice of the operators.

A first 'Kaiten' model ('Type 1') was ready by early 1944 and in October of the same year, when the use of 'kamikaze' aircraft began to spread, arousing the growing interest of young Japanese pilots, the first volunteers for the 'Kaiten' were enrolled. Their lifestyle, the psychological preparation and the emotive ceremonial of investiture and farewell to the companions before the one and last mission were identical to those of the 'kamikazes'.

'Kaiten' on the deck of a big Japanese submarine.

The 'Kaiten' were normally transported to the theatre of action by other units: large submarines, but also surface ships like the cruiser *Kitakami*. The latter launched the submarines from special slides; the large carrier submarines – which transported between three and six 'Kaiten' on deck – instead, were forced to use a more complex release manoeuvre that, however, produced good results. During the missions, the 'Kaiten' pilots lived inside the mother-submarine until the opportunity for action arose. Then they moved to their craft through special watertight trunking, and locked themselves in. Through the following phase of approach to the targets, the pilots remained in telephone contact with the submarine control room to receive the latest data on course and speed of the targets and any special instructions. The order to start, detach from the submarine and attack was given to the 'Kaiten' at about 7000 metres from the targets. During the approach, just below the surface, the pilots could correct the course of the craft by observing the target through a small periscope; after setting a correct collision course with the enemy ship, the pilots dived the torpedoes to a depth of four metres and locked the controls at about 500 metres from the impact point. The explosion of the charge against the hull of the target was enough to sink a medium-sized ship, with much more destructive results than those of the 'kamikaze' and the 'Shynyo'.

The first operational use of the 'Kaiten' took place in November 1944, and continued at an increasing rate until the last days of the war, employing all the surviving ocean-going Japanese Navy submarines as carriers. However, the overall results achieved by the 'Kaiten' were rather modest. This was probably the result of the insufficient and hasty training of the pilots, and the difficulties of manoeuvring a craft that did not stabilise on the target course with sufficient speed and precision, besides being unable to correct course in the final stage of the fast run.

By the end of the conflict many of these underwater craft were found in Japanese bases, ready for the desperate defence against the expected final enemy attack. Overall, from mid-1944 to August1945, several hundred 'Kaiten' were built, but only about fifty were actually employed in war operations.

Equivalent Ranks

Italian Navy[1]	Royal Navy	US Navy
Grande ammiraglio	Admiral of the Fleet	Fleet Admiral
Ammiraglio d'armata	Admiral	Admiral
Ammiraglio di squadra	Vice Admiral	Vice Admiral
Ammiraglio di divisione	Rear Admiral	Rear Admiral (upper half)
Contrammiraglio	Commodore	Rear Admiral (lower half)
Capitano di vascello (cv)	Captain	Captain
Capitano di fregata (cf)	Commander	Commander
Capitano di corvetta (cc)	Lieutenant Commander	Lieutenant Commander
Tenente di vascello (tv)	Lieutenant	Lieutenant
Sottotenente di vascello (stv)	*(No corresponding rank)*	Lieutenant, junior grade
Guardiamarina (gm)	Sub-Lieutenant	Ensign
Aspirante guardiamarina (asp gm)	Midshipman	Midshipman
Capo di 1ª classe (C° 1ª c)	Chief petty officer, 1st class	Chief petty officer, 1st class
Capo di 2ª classe (C° 2ª c)	Chief petty officer, 2nd class	Chief petty officer, 2nd class
Capo di 3ª classe (C° 3ª c)	Chief petty officer, 2nd class	Chief petty officer, 2nd class
2° Capo (2° c)	2nd Chief petty officer	2nd Chief petty officer
Sergente (serg)	Sergeant	Sergeant
Sottocapo (sc)	Leading Seaman	Leading Seaman
Comune di 1ª classe (mar)	1st class Seaman	1st class Seaman
Comune di 2ª classe (mar)	2nd class Seaman	2nd class Seaman

1. Officers of the Technical Corps (Engineer Corps, Naval Weapons Corps, Medical Corps, etc, equivalent ranks in the Italian Army): Generale Ispettore = Amm sq; Tenente generale = Amm div; Maggior generale = Contramm; Colonnello (col) = Cap vascello; Tenente colonnello (t col) = Cap fregata; Maggiore (mg) = Cap corvetta; Capitano (cap) = Tenente vasc; Tenente (ten) = S Ten vasc; Sottotenente (s ten) = Guardiamarina. 'Operaio mil' were civilian technicians under military control. There were several in the X Mas, drafted from the manufacturers of craft and equipment.

Note: The operators are listed using the common abbreviations then in use, and the rank at the time of the mission.

For the main decorations, the following abbreviations are used:
MO: Gold Medal of Military Valour
MA: Silver Medal of Military Valour
MB: Bronze Medal of Military Valour
CVM: War Cross of Military Valour
OMS: Military Order of Savoy (today OMI - Military Order of Italy)
A/P: Rank advancement or promotion
The (+) and (°) marks after each name mean respectively: Killed in action and Captured.

Chronology and summary of the main actions carried out by Italian assault craft (1918 and 1940–1945)

13 MAY 1918

Target: Warships moored in Pola
Grillo 'jumping' boat

From Venice with the support of torpedo boats *9 PN* and *10 PN*, of *MAS 95* and *96* and the distant escort of 5 destroyers.

Crew: tv Mario Pellegrini MO (°)
2° c Antonio Milani MO (°)
sc Giuseppe Corrias MO (°)
mar Francesco Angelino MO (°)

Discovered while overcoming external obstructions of Pola, the boat was badly damaged by enemy fire and its sinking was accelerated by the crew activating the self-destruct charges.

Failed mission.

Wreck of the *Grillo* recovered by the Austrians a few days after the 13 May 1918 action, on a Pola harbour quay. *(A Molinari collection)*.

Before 13 May 1918, 'jumping' boats had attempted two unsuccessful actions against Pola:

8 APRIL 1918
Boats *Grillo, Pulce, Locusta* and *Cavalletta*

Under the command of tv Pellegrini, Da Zara, Castellani and Speziale, the small boats left Venice towed by torpedo boats *13, 15, 16, 18, 48 OS* and *14 PN* with the distant escort of the scouts *Aquila* and *Sparviero* and two destroyer squadrons. As a result of the complexity of the fleet there were delays in the approach navigation to the target and, given the advanced hour close to the sunrise, the mission was aborted.

12 APRIL 1918
Boats *Cavalletta* and *Pulce*

From Venice towed by *MAS 95* and *96*, the support of torpedo boats *13, 16* and *18 OS* and the same distant escort of the previous mission. Released too far from the target and no longer able to reach it before dawn, the commanders of the boats decided to return to the waiting Mas. The operation to take them in tow added further delay and, to avoid the risk of being discovered and compromising future actions, the two boats were scuttled and the rest of the force returned undiscovered to base.

Three other attempts were made by *Grillo* alone on 6, 9 and 12 May 1918, but the first two had to be cancelled due to adverse weather conditions and the third because of an unrepairable failure of the torpedo rack.

31 OCTOBER 1918
Target: Major naval units moored in Pola
Rossetti S.2 semi-submersible craft (nicknamed '*Mignatta*')

From Venice aboard torpedo boat *65 PN* and then in tow of *MAS 95* (C° Gino Montipò) with capitano di vascello Costanzo Ciano aboard as mission leader.

Operators:

mag (engineer) Raffaele Rossetti	MO and A/P (°)
ten (doctor) Raffaele Paolucci	MO and A/P (°)

Penetrating Pola harbour undiscovered, the two operators targeted the dreadnought *Viribus Unitis* (21,370 tons) with their first charge, causing her sinking. Discovered, they left the *Mignatta* in motion with the last charge triggered; the device ended up under the

Battleship *Viribus Unitis* sinking in Pola.

stern of the big liner *Wien* (7400grt), that was seriously damaged and partly sank; later recovered, it resumed passenger service under the Italian flag with the name of *Vienna*.

Fully successful mission.

AUGUST 1940

Operation GA 1. Target: Alexandria
'Approacher': submarine *Iride*

Submarine commanding officer:
tv Francesco Brunetti
Mission leader: cv Mario Giorgini

Leaving La Spezia on the 12th, reached Messina on the 14th, then headed for the Gulf of Bomba, in Cyrenaica, on the 16th, meeting the requisitioned motorship *Monte Gargano* and torpedo boat *Calipso* (tv G. Zambardi) that had transported four SLC type craft from Italy to be transferred aboard the *Iride* and released with their operators near the target on the night of the 25th.

Lieutenant Luigi Durand de la Penne who did his utmost to save crewmen from submarine *Iride*, sunk by British aircraft in the Gulf of Bomba on 21 August 1940.

SLC operators:

tv Gino Birindelli	MA
tv Alberto Franzini	MA
cap Teseo Tesei	MA
cap Elios Toschi	MA
C° 3ª cl. Enrico Lazzari	
2° c Damos Paccagnini	MA
2° c Emilio Bianchi	MB
serg Alcide Pedretti	MB

Reserves:

stv Luigi Durand De La Penne	MB
serg Giovanni Lazzaroni	MB
operaio mil Pietro Biradelli	MA

Around 12.00 on the 21st, an attack by three British torpedo bombers on the Gulf of Bomba sank both the motorship and the submarine, that was surfacing after a trial dive with the assault craft secured to saddles on deck. The submarine was broken in two and sank immediately; the SLC operators rushed in immediately and were the decisive factor in the rescue of some crews trapped in the wreck. The four SLC sunk without serious damage with the *Iride* were immediately recovered and re-embarked on *Calipso* which brought them back to La Spezia.

Failed mission.

SEPTEMBER 1940

Operation GA 2. Target: Alexandria
'Approacher': submarine *Gondar*

Submarine commanding officer:
tv Francesco Brunetti (MB) (°)
Mission leader: cv Mario Giorgini (°)

Left La Spezia on the 21st with three SLCs stored in waterproof cylinders on deck, reached Messina on the 23rd to embark the assault operators. After a stop in Tobruk, on the 29th, the submarine was discovered about 100 miles from the target, and attacked with depth charges by destroyers *Stuart* (Australian) and *Diamond* (British) with the support of a Sunderland

Submarine *Gondar* sinking off Alexandria on 30 September 1940. Only the tip of the bow is visible. *(Imperial War Museum)*

flying boat. On the morning of the following day, after 14 hours of continuous hunting, the damaged boat was forced to surface and scuttled; many wounded and one killed (electrician Luigi Longobardo, MO) amongst the crew. All survivors were captured.

SLC operators:

tv Alberto Franzini	CVM
gm Alberto Cacioppo	CVM
cap Elios Toschi	CVM and OMS
serg Umberto Ragnati	CVM
cap Gustavo Stefanini	CVM
serg Alessandro Scappino	CVM

Reserves:

serg Aristide Calcagno	CVM
2° c. Giovanni Lazzaroni	CVM
c° 2a c. Cipriano Cipriani	

Mission failed.

Operation BG 1. Target: Gibraltar
'Approacher': submarine *Sciré*

Submarine commanding officer:
cc Junio Valerio Borghese

The submarine left La Spezia heading for Gibraltar on 24 September 1940 with three SLCs aboard. On the 29th, still about 50 miles from the target, the order to head back was received, as the major British ships had put to sea. Following a brief stop in La Maddalena from 3 October, *Scirè* returned to La Spezia.

SLC operators:
tv Gino Birindelli
cap Teseo Tesei
stv Luigi Durand De La Penne
2° c Damos Paccagnini
serg Alcide Pedretti
2° c Emilio Bianchi

Reserves:
ten Gastone Bertozzi
serg Enrico Ario Lazzari

Mission cancelled.

OCTOBER 1940

Operation BG 2. Target: Gibraltar
'Approacher': submarine *Sciré*

Submarine commanding officer:
cc Junio Valerio Borghese MO

Transporting three SLCs and their operators, the submarine left La Spezia on the 21st, forcing the Strait of Gibraltar on the night between 28 and 29, and entering the haven where the operators and craft were released at 02.19. Heading back to the base, the *Sciré* resurfaced after about 40 hours of underwater navigation, finally reaching La Spezia on the evening of 3 November.

SLC operators:

tv Gino Birindelli MO (°)
cap Teseo Tesei A/P
stv Luigi Durand De La Penne rewarded with promotion from reservist to Permanent Commission
2° c Damos Paccagnini MA (°)
serg Alcide Pedretti A/P
2° c Emilio Bianchi A/P

Reserves:

Ten GN Gastone Bertozzi
2° c pal Giuseppe Viglioli

The Birindelli/Paccagnini team arrived close to the battleship HMS *Barham* moored in the military harbour, but was forced to give up the attack due to craft failure. Despite a failed attempt to drag the SLC along the bottom, it had to be abandoned after the time charge fuse was activated; the explosion caused no damage to ships. The two operators were captured.

The Tesei/Pedretti and De La Penne/Bianchi teams were also forced to abandon their craft because of failures, again after activating self-destruction. Therefore they swam towards the Spanish coast near the town of La Linea, where they were recovered by the prearranged Italian clandestine organisation, and repatriated.

British divers managed to recover part of the heavily damaged wreck of the Birindelli/Paccagnini craft, while the Spanish authorities recovered Tesei's SLC almost intact after it had run aground on the coast near La Linea, probably because of the failure of the self-destruction charges. This craft would be returned to the Italian Navy only after the war, in 1975, and is preserved as a memorial at the Comando Subacquei e Incursori at Varignano, La Spezia.

Mission failed.

MARCH 1941

First 'explosive motorboats' mission.
Target: shipping in Suda Bay (Crete)
'Approacher' craft: destroyers *Francesco Crispi* and *Quintino Sella*

Motorboat group leader: tv Luigi Faggioni

First explosive motorboats mission. By the end of December 1940, the eight MT for the operation were transferred from Augusta to the island of Leros (Parteni Bay) aboard the destroyers *Dardo* and *Strale*, but the destroyers *Crispi* (cf Ferruta) and *Sella* (cc

A view of the entrance to Suda Bay as it appeared in the early 1990s from offshore. *(S Bagnasco)*

The SLC used by the Tesei/Pedretti team in operation BG 2 against Gibraltar recovered nearly intact by the Spaniards. The craft is shown after substantial modifications by the Spanish Navy, which tested it for a long time. It is pictured aboard the ship bringing it back to Italy in 1975.

Redaelli), based in the Dodecanese, were designated final 'approachers' instead.

The operation was initially planned for January 1941, then postponed to February and finally performed in March. Shortly before the start of the expedition, an air strike damaged two motorboats, which were left ashore upon departing from the island of Stampalia at 17.30 on 25 March.

Shortly after midnight on the 25th the six remaining boats were put in the water about 6 miles from the entrance to Suda Bay, beginning the last phase of the slow-motion approach. Passing the double line of external obstructions without raising the alarm, and after a long journey down the deep inlet, the craft passed the last obstruction silently. Targets assigned, the individual attacks were performed at dawn, in a quick sequence starting at 05.30:

- tenente di vascello Luigi Faggioni (MO), tried to hit the light cruiser HMS *Coventry*, sighted suddenly and underway at slow speed, but the attack failed and the boat exploded against a dock;
- sottotenente di vascello Angelo Cabrini (MO) hit the moored heavy cruiser HMS *York* (8250 tons) with his craft;
- capo di 3a c Tullio Tedeschi (MO and P/A) also exploded his boat against the *York*;
- capo di 3a c Alessio De Vito (MO and P/A) launched his craft, which hit no target;
- 2° capo Lino Beccati (MO and P/A) hit the tanker *Pericles* (8234grt) with his boat;
- sergente Emilio Barbieri (MO and P/A) launched his craft, which hit no target.

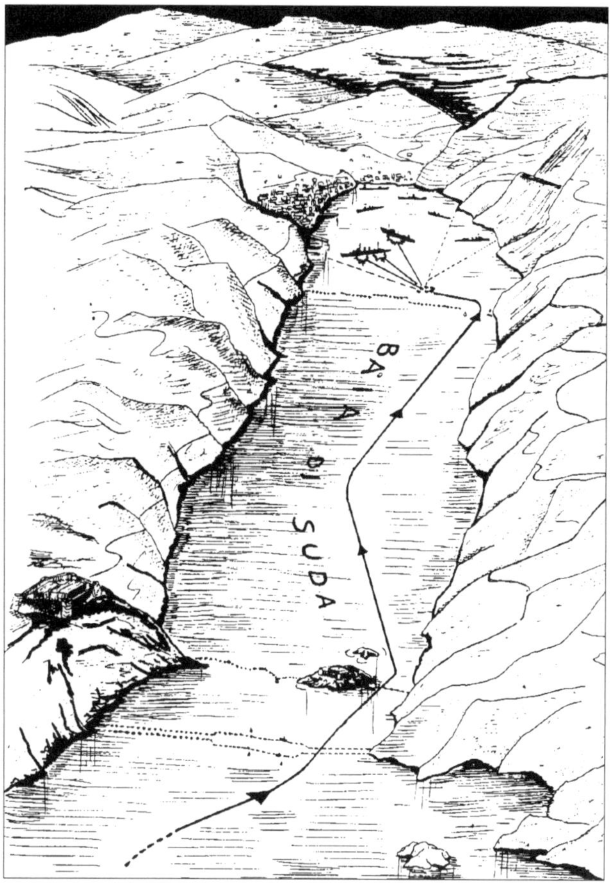

The forcing of Suda Bay Souda by explosive motorboats on the night of 25/26 March 1941.

Altogether, three of the MT exploded against their targets, two were destroyed upon hitting the coast, one was recovered unexploded by the British,

The wrecked cruiser HMS *York* taken in Suda in spring–summer 1941.

Another view of the wrecked cruiser HMS *York* taken in Suda in spring–summer 1941.

but exploded shortly after, during inspection.

All the operators, unscathed, were taken prisoner (°).

HMS *York* was badly damaged and, with the engine rooms completely flooded, settled on the bottom almost upright. Immobilised, the cruiser was heavily hit by German air raids in the following days and reduced to an unusable wreck. The tanker *Pericles* was seriously damaged too, but did not sink; hastily repaired, it was evacuated from Crete the following month, sinking after structural failures before reaching Alexandria.

Mission successful.

The heavily damaged tanker *Pericles*.

APRIL 1941

Combat reconnaissance with 'light motor torpedo boats'. Target: Corfu waters

Mission leader:
cf Vittorio Moccagatta aboard *MAS 539*

A combat reconnaissance of the Corfu, Sarandë and Porto Edda moorings was organised to test the capabilities of the first light torpedo motorboats (MTS). Leaving Brindisi on 2 April, *MAS 539* and *535* reached Sazan island, in Albania, towing two MTS crewed by the following pilots:

MTS 2: cc Giorgio Giobbe, stv Aldo Massarini;
MTS 4: stv Renato Iovine; 2° Enrico Cerruti

During the night of 4/5 April, the Mas reached the point of expected release, cut the tow and continued along the coast. Discovered, framed by some searchlights and subjected to fire from the coast, the MTS were forced to retreat: *MTS 2* made it back to the waiting Mas, while *4* (jettisoning its two small torpedoes to increase speed) returned to Sazan.

Mission failed.

MAY 1941

Operation BG 3. Target: Gibraltar, merchant shipping moored in the harbour
'Approacher': submarine *Sciré*

Submarine commanding officer:
cc Junio Valerio Borghese

Leaving La Spezia on 15 May with 3 SLCs inside their special watertight cylinders, but with no operators aboard, the submarine passed the Straits of Gibraltar between the 22nd and 23rd. After spending many daylight hours lying on the bottom, it entered the river Guadalete under cover of darkness, ran up to the Spanish port of Cadiz, and tied up alongside the Italian tanker *Fulgor* (code-named secret base 'C') which had been interned since June 1940. Having embarked the operators (who had clandestinely reached the ship in the previous days) and verified the efficiency of the three self-propelled craft already on board, *Sciré* tried to reach the deep bay of Algeciras on the 25th but, hampered by a strong contrary current, had to give up. It tried again on the 26th with better luck, emerging at the centre of the vast bay off the mouth of the Rio Guadarranque, where operators and craft were released.

After that the *Sciré* retired, reaching La Spezia on 31 May.

SLC crews:

SLC 130 tv Decio Catalano	MA
sc Giovanni Giannoni	MA
SLC 120 tv Amedeo Vesco	MA
sc Amelio Franchi	
(taken ill, replaced by cap A Marceglia)	
SLC 160 stv Licio Visintini	MA
sc Giovanni Magro	MA

Reserves:

ten Antonio Marceglia	MA
sc Spartaco Schergat	MB

Mission medical officer: ten Bruno Falcomatà

The 'pig' assigned to the Vesco/Marceglia pair did not start through motor failure. It was sunk, and the extra warhead entrusted to Visintini's SLC, which embarked even Vesco himself, while Marceglia joined the Catalano/Giannoni team. During the attack on a merchant ship at anchor, Marceglia was suddenly

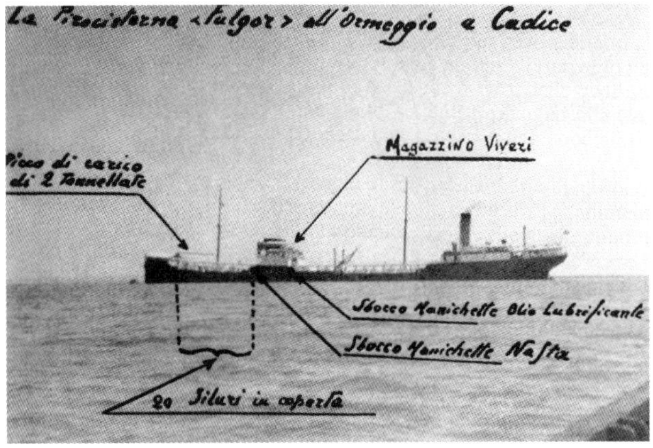

Tanker *Fulgor* anchored in Cádiz in an Italian Navy Information Service picture. *(USMM)*

taken ill, while the *SLC 130* sank, and was lost. All three operators of this self-propelled craft managed to swim to land, and were recovered and then repatriated.

Visintini, after discarding several targets (a hospital ship, a neutral, etc), was attacking a steamer when his 'pig' lost buoyancy and sank. The crew of this craft was also recovered as soon as it landed and returned to Italy.

Mission failed.

SPRING 1941

A temporary surface assault craft base was established in Augusta for preparing an attack against the main Malta anchorages. A group of MT type explosive motorboats was deployed from La Spezia, while some MTS (probably two) arrived from Brindisi.

JUNE 1941

Operation Malta 1. Target: Valletta harbour

Mission leader: cf Vittorio Moccagatta

24 June

MAS 451 and *452* carrying the MT pilots tasked to attack Valletta harbour carried out a coastal reconnaissance mission off the island.

28 June

Capitano di fregata Moccagatta, with the two Mas cited above and the support of *MAS 509*, *556* and *562* attempted the attack with a group of eight MT explosive boats and an MTS motor torpedo boat skippered by cv Giorgio Giobbe. The accidental sinking of an

MT and other failures forced the mission to be aborted, and the force returned to Augusta.

30 June

The mission left Augusta again at 15.00, with fresh wind and sea; shortly after, an MT began to take on water, and cv Moccagatta ordered its return, towed by a Mas. Convinced that wind and sea conditions would improve later, the commander chose to go on; then the engine of the explosive boat designated to attack the surface obstructions failed. Still not persuaded to cancel the operation, the approach continued until a Mas engine also failed; then, considering also the late hour, the return was ordered.

JULY 1941

Operation Malta 2. Target: Valletta harbour

Mission leader: cf Vittorio Moccagatta MO (+)

Compared with 'Malta 1', the organisation of the operation was heavily modified, becoming much more complex and interconnected. At sunset on 26 July the following departed Augusta:

Armed Fast Yacht *Diana* cc Mario Di Muro (MA)
with 9 MT aboard and an MTL under tow;
MAS 452 tv Giobatta Parodi MA (+)
tasked with MTS recovery, with cf Moccagatta and ten Bruno Falcomatà MO (+) aboard;
MAS 451 stv Giorgio Sciolette MA (°)
tasked with the second phase of MTL tow;
cc Giorgio Giobbe MO (+);
sc Leonildo Zocchi MB (+);
sc Luigi Costantini MB (+);
craft tasked with MT guidance;
MTL sc Tindaro Paratore MA (°);
with two SLC aboard:

Lieutenant Commander Giorgio Giobbe in Augusta in spring 1941.

Commander Vittorio Moccagatta aboard *MAS 452* leaving Augusta for an exercise in preparation for the attack on Malta. To his right is Major (eng) Teseo Tesei in grey overalls, and to his left Lieutenant Giovanni Battista Parodi, Mas commanding officer. *(USMM)*

Chief petty officer, 2nd class Pietro Zaniboni pictured in Augusta aboard his MT type explosive motorboat.

St Elmo bridge at the entrance of Valletta harbour in Malta with a span collapsed after the attack of 26/27 July 1941.

The broken-down *MT 16* captured by the British off Malta.

1° SLC mag Teseo Tesei MO (+);
2° c Alcide Pedretti MO (+);
target: obstructions under St Elmo bridge;
2° SLC tv Franco Costa MA (°);
serg Luigi Barla MA (°);
target: Marsa Muscetto submarine base;
1° MT stv Carlo Bosio MO (+);
charge set to detonate at 5 metres;
2° MT stv Roberto Frassetto MO (°);
charge set to detonate at 1.5 metres;
3° MT s ten AN Aristide Carabelli MO (+);
charge set to detonate at surface;
4° MT Vittorio Marchisio MA (°);
charge set to detonate as 1° MT, as all the following;
5° MT 2° c Vincenzo Montanari MA (+);
6° MT 2° c Alessandro Follieri MB (°);
7° MT 2° c Enrico Pedrini MA (°);
8° MT c° 3a c Pietro Zaniboni MA (°);
9° MT c° 3a c Fiorenzo Capriotti MA (°)
craft tasked with attacking defence positions;

Reserves
cap Vincenzo Martellotta MA;
cap Gastone Bertozzi MA;
tv Pietro Miniat MB;
gm Vittorio Pinto MB;
c° 3a cls Mario Marino MB;
c° 3a cls Francesco Malfa MB;
Corrado Gianni CVM.

At 23.00 on the 26th the force reached the established point 'C' (20 miles off Valletta). The *Diana* put the MTs into the water, but some accidents caused delays (a cable fouled *MAS 451*'s propeller, and the MTL was slightly damaged by collision). At 02.00 some Malta searchlights came on briefly. One hour later, and already late, the 'pigs' were launched from the MTL; Costa's floated stern-down because of a failed transfer pump, and after several attempts it was decided to sink it.

Around 04.30 Tesei and his SLC should have been close to the wire mesh obstruction placed under the bridge of St Elmo to blow it up, and the MTs should have started their attacks at 04.40. As result of closely spaced explosions (two boats in rapid succession and perhaps the charge of Tesei's 'pig'), a span of the bridge collapsed into the water blocking the entry of other boats into the harbour. At the same time the harbour defences, already on alert for some time, began a fierce response that lasted until 04.50. All the explosive motorboats were lost except *MT 16*, broken down and later captured by the British. The two Mas, the MTS and the MTL moving away from the island were strafed by numerous British fighters: of about 50 men who had participated in the action only 11 returned: all the others were killed, or ended up prisoners. *MAS 451* was sunk and *452*, left adrift after the loss of most of the crew, was captured. The damaged MTL was scuttled while the MTS managed to reach the *Diana* unscathed, with some *MAS 452* survivors on board.

The main reason for the failure of this operation was the complete lack of surprise, the raiding force being discovered at great distance, thanks to the presence on Malta of radar stations and the British

MT 16 transferred to a Grand Harbour quay to be inspected. *(NWM, Malta)*

Two pictures of the wreck of the Costa/Barla team's SLC that was sunk off Marsamxett and later recovered split in three parts by the British.

hydrophone network, which had alerted the coastal defences in good time.

Mission failed.

SEPTEMBER 1941

Operation BG 4. Target: Gibraltar (military harbour)
'Approacher': submarine *Sciré*

Submarine commanding officer:

cc Junio Valerio Borghese	A/P

The submarine left La Spezia on 10 September, with three 'pigs' aboard:

SLC 140 tv Decio Catalano	MA
sc Giuseppe Giannoni	MA and A/P
SLC 210 tv Amedeo Vesco	MA
sc Antonio Zozzoli	MA and A/P
SLC 220 tv Licio Visintini	MA
sc Giovanni Magro	MA and A/P

Reserves

cap Antonio Marceglia	CVM
Sc pal Spartaco Schergat	CVM
S ten Giorgio Spaccarelli	CVM

Operators and reserves arrived in Cadiz by air and embarked secretly on the tanker *Fulgor*. *Sciré* passed the Strait of Gibraltar on 16 September and on the 18th reached Cadiz and came up alongside the *Fulgor*. The next day the submarine entered Algeciras Bay, released the operators and their craft around 01.07 on the 20th, then retreated towards blue water, reaching La Spezia on the 25th.

Vesco/Zozzoli team. Intended to operate against battleships, they were discovered by patrol boats about fifty metres from the boom defences of the military harbour, so attacked the tanker *Fiona Shell* (2444grt) at anchor in the roadstead. When the charge exploded, the ship broke in two. Having activated the craft's self-destruct timer, they reached land but were stopped by Spanish sentries to whom they claimed to be shipwrecked.

Snapshot of Lieutenant Commander Junio Valerio Borghese taken in Bocca di Serchio in 1941.

Close-up of the conning tower of the submarine *Sciré* in late 1941. Compared to its original configuration, the structure has been heavily modified with reduced height and bulk, making it less visible on the surface.

Catalano/Giannoni team. Although also intended to operate against battleships, the vigilant defence forced them to attack a merchant ship at anchor in the roadstead. The first chosen target turned out to be a requisitioned former Italian ship so the attack was directed at the British ship *Durham* (10,900grt) that was beached after the explosion of the charge and later recovered.

Visintini/Magro team. Target assigned: aircraft carrier HMS *Ark Royal.* Prevented from approaching the carrier by the explosions of charges dropped by the patrol boats, so attacked the military tanker *Derbydale* (8145grt) which, though severely damaged, would not sink.

All operators reached the coast, were recovered and quickly repatriated.

Partially successful mission.

DECEMBER 1941

Operation GA 3. Target: Alexandria 'Approacher': submarine *Sciré*

Submarine commanding officer:
cf Junio Valerio Borghese OMS

The *Sciré* left La Spezia on 3 December with three SLCs aboard, heading for Messina. It arrived at Leros on the 9th, mooring in the Submarine dock of the Porto Lago base where, thanks to the work of five specialised technicians flown in from Italy, the 'pigs'

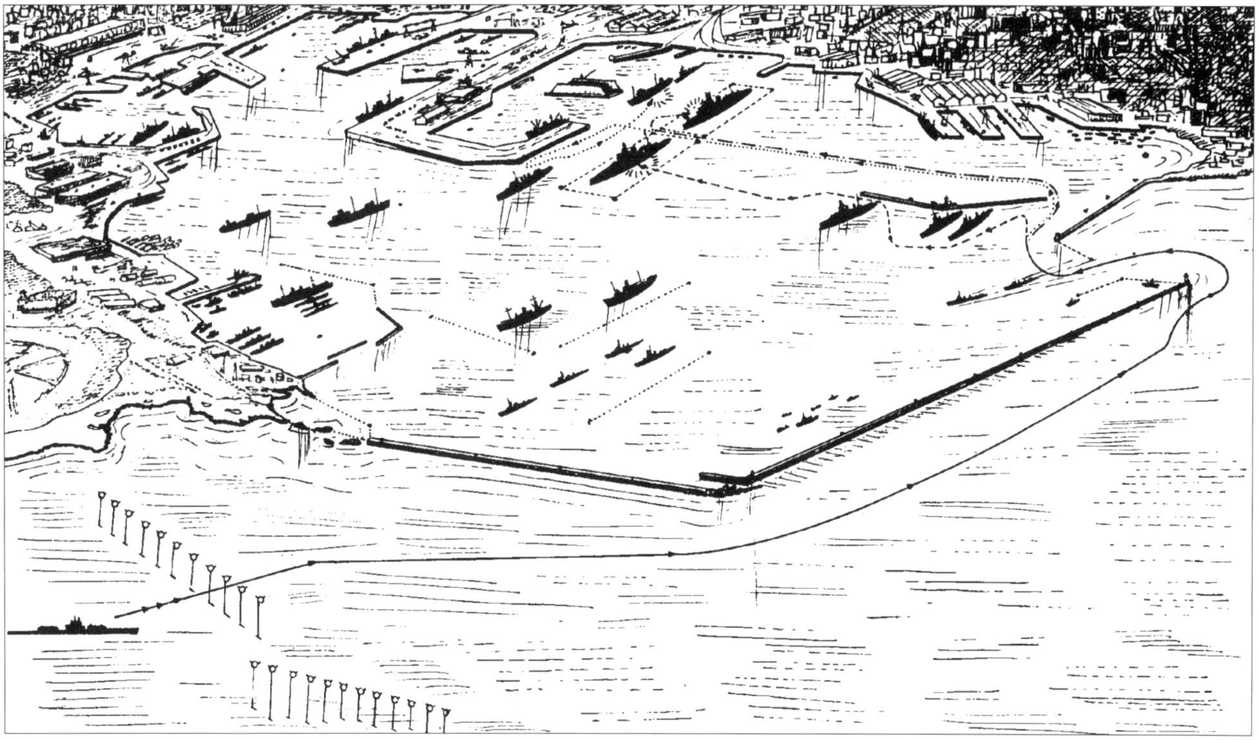

Operation of 18/19 December 1941. General scheme of the penetration of Alexandria harbour by the three SLC 'approached' by submarine *Sciré*.

Battleship HMS *Queen Elizabeth* at a mooring in Alexandria, where it was heavily damaged on 19 December 1941 by the explosion of the warhead of *SLC 222* crewed by Marceglia and Schergat.

were carefully checked while the operators arrived, again by air:

SLC 221 tv Luigi Durand De La Penne MO + A/P (°)
c° 1a c Emilio Bianchi MO + A/P (°)
SLC 222 cap Antonio Marceglia MO + A/P (°)
sc Spartaco Schergat MO + A/P (°)
SLC 223 cap Vincenzo Martellotta MO + A/P (°)
sc Mario Marino MO + A/P (°)

Reserves
ten Luigi Feltrinelli MA
sc Luciano Salvaré MB
s ten Giorgio Spaccarelli MA
sc Armando Memoli MB

Leaving Leros on the 14th after having receiving radio confirmation of the presence in Alexandria of two battleships, on the 18th the *Sciré* reached the point set for the release of the divers (on a bearing of 356° 1.3 miles from the west light of the merchant harbour), after an underwater passage of the extensive minefields set up to defend the British base.

The off-loading took place around 20.40 with the submarine semi-surfaced; helped by the reserves, the three crews extracted the SLCs from the cylinder containers. Following the operation – and some difficulty in closing one of the cylinder doors – the boat dived and began the navigation that brought it to La Spezia on the 29th, after a brief stop in Leros.

The three SLCs proceeded together for a first stretch then, after penetrating the boom defences in the wake of some destroyers returning to harbour, they separated around 01.00 on the 19th, each heading to its target.

De la Penne/Bianchi team. Once through the booms they reached the battleship HMS *Valiant* (30,600 tons) at a mooring protected by a fence of torpedo nets that were crossed on the surface. Fifty metres from the battleship, the 'pig' froze, sinking in 17 metres and the two operators lost contact. De la Penne began pushing the craft with his arms, crawling on the bottom and heading towards the target by listening to the sound of a pump running on the ship. After about forty minutes of extreme effort he succeeded in dragging the craft under the hull; then

Battleship HMS *Valiant* pictured at Gibraltar in late June 1943 by a Regia Marina Secret Information Service agent. After the attack at Alexandria in December 1941 this ship was not fully repaired until the middle of the following year.

the fuses were activated and he reached the surface to try to get away. However, he was sighted, captured and brought on board the battleship where he found Bianchi who had floated to the surface unconscious, and had been immediately picked up. The two operators went through a first interrogation, and were then locked up in a hull compartment.

With the time set for the explosion of the charge approaching, De la Penne asked to meet the commander of the ship, warning him of the imminent danger so he could save the crew. The explosion took place at 06.15 severely damaging the vessel, but she remained afloat.

Marceglia/Schergat team. Shortly after entering the harbour together with the other two self-propelled craft, they identified their target: the battleship HMS *Queen Elizabeth* (30,600 tons) moored astern of the *Valiant* in its own torpedo net enclosure. Finding a gap in the net, they dived and headed for the ship. Then they detached the charge, which was suspended between the two bilge keels. Once the fuses were set around 03.25, they left and reached the land, after activating the charges for scuttling their craft. They succeeded in leaving the harbour, but were later identified by the Egyptian police and arrested. Meanwhile the charge of the *SLC 222* had exploded, seriously damaging the battleship that settled on bottom of the harbour, a few metres beneath the hull.

Martellotta/Marino team. The primary objective should have been an aircraft carrier, but no carrier was present so the oil tanker *Sagona* (7554grt) was assigned to the *SLC 223* as a target. It would be seriously damaged by the explosion of the charge of the 'pig, together with the destroyer HMS *Jervis* (1690 tons) moored alongside. After destroying the SLC, the two operators were arrested while trying to walk out of the harbour.

Destroyer HMS *Jervis*, damaged in Alexandria in December 1941 and later repaired, in a post-war picture.

The only two battleships of the Mediterranean Fleet were seriously damaged and remained out of service for many months: HMS *Queen Elizabeth* was in drydock at Alexandria until June 1942, then transferred for further repair work to the United States, returning to action only by June 1943; HMS *Valiant*, hastily repaired, was partially operational again towards the middle of 1942.

Fully successful mission.

MAY 1942

Operation GA 4. Target: Alexandria
'Approacher': submarine *Ambra*

Submarine commanding officer:
tv Mario Arillo MA

With three SLCs on board, the *Ambra* (recently converted to assault craft transport) left La Spezia on 29 April 1942 heading to Leros, where the operators came on board. On 12 May it continued towards Alexandria, its primary target being the floating dock where the battleship HMS *Queen Elizabeth*, seriously damaged during the 'GA 3' operation the previous December, was under repair.

SLC crews

cap Egil Chersi	MA (°)
sc Rodolfo Beuck	
ten DM Luigi Feltrinelli	MA (°)
sc Luciano Favale	MA (°)
s ten Giorgio Spaccarelli	MA (°)
serg Armando Memoli	MA (°)

Reserves

gm Giovanni Magello	MA (°)
2° c Giuseppe Morbelli	MA (°)
2° c Enrico Ario Lazzari	

Mission medical officer: s ten Elvio Moscatelli

At the last moment the roles of the Chersi/Beuk and Magello/Morbelli pairs were swapped, and cap Chersi was used as relay, connecting by telephone with the

Alexandria harbour photographed from a high-flying German reconnaissance aircraft on 17 May 1942 after the failure of operation GA 4.

submerged submarine to direct it during the final approach phase.

At the time of the craft release it was found that the boat was somewhat westward of the expected position, and British surveillance in the area was very intense. The three 'pigs' were pulled from the cylinders between 20.30 and 20.56 on 14 May; shortly thereafter, *Ambra* began the return voyage, arriving in La Spezia on the 24th.

Feltrinelli/Favale team. Delayed by problems extracting the craft from the cylinder and having found it broken down, they were forced to scuttle it. Swimming to land, they were assisted by local Italian agents, and hid in the city until 29 June, but then ended up in the hands of the British military police.

Spaccarelli/Memoli team. Because of the incorrect starting position, they could not find the harbour entrance; over-schedule, they destroyed the 'pig' and swam to the coast, where they were captured.

Magello/Morbelli team. Failed to find the harbour entrance for the same reason as the pair above; with dawn approaching, they took temporary refuge in the wreck of a half-sunken ship but later – after destroying the SLC – they were captured as well.

Mission failed.

Reconnaissance with light motor torpedo boats
Target: Malta coast

In support of a planned invasion of the Maltese archipelago through an amphibious operation, a group of MTSM was deployed to Augusta in Sicily to perform reconnaissance and ambush missions along the Malta coasts.

On the evening of 17 May 1942 the torpedo boat *Abba* left Augusta with *MAS 574* and *576* escorting a pair of light motor torpedo boats tasked with two separate operations in Maltese waters:

Operation 110

MTSM 218 tv Giuseppe Cosulich (MB)
2° c Aldo Pia

The craft headed for Marsaskala with diver Giuseppe Guglielmo (MA) (°) of the X^{a} Mas 'Gamma' Group who landed under the cover of darkness using an

Left to right: Admiral Aimone di Savoia, duke of Aosta, chatting with commanders Forza, Borghese and Todaro of Decima Flottiglia Mas.

inflatable raft, which he then deflated to perform a night reconnaissance on foot. On his return, the operator could not regain contact with *MTSM 218* (which had waited until nearly dawn, then had been forced to leave) and was subsequently captured.

Operation 111

MTSM 214 stv Ongarillo Ungarelli
Sc mot Arnaldo De Angelis

This motorboat proceeded together with *MTSM 218* until Marsaskala, then alone up to well beyond Marsaxlokk, skirting the Maltese southern coast and in a hidden cove releasing an agent on an inflatable raft about 150 metres offshore. He was Carmelo Borg Pisani (MO) (°) (+), a Maltese but resident in Italy, and s ten of Milmart with the cover name Caio Borghi. Equipped with a two-way radio, he should have remained hidden in the hills, but was captured and subsequently recognised as a Maltese citizen. He was sentenced to death and the sentence was executed five months later.

Failed missions

The MTSMs from Augusta subsequently carried out some ambush missions along the Valletta approach routes, which however proved fruitless.

'Comandante Moccagatta' land convoy Black Sea: May 1942–March 1943

Craft (official designation: 101ª Squadriglia)
5 light motor torpedo boats *(MTSM 204, 206, 208, 210 & 216)*
5 MTM type explosive motorboats

Pilots:

cc Salvatore Todaro	MA
cc Aldo Lenzi	MA
tv Roberto Romano	MB
tv Aldo Massarini	MA
stv Luigi Cugia di Santorsola	MB
gm Roberto Peliti	MB
cap Guido Cattaneo	MB
s ten Silla Volonteri	
s ten Renato Ciravegna	
2° c Eliodoro Grillo	MB
2° c Alfredo Montanari	MB
serg Osvaldo Ferrarini	CVM
2° c Mario Lavoratori	CVM
c° 2a c Cesare Barberi	MB
2° c Ernesto Berti	
serg Dionisio Pascolo	MA
serg Carlo Zane	CVM

Preparations to launch an MTSM light motor torpedo boat from a slipway in the Foros (Crimea) base in June 1942.

The craft is launched.

sc Pietro Tosino	CVM
c° 3a c Amerigo Dini	
serg Pietro Testini	

Together with 8 Mas (XVII and XIX Squadriglia) and 6 CB type mini-submarines (1ª Squadriglia), 10 surface assault craft divided equally between torpedo and explosive motorboats were sent in a special convoy to the Black Sea, operating under the control of IV Flottiglia Mas (cf Francesco Mimbelli) until February 1943.

The most significant actions of these motorboats, all conducted as part of the operations for the conquest of Sevastopol, were:

- an attack on the Soviet destroyer *Tashkent* carried out by *MTSM 216* (stv Aldo Massarini) off Sevastopol on 10 June 1942 which was unsuccessful because the torpedo – maybe launched too close – failed to explode;
- an equally unsuccessful attack carried out by *MTSM 210* (cc Salvatore Todaro) the next day against a small military unit;

The boat crew, with life jackets, ready to board.

An MTSM in Balaclava harbour on 2 July 1942.

- a second attack conducted by *MTSM 210* (stv Aldo Massarini; 2° c Eliodoro Grillo) on 13 June that severely damaged a large motorship, later sunk by aircraft while being towed to Sevastopol.

Except for *MTM 80* (c° 2ª c Cesare Barberi) that was used in a demonstration action in the Balaclava area, all craft and personnel returned to Italy in March 1943.

JULY 1942

Operation GG 1. 'Gibraltar Gamma'
Bases: *Fulgor*, *Olterra* and Villa Carmela

'Gamma' divers

stv Agostino Straulino	MA
stv Giorgio Baucer	MA
c° 2a c Alfredo Schiavoni	MA
2° c Alessandro Bianchini	MA
sc Giovanni Lucchetti	MA
sc Carlo Del Valle	MA
sc Giuseppe Feroldi	MA
sc Vago Giari	MA
sc Evideo Boscolo	MA
mar Bruno di Lorenzo	MA
mar Rodolfo Lugano	MA
mar Carlo Bucovaz	MA

Given their number, the dispatch of operators from Italy to the operational area was rather complex, but well organised. Of the twelve 'Gamma' chosen, six were transferred to Spain from Bordeaux (Betasom), walking across the Pyrenees and then hidden in a double bottom under a truck; six were embarked as ordinary seamen on the steamer *Mauro Croce* headed for Barcelona, where they 'deserted'. Everyone reached a secret Madrid meeting centre, then drove to Cadiz

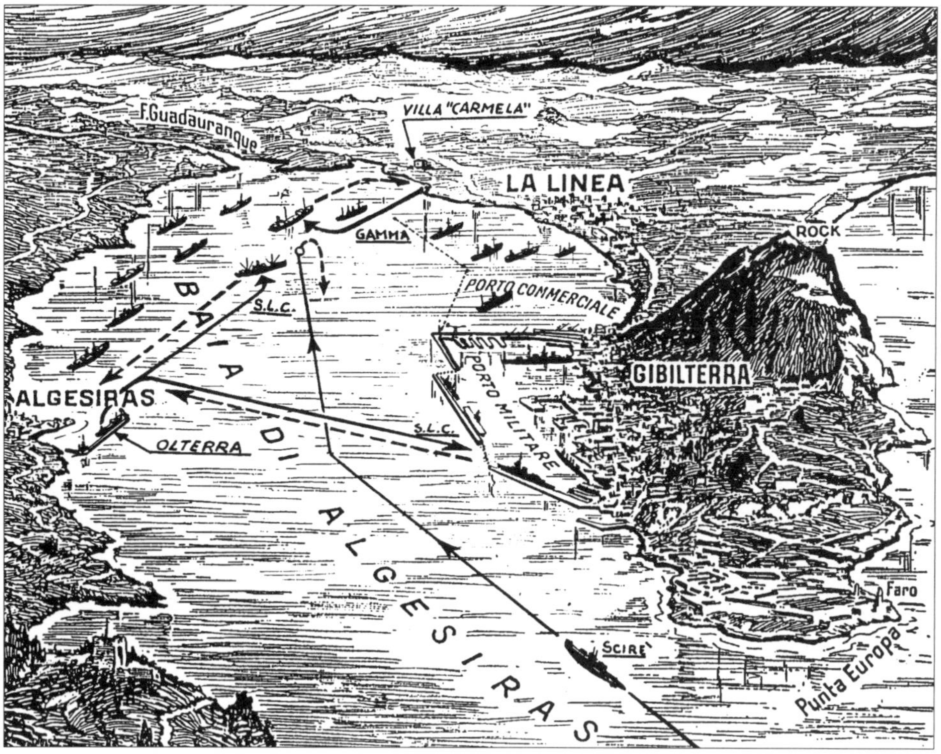

The Decima advanced bases 'system' in the Gibraltar area, from which SLC and 'Gamma' operated; and also the approach route previously used by *Sciré* for SLC release.

harbour posing as crew replacements for the tanker *Fulgor*. From here the 'Gamma' personnel transferred in small groups to the tanker *Olterra*, moored in Algeciras, pretending to be workers carrying out ship repairs. Finally, on 13 July, the group reached Villa Carmela where they picked up the equipment. From 03.00 on the 14th, they made it to the beach undiscovered and set off towards the merchant ships at anchor in the harbour. It took about three hours for the 'Gamma' to carry out their attacks; on coming ashore some were stopped by the Spanish police but, thanks to the intervention of Italian consular authorities, all of them were finally repatriated to Italy.

This first 'Gamma' operation was successful, completely escaping British surveillance, but the results were poorer than expected, because of the failure of some of the small charges carried. Nonetheless, four small merchant ships were damaged (*Meta*, 575grt; *Shuma*, 1494grt, *Empire Snipe*, 2497grt and *Baron Douglas*, 3,889grt; all, however, were be saved by beaching them quickly.

Partially successful mission.

Operation *Cefalo* 1

Manned by a militarised civilian crew, the requisitioned fishing trawler *Cefalo* (302grt) left La Spezia on 14 July with *MTSM 222* and *230* hidden under nets and other fishing equipment. Crew chiefs of the boats were tv Corrado Dequal and stv Corrado Garutti. The mission was to patrol the waters south of the Balearic Islands pretending to be fishing, and attack with light motor torpedo boats the aircraft carriers that sometimes launched aircraft for Malta from there. Remaining in the area for 16 days, with the rough sea at times, the *Cefalo* returned to the base without using its assault craft for lack of sightings.

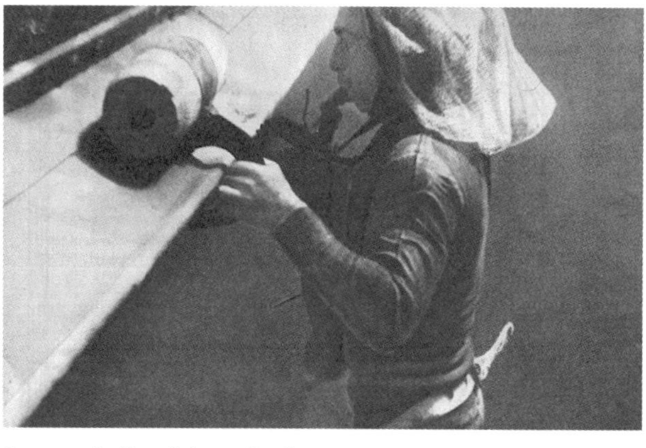

An assault diver fixing a 'bedbug' type charge to a target bilge keel during a training exercise. The operator is wearing no mask and using just the rebreather mouthpiece; his head is wrapped in a camouflage net.

AUGUST 1942

Operation *Cefalo* 2

From 5 to 8 August the *Cefalo* repeated an operation similar to that carried out in July, in the same waters and equally with no results.

Operation SL 1. Target: Haifa
'Approacher': submarine *Sciré*

Submarine commanding officer:

cc Bruno Zelich	MA (+)

On 27 July 1942 the *Sciré*, of which cf Borghese had given up the command the previous spring, left La Spezia with the materials needed for the action of 8 'Gamma' assault frogmen, who would be embarked later, together with three other operators with special assignments:

The *Sciré* wreck, lost during operation SL 1, pictured a few years ago off Haifa.

'Gamma'

2° c Eugenio Del Ben	CVM (+)
2° c Aurelio Morgan	CVM (+)
serg Delfo Caprili	CVM (+)
serg Lauro Mengoni	CVM (+)
sc Emilio Fioravanti	CVM (+)
mar Guido Fontebuoni	CVM (+)
mar Paolo Baroncellli	CVM (+)
mar Luca Ricciardi	CVM (+)

'decoy'

cap Egil Chersi	MB (+)
serg Rodolfo Beuck	MB (+)

medical officer:

s ten Pier Ermesto Gnecco	MB (+)

Sciré reached Leros on 2 August, leaving on the 6th after embarking the operators who had arrived by air from Italy, and planning to be – according to the operational orders – 1.5 miles from the entrance of the Haifa harbour on the evening of the 10th. According to the interpretation of aerial reconnaissance photos, many British naval and merchant ships were in the Palestinian harbour. The targets assigned to the 'Gamma' were, in order of precedence: submarines, cargo ships, destroyers and frigates, cruisers, troop carriers, support vessels, tankers and patrol ships.

The last radio contact with the *Sciré* was on 9 August, and it was only after the end of the conflict that the circumstances of its loss with no survivors became known. The submarine had arrived as scheduled off Haifa and, at around 10.15, had been targeted with depth charges by the coastal escort HMS *Islay*, an 'Isles' class trawler (460 tons launched in April 1941). Badly damaged, the *Sciré* had been forced to surface and came immediately under fire by three guns of the Anglo-Palestinian 14th Coast Regiment, which hit from the first rounds, sinking the submarine with the loss of all 11 operators and 48 crew members.

Failed mission.

AUGUST–SEPTEMBER 1942

Theatre: Northern Africa
'Approacher': *Sogliola* and *Costanza* fishing trawlers
'Comandante Giobbe' land convoy

Operation leader: cf Ernesto Forza

Launch of an MTSM at the Ras El Daba advanced base, just west of El Alamein. *(F Petronio collection)*

MTM pilots

tv Corrado Dequal	
tv Giuseppe Cosulich	
stv Corrado Garutti	
stv Piero Carminati	MA
stv Mameli Rattazzi	
stv Edoardo Longobardi	
s ten Elio Scardamaglia	
C° 2a c Renato Garrone	
C° 3a c Giovanni Rossi	
2° c Ugo Patrizi	
2° c Francesco Malfa	
2° c Demetrio Raffa	
2° c Aldo Pia	
2° c Alberto Grilli	
serg Alcandido Mazziol	MB
sc Gastone Michelacci	
sc Cesare Sani	MA – A/P
sc Pio Fanella	
sc Goffredo Cerolini	

Using a group of explosive and light motor torpedo boats, intensive operations were carried out close to the frontline to undermine and disrupt naval movements in support of land operations.

The main success was the serious damaging of the destroyer HMS *Eridge* ('Hunt' class, 1050 tons), torpedoed by *MTSM 228* (stv Carminati and sc Sani) of the 'Giobbe' land convoy, on 29 August in the waters of Ras El Daba, about 50km west of El Alamein. The British destroyer was towed to Alexandria, but, due to the considerable damage suffered, never returned to active service.

Escort destroyer HMS *Eridge* entering Alexandria heavily damaged by a torpedo from *MTSM 228*, which attacked the ship off Ras El Daba on 29 August 1942.

On the other hand, the cruises of the trawlers *Sogliola* and *Costanza* with surface assault craft were not successful.

Operation GG 2. Target: Gibraltar roadstead
Bases: *Olterra* and Villa Carmela

'Gamma'

tv Agostino Straulino	MB
mar Bruno Di Lorenzo	MA
sc Vago Giari	MB

Reserves

Mar Rodolfo Lugano
2° c Oreste Botti

Arriving on the *Olterra* from Italy, the three operators reached Villa Carmela from where, at 23.40 on 14 September they entered the water to attack the three merchant ships anchored in the harbour. Because of the intensified British surveillance, only diver Di Lorenzo succeeded in securing his charges to the hull of the steamer *Raves Point* (1787grt) which sank. All the 'Gamma' who had taken part in the action were repatriated, by different routes and times.

Partially successful mission.

NOVEMBER 1942

Operations GM 1 and GM 2. Target: Malta, Marsamxett

Actions planned against the units at the Marsamxett submarine base to be carried out by 5 'Gamma' transported and 'approached' by *MTSM 240, 246* and *256* launched from Augusta.

The first mission, scheduled for around mid-November, was cancelled due to persistent unfavourable weather conditions. The second, which began on 30 November, had to be called off due to failure of one of the 'approacher' craft.

Two other similar operations, planned for 1 and 8 April 1943 had to be cancelled due to adverse weather conditions.

Aborted missions.

DECEMBER 1942

Operation BG 5. Target: Gibraltar military harbour
Base: tanker *Olterra* moored in Algeciras

First operation with 'pigs' departing from the *Olterra*; the self-propelled craft had arrived dismantled from Italy and were reassembled in the secret workshop set up aboard the tanker interned in the Spanish port of Algeciras, in sight of the Gibraltar Rock. Through a special flooded hold, connecting to the sea, *SLC 228, 229* and *236* left at 23:30 on 7 December with the following crews:

SLC operators

tv Licio Visintini	MO (+)
serg Giovanni Magro	MO (+)
gm Girolamo Manisco	MO (°)
sc Dino Varini	MA (°)
s ten Vittorio Cella	MA
serg Salvatore Leone	MA (+)

Targets were the battleship HMS *Nelson* and the aircraft carriers HMS *Formidable* and HMS *Furious* at moorings in the British military harbour at the foot of the Rock. Besides the standard explosive warhead, each of the SLCs also carried some 'bugs' to be used against any secondary targets. Shortly after leaving *Olterra*, it was found that the rudder cables of all three craft had been inverted while being connected; it was then necessary to go briefly back for the appropriate corrections, then take to the sea again.

Visintini/Magro team. Nothing was heard after the second start, and the operators were posted missing. From later information it turned out that, as soon as their 'pig' had penetrated the booms of the military harbour, it had been overwhelmed by one or more explosions of underwater bombs, systematically launched by surveillance motorboats. The two operators were killed, and their bodies surfaced a few days later in the waters of the harbour. Recovered, they were buried by the British with military honours.

Manisco/Varini team. Spotted by a sentry on the harbour quay, they were first targeted by small-arms fire, then by a large depth bomb; forced to activate the self-destruction of the craft, they were taken prisoner soon after.

Cella/Leone team. Leaving the *Olterra* last, they arrived near the military harbour when the general alarm was already in force, after the sighting of the Manisco/Varini craft. Only s ten Cella returned to the base with his 'pig', while his 'second' went missing, probably killed by an underwater charge from the

Lieutenant Licio Visintini, killed in action off Gibraltar on 8 December 1942.

surveillance motorboats after being thrown from his seat on the craft.

Failed mission.

Operation NA 1. Target: ships in Algiers roadstead
'Approacher': submarine *Ambra*

Submarine commanding officer:

cc Mario Arillo	MO

First combined mission of 'Gamma' and SLC; these were equipped with a double head (150kg each element), more suitable for attacking merchant ships, rather than the original single 300kg (shell + charge) element.

SLC operators

tv Giorgio Badessi	MA (°)
sc Carlo Pesal	MA (°)
ten Guido Arena	MA (°)
sc Ferdinando Cocchi	MA (°)
gm Giorgio Reggioli	MA (°)
sc Colombo Pamolli	MA and A/P (°)

'Decoy' and reserves:

tv Augusto Jacobacci	MA
2° c Armando Battaglia	CVM

'Gamma':

s ten Agostino Morello	MA (°)
2° c Oreste Botti	MA (°)
serg Luigi Rolfini	MA (°)
sc Giuseppe Feroldi	MA (°)
serg Gaspare Ghiglione	(°)
sc Evideo Boscolo	MA (°)
serg Alberto Evangelisti	MA (°)
mar Rodolfo Lugano	(°)
mar Giovanni Lucchetti	(°)
Private Luciano Luciani (Army)	MA (°)

Ambra had left La Spezia on 4 December with craft and operators aboard, arriving off Algiers on the 8th, but had to wait in the area until the morning of the 11th, when improved sea conditions permitted the final approach in shallow waters. At 17.00 on the 11th tv Jacobacci surfaced; equipped with a phone he began to guide the navigation of the submerged submarine as it moved slowly across the seabed. At 21.15 *Ambra* stopped in the centre of the harbour, in the middle of a group of large merchant ships at anchor. The 'Gamma' left the submarine around 22.24, followed by the three SLCs by 23.04. Having waited in vain for the return of at least some of the operators, the submarine began to withdraw at 03.00 on the 12th as arranged, moving always submerged and re-surfacing only at

Lieutenant Commander Mario Arillo aboard *Ambra*.

Steamer *Harmattan* (6587grt) sunk in Algiers during operation NA 1.

19.45, after 36 hours underwater; the return voyage ended at La Spezia on the 15th.

During the operation, the merchant ships *Ocean Vanquisher* (7174grt) and *Berto* (1493grt) were sunk, while the *Empire Centaur* (7041grt) and the *Harmattan* (6587grt) were damaged. After the operation, none of the 16 operators could find the 'decoy' or the submarine; all were taken prisoner.

The action of two of the three 'pigs' was marred by failures in the breathing apparatus and the craft themselves, and that of the 'Gamma' was compromised by the almost immediate capture of one of the assault divers, who had given up the attack, providing an early warning to the roadstead security forces.

However, the precise execution of the approach navigation by the *Ambra* and the large number of attackers employed in the action was reason to hope for far greater success than that achieved. Nevertheless, it resulted in more than 20,000grt of merchant shipping destroyed or damaged.

Partially successful mission.

Operation BO G 1. Target: ships in Annaba harbour
'Approacher' craft: *MTSM 268* from La Galite island

On 12 December the mission was cancelled due to adverse sea conditions but was retried the following day with *MTSM 268* (cc Salvatore Todaro), with three 'Gamma' (seated in the torpedo compartment after the weapon had been landed) accompanied by two more light motor torpedo boats with the escort role. Failures to one of the escorts, and deteriorating weather conditions, led to the mission being interrupted again and the units returned to Galite. In the meantime, the fishing trawler *Cefalo*, acting as support vessel for the torpedo boats, had arrived. Shortly after two enemy fighter-bombers carried out a sudden low altitude attack, killing cc Todaro and sinking the vessel which, however, was raised in the following days.

Cancelled mission.

APRIL 1943

Operation BO G 2. Target: ships in Annaba harbour
'Approacher' craft: *MTSM 262* and *263* (with *MTSM 264* as escort)

MTSM 262
tv Giuseppe Cosulich MB
c° 3a c Francesco Malfa

MTSM 263
tv Edoardo Longobardi MA
stv Mameli Rattazzi

MTSM 264
tv Corrado Garutti
c° Giuseppe Barabino

'Gamma'
ten Aldo Coceani
sc Vago Giari
sc Ferdinando Pacciolla
2° c Giovanni Maestrale
2° c Walter Fabbri
sc Giovanni Mistroni

This was substantially a repetition of Operation BO G 1 of the previous December. On the night of 6 April, the craft were discovered shortly before the release of the 'Gamma' and had to withdraw, aborting the action.

Failed mission.

APRIL–JUNE 1943

Operation G O G. Target: merchant ships in the harbour of Huelva (Spain)

'Gamma'
sc Salvatore Nizzi (MA)
mar Carlo Vianello

The two assault divers, based on the Italian steamer *Gaeta* (4457grt) interned in Huelva, placed mines on some enemy merchant ships. However, the ships from Huelva unexpectedly put in to Gibraltar where the mines were cleared by British security.

Failed mission.

Lieutenant Commander Ernesto Notari, 1st operator aboard a 'pig' during an exercise. Note the number *150* painted up in an unusual position.

MAY 1943
Operation BG 6
Target: merchant ships, Gibraltar roadstead
Base: tanker *Olterra* in Algeciras

SLC operators

cc Ernesto Notari	MA
sc Ario Lazzari	MA
ten Camillo Tadini	MA
sc Salvatore Mattera	MA
s ten Vittorio Cella	MA
sc Eusebio Montalenti	MA

The three SLCs left the *Olterra* to operate in the night of 7/8 May, fitted with double warheads and some 'trunks' (small explosive charges – see Appendix 1L) each. The action was carried out during a storm in the Gibraltar area: the 'pigs', although hampered by a strong current, went completely unnoticed by British surveillance.

Notari/Lazzari team. Attacked a merchant ship by attaching a warhead and a 'trunk' on the hull, returning to the *Olterra* with the craft at 03.45 on the 8th.

Tadini/Mattera team. Managed to attach a head and a 'trunk' to the hull of a merchant ship, returning to the *Olterra* with the craft at 04.15.

Cella/Montalenti team. Placed a head and a 'trunk' under the hull of a merchant ship, returning to the *Olterra* at 02.15.

All charges exploded regularly between 06.15 and 07.30 seriously damaging the following ships: *Pat Harrison* (7191grt, American 'Liberty' type); *Mashsud* (7540grt) and *Camerata* (4875grt). The steamers were towed to shallow waters off the Spanish town of La Linea to avoid total loss.

This was an excellent and definitive test of the advanced base established on the *Olterra*. The bad weather conditions on the one hand favoured the stealth of the raiders but on the other it slowed their navigation, so that only half of the available charges were placed.

Successful mission.

JUNE–AUGUST 1943
Operation 'Stella' ('Star').
Target: merchant ships in the harbours of Iskenderun and Mersin (Turkey)

'Gamma' ten Luigi Ferraro	MO

Given the cover role of a clerk at the Iskenderun Italian

Luigi Ferraro, Gold Medal for his endeavours at Iskenderun and Mersin ('Operation Stella'), in a post-war picture.

Norwegian steamer *Fernplant* (5274grt) attacked and sunk by Ferraro in Iskenderun.

Consulate, Ferraro managed to attack 4 enemy merchant ships, sinking two and severely damaging a third (*Kaituna*).

Iskenderun 30.6.1943	*Orion*, Greek (4798grt)
Mersin 9.7.1943	*Kaituna*, British (4914grt)
Iskenderun 1.8.1943	*Fernplant*, Norwegian (5274grt)

The fourth steamer (*Sicilian Prince*, British, 3489grt), attacked in Mersin on 30 July 1943 was saved by the removal of the charge ('trunk') following a hull inspection by British divers. After the action of 1 August 1943 Ferraro returned to Italy.

Successful missions.

JULY 1943

First MTR operatio. Target: Syracuse
'Approacher': submarine *Ambra*

Submarine commanding officer: cc Renato Ferrini

British steamer *Kaituna* (414grt), heavily damaged by Ferraro's attack in Mersin.

MTR pilots:
tv Corrado Garau
c° 2a cls Amleto Tonissi
c° 3a cls Salvatore Guercio
serg Giuseppe Derin

Ambra, with three reduced-type explosive motorboat (MTR) inside the waterproof cylinder normally used for transport, left La Spezia on 14 July, four days after the Allied landings in south-eastern Sicily, bound for Syracuse to attack the enemy ships at anchor in the roadstead outside that port recently conquered by British forces. The submarine was discovered on the surface by an aircraft around 03.00 on the 18th, and attacked with bombs. Heavily damaged, *Ambra* was forced to retire, and the mission cancelled. After a brief stop in Messina, *Ambra* slowly headed for Naples, arriving under tow of the torpedo boat *Partenope*. After some repairs, the submarine finally reached La Spezia on 27 July, entering the dockyard to be repaired.

Cancelled mission.

JULY–AUGUST 1943

Surface assault craft
Various bases in Sardinia and Sicily

Anticipating the probable landing of the Allies in one of the two major Italian islands, some MTSM and MTM were deployed to Sardinia (Cagliari, Carloforte and Bosa Marina) under the command of cc Aldo Lenzi with tv Corrado Dequal and Aldo Massarini, as subordinates.

In Sicily the main base was Augusta – where the surviving motorboats formerly in the 'Moccagatta' and 'Giobbe' land convoys had gathered – under the command of stv Ongarillo Ungarelli. When the Allies began the invasion of Sicily on 10 July, the Sardinian bases were decommissioned while the craft in Augusta were almost immediately forced to retreat rapidly northwards, concentrating the light motor torpedo boats and the explosive motorboats in Mazzarò, near Taormina, where they were joined by commander Lenzi, who had been immediately moved from Sardinia.

The light motor torpedo boats attempted some attacks on enemy shipping operating along the coasts of eastern Sicily, but did not achieve any direct results. With the front retreating, the craft moved first to Messina (from where *MTSM 262* was the last Italian

Surface assault craft (MTM and MTSM) based at Mazzarò di Taormina in summer 1943. Note those undergoing maintenance using improvised facilities.

unit to leave the waters of the island now totally in Anglo-American hands), then to Gioia Tauro and finally to Amalfi.

AUGUST 1943

Operation BG 7. Target: merchant ships, Gibraltar roadstead
Base: tanker *Olterra* in Algeciras

Operation performed on the night of 3/4 August 1943 by three SLCs with the same procedures and the same operators as 'BG 6' except for the replacement of 2° c Lazzari with sc Andrea Gianoli. All operators returned to the *Olterra* except for sc Gianoli, and were decorated with the Silver Medal for Valour.

Notari/Gianoli team. Left at 22.53 on 3 August and headed towards a 'Liberty' ship anchored in the roadstead. After the charge had been placed the 'pig' sank to the bottom and Gianoli lost contact. Notari succeeded in bringing the craft back to the surface, and returned to the *Olterra* while Gianoli was taken prisoner. The explosion of the charge sank the target, the American SS *Harrison Gray Otis* of 7176grt.

Cella/Montalenti team. Left the *Olterra* at 23.55 on the 3rd and at 01.30 on the 4th attacked the Norwegian tanker *Thorshovdi* of 9944grt that later broke into two sections and sank.

Tadini/Mattera team. At 01.45 on 4 August they concluded their attack on the British SS *Stanridge* of 5975grt, which sank at 05.10, an hour after they had returned to the *Olterra*.

British steamer *Stanridge* (5975grt) sunk at Gibraltar by the Tadini/Mattera team's SLC during operation BG 7.

Successful mission.

SEPTEMBER 1943 – MAY 1945

As an immediate consequence of the armistice, proclaimed on 8 September 1943, within a few days Italian territory found itself separated into two parts, the southern occupied by the Allies and the central-northern by the Germans, with a fighting front that, south of Rome, extended from the Tyrrhenian to the Adriatic. The Kingdom of Italy, with Brindisi as its first provisional capital, began a co-belligerency with the Allies which continued until end of the European conflict in May 1945; in the North, the Italian Social Republic (RSI) was established, governed by Benito

Motor torpedo boat *MS 74* moored at the quay of San Vito di Taranto, Mariassalto headquarters, in 1944.

Mussolini, who maintained the alliance with Germany – albeit in subordinate position – with a co-belligerency substantially similar in form to that in the South.

Obviously, the organisation of the assault craft also reflected this dichotomy.

In the Decima's La Spezia headquarters Commander Borghese (who had taken command of the flotilla on 1 May 1943) succeeded in preventing the disintegration of the unit and initially established a direct 'alliance' agreement with the local German military authorities, later joining the Republican Armed Forces while maintaining a degree of autonomy. The unit continued to be called 'Xª Flottiglia Mas' and its naval component remained, in truth, of quite modest size; but this was not so for the new Marine Infantry component, which was quickly established to employ the significant numbers of volunteers who immediately began to flock to the Decima banner.

Many craft and special materials were found in La Spezia and in the flotilla training centres, all located in the North; more were recovered in the production factories, or were later transferred by the Germans who took them from their own production. Overall, from the end of 1943 to May 1945, the 'Xª MAS' would commission nearly seventy surface assault craft, divided between light torpedo and explosive motorboats, alongside twenty underwater craft of the SLC and SSB types.

Although some operations with 'pigs' and 'Gamma' were attempted or planned, the main activity was carried out by surface craft, generally no longer employed in forcing enemy harbours, but in coastal-water attacks against enemy ships; these craft operated mainly from four bases (codenamed 'South', 'West', 'East' and 'X').

In the south, the Regia Marina reconstituted a unit similar to the original Xª Flotilla Mas, named 'Assault Craft Command' (Mariassalto), based in Taranto and under the orders of Captain Ernesto Forza. The craft available were only those operating in southern Italy and in Sardinia on the date of the armistice; there was no chance of acquiring new ones, as the related technology (workshops, production sites, etc) was all in the North. These comprised about twenty surface craft divided between MTSM and MTM, no underwater craft, and few breathing sets for 'Gamma' divers. The activity of Mariassalto was therefore limited to some reconnaissance of beaches ahead of Allied amphibious operations, transport and recovery of agents in territories occupied by the Germans, and two forcing operations of major Ligurian harbours in collaboration with British operators and craft.

'Xª MAS' (National Republican Navy, MNR – RSI)

JANUARY–JUNE 1944

'South' Base (formerly 'X' Base)

The first operational base was Terracina where in the first days of January 1944 some MTM and MTSM with their pilots were sent in a land convoy, from the Sesto Calende School to operate in the Gulf of Naples area. After the landing of the Allies at Anzio in the beginning of February, the base was transferred to Fiumicino with the headquarters in Villa Torlonia. At that date the available craft were 5 MTSMA and 8 MTSM, while the MTM had been withdrawn to La Spezia.

The first actions in the waters off Anzio began on

20 February 1944 and continued until the end of May, when, with the front receding, the base was decommissioned and the surviving craft and personnel returned in La Spezia. The base was commanded by Lieutenant Gustavo Fracassini from its establishment on 29 April 1944, and later by Lieutenant Sergio Nesi. The operational craft were *MTSM 206, 208, 216, 226* and *264* (of which the first four were lost) and *'SMA 302, 304, 308, 310, 312, 314, 318, 336/3, 358/14* and *362/16* (of which five were lost).

The most significant actions off Anzio were:

- 20 February 1944: *MTSM 206* (serg Rocco Chiarello and mar Guido Candiolo) may have sunk the British tank landing ship *LST 305* with a torpedo (this success was also claimed by the German submarine *U-230*) and then damaged the minesweeper USS *Pioneer* (AM 105), with depth charges.
- 13 May 1945: the *'SMA 318* (tv Sergio Nesi and serg Cesare Zironi) damaged the patrol ship USS *PC 626* with the launch of a depth charge, putting it out of action for a few days.

JUNE 1944–APRIL 1945
'X' Base

Also known as the 'Base for connections with occupied Italy', it was established in La Spezia in June 1944 under the command of tv Gustavo Fracassini and operated until 22 April 1945 with some MTSMA (*'SMA 304, 312, 324, 326* and *501*) especially in dropping and recovering agents behind the lines.

AUGUST 1944–APRIL 1945
'West – Com te Domenico Mataluno' Base

Established in August 1944 immediately after the Allied landings in Provence, with two MTSMA (*'SMA 334/8* and *348/9*) transferred from La Spezia and reinforced shortly after by 10 more boats of the same type and 10 MTM sent in a land convoy from Sesto Calende.

The first operational headquarters was Villefranche, from where the first mission was carried out on 24 August. On 30 August, with the stabilisation of the front almost on the line of the old Italian-French border, the base was transferred to San Remo, with headquarters at the Parigi-Corso Hotel, warehousing in the old San Tecla fort and technical-logistic services in the requisitioned villas Zirio and Nobel. The command of the base was initially entrusted to cap Umberto Andreoli di Sovico who was replaced by tv Gustavo Fracassini at the beginning of 1945.

Craft from the 'West' base operated mainly against light enemy shipping supporting the operations along the frontline and, later, shelling western Ligurian harbours.

Although strongly affected by continuous air and sea bombing leading to the loss of many motorboats, the activity of this base continued, along with that of similar German craft, until 24 April 1945 when the last mission was carried out by 6 MTSMA and 7 MTM in collaboration with some Mas. The following day all the remaining effective boats were sunk, and the staff began the retreat towards the Po valley.

Operational craft:
MTM 3b, 4b, 15b, 16b, 26b, 28b, 30b, 33b, 48, 63b, 517, 545, 549, 552, 555 and *558.*
'SMA 312, 334/2, 336/3, 348/9, 358/14, 366/18, 380/25, 404/39 and *405/40.*

Most significant actions:
- 25 August 1944: the *'SMA 336/3* (gm Carlo Sicola and sc Giuliano Gregorat) probably damaged a destroyer.
- 16/17 April 1945: during a mission by *'SMA 312* and 6 MTM, one of the latter (probably *26b* or *28b* piloted by sc Sergio Denti) severely damaged the French destroyer *Trombe* (formerly *FR 31*), which managed to return to Toulon, but was not repaired and quickly decommissioned. The pilot of the craft was later recovered at sea by a French patrol ship, and taken prisoner. This action would be the only 'hit' obtained by an explosive motorboat against a moving target. The destroyer did not sink, as the

Republican Xa Mas *MTSMA 320* in 1944.

French destroyer *Trombe*, heavily damaged by the explosion of a republican Xa Mas MTM off the Ligurian coast on the night of 16/17 April 1945, decommissioned in Toulon in the early post-war period.

Close-up of the damage to *Trombe*, whose hull was breached on both sides.

main charge exploded on the surface, causing extensive damage to the ship's topside only.

Operational underwater group – La Spezia

Based near the 'Castagna Battery' on the western side of the Gulf of La Spezia, close to Varignano fort, this unit's main operation was an attempt to force the port of Livorno – very important to the Allied supply line – by *'SMA 501* (tv Gustavo Fracassini and 2° c Luigi Scarpino) as escort craft to *MTL 476* (ten Salvatore Uras) with two SSB aboard (operators: tv Augusto Jacobacci and sc Antonio Toma; ten Sergio Pucciarini and 2 c Bruno Bonato). The mission, led by cc Mario Arillo aboard *'SMA 501*, left La Spezia on the evening of 7 November 1944, but was forced back shortly after by a failure of the MTL.

The action should have been repeated in January 1945 with *MTL 571*, but was cancelled because of adverse weather conditions and various technical problems.

In the same period, two more actions were attempted against Livorno with a total of four 'Gamma' transported by *'SMA 501* on 17 November and 12 December 1944, but both failed.

BEGINNING 1945 – APRIL 1945
'East' base

This should have been established in Portorož, in Istria, under the command of tv Sergio Nesi but was actually set up on Veliki Brijun island, just north of Pola. It was intended to have had some MTM and four MTSMA, but none of these craft arrived before the end of hostilities.

The most significant action was a mission to land an agent in the Ancona area and then attempt to force that port on 13 April with two SMA loaned by the local German assault unit. The two motorboats (tv Sergio Nesi and serg Sergio Perbellini; 2° c Flavio Mauceri and sc Roberto Bratti) managed to land the agent but were discovered, the craft scuttled and the crews taken prisoner.

A republican Xa Mas SSB at La Spezia in 1944–1945.

Mariassalto – Italian Royal Navy

JANUARY 1944
Target: German ships in Suda Bay (Crete)
'Approacher': destroyer *Grecale*

Assault craft: 2 MTM and 2 MTSM (commanded by tv Edoardo Longobardi)

With the craft carried in saddles on deck, the destroyer left Taranto in mid-January 1944 heading for Tobruk, where it remained from the 21st to 30th of the same month, waiting for the order to carry out the mission. However, the weather conditions in the Crete area remained adverse throughout the period, and the operation was finally cancelled. At the same times similar missions were planned – but not carried out – against various anchorages in Leros, Rhodes and Samos.

APRIL–MAY 1944
Agent landing and recovery operations along the Albanian coast

Craft employed: *MTSM 212, 220, 244, 248, 250* and *256*

Crews: tv Edoardo Longobardi MA, Corrado Dequal and Luigi Cugia di sant'Orsola; stv Mameli Rattazzi

Sesto Calende, 1944. Trials of a 'self-propelled raft' for operational towing of 'Gamma' divers.

(later killed during an underwater training mission in Taranto); gm Carlo Goda and Andrea De Angelis; c° 2a cls Luigi Zoppis, c° 2a cls Pietro Castelli, 2° c Italo Mazzoni; 2° c Italo Mazzoni, sc Luigi Gattorno MB.

JUNE 1944

Operation 'QWZ'. Target: La Spezia roadstead
'Approacher' craft: destroyer *Grecale* (cf Benedetto Ponza di San Martino) with 2 MTSM aboard; motor torpedo boat *MS 74* (tv Pietro Carminati, MA) with 2 British 'Chariots' Mk I (*LVIII* and *LX*) aboard

MTSM crews:
tv Luigi Durand De La Penne, A/P and c° 2a cls Luigi Zoppis, MB;
tv Luigi Cugia di Sant'Orsola, MB and sc Luigi Gattorno, MB;

on the motorboats, for support and possible 'Gamma' recovery: gm Girolamo Manisco, MB and sc Evelino Marcolini, CVM.

'Gamma' (aboard MTSM):

gm Francesco Berlingeri	MA
asp gm Andrea De Angeli	MA
sc Corrado Giani	MA and A/P

British Chariot operators:
Sub Lieut M R Causer and Able Seaman H Smith; Petty Officers C Bercy and W Laurence

The Italian-British operation left Bastia, in Corsica, on the evening of 21 June 1944. The MTSM were put into the water off Gorgona island, and headed for La Spezia together with *MS 74*. The underwater craft and the 'Gamma' went into the sea close to the booms, which were partly open and barely monitored. The targets for the Chariots were the heavy cruisers *Gorizia* and *Bolzano*, moored in the roadstead and then abandoned and partly dismantled, to prevent them from being scuttled to block the harbour further. The 'Gamma' were to attack lesser targets, or as a final resort submarines moored in the Muggiano area.

Bercy/Laurence team. Was forced to abandon the craft before reaching the target because the batteries were completely dead.

Causer/Smith team. Attacked the *Bolzano* that sank on its side inside its own torpedo nets roughly in the centre of the roadstead.

Both Chariots were scuttled but only petty officer Bercy managed to get through the lines while the other three operators were taken prisoner.

The results of the 'Gamma' action were negative and conflicting versions of its implementation still remain.

APRIL 1945

Operation 'Toast'. Target: Genoa harbour
'Approacher' craft: destroyer *Legionario* with 2 MTSM aboard; motor torpedo boat *MS 74* (tv Pietro Carminati, MA) with 2 'Chariots' aboard; British motor gunboat *MGB 177* as escort.

The wreck of the cruiser *Bolzano*, capsized to port, emerging from the waters of La Spezia roadstead in an early post-war photo by Aldo Fraccaroli.

A pair of underwater operators training aboard an SLC.

Sub-lieutenant Nicola Conte at the end of a demanding exercise on a 'pig'.

MTSM 230	
tv Corrado Dequal	MA
c° 2a cls Pier Luigi Zoppis	
MTSM 232	
tv Luigi Cugia di Sant'Orsola	MA
2° c Pietro Castelli	MB

Chariot operators:	
stv Nicola Conte	MO
sc Evelino Marcolini	MO
gm Girolamo Manisco	MB
sc Dino Varini	MB

Reserves:	
gm Franco Robustelli	CVM
gm Mario Pomponi	CVM
ten Renato Ciravegna	CVM
sc Carlo Pesel	CVM

The action was conceived and planned by Mariassalto which, amongst other things, regarded an important success to be politically very useful for the Regia Marina before the imminent end of the hostilities

The MTSM were assigned the task of escorting the Chariots close to the harbour defences and to attempt the recovery of the operators once the mission was accomplished. The two Chariots were temporarily loaned by the Royal Navy to Mariassalto, which had no SLCs or SSBs. Their target was the unfinished large aircraft carrier *Aquila* (former liner *Roma*) of 23,300 tons, which was to be sunk at its isolated mooring, thus preventing the Germans from scuttling it to further block the harbour.

The Chariots were taken from a group of ten decommissioned at Malta since June 1944. They were only turned over to Mariassalto on 12 April in Livorno and the expedition left that harbour heading for Genoa at 14.15 on the 18th. Therefore the operators only had a limited time to test them, even if they were already familiar with this kind of craft (a not very effective copy of the first series of Italian 'pigs'), having previously trained on a couple of Chariots in the Mariassalto base in San Vito di Taranto where, however, they were still entrusted to British technicians.

At 23.30 on 18 April *MS 74* put the two craft into the water off the eastern entrance to Genoa harbour.

The crews immediately headed towards the barriers together with the MTSM. The Manisco/Varini team's Chariot came to a halt about 800 metres from the booms because the batteries were completely flat. It was therefore scuttled, and the operators boarded one of the motorboats, while the other underwater craft proceeded towards the harbour.

The Conte/Marcolini team managed to overcome the barriers with relative ease, even though the self-contained breathing apparatus of the 'second man' (and the reserve, too) functioned poorly. At 00.15 of 19 April the craft arrived near the target but, failing to attach the charge to the hull, it was deposited on the bottom near it. After initiating the fuses, the crew began retiring, reaching *MTSM 230* just off the booms. Once the craft was scuttled, the operators made for the safety of the motorboat: this was the first time the crew of an underwater assault craft was recovered after an action.

Despite the commitment and determination of the two operators, however, the *Aquila* did not sink. If the charge actually exploded, then damage to the ship, which was protected by large anti-torpedo bulges, was not serious; but it is also possible that, for some unknown reason, the fuses did not work. Though abundantly mined, through a series of fortunate circumstances, the *Aquila* was not sunk, even by Germans, although in the days after 19 April they had moved it to block the narrow passage that then divided Genoa harbour into two parts. When the first British forces occupied the harbour, towards the end of April 1945, they found the ship afloat and, with some difficulty given the size of the vessel, moved it to its old mooring place.

The unfinished aircraft carrier *Aquila*: the hull is still afloat, though listing to starboard, in a picture taken in Genoa in early May 1945. *(US Navy)*

Part 2

DESCRIPTION OF ITALIAN ASSAULT CRAFT

MEZZI DI SUPERFICIE

Scafi progettazione CATTANEO-BAGLIETTO. Costruzione legni BAGLIETTO. Armamento totale CATTANEO.

Documentazione CATTANEO G.

Tipo Motoscafo	Lungh. fuori tutto (m)	Largh. fuori tutto (m)	Anno di costruz.	Motore (1)	Disloc. a pieno carico (Kg)	Carico utile (2) (Kg)	Velocità max. (nodi)	Uomini (3)	Armamento (4)	NOTE
MT	4.700	1.460	1938	1*	1300	300	32	1	Carica 300 Kg	Carena a gradini. Motore a sogliola. Trasporto con idrovolante S.55
MT	4.700	1.460	1938	1*	1300	300	32	1	"	Trasformato con motore verticale
MTM	5.400	1.676	1940	1*	1400	300	33	1	"	Edizione definitiva dell'MT con nuova carena più marina
MTR	5.415	1.080	1942	1*	1250	300	32	1	"	MTM trasformato per essere contenuto in un tubo porta SLC (maiali) dei sommergibili
MTS	6.500	2.200	1940	1*	1750	600	29	2	2 Siluri	Scafo silurante con 2 silurotti ad aria fredda produzione SAN BARTOLOMEO – CATTANEO
MTMS	7.800	2.200	1942	2*	3300	300	32	2	1 "	Un solo siluro SAN BARTOLOMEO Ø 450 lungh.330
SMA	8.200	2.320	1943	2*	3760	530	29	2	1 "	" " " " " " " " " e 2 bombe di profondità
MTL	10.720	2.850	1942	1 elettrico	7300	2600	5	6	2 SLC	Scafo lento per trasportare 2 SLC (maiali) Rimorchio + propulsione elettrica

* Motopropulsore entrofuoribordo brandeggiabile CATTANEO, Motore ALFA ROMEO 2500cc 90 CV, trasformato marino CATTANEO

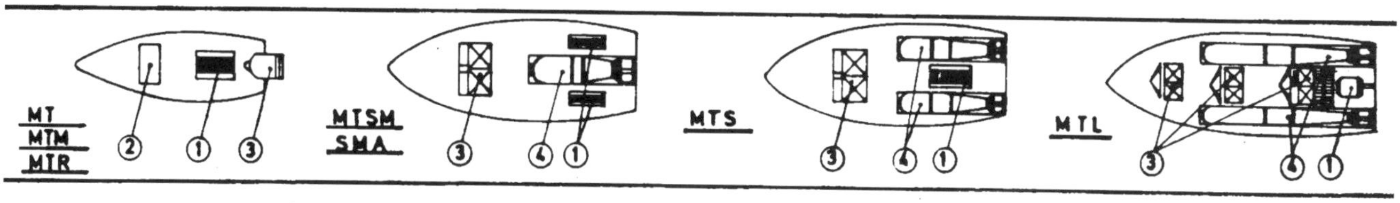

MEZZI SUBACQUEI

Documentazione CATTANEO G.

Tipo	Lungh. fuori tutto (m)	Largh. fuori tutto (m)	Anno di costruz.	Motore	Disloc. a pieno carico (Kg)	Carico utile (Kg)	Velocità max. (nodi)	Uomini	Armamento	NOTE
SLC maiale	5.900	0.533	1938	1 elettrico	1300	200	2.5	2	Carica 200 Kg	2 uomini a cavallo. Costruzione CATTANEO-SAN BARTOLOMEO
SSB	7.050	0.780	1943	"	1860	300	4	2	Carica 300 Kg	2 uomini all'interno dello scafo costruzione SAN BARTOLOMEO

Reproduction of a synoptic table compiled post-war by CABI of Milan, showing the main characteristics of Italian assault craft used in the Second World War. (For underwater craft, the SLC length is with no warhead, while that of the SSB is with multiple, double-charge warhead.)

SURFACE CRAFT

MAT/MA (Airborne Motorboat/ Assault Motorboat)
MT (Touring Motorboat – Explosive motorboat)
MTM (Modified or Improved Touring Motorboat – Explosive motorboat)

The idea of explosive motorboats was born in the autumn of 1935, at the height of the Ethiopian crisis, when Italian-British relations were tense and the Royal Navy had deployed large parts of the Home Fleet to the Mediterranean. In its embryonic form, the concept was the brainchild of air force General Amedeo di Savoia, Duke of Aosta, who suggested it to his brother Aimone, a senior officer of the Regia Marina: he quickly developed it and made it technically feasible with the help of two collaborators. On 27 November 1935 Admiral Aimone di Savoia-Aosta, Duke of Spoleto, submitted to the Navy ministry a study compiled with the assistance of Commanders Giorgio Giorgis and Carlo Margottini, describing a series of light, fast single-seater motorboats, with a strong explosive charge in the bow, to be launched against enemy ships at their moorings, and transported close to enemy bases by Savoia Marchetti S.55 flying boats.[1]

The study began with a brief description of the proposed operation:

a) Six small light and fast single-seat motorboats (about 40 miles per hour) equipped with an explosive TNT charge of about 300kg (torpedo head) are suspended beneath six SM. 55 (Atlantic) flying boats, between the [twin] hulls.
b) On a calm night the six flying boats carry the motorboats close to naval base to attack, landing in open water at far enough from the land (some tens of miles) [as to] exclude the chance of an early discovery by the enemy watch.
c) Once at sea, disengaging from the planes, the six motorboats head for the enemy base. At the

1. This was the same type of aircraft that General Italo Balbo used for the well-known transatlantic formation flights that achieved worldwide renown in the early 1930s. The SIAI S.55 was a catamaran flying boat with cantilever wing, double tail booms and twin tails, originating from a 1923 specification for an 'offshore torpedo seaplane', and was designed by engineer Alessandro Marchetti; 16.5m long and with a 24m wingspan, its full load weight was about 9500kg. It was built in several versions: the 'M' for maritime reconnaissance and bombing was the most numerous. Equipped with two 500-700hp 'tandem' engines, the maximum speed of the S.55 M was 265 km/h, and normal load range around 2000km.

MAT/MA prototype – 'Gamma Device' (CABI drawing A.30, 8.9.1936).

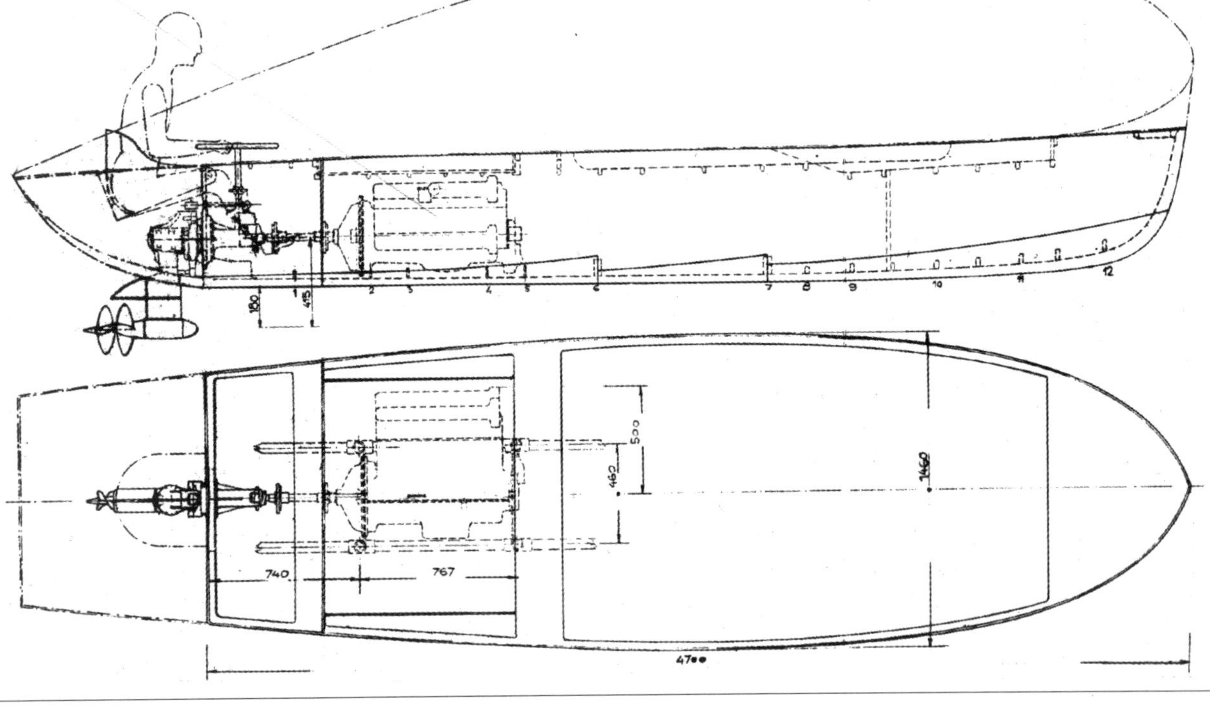

mouth of the harbour the leader heads for the boom defence at full speed. 50–100 metres from it the helmsman jumps into the sea, letting the motorboat continue and explode on impact against the boom, destroying a section.

d) The following motorboats pass through the gap thus opened in the boom, the location of which will be shown by a light signal left on the sea by the first motorboat together with the helmsman. In case there is another boom the second motorboat repeats the destructive operation already carried out by the leader on the first boom.

e) The surviving motorboats, penetrating into the harbour, head for the moored ships. Each helmsman jumps into the sea at 50–100 metres from his target, while the motorboat goes on, exploding against the ship.

One of two MAT/MA prototypes during outfitting in the Baglietto Shipyards in Varazze (Savona).

Varazze, 2 November 1936. Tests of an MAT/MA prototype.

f) Nothing prevents the operation from being performed with a greater number of motorboats (nine–twelve) and also repeated after a short interval, since it is not easy to set up an unbreachable defence in a few days ...

The outline went on to deal with all the aspects of the proposed operation in detail, and above all the various technical problems: the range and operational capabilities of the S.55; size and general characteristics of motorboats; burst charge; destruction of boom defences; destructive potential of the explosive charge against the hulls; rescue of helmsmen, as the future 'Pilots' were then called, etc. It ended with the sentence: 'The present study was compiled by the undersigned together with cf Giorgis and Margottini. It is a strong desire of all three, in case of favourable acceptance, to be selected for its practical implementation'.[2]

Given the moment of international tension, the Italian Navy was looking for every new weapon that could somehow compensate for its materiel inferiority in case of confrontation with the British and French, so the Ministry received the project with great interest.

Two famous boatyards (Baglietto of Varazze and Picchiotti of Limite d'Arno) were immediately consulted about the hulls; they specialised in the construction of very fast motorboats and Mas, but were only provided with the general characteristics of the desired craft without specifying its purpose and operational use. In a meeting held on 29 February

2. Fate decided otherwise. Subsequently promoted Captains, Margottini and Giorgis (both awarded the Gold Medal posthumously) were killed in action, respectively in command of a destroyer squadron in the Central Mediterranean in October 1940, and of the cruiser *Fiume*, sunk at the battle of Cape Matapan in March 1941.

1936 in Rome in the headquarters of the Ship Projects Committee (Maricominav, presided over by General Giuseppe Pugliese, the well-known designer of, amongst other things, the *Littorio* class battleships), engineer Vincenzo Baglietto, owner of the yards of the same name, was commissioned to complete the design of a small speedboat with speed as high as possible (no less than 30 knots) that could be carried between the floats of an S.55 type flying boat, thus with precisely established weight limits and mandatory maximum dimensions.

In particular, the weight could not exceed a total of 1000kg, including 300kg of payload and 150 between petrol and pilot. Another peculiar feature was the need for a mechanical system that somehow allowed propeller and rudder lifting, to facilitate overcoming the barriers and floating obstructions which were bound to be present in the harbours that the craft was designed to assault. Furthermore, maintaining a steady course was required even after the boat had been abandoned by the pilot who would lock the rudder amidships. A few months earlier engineer Baglietto, together with engineer Guido Cattaneo[3] had designed and built the 'Asso RB' racing speedboat, equipped with a special 'Z' shaped transmission designed and produced by CABI–Cattaneo of Milan; this was capable of modification to make it pivot on the horizontal axis as well. Once authorised, the Baglietto shipyards introduced CABI to the issue, starting that close collaboration in the manufacture of surface assault craft that would produce excellent results and continue until the end of the conflict. Engineer Cattaneo took responsibility for the design and implementation of the propulsion system featuring a swivelling and lifting stern drive equipped with counter-rotating propellers to eliminate the heeling torque and to ensure the motorboat kept a good steady course. The problem represented by the minimal hull depth, which had to be less than the limited space between the two floats and the wing centre section of the aircraft (about 0.80m), was solved by fitting the chosen engine – a 90hp Alfa Romeo '6c 2300' similar to those used as auxiliaries on the '500' class Mas boats, then under construction – in a 'lying down' position, rotated 90° on its horizontal axis.

While the definition and drafting stage of the general project was in progress, the Regia Marina ordered the building of a wooden mock-up of the 'barchino' (light boat, as the new craft was then named) for the first transportation tests with the S.55 flying boat. The mock-up was ready by 23 March 1936 and immediately transferred to the Regia Aeronautica Orbetello seaplane base, where tests began with due secrecy shortly after. Flotation, take-off and landing trials were carried out until the following June. From the first attempts, however, it was clear that the conversion and use of flying boats for the transport and release of motorboats presented aspects of considerable complexity, and operating limitations that would be hard to overcome completely. On the whole, however the tests did not exclude the possibility of using the S.55 as 'carriers' (or 'approachers') for the light motorboats.

As soon as the designs were ready, including the changes dictated by the results of the first experiments with flying boats, on 15 June 1936 the Regia Marina commissioned the Baglietto yard in Varazze to construct the hulls of two prototypes, whose mechanical parts would be supplied by CABI–Cattaneo while the final outfitting (explosive charge, fuses etc) would be completed by the Navy in its own yards for reasons of secrecy.

The two prototypes, built in Varazze and partly set up in Milan, were ready for tests by the following November. As the weight reached 1050kg by the end of outfitting, some weight-reduction measures were taken, such as the replacement of the mahogany deck with aluminium and waterproofed canvas (in the bow area), and the cutting of lightening holes in the transverse bulkheads, etc; these brought it back to 950kg as planned.

At the trials carried out in Varazze on 23 November 1936 with a single unit (the other was unavailable due to shaft line revision work), the maximum speed obtained was 32.4 knots. – a satisfying result, though the endurance test (one hour at $\frac{9}{10}$ power) showed insufficient ventilation of the engine due to the restricted size of dynamic air intakes. After the necessary changes, the two prototypes were transferred to La Spezia dockyard to complete the outfitting.

3. It is interesting to note an unlikely series of personal connections that facilitated the success of the initiative: Admiral Aimone di Savoia Aosta, because of his involvement in amateur speedboat competitions, had known the engineer Guido Cattaneo for a long time. The latter was a well-known champion of those years, and the son of the owner of CABI-Cattaneo of Milan that collaborated with the Baglietto shipyards in Varazze in producing the hulls that allowed him to win a number of world records. Commander Giorgis, in turn, was the brother of an Alfa Romeo technician; and engineer Romeo, a former Lieutenant Colonel of the Air Force. Therefore, the project became something of a 'family business' with undeniable advantages in the mutual trust necessary to keep it confidential.

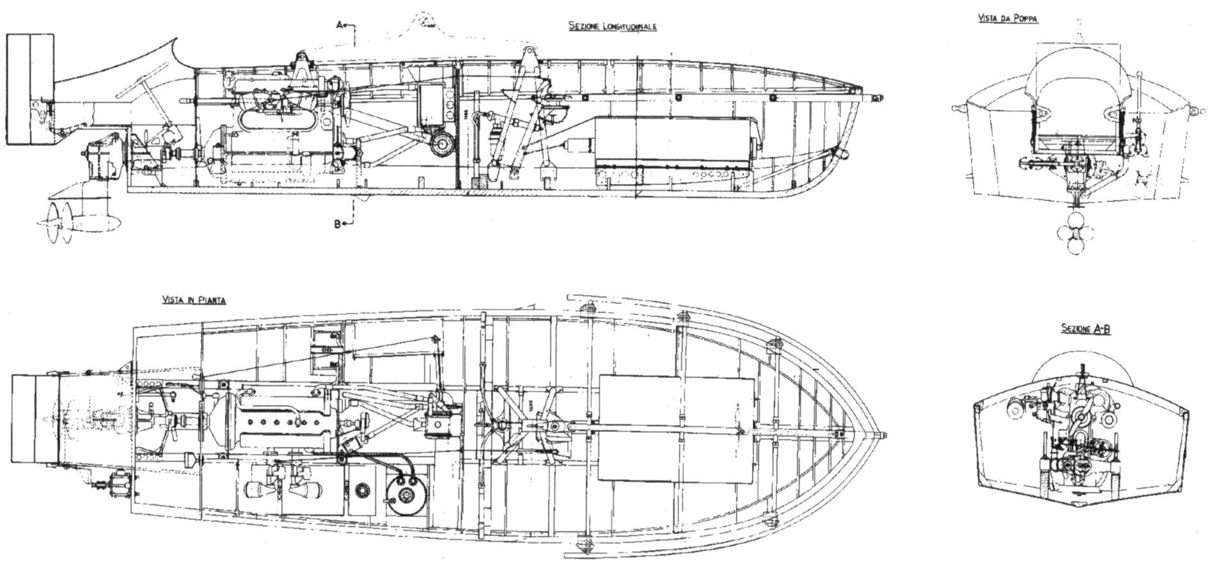

'Gamma 3' project (CABI drawing A.253, 25.1.1940).

'1-ton light motorboats' was adopted as a cover name for these units, while the official classification (restricted) was 'Motoscafi Avio Trasportati' (MAT = Air-portable Motorboats), but on some documents of that time 'Assault Motorboats' (MA) also appears. Moreover, a probably temporary cover name appears on some blueprints: 'GAMMA Device' (*eg* CABI. A.30 of 15.9.1936, provisional).

With the outfitting complete, the main features of these craft were:

Hull:
in wood, hard chine with a low 'V' bottom and two steps at frames 6 and 7, internally divided by two non-watertight transverse bulkheads separating the engine room from that of the explosive charge, at the bow, and from the steering position, in the extreme stern. The deck was in waterproof canvas in the bow area and in aluminium over the engine.
Length: hull 4.70m; overall 5.25m.
Width at the main beam: 1.460m
Hull depth: 0.65m

Propulsion system:
One Alfa Romeo '2300/1' internal combustion engine, 6-cylinder, about 75hp at 4400rpm, forward gear only, 'lying' on its left side at about 10° to the horizontal.

The gases exhausted through a silencer; the carburettors were on the upper side, while the starting motor and generator were (very awkwardly) on the lower side. The forward-only motion was through a half-axle joining the engine and the stern drive/rudder unit designed by CABI. This drive included two contra-rotating propellers (a three-blade, left-handed one ahead of a two-blade, right-handed one) and a small fin. It could be rotated 18° on each side, and upwards, to a clearing position, to about 98°. The fuel (petrol) tanks were in the engine room, and provided about 80 miles range at the maximum 32 knots speed.

Steering:
The steering position was at the extreme stern. The wheel was spoked, similar to that of a truck, with its vertical column keyed to the front (fixed) side of the drive block, which also included the device for lifting the 'foot' and the lock to keep the craft on a constant heading after the pilot abandoned ship. The latter sat on a small seat cantilevered out from the transom and tilting backwards to make it easier for the operator to drop into the sea after pointing his craft towards the target. Given the absence of a reverse gear, all manoeuvres had to be carried out using only forward motion, and a small oar or paddle. The steering position, besides the helm and engine controls, and various safety devices, also contained a small magnetic compass and all the engine monitoring instruments.

Explosive charge and other special fittings:
The burst charge consisted of a cylindrical case holding about 300kg of Tritolital right forward.

Immediately aft was a ring of small explosive charges known as the 'cannon'. At the moment of impact against the side of the enemy ship, a mechanical device called the 'palmola', placed at the bow at the height of the deck stringer, activated the fuses of the 'cannon' charges, whose explosion split the craft in two, immediately sinking the bow containing the main charge. The explosion of the latter took place underwater, triggered by a hydrostatic pressure device. This meant it was possible to achieve the maximum destructive effect of the shock wave against the hull of the unit attacked. Should the hydrostatic plate fail, the explosion of the charge occurred on the bottom – generally shallow inside harbours – after about a minute and a half, activated by a time device. For the possible use of light motorboats to open up a gap in floating boom defences, the explosion of the main charge instead occurred at the moment of impact, at sea level or just below. This was achieved with a special 'whisker' device, placed in front of the stem and hinged at deck level, which replaced the 'palmola-gun' system.

International tension decreased following the conclusion of the Ethiopian war in the spring of 1936, and the two light motorboat prototypes were laid up in the 'Cottrau' range area by the Permanent Commission for experiments with war material (Mariperman) in the La Spezia base. The use of explosive motorboats was only considered again by the Regia Marina at the end of 1938, after a study section devoted to the development of new weapons was formed within the Office of Operational Plans of the General Staff in Rome. At the same time the Headquarters of the 1st Flotilla Mas in La Spezia was given the task of continuing the experiments with existing material in complete secrecy.

On 29 September 1938 the General Staff proposed to the Ministry of the Navy the construction of a new series of 12 motorboats similar to the two prototypes already built, but with some modifications: increase in the hull length of about forty centimetres (from 5.25 to 5.62 metres overall); elimination of one of the two bottom steps in an attempt to improve the course stability, while accepting a slight decrease in maximum speed, partly compensated by the adoption of a higher power engine: the 90hp Alfa Romeo '6c 2500'. The proposal was partially accepted, and the following October Cantieri Baglietto was ordered to build 6 light motorboats, with the new chosen cover name of 'Touring Motorboats' (MT) that would mark all Italian Navy surface assault craft thereafter.

As for the 'MA/MAT', the manufacture of the mechanical parts for the 6 new MT was entrusted to CABI–Cattaneo of Milan, while the final outfitting remained a responsibility of the technical units of the Navy. One of the two existing light motorboats was sent back to the Varazze shipyards as an example, but devoid of any equipment that could reveal its actual use.

Officially the 6 MT should have been delivered to the Navy for final outfitting on 15 December 1938 but for various reasons their construction suffered some delays, and mechanical fitting-out could not start before February 1939. At the same time, however, contracts were placed with the interested companies for the building of a new series of 12 light motorboats identical to those under construction. The order was finalised in March 1939 while the 6 first series MT were delivered in late spring.

Once the craft were finally outfitted, a new cycle of trials was started in La Spezia, which highlighted some technical deficiencies likely to compromise the efficiency of the boats. These referred especially to the bow canvas cover, which had proven too weak, and to

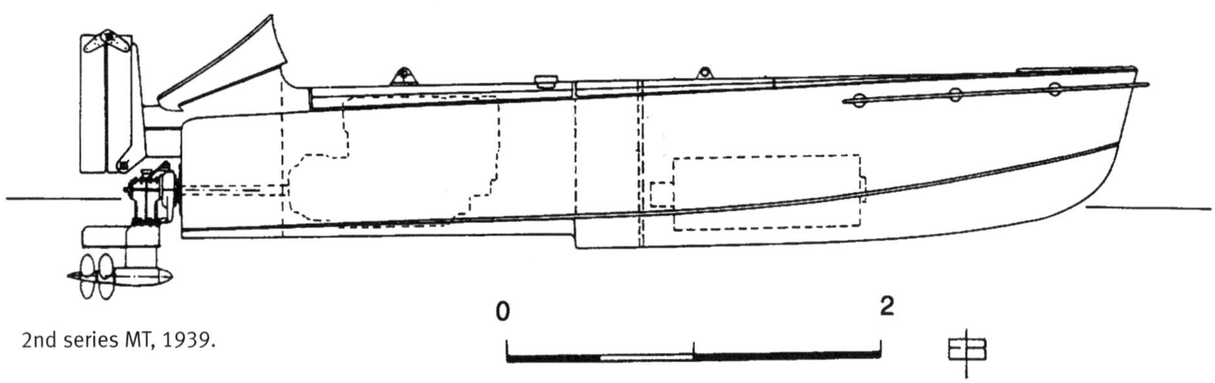

2nd series MT, 1939.

Two pictures of *MT 16* found broken down (resulting from an engine starter motor short-circuit) by the British off Malta in July 1941. *(NWMA, Malta)*

the position of the engine on its side, where some delicate electric accessories were in contact with bilge water.

For various reasons, the weight and space limitations that had determined these solutions had been removed – by then, the light motorboats were no longer expected to be transported by S.55 flying boats, but by naval units – so appropriate modifications were investigated. Towards the end of summer 1939 the 6 first series MT were therefore returned to the building companies for replacement of the waterproof canvas cover with plywood, and turning the engine upright, which raised the construction depth to about 0.90 metres. Furthermore, it was decided to adopt a particular type of lifebuoy or rigid raft for the pilot which, when folded, constituted the back of the pilot's seat, and was released at the moment of his 'dive'.

The building of the 12 MT of the 2nd series was halted pending the practical testing of the changes made to those of the 1st, and would not be resumed before mid-1940, after the trials had given satisfactory results. Thus the 2nd series of light motorboats were identical to those of the modified 1st series, but were only ready for use by the end of 1940.

Meanwhile, CABI and the Baglietto shipyards continued studies intended to improve the characteristics and performance of the explosive motorboats. Some designs were prepared: the 'Gamma III' of January 1940 and the MTU ('Unified MT') of that June, characterised by a notably convex deck cross-section and an overall length reaching 5.75m in the MTU. Hull shape and general arrangements of the engine and systems related to the explosive charge were similar to those of the MT after the last modifications. These two models were not proceeded with because, in the course of further trials with the MT, it

The same *MT 16*, hastily repaired, in British hands.

became clear that the original design required substantial modifications to improve, above all, the seakeeping qualities and course stability.

It was therefore decided to eliminate the last remaining hull step, and increase the length significantly, as well as other changes to internal arrangements, explosive charge-related devices and steering position. CABI, in collaboration with Baglietto shipyards, was in charge of building the prototype (CABI A. 326 design of 11.25.1940 for '5.4m experimental MT') 'Modified or Improved Touring Motorboat', initially also called 'Marino', from which the new MTM designation was derived.

In particular, compared to the previous series MT, the new project proposed to:

- lengthen the hull to 5.40m (6.15m overall) and to increase breadth by 0.30m;
- adopt a new, stepless hard-chine hull, with a rather deep 'V' at the bow, to get better seaworthiness and increase course stability;
- fit the engine with reversing gear, to ease the approach manoeuvres to obstructions, and increase endurance to 3 hours at full power;
- secure the main charge case to the floor rather than the keel;
- adopt an electric trigger system for the boat separation device ('cannon');
- move the 'palmola' up to the deck at the bow from inside the hull to prevent water infiltration through the openings required;
- equip the 'palmola' with the 'whisker' device, to allow the light motorboat's employment against either naval units or obstructions via an easy and quick operation carried out from inboard;
- fit the hull with a new central transverse bulkhead, at the centre of gravity, with a single eyebolt for hoisting the craft;
- make the cockpit bulkhead watertight;
- modify the steering position arrangements appropriately to give the pilot a more comfortable position and protect him better from spray.

Using the engine of one of the two experimental MA/MAT that had been expended in a live test (with reduced charge) against the hull of the old decommissioned cruiser *Quarto* in La Spezia on 13 November 1940, the prototype of the new MTM was tested with satisfactory results at the Milan seaplane base on 1 March 1941. During these trials, a maximum speed of 33 knots, and much improved course stability, was achieved with the boat at full load (1100kg).

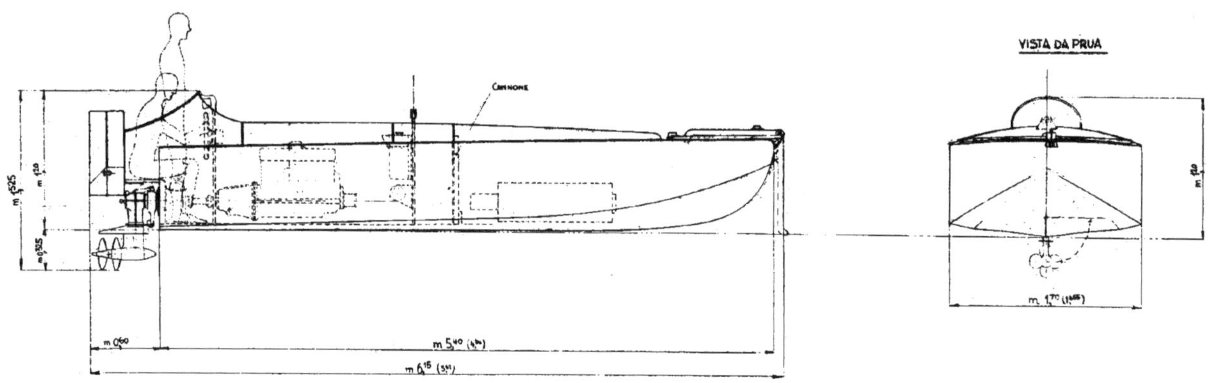

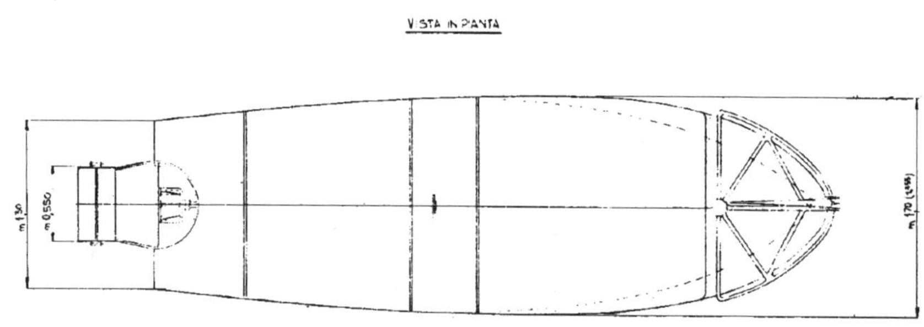

Experimental MTM (CABI drawing A.326, 26.11.1940), 'MT 5.4m'.

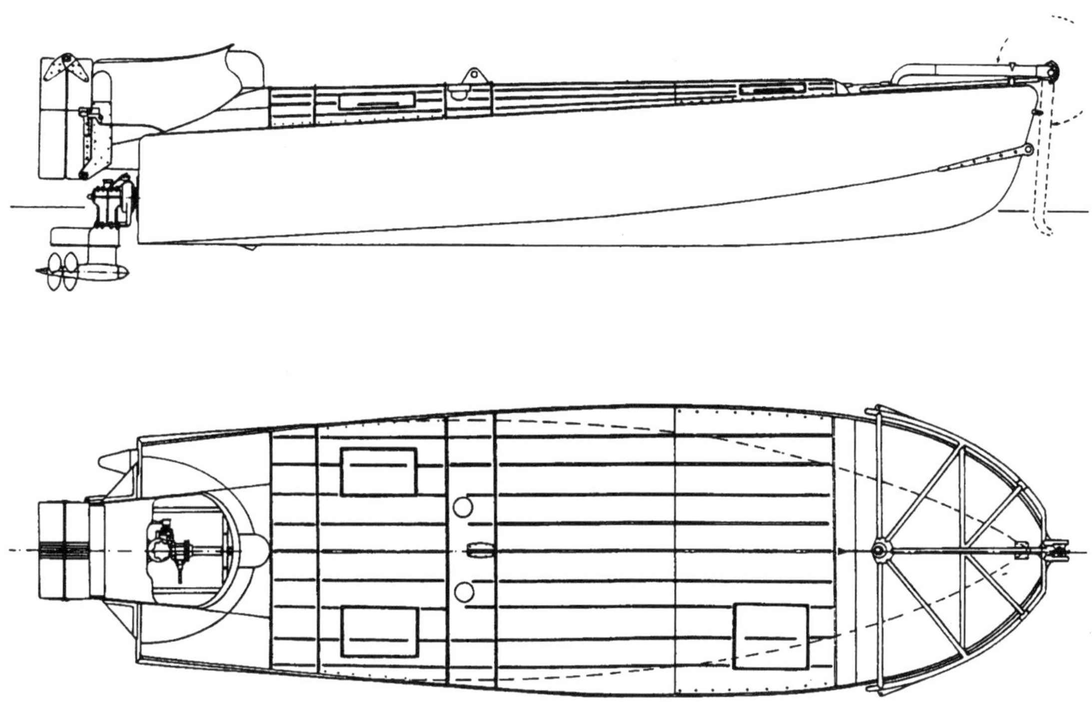

4th series MTM, 1942, external views.

A few days later, on 25/26 March, 6 MT of the 1st and 2nd series successfully carried out their first action of the war by forcing Suda bay on the island of Crete.[4]

In the same month of March 1941 the Regia Marina ordered from CABI the first series of 12 MTM, with Baglietto-built hulls, and invited the same company to design a type of explosive boat of reduced dimensions – transportable in the watertight cylinders used for SLCs aboard 'approacher' submarines – from which the MTR would be born.

The first MTM needed some changes suggested by operational use so could not be ready before autumn 1941 and the unfortunate action against Malta of 26 July 1941 had to be carried out with 9 of the remaining MT. The failure of the attack on Valletta harbour demonstrated, among other things, that the transport of light motorboats close to enemy bases by surface ships constituted a serious risk to the operation, as they could be located at a great distance by radar, whose existence was known by that time; this destroyed the element of surprise on which assault craft depended. Therefore, speeding up development of small submarine-transportable boats (MTR) was requested but, at the same time, the X Flottiglia Mas did not give up work on MTM with gradually improved characteristics, which were mainly used from coastal bases and advanced mobile sites (land convoys, support ships, etc).

Overall, between March 1941 and September 1943 the Regia Marina ordered from CABI (prime contractor) about 40 MTM of which the first 12 were delivered in the autumn of 1941 (series III, according to a progression that also considered the two previous series of MT) and the rest (series IV on, probably up to VIII) by the date of the armistice.

There is insufficient evidence to attempt a reliable reconstruction of the numbering of individual craft. It has been ascertained, however, that the distinguishing numbers assigned by the Regia Marina were between 1 and 199, generally using even numbers only. After the armistice, the X^{a} Mas of the RSI commissioned both MTM built before September 1943 and light motorboats built thereafter. The former were identified with the old numbering (*42, 98, 114,* etc) while the latter also carried odd numbers, always followed by the letter 'b' (*2b, 16b, 17b, 33b,* etc) for those with Baglietto hulls, or '500' series numbers (*517, 549,* etc) for the group of MTM built by SIAI of Sesto Calende as a CABI subcontractor; these were transferred to the X^{a}

4. Examining the results obtained in that action where, despite the three hits against the heavy cruiser HMS *York* and a tanker, two of the three other motorboats missed relatively large and close targets, it could be deduced that this was essentially due to the poor course stability of the MT – something the MTM had to remedy.

Mas of the republican Navy from production runs ordered by the German Navy.[5]

After the armistice the Regia Marina (Mariassalto) only retained a little over a dozen MTM, located in Amalfi and Sardinia, but these were no longer employed in war operations.[6] Only two MTM were to be used – together with one MTSM – for an attempt at forcing Suda in January 1944 but the action was cancelled at the last moment.

The MTM, familiarly abbreviated to 'emme' in the assault craft world, became the standard X^{a} Mas explosive motorboat after the end of 1941, and also the one that was built in the greatest numbers.

The main dimensions of the MTM (CABI A. 383 drawing of 1.7.1941, series IV–VII) were as follows:

- Overall length (life-raft and 'whisker' of the 'palmola' included) 6.110m
- Hull length 5.385m
- Maximum breadth (with the small side 'whiskers' of the 'palmola' extended) 1.665m
- Depth 1.040m
- Total weight (at full load) 1200kg

For the main performance details please refer to the table on page 85 but, given the peculiarity of the design, we provide some detailed information about its constructive characteristics below.

Hull:

Wood, unstepped hard-chine hull, reinforced by two walnut keelsons on which the frames were fixed, and divided along its length into four compartments. The planking consisted of a double layer of 1.5mm beech plywood strips, fixed with copper and brass pins, with a layer of waterproofed canvas between them.

The deck had a slightly convex cross section except at the forward end (about 1.10m long) which was flat to support the 'palmola'. A series of hemispherical section strips was arranged longitudinally on the deck to provide a walkway and strengthen the deck itself; depending on the different series, these were arranged

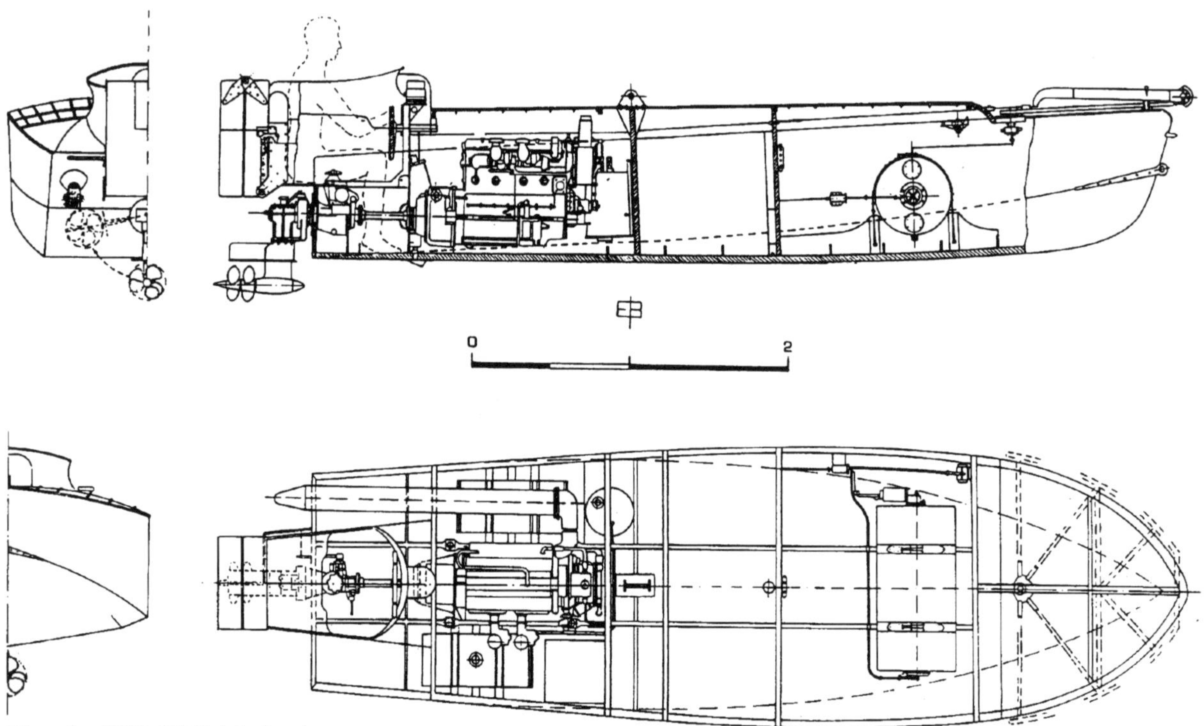

4th series MTM, 1942, interior views.

5. A total of 29 MTM served with the 'X^{a} Mas' of the RSI from autumn 1943 to April 1945 (see table on page 35). A dozen were lost in action (one hit and severely damaged the French destroyer *Trombe* in April 1945) or in accidents; the surviving units were destroyed or abandoned at the end of hostilities. In Sesto Calende, at SIAI or at the nearby former 'Sant'Anna' seaplane base – home of the X^{a} Pilots School – in May 1945 there were 22 MTM in various stages of construction forming part of a German contract, and 6 MTM already belonging to the School (*MTM 98, 110, 50, 92*, etc), some with engines missing or damaged.

6. See table on page 35.

3rd series MTM hull ready to be shipped from Varazze to Milan for outfitting by CABI.

in variable numbers (up to ten) and constantly spaced, or grouped together in three or more groups of three or four items each.

The deck sections over the warhead and engine compartments were removable and fixed along the stringer with wing nut screws or hexagonal headed bolts. Two rectangular hatches above the engine compartment could be opened to allow access to the

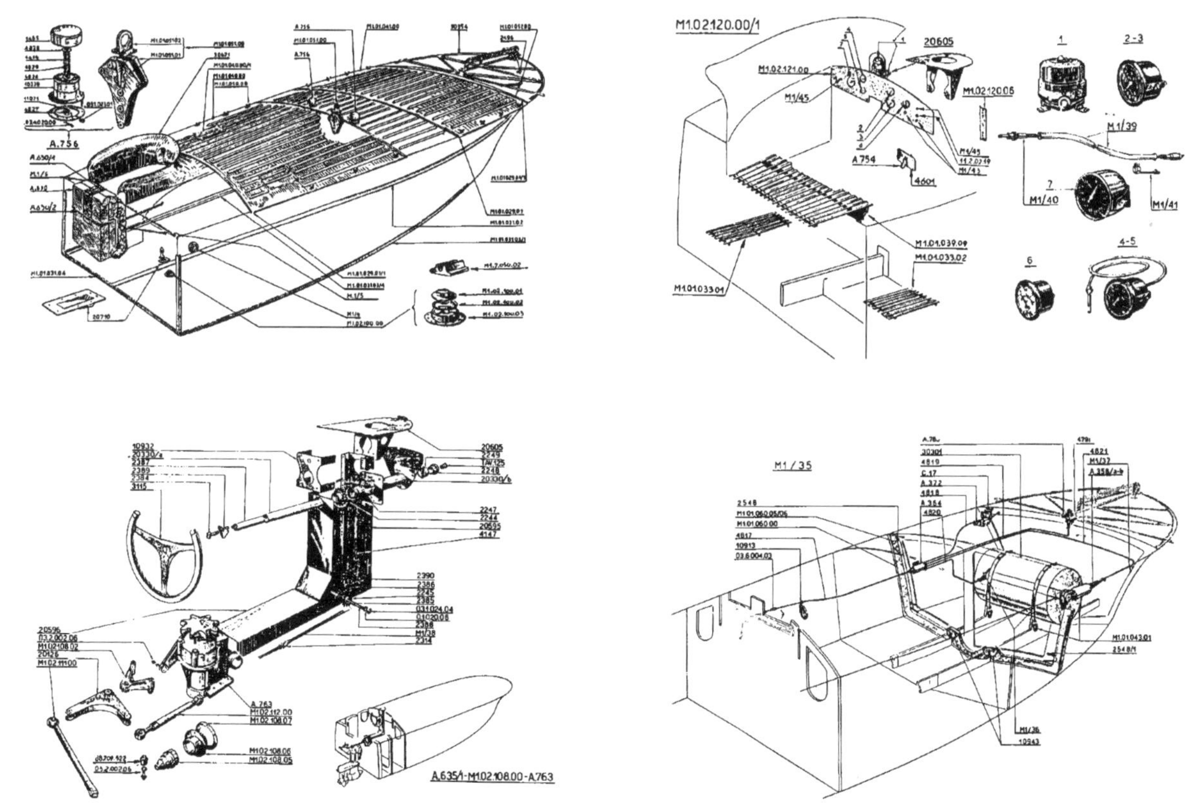

Clockwise from top left. MTM External fittings and hull hatches. MTM Instrument panel. MTM Explosive charge arrangement. MTM Steering. *(From the spare parts catalogue for 'M 1' type assault motorboats, published by SIAI-Marchetti, 1941.)*

Two stills of the MTM pilot 'jump' sequence from a spring 1944 propaganda film shot in Sesto Calende. *(M Spertini collection)*

carburettors and fuel tanks. A double plate with eyebolt was bolted at the stem-head, for towing the craft.

The stern drive emerged from the bottom of the transom, and the propeller-rudder unit could tilt 75-80° to the right; the truncated-cone of the muffler end – which expelled the exhaust gas and engine cooling water – was in the upper left corner of the transom. The aft part of the cockpit and the folded life-raft were cantilevered over the stern.

Engine unit:
One Alfa Romeo 90 hp '6c./2500' petrol engine (see description in Appendix A) equipped with a reverse gear gave the craft a 31-knot maximum continuous speed with a corresponding endurance of about 3 hours. The engine was upright and fixed to the two keelsons. Power was transmitted via a short shaft to the stern drive, equipped with two contra-rotating propellers. Two cylindrical fuel (petrol) tanks were fitted sideways in the engine compartment, with a capacity of about 50 litres each.

Explosive charge and other special arrangements:
The charge of about 300–330kg of Tritolital[7] was contained in a cylindrical sheet metal case (50 x 100cm) weighing about 20-30kg. This was fitted on the bow compartment floor and fixed on wooden saddles which rested on the two keelsons. On the two bases of the case were an electromechanical bursting device to the left, and a hydrostatic plate for controlling the charge explosion when calibration depth was reached (8-12 metres for stationary and 3-4 metres for moving targets) to the right.

An essential element for shearing the light motor-boat in two on impact, and the consequent explosion

7. Enhanced derivative of TNT (or trinitrotoluene) normally produced by SIPE (Soc Italiana Prodotti Esplodenti). It was an explosive with excellent stability, moisture resistance, etc, widely used for the underwater charges of Regia Marina weapons.

Two pictures of *MTM 8B*, outfitted by CABI (MTM type 'D') on German orders, captured by a US ship off Provence in October 1944. *(US Navy)*

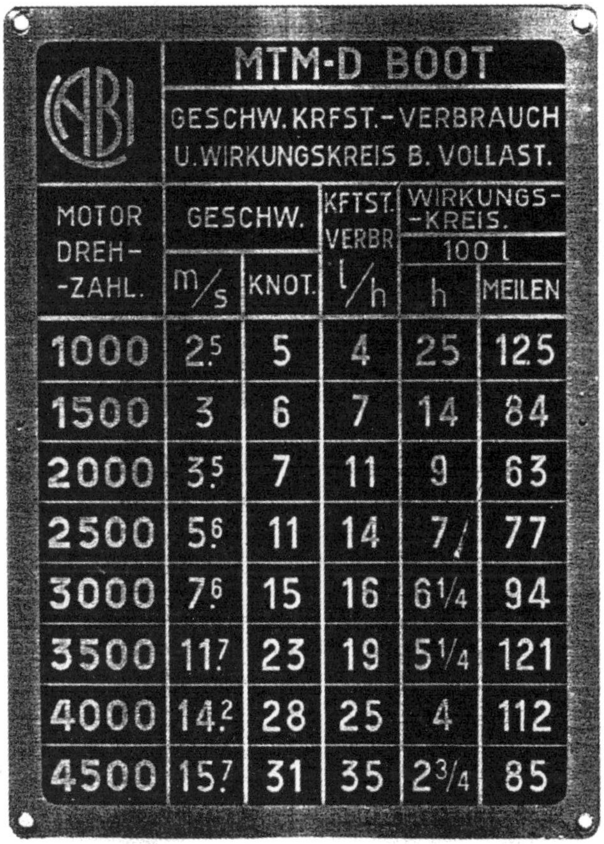

CABI — MTM-D BOOT — GESCHW. KRFST.-VERBRAUCH U.WIRKUNGSKREIS B. VOLLAST.

MOTOR DREH- -ZAHL.	GESCHW. m/s	GESCHW. KNOT.	KFTST. VERBR l/h	WIRKUNGS- -KREIS. 100 L h	WIRKUNGS- -KREIS. 100 L MEILEN
1000	2.5	5	4	25	125
1500	3	6	7	14	84
2000	3.5	7	11	9	63
2500	5.6	11	14	7	77
3000	7.6	15	16	6¼	94
3500	11.7	23	19	5¼	121
4000	14.2	28	25	4	112
4500	15.7	31	35	2¾	85

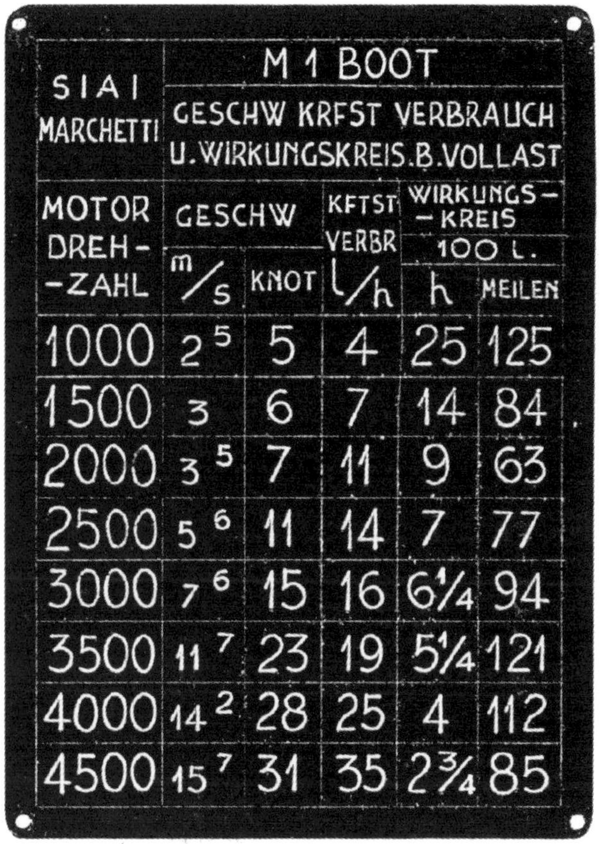

SIAI MARCHETTI — M 1 BOOT — GESCHW KRFST VERBRAUCH U.WIRKUNGSKREIS.B.VOLLAST

MOTOR DREH- -ZAHL	GESCHW m/s	GESCHW KNOT	KFTST VERBR l/h	WIRKUNGS- - KREIS 100 L. h	WIRKUNGS- - KREIS 100 L. MEILEN
1000	2 5	5	4	25	125
1500	3	6	7	14	84
2000	3 5	7	11	9	63
2500	5 6	11	14	7	77
3000	7 6	15	16	6¼	94
3500	11 7	23	19	5¼	121
4000	14 2	28	25	4	112
4500	15 7	31	35	2¾	85

Reproduction of two original plates showing fuel consumption, speed and range corresponding to different engine rpm on 'MTM-D' (CABI) and 'M 1' (SIAI) explosive motorboats. *(M Spertini collection)*

of the main charge, was the so-called 'palmola', a unique form of striker. On the MT it consisted of an arched metal tube frame placed at stringer height in the bow area and held in extended position by counter-balanced springs acting on the frame tubes, which emerged from apertures in the planking.

On the MTM this structure, connected to the electromechanical burst devices, was placed outside the hull, at the forward end of the deck.

To increase the angle of incidence, and at the same time to make it easier to catch any cables hanging from defensive booms or from the hull of the target,

Details of main charge case and instrument panel of *MTM 8B* (CABI type 'D').

small side 'whiskers' were arranged along the outer edge of the 'palmola' in variable numbers (generally two). To operate against obstructions the 'palmola' was also equipped with a folding central element, also called a 'whisker', which, when armed, hung vertically over the bow, with the head just below the water surface to engage horizontally arranged cables etc, thus activating the main charge burst system.

In late model MTM the main charge could be set to explode in three modes: immediately against the target (light structures, etc); at a predetermined depth (ships) after the sinking of the bow section of the light motorboat following the impact due to the chain reaction of the 'cannon'; or by an 'end of run' timing

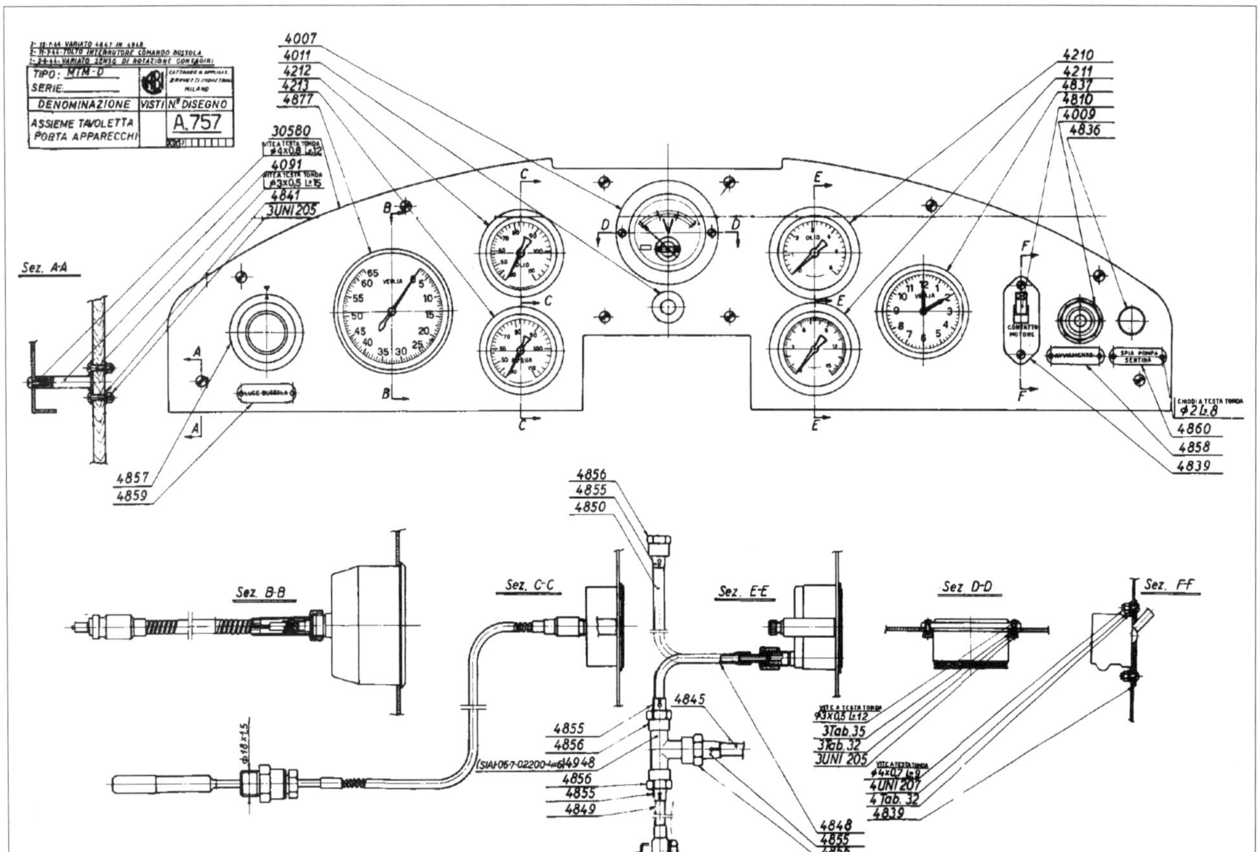

'MTM type D' instrument panel (CABI drawing A.757).

device that came into operation in case the motorboat missed the target, to prevent its capture. The so-called 'sausages' containing the small charges of the 'cannon', intended to blow the boat in two, were placed in contact with the planking around the bulkhead between the forward and central compartments, and were electrically connected to a junction box fixed on the same bulkhead, which also included electric cables of the main bursting device activated by the 'palmola'. A security system prevented accidental activation of the various triggers and was connected to the 'burst lever' in the steering position; this overrode the safety system itself, thus arming the charges.

Steering arrangements:
The steering position, sometimes and improperly called 'cabin', but much more often 'cappottina' ['canopy'], was at the extreme stern and had a non-magnetic metal wash strake in front, with rounded edges and facing towards the bow to act as a spray deflector. Ahead of this structure was a niche on the centreline containing the magnetic compass. On the front bulkhead dividing the steering position from the engine compartment were the dashboard and steering column; the wheel consisted of a duralumin sector of about 270° with three spokes.

A horizontal cog on the steering wheel column, acting on a chain with rollers which in turn, through a countershaft system, acted on the steel rods that crossed the transom, controlled the turning of the stern drive on its vertical axis. The automobile type dashboard contained the main engine control instruments (tachometer, oil and cooling water temperature, batteries voltmeter, engine and inverter oil pressure indicators, fuel level gauge etc) as well as the knob for releasing the 'whisker' of the 'palmola', various warning lights, etc.

On the right was the engine throttle and on the bulkhead the inverter lever with its three positions (forward, neutral and rear). On the left was the red-painted 'burst lever' which armed the various charge priming devices, and released the life-raft at the same time. Also attached to the bulkhead was a metal plate which summarised speed data, endurance etc, at different engine rpm settings. Between the pilot's legs was the 'lock screw' of the propeller-rudder drive block, which was tightened after aiming the light motorboat towards the target, shortly before the 'jump'. A handwheel for lifting the 'drive itself was fixed to the same block.

Close-up of the 'palmola' aboard *MTM 8B* with 'whisker' raised, and another with it lowered. *(US Navy)*

After the 8 September 1943 armistice, in addition to some MTM type explosive motorboats built previously for the Regia Marina, the Xª Mas commissioned many newer 'emme', from a batch of 170 light motorboats ordered by the Kriegsmarine from CABI, which delivered 143 before the end of hostilities.

These were a variant of the MTM (MTM-D defined as MTM-M1). This variant (CABI 729 drawing probably dated February 1944) used SIAI instead of Baglietto hulls: the Sesto Calende company applied their own experience and techniques, derived from aeronautical construction, in the building. The hull construction was no longer planked, but hot moulded with aeronautical plywood sheets, saving cost and time while eliminating or reducing hull reinforcements, screws, rivets etc. The various parts were combined using special synthetic resins (for example 'Kaurit'), overlapping up to four layers of canvas normally used for aircraft; even though the thickness remained around 15mm, it had greater compactness and good waterproofing. The hull was also more rigid compared to the elasticity of the traditional construction system, although this caused some minor inconvenience (vibration, etc) at times.

The main dimensions of the light motorboat remained almost unchanged, as with the identical propulsion system and other general characteristics. Only the weights had increased:

Hull only	830kg
Fuel and oil	100kg
Charge and related devices	320kg
Pilot, etc	90kg
Total weight	1340kg

The hull shape was very similar to that of the Baglietto model, except for a slightly higher stringer plate in the bow area. The MTM-D (or 'M1' for SIAI-Marchetti) remained in production until the end of the conflict and was largely employed by the Kriegsmarine. Some SIAI-Marchetti documents (bilingual spare parts catalogue for M1 type assault motorboat) show that, after the fortieth unit built by the company in Varese, the engine reversing gear was deleted to reduce production costs.

In the second half of 1944 both CABI and SIAI were commissioned by X^{a} Mas and the German Navy to begin developing a new model of light explosive motorboat following the general characteristics of the MTM but cheaper and easier to build, eliminating, amongst other things, the stern drive; this had lost much of its original importance – to allow the propeller to be easily lifted over any obstructions in harbour forcing operations – since the motorboats were now almost exclusively employed in the open sea.

Towards the end of 1944 SIAI (M/1 drawing of 2.9.44 for an 'Improved MTM explosive motorboat') and CABI (A.797 drawing of 7.11.1944, experimental 'MTM-D') presented their respective designs which, however, were not realised before the end of the conflict. For the record, some basic data are given here:

Improved MTM (SIAI)
Overall length 5.80m
Overall width 1.65m
4-cylinder engine, no inverter, with three-bladed propeller and traditional rudder

Experimental MTM-D (CABI)
Overall length 5.30m
Overall width 1.80m
'AR 6c. 2500' engine, no inverter, 'V-drive' transmission with traditional propeller and rudder.

Another study conducted by CABI, which did not get beyond the experimental phase, was the design of a small outboard electric motor to be installed on the MTM for short silent passages.

Given the peculiar nature of these craft, the following information (mainly from memories and notes by the author's old friend Marco Spertini) about the operational methods and features of the explosive motorboats must be of interest.

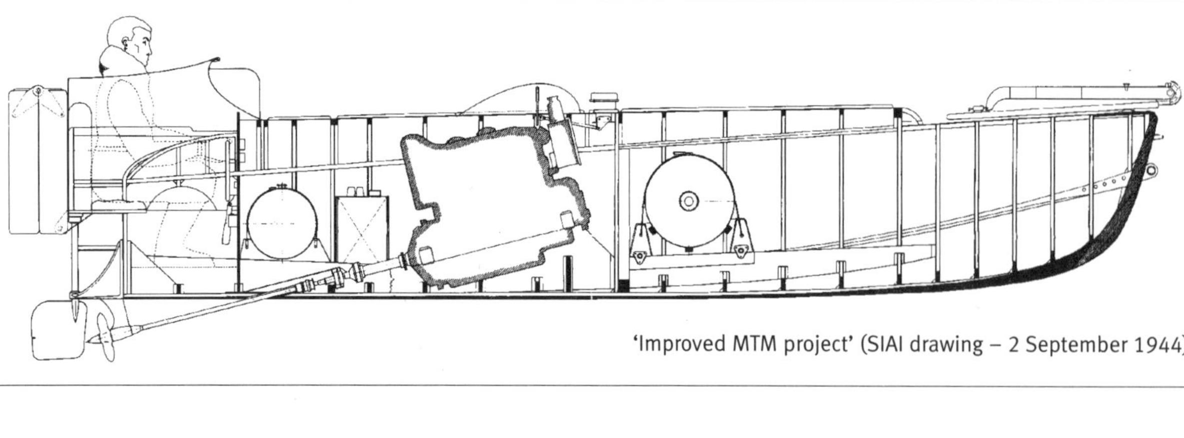

'Improved MTM project' (SIAI drawing – 2 September 1944).

Born to be employed in surprise attacks against stationary targets within smooth harbour waters, the light motorboats ended their career employed almost exclusively against moving targets offshore, and not always in optimal weather conditions. There was a substantial difference between the two techniques of use, as might be guessed: in the first case, target aiming was relatively easy, while in the second the pilot had to steer the craft on a collision course with the target, to be calculated instinctively and checked and refined with subsequent correction of the relative positions. Indeed, it was still a case of solving a kinematic problem similar to that of a torpedo launch, with the peculiarity that the craft itself was the weapon to be brought into contact with the target, with the one simplification represented by the shorter distances involved.

Assuming that the 'collision course' was easily determined thanks to the operator's training, there was still another problem: that of course stability of the light motorboat in the last short part of the race towards the target, after being abandoned by the pilot with the rudder locked. Factors that could push the craft off course essentially derived from the strength and direction of wind and sea, propeller torque and, finally, a poorly executed 'jump' by the pilot. The effect of sea and wind was only minimal if exactly from ahead: from all other directions it could cause even substantial deviations. Propeller torque, despite contra-rotation, was remarkable even if measurable, in smooth waters, depending on the speed:

- at 3000 rpm: nearly straight path for several hundreds of metres;
- at 3200 rpm: course kept for about 300m, then the craft began to turn right;
- at 3500 rpm: strong rightward deviation.

Avoiding possible harmful lateral thrusts imposed on the craft's stern by the pilot at the time of launch depended primarily on strict training, as well as keeping a cool head during the action. The choice of the moment and the execution of the 'jump' actually constituted the most delicate aspect of the operation: aiming the craft in the desired direction, and reaching the optimal distance, the pilot checked the speed one last time, and tightened down the rudder lock 'screw'; he then crouched on his toes on the seat, leaning back on the raft; finally, he firmly raised the 'burst lever' with the left hand and, while the trigger circuits were activated, the raft and pilot fell into the wake of the craft,

Two pictures of a group of SIAI-built 'MTM – M 1' explosive motorboats ready for delivery in Sesto Calende at the end of 1944. These are '500' series units, produced for the Kriegsmarine which later transfered some to the republican Xa Mas.

that continued on its way. After a short dive the pilot, supported by a 'Belloni suit', re-emerged pulling the line connected to the raft, which in the meantime had opened; he climbed over it quickly to get completely out of the water, just at the moment, if he had been skilled and lucky, the main charge of the craft exploded under the target.

At the end of the conflict, almost all the explosive motorboats still in operational condition in X^{a} Mas service were deliberately destroyed; but many of those already commissioned by the Germans, or at various outfitting stages at construction sites, could be recovered. To these must be added the dozen MTM supplied to Mariassalto.

The Allies took possession of some units, in addition to those they had managed to capture during the conflict. Half a dozen MTM ended up in Israeli hands; after a period of training on Lake Tiberias assisted by an Italian veteran, they used them in the 1948 war with some success.

Today an MTM in excellent condition is exhibited in the Tel Aviv War Museum; others are kept as memorials in Italian naval museums (La Spezia and Venice), at the Museum of Science and Technology in Milan, and the Valletta War Museum in Malta.

MTR (Motoscafo Turismo Ridotto – Reduced size Explosive Motorboat)

As mentioned previously, as early as the beginning of 1941 it had seemed a good idea to find a different system for approaching the targets, by simplifying the procedures and reducing the risks of sighting that derived from the use of surface units as 'carriers'. As had already happened with the SLC, it was proposed to employ submarines as 'approachers', using the same watertight cylinders used for the transportation of underwater self-propelled craft.

The main obstacle was the overall size of the standard explosive motorboats; a version with reduced size was therefore designed, officially named MTR while in current language the staff called them more simply 'erre' (R). Based on the experience gained with the MTR, an improved type named MTRM was under development before the armistice.

One of the first technical documents relating to the new 'downsized' motorboats is CABI drawing A.550 of 28 February1942. The length of the boat did not differ significantly from that of the MTM while the breadth was about 60cm narrower. As for the 'emme', the 'erre' hull was hard-chined and unstepped. With a fully loaded weight of 1250kg, they had an overall length of 6.185m, a breadth of 1.080m and a depth of 1.14m (measured with the stern drive raised, but temporarily removing both the windshield and compass, which had to be refitted at the time of launch).

Considering that the 'container cylinders' of the submarines had a length of about 6.60m and an internal diameter of about 1.15m, all available space was obviously exploited; also each section of the life-raft (very different from that of the 'emme') had been shortened to 0.425m with a 0.50m width, leaving unchanged the 0.150m depth of each element. Again because of 'loading gauge' limitations, the sides were not almost vertical as in the 'emme' but had a pronounced convexity. Consequently, the charge and the cylindrical petrol tank (37 x 50cm) were seated on the keel and no longer on the floor. The refuelling nozzle was concealed inside a well on the deck, which was therefore free of bumps or protrusions as the air intakes were replaced by a rectangular hatch that could be lifted at the front; the ventilation inlet was opened by a moveable support rod. The lubrication oil tank and battery were moved against the right side of the engine compartment.

As a result of the increased waterline length/breadth ratio, the already modest seakeeping qualities of the explosive motorboats declined steeply in the MTR. However, poor seaworthiness was relatively unimportant, considering that the 'erre' only navigated the short distance between the release point and the attack target. In order to improve performance, a longer and wider flap was applied to the stern drive, so that the action of the coaxial propellers and the water flow were best exploited.

The 'palmola' of the MTR was simplified compared to that of the MTM and had a higher number of side 'whiskers': in fact, it carried five on each side.

The weight breakdown for the 'erre' was as follows:

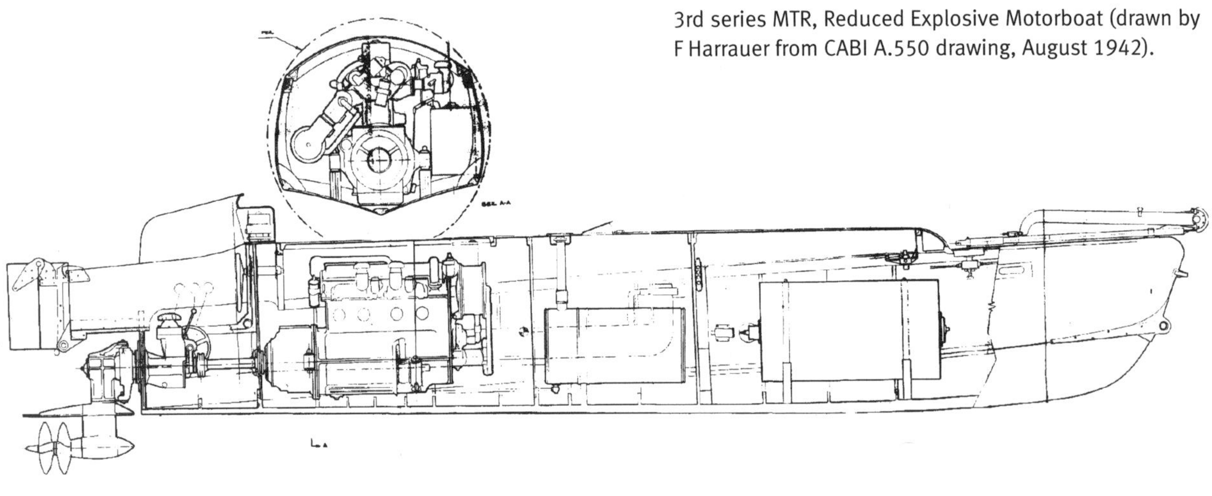

3rd series MTR, Reduced Explosive Motorboat (drawn by F Harrauer from CABI A.550 drawing, August 1942).

Two pictures of *MTR 14* being shown to a group of admirals visiting the Muggiano Decima Flottiglia Mas base in early spring 1943. On the hull sides there is a series of recessed handles to ease extraction from the cylinders of 'approacher' submarines. *(F Bargoni collection)*

Hull only	680kg
Pilot	80kg
Fuel and oil	80kg
Raft-lifesaver	21kg
Case and explosive charge	350kg
Various devices	39kg
Normal displacement	1250kg

Propulsion was by the usual 'AR 2500', which allowed a maximum speed of 31 knots, with a corresponding range of about 67 miles.

Despite their design being finalised by the early months of 1942, the 'erre' had no opportunities for action. Nevertheless, the command of X Flotilla Mas had high expectations for the MTR: by the date of the

The hull of *MTR 020*, minus explosive charge, engine and cockpit 'screen', in an early post-war picture.

EXPLOSIVE MOTORBOATS – UNIT/MODEL SUMMARY

Model	*Series*	*Number*	*Building period*	*Notes*
MA	Mock-up		February/March 1936	Used for tests with S.55 flying boat
MA/MAT	Prototypes		June/November 1936	('1-ton light motorboats')
MA/MAT (later MT)	1st		October 1938/May 1939	Converted to MT: late summer 1939/mid-1940
MT	2nd		March 1939 then stopped; mid-1940/end 1940	Identical to above after the 1939/40 modifications
MTM	Prototype		November 1940/ March 1941	Used the engine from an MT/MAT destroyed during tests in November 1940
MTM	3rd		March 1941/autumn 1941	
MTM	4th, 5th, 6th, 7th, etc	~30	Summer 1941/summer 1943	
MTM-D and MTM/M-1	–	~140	Early 1944/spring 1945	Kriegsmarine order for 170 units; 25 were loaned to the republican 'Xª Mas' MTM-D = Baglietto hull MTM-/M-1 = SIAI hull all = CABI outfitting
MTR	Prototype		Late 1941/early 1942	
	1st series		42	
	2nd series			
	3rd series		/43	
MTRM	–		/45	A single unit delivered to the republican 'Xª Mas'

armistice of 8 September 1943, operations were being studied with 'erre' carried by submarines against Gibraltar, Freetown, Cape Town and even New York.

The only mission attempted – with three MTR approached by the submarine *Ambra* – was part of attempts to counter the Allied landings in Sicily in July 1943; however, it was cancelled because an air attack damaged the submarine. Finally, what would have been a revolutionary MTR action was planned for the first days of October 1943, but against a traditional target: Gibraltar. The new submarine *Murena*, equipped with four watertight 'cylinders', would have brought as many 'erre' close to the Rock at night; they were to be hidden among the rushes at the end of Algeciras harbour, to attack with total surprise in daylight at 11 am, heading at full speed against the many merchant ships at anchor in the harbour.

As a result of the alarm caused by the sudden attack, it was predicted that the defence forces would immediately leave the military harbour: then an SSB underwater self-propelled craft from the *Olterra*, waiting near the booms, would exploit the opening of the latter to sneak into the area where the major warships moored.

The date scheduled for the action was 2 October 1943, but in consequence of the armistice the project was abandoned.

Thirteen MTR were built in total: a prototype and 12 operational units in three successive series with few variations between them. The prototype was probably built between the end of 1941 and the first months of 1942; after the trials, it was used for other experiments.[8] Up to 8 September 1943 the Regia Marina ordered from CABI a total of 12 series MTR, all delivered before that date.[9]

The numbering assigned to these 12 craft was preceded by '0' and between 02 and 024 with the usual

8. In 1944 an 'erre', or rather its framework without plating, was used as a teaching aid by engineer Guido Cattaneo in the classroom of the Pilot School of 'Xª MAS' in Sesto Calende. Most likely it was the prototype, or a series unit recovered after some accident.

9. A 20 October 1942 situation report on surface craft supplied to the X Mas Flotilla shows that the MTR were 9 in total.

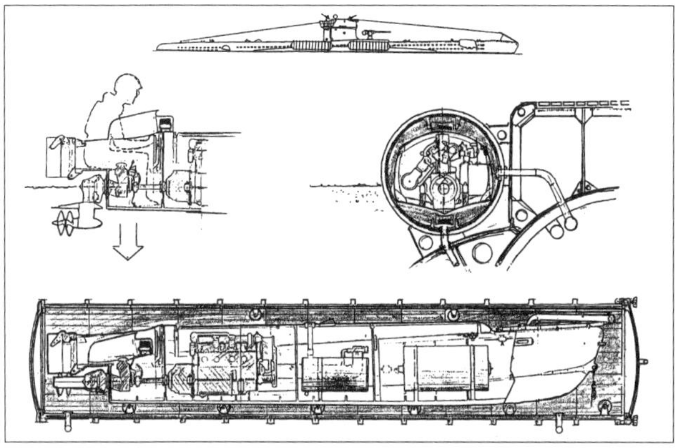

Two drawings by Franco Harrauer showing MTR arrangement and extraction from the cylinders of *Flutto* class 'approacher' submarines (*Murena, Sparide* and *Grongo*).

exclusion of odd numbers. It seems that the first 'erre' produced were not painted, but left by the builder in their natural dark wood colour; however, they were later painted light blue-grey as all other Italian surface assault craft. After the armistice almost all the 'erre' should have been concentrated at La Spezia, the base for the 'approacher' submarines.

A few were commissioned by the republican 'X^a Mas', except perhaps a few units taken (but not used) by the Germans; another nine 'erre' (probably 'modified' MTRM) were ordered from CABI but just one was delivered before the end of the war.

By the beginning of April 1945 four hulls (*MTR 02, 04, 014* and *020*) still existed, though not all were ready for use. They were in fact discovered with no engine at the 'X^a Pilot School' at Sesto Calende in May 1945.

Light Motor Torpedo Boats

The progressive increase in the size of Mas craft was driven by the need to achieve particularly high speeds

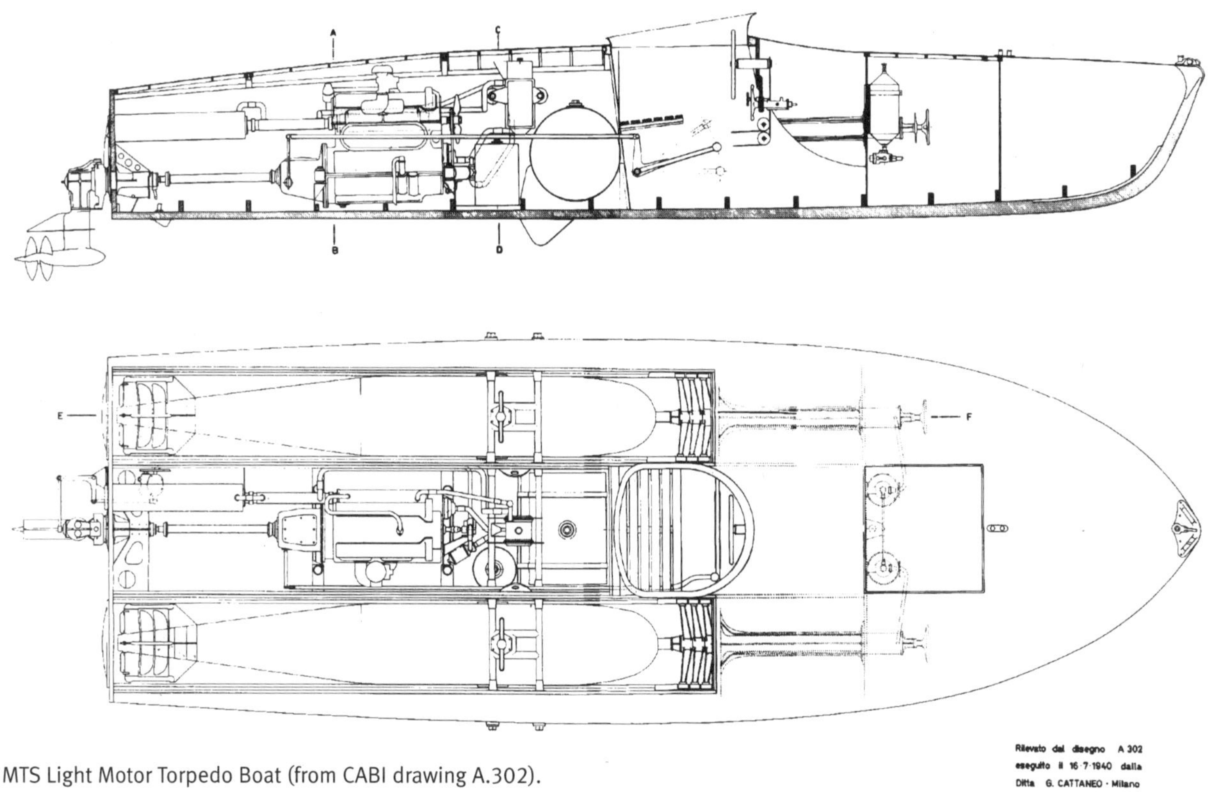

MTS Light Motor Torpedo Boat (from CABI drawing A.302).

while at the same time retaining sufficient nautical qualities and adequate range; this decisively contributed to directing their use increasingly towards offshore torpedo actions, almost entirely at the expense of the kind of intruder operations into enemy anchorages that were the origin of their activities in the First World War.

There remained, however, a need for very small and fast low-cost units to employ in large numbers for attacks in restricted waters, maritime choke-points, and the like. This was the inspiration for the birth of light motor torpedo boats in Italy at the end of 1939. Unlike the explosive motorboats, the light motor torpedo boat formula was not entirely new: in fact it was inspired by what had been the basis of the first torpedo Mas in 1915 and of the British CMB (Coastal Motor Boat), which in turn derived from small coastal torpedo boats of the previous century.[1]

In the 'Decima' milieu the MTS and light motor torpedo boats were called 'esse' for short, the MTM explosive motorboats were called 'emme' and the MTR just 'erre'. For the MTSMA the regular abbreviation was 'SMA.

MTS (Torpedo Touring Motorboats/ Light Motor Torpedo Boats)

The development of the craft, conceived as a small single- or two-seater motorboat armed with torpedoes of reduced length and charge, was entrusted by the Regia Marina General Staff to CABI of Milan, in collaboration with Baglietto Shipyards of Varazze for the hull design.

Known as the 'Omega Project', the first configuration of the new craft dates from January 1940 (CABI drawing N^O A.255 on page 108). It was a wooden, hard-chined hull with low 'V' bow section, 6.5m long and 2.2m wide, whose maximum depth (from the keel to the upper edge of the cockpit cover) was 1.75m. The overall length reached 7.15m due to the same MT type stern drive and its related tubular metal guard. The engine was a petrol Alfa Romeo '6c 2500' with an expected maximum power of about 90hp, mounted amidships in the central-stern area of the hull. Equipped with an inverter (reversing gear), it was connected by a half-axle about 70cm long to the stern drive which, unlike that of explosive motorboats, could not swing sideways.

The maximum expected speed was in the order of 28 knots with a corresponding endurance of about 3½ hours on the move, equal to about 98 miles. The intended torpedoes were two of 450mm, reduced to 3.2 metres in length and modified for propulsion by a cold air turbine, with a unit weight of about 300kg,[2] arranged with the head facing forward in special compartments either side of the engine.

The launch would be sternwards, pushed by a pair of telescopic pistons moved by compressed air in cylinders. The sternwards torpedo launching system had been studied previously for the Mas, but then abandoned; however, it had been adopted by the Royal Navy for various models of Thornycroft-produced Coastal Motor Boats starting from the Great War years. In 1930 the system had been tested again aboard *MAS 551* (1st), an old hull reactivated for these tests only, though using explosive-activated torpedo launchers and standard 450mm weapons.

In operation the torpedo entered the water with the propellers first instead of the head as was usual.[3] As soon as it was in the water the propellers first stopped any possible torpedo backwards motion, then set it on its run along the launch course. Actually the weapon entered the water at very low relative speed, as it was launched with the motorboat moving rapidly forward. The initial 'sag' – that is the dive deeper than set by effect of the launch impulse – was quite limited, and the torpedo could quickly stabilise at the set direction and depth parameters. To avoid accidents due to possible porpoising of the weapon, the motorboat turned sharply to one side just after the launch, thus freeing the torpedo route (normally that of the craft at the time of the launch), which was maintained by the gyroscopic 'torpedo guide' of the weapon itself.

The weight of the complete craft was not to exceed 1750kg including armament and equipment. The steering position of the early torpedo boats was uncovered, with a steering wheel in the centre and a simple

1. It is interesting to note how the light torpedo boat formula (also developed by the Kriegsmarine with the Leichte Schnellboote initially embarked aboard German Armed Merchant Cruisers) has not been abandoned even after the end of the Second World War. In the 1960s and 1970s (the then) East Germany commissioned many fast units ('Iltis' class) which – in terms of size and technical solutions adopted – were clearly inspired by Italian motor torpedo boats. Even in more recent times, the small boats of the Iranian Pasdaran (or Guardians of the Revolution), armed with portable rocket launchers and operating with speed and surprise in the coastal waters of the Persian Gulf in the late 1980s, can be seen as nothing but a new version of assault craft.

2. These weapons were produced by the San Bartolomeo Torpedo Works (La Spezia) and modified by CABI, reducing the length (and therefore the capacity) of the compressed air tank (contained in the central section) and the warhead length, with a reduction of the explosive charge to 150kg (CABI A.344 drawing of 15.11.1940).

wooden slat seat. It was protected frontally by a simple semi-circular wash strake. Its sides and back had a rectangular section and but the upper edge was noticeably rounded outwards to form a wind and spray deflector. As the seat was just 70cm wide, it can be assumed that the initial plan was for a single operator.

Some changes were quickly introduced to this preliminary design, then the Regia Marina ordered a first series of 5 units that were named 'Torpedo Touring Motorboats' (MTS) from Baglietto Shipyards (for the hulls) and CABI (for mechanical parts and outfitting). The construction of *MTS 1–5* began in spring 1940 and the prototype was ready for the first trials by the summer of the same year, after the war had broken out. Changes to the original design can be seen in the almost definitive MTS plans (CABI drawings A.302 and A.303 of July 1940), the most significant being:

Hull:
- installation of a small keel stabiliser fin;
- in the cited drawings the steering seat (there were two MTS pilots) is again shown as 70cm width, but it is believed to have been modified later.

Engine:
- an Alfa Romeo 4-cylinder inline is indicated in the drawings; it seems from other documents that the engine installed on the 'esse' was a 6-cylinder Alfa Romeo 2300.

Propeller-rudder unit:
It was made liftable (by rotating 90° to starboard); the metal guard structure was eliminated.

Torpedo Launch arrangements:
- installation of pneumatic-opening hatches on the torpedo bays' rear side;
- installation of rollers in the torpedo bay to ease weapon launch;
- installation of two compressed air cylinders for torpedo launch operations in the bow compartment;
- installation of a control valve for the launch device, operated by a knob located under the steering wheel column.

After a long series of trials[4] during which some other changes were made, the first three MTS were ready for service by the beginning of 1941. The first war action by these craft involved *MTS 2* and *4* in an offensive reconnaissance in the Porto Edda and Sarandë anchorages (Corfu Island), attempted in the night of 4/5 April 1941. This brought no results, as the craft were discovered just before reaching the target and when subjected to a violent response from the land they had to withdraw. Another MTS was used as a support craft for the MT explosive motorboats in the series of attack attempts against Malta culminating in the ill-fated action of 26 July 1941. This MTS was the only craft to take part in the final approach and action phase, and reached the armed fast yacht *Diana* with some *MAS 452* survivors.

Despite the changes made, the initial trials and later the early war operations showed that the MTS were far too slow for successful torpedo attacks against moving targets. This was mainly because they were underpowered in relation to the high war load; therefore, it was decided to consider a twin-engine craft, sacrificing one of the two torpedoes, for greater range and much better seaworthiness.

For these reasons the Navy ordered the suspension of work on the last two MTS which at the time were still at the builders. Following the good results obtained by the prototype of the next modified light motor torpedo boat model with two engines and a single torpedo (MTSM), the outfitting of these two MTS was abandoned and CABI delivered the customer the bare hulls with no engine: they were probably assigned to other tasks or scrapped.

MTSM (Modified Touring Motor Torpedo Boat/ Light Motor Torpedo Boats)

Major shortcomings in the design had already emerged during the trials of the MTS prototypes, specifically poor seakeeping and insufficient speed. This was essentially a product of the excessive load (2 torpedoes and 2 men) compared to the size and power of a single 90hp engine, but also a result of the unfortunate hard-chined hull shape, with a low 'V' in the bow area.

Studies were therefore begun on a new type of craft that, while following the original lines, made significant changes to overcome the earlier defects. The design of a modified (or 'marine' or 'improved') light motor

3.The British call this system *tail-first*.

4. During one of these trials held at the 'Cottrau' battery in La Spezia, one of the craft (crewed by the engineer Guido Cattaneo, owner of the CABI, and his assistant technician Pinti) had launched a torpedo against the Tino island cliffs. The torpedo was released at the planned distance and the motorboat turned sharply to one side as expected but, much to the surprise of the pilots, the boat's speed increased significantly. It was actually being pushed by the torpedo: due to the failure of some of the seals, it was jammed with only the stern in water, but with its propellers turning since its movement had been enough to operate the 'register valve' lever and start the motor.

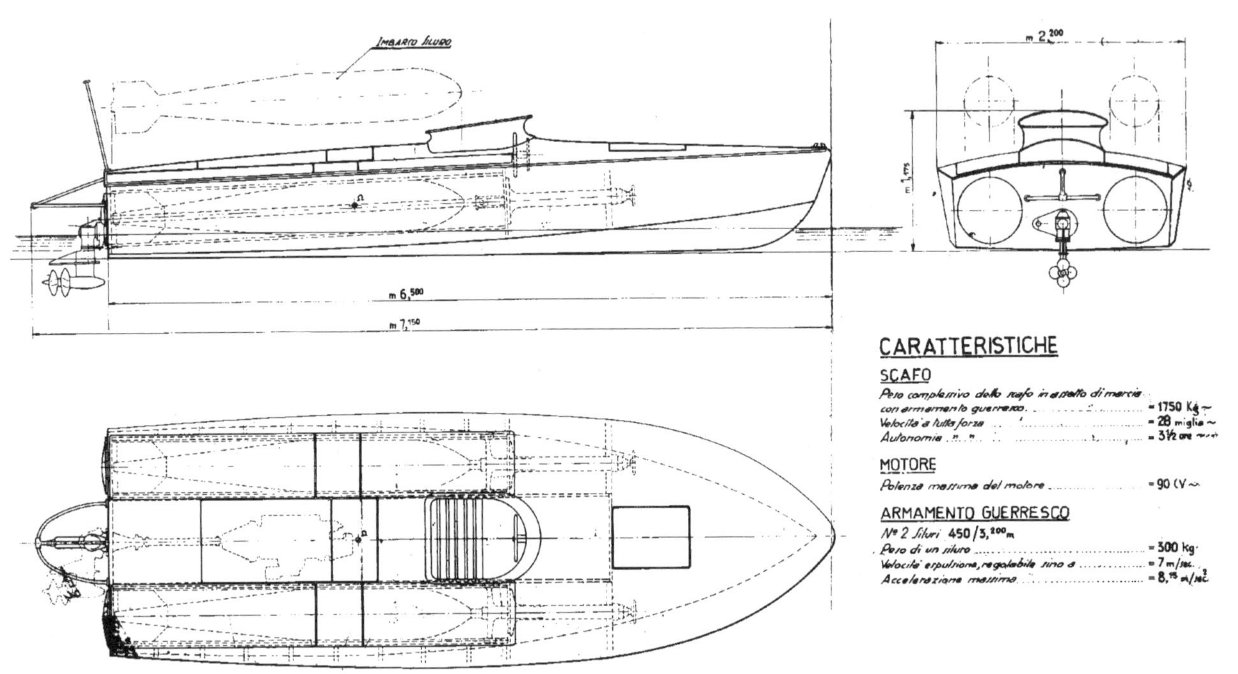

'MTS – Project Omega' (CABI drawing A.255, January 1940).

torpedo boat was again entrusted to CABI, still in collaboration with Baglietto Shipyards for the hull. The design was completed by June 1941 and immediately proposed to the technical departments of the Regia Marina in charge of 'special craft' development.

It was an improved version of the MTS, with major changes as follows:

- increase in hull length from 6.50m to 7.80m, which including the stern drives reached 8.3m overall;
- adoption of new hull lines, hard-chined again, but with a more pronounced 'V' in the bow area;
- fitting of two 90hp Alfa Romeo 6c-2500 engines instead of one;
- reduction of embarked small torpedoes (and related launch equipment) from two to one, placed on the centreline abaft the cockpit, between the two engines;
- addition of a small fin keel to improve course stability and reduce heeling and side drift in tight turns at speed;
- addition of two 50kg depth charges for anti-ship use on side deck saddles;
- fitting a small Garelli compressor with two-stroke engine to provide the necessary air for torpedo launching;
- fitting a radio transceiver with folding whip antenna;
- creation of a covered operators' cockpit;
- reduction of the military payload from 600kg (2 torpedoes) to about 400kg (one torpedo and two depth charges).

The construction of a first prototype was immediately ordered, followed shortly after by a second unit. The conventional classification initially assigned to the new type was 'Marine Touring Motor Torpedo Boat', later changed to 'Modified Touring Motor Torpedo Boat'.

Trials of the first MTSM took place in autumn 1941 with entirely satisfactory results. Despite the full load displacement now exceeding 3 tons, the doubling of available power compared to that of the MTS produced a speed of 32/34 knots with a corresponding range in the order of 200 miles. Furthermore, seaworthiness, manoeuvrability and course stability were significantly improved.

Shortly after the trials of the two prototypes, the Regia Marina ordered a first series of 10 motorboats from CABI and Baglietto Shipyards, requesting only minor alterations to the design. Designated *MTSM 204–222* (excluding odd numbers), these units were delivered to the X^{a} Mas Flotilla at La Spezia almost certainly within March 1942. This first series included the 5 light motor torpedo boats (*MTSM 204, 206, 208, 210* and *216*) which operated with the Moccagatta land convoy in the Black Sea from May 1942 to winter 1942/43.

These craft had good general characteristics, and a few constructional details are outlined below.

The hull was made of wood, with diagonal planking riveted in brass or copper, with an almost flat bottom in the central-stern area and 'V' shape at the bow, divided longitudinally by two keelsons and bulkheads into three compartments, for housing the torpedo (on centreline, about 55cm wide) and the two engines (on either side, about 85 cm wide). Transverse bulkheads – partial in some cases – divided the interior into distinct spaces: anti-collision bow tip, forepeak (mooring equipment), steering cockpit (called the 'canopy'), fuel tank, engine room and after peak. The deck had a slightly convex cross section at the bow, its curvature increasing in the centre-stern area.

In the bow section, a hatch, which could be opened against the wind, gave access to the forepeak, delimited by the collision bulkhead and the second watertight bulkhead that closed the cockpit front. The deck aft of the latter was formed by removable plywood sheet panels (hatches) corresponding to the various torpedo and engine rooms to ease maintenance operations, repairs etc. Aluminium covers hinged at the outer sides and laying upon raised coamings over the engines allowed access for appropriate checks and minor repairs even while under way.

Two wooden hatches – hinged towards the stern and

An MTSM at speed.

secured by wing or hexagonal nuts – allowed access to the 'wells' containing the drive shafts and stern drive lifting gears. The engines were ventilated by two aluminium dynamic air intakes, located on the centreline: the front one had its rectangular opening facing towards the bow, while the rear one opened aft. When in motion an air flow penetrated the torpedo bays and flowed to the engines through openings cut in the bulkheads between the same compartment and those of the engines. There was an eyebolt for towing or mooring at a buoy fixed on the cutwater with riveted metal bands. Two pairs of eyebolts were fitted at the extreme stern and a little aft of the pilots' cockpit for attaching the

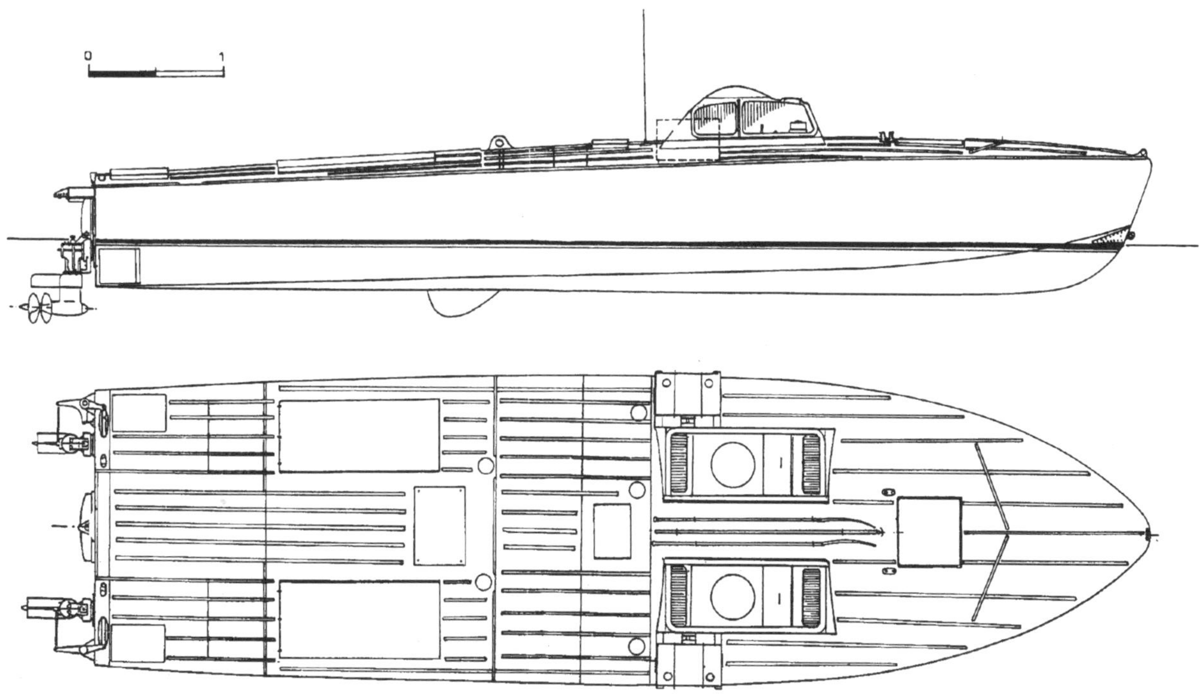

MTSM Modified Light Motor Torpedo Boat, 1st series *(drawn by author)*

Two pictures of MTSM on loan to the republican Xa Mas Pilot School cruising on Lake Maggiore in spring 1944. *(M Spertini collection)*

steel cable bridle used for lifting the craft. The positions of these eyebolts were barycentric, but when complete with all equipment the craft was not always properly balanced: at least one of the two crew members had to stay aboard during the manoeuvre and move forward to act as mobile compensating ballast.

The 'canopy' that covered the two pilot seats protruded from the deck forward of the centre of the hull. On these first series craft (including those used in the Black Sea) the structure was divided in two, made of light sheet metal, mostly glazed and with rounded corners. The pilots lowered themselves into their side-by-side seats through an upper door, hinged towards the stern, which could be closed from the inside with a handle. A rubber gasket guaranteed waterproofing. Normally, operators preferred to steer standing upright, with upper body emerging from the 'canopy': though exposed to wind and spray they enjoyed better visibility. Later the 'canopy' shape was modified to a single piece, and no longer divided; its plan shape became trapezoidal, yet the upper access hatches remained separate. This modification was gradually extended to many previously built craft.

The windows had sheet metal screens: the front ones could be lifted and fixed to obtain a splash

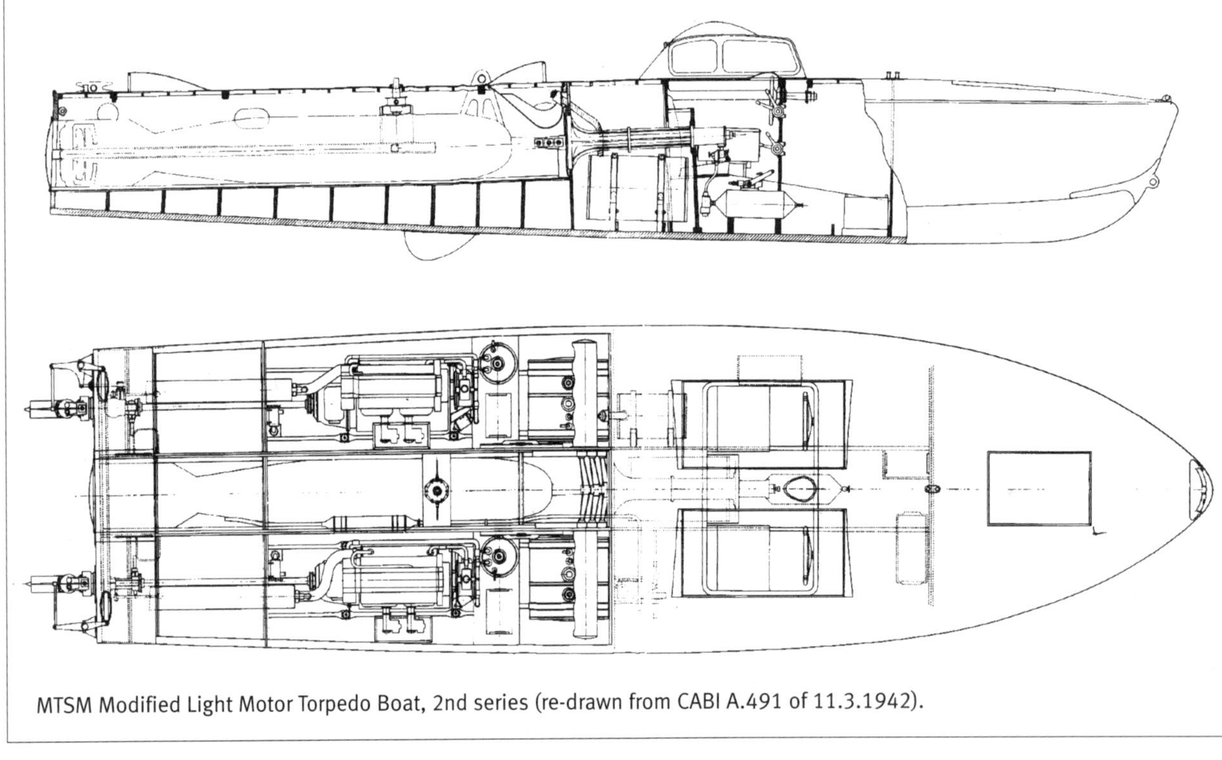

MTSM Modified Light Motor Torpedo Boat, 2nd series (re-drawn from CABI A.491 of 11.3.1942).

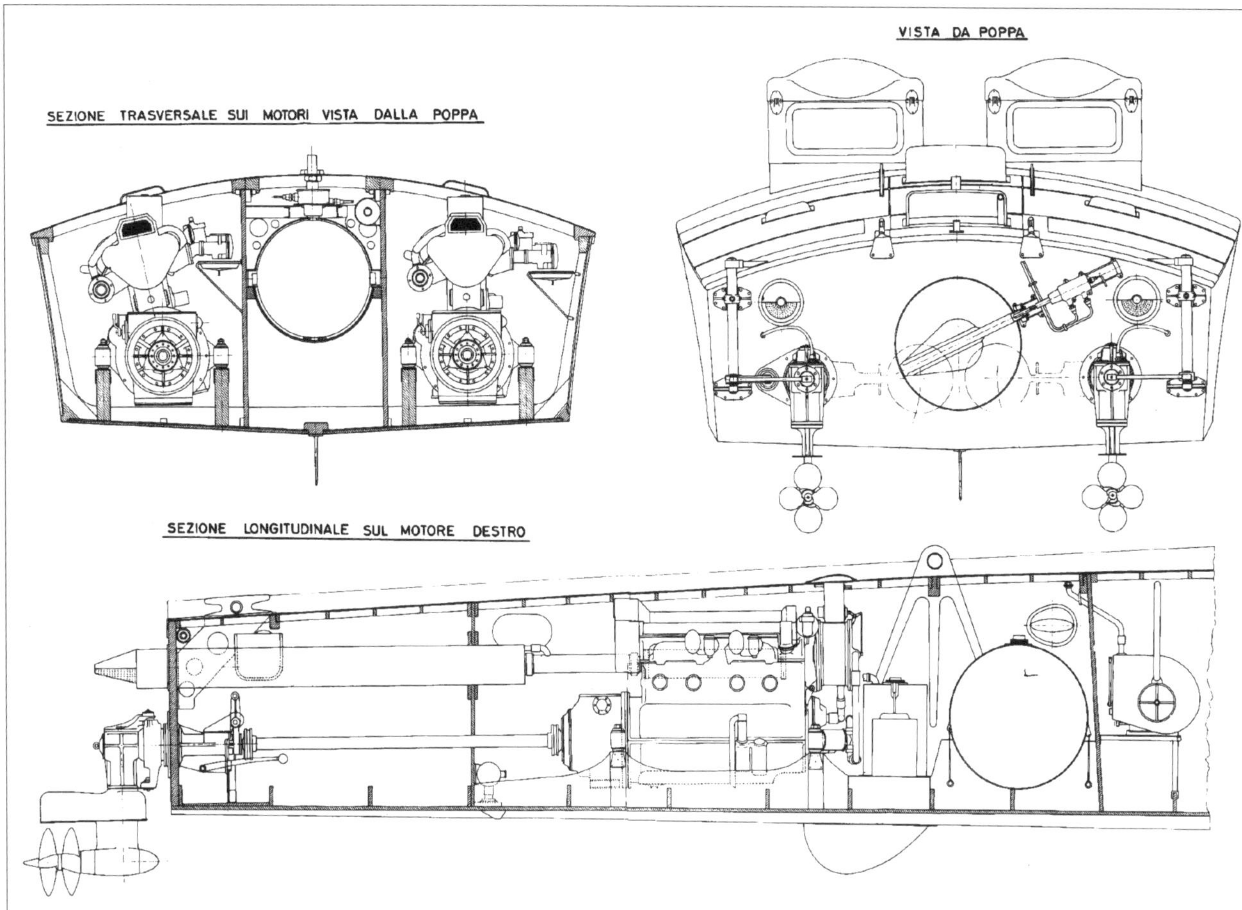

MTSM Modified Light Motor Torpedo Boat, 2nd series: details (re-drawn from CABI A.491 of 11.3.1942).

guard, while the side ones were in two sections hinged in the middle to fold them down, and could be locked high with a simple button; if necessary they could serve as deadlights at night to prevent wheelhouse lighting or portable flashlights from being seen outside.

In each of the two steering positions was a comfortable padded seat, sprung and adjustable, covered in automobile-type synthetic leather.[5] The inside of the steering position was fitted with:

5. It would seem that the first MTSM were fitted with motorcycle-type seats on metal tube frames that, while allowing greater freedom of movement to the pilots, must undoubtedly have been less comfortable.

Two pictures on an MTSM at Malta during the Italian co-belligerency with the Allies.

MTSM assault boat - outline by US Navy technicians (1945).

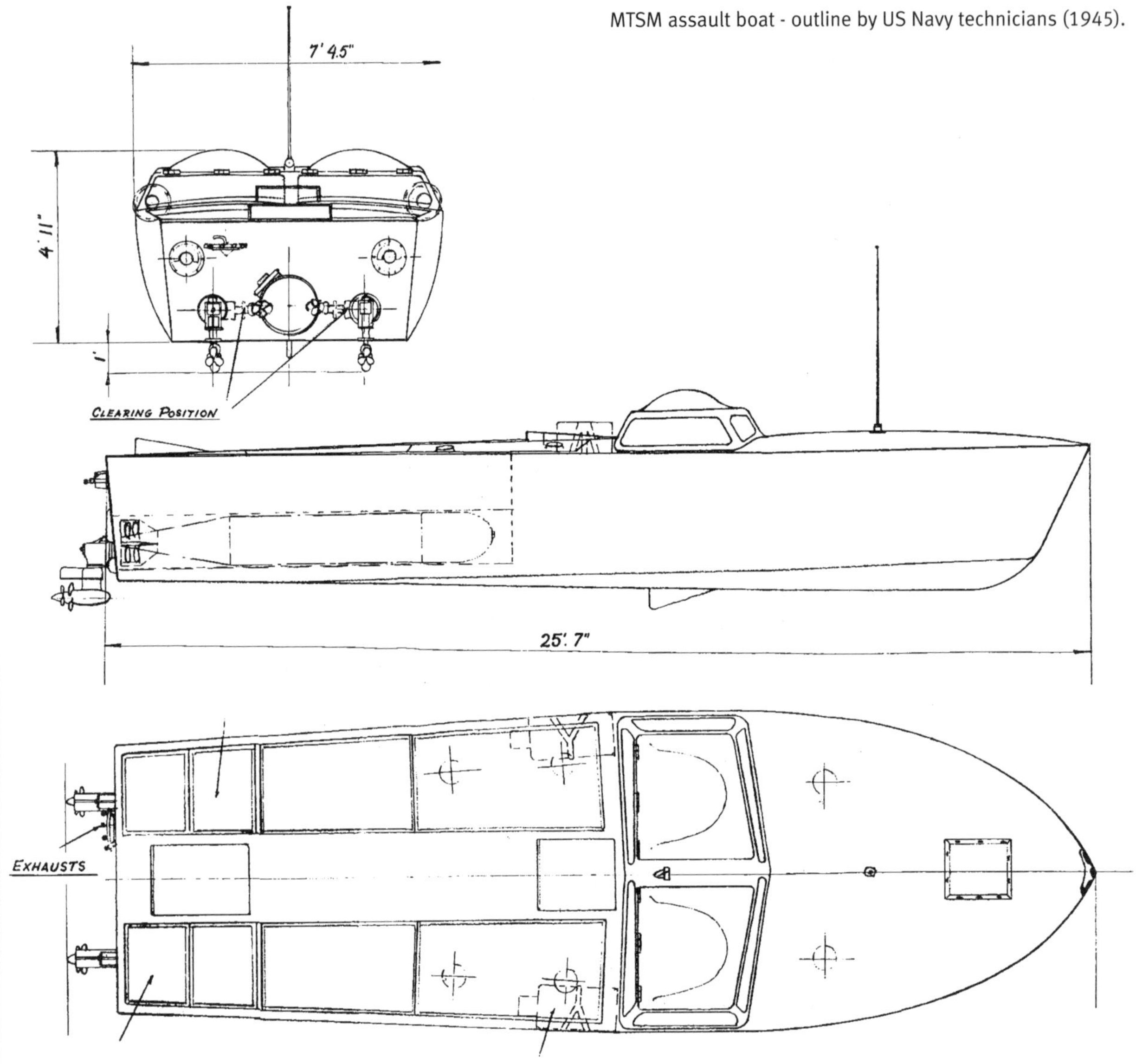

Fixed to the front bulkhead:

– The two rudder half-wheels (270°), placed vertically;
– a magnetic OMI type compass (raised, on the centreline);
– a dashboard (somewhat similar to that already described for the MTM, but 'double' as gauges were provided for each engine);

On the longitudinal 'bridge' between pilots' seats (and therefore accessible to both):

– two twin control levers (one set for each engine): the throttles at the front, and the inverter at the rear, with notches corresponding to forward, neutral and reverse;
– between the two pairs of levers, a crank and control for depth adjustment of the torpedo run;

Hull floor (on the centreline):

– the cylindrical compressed air tank for the torpedo launch system with release handle and air pressure gauge;
– taps to open or shut off the fuel tanks, used to maintain a correct trim;

Under the dashboard on the starboard side:

– small Garelli compressor, with a short vertical exhaust pipe extending to the deck, protected from water infiltration by a characteristic mushroom that also acted as a silencer; on the early types it was placed at the rear and the exhaust vented inside the torpedo compartment;
– possible support for the radio transceiver (an Italian Army model for tanks), with Morse key and power

MTSM 230 with modified hood during a drill on Lake Maggiore. *(M Spertini collection)*

supply battery; sometimes it was equipped with a jack to insert the microphone for voice communications;

On the centreline, externally and behind the 'canopy':

- tube holder for the swivelling blue light for making signals; its related Morse key was on the bridge described above.

The engines were two Alfa Romeo 6c-2500 (90hp each). A peculiarity of the 'emme' was the outward tilting (about 5°) of the left engine block (to fit its asymmetrical shape into the available space), while the starboard block was vertical.

In the cabin, behind the back of the left seat, was a small cylindrical tank with pipe inlet on deck, for crew drinking water if required. Also in the cockpit were supports for a small chart table and related lighting.

There were two fuel (aviation gasoline) tanks, cylindrical in shape (capacity approximately 95 litres each), placed forward of each engine.

On the transom were the silenced exhausts, the torpedo launch hatch with its hydraulic-mechanical opening system, the stern drives and control rods to swing them from the clearing to working positions.

Almost simultaneously with the delivery of the first ten, an order was placed for a second series of 8 units (*MTSM 224–238*, again with the exclusion of odd numbers). The 2nd series (CABI A.491 drawing of 1.3.1942 and A. 492 of 30.4.1942) did not show substantial changes from the 1st, which were introduced on the later (3rd series) instead.

The first operations of the 'emme' in the Black Sea with the 'Moccagatta' land convoy[6] and in the Strait of Sicily would lead to some improvements, such as among other things the modification of the cockpit by combining the twin 'canopies' into a single structure.

Close-up of deck and modified hood of the same boat as in the previous picture. *(M Spertini collection).*

Shortly after the 2nd series motorboats had been ordered in the late spring of 1942 (probably at the end of May), the Regia Marina ordered the construction of a 3rd series of 14 light motor torpedo boats (*MTSM 240–268*, as always excluding the odd numbers).

However, the decision to modify these boats in the light of war experience with the 1st series delayed the start of their construction until the end of summer 1942, when the plans were prepared and approved (CABI A.548 and A.549 drawings). An analysis of these documents shows the main changes compared to 1st and 2nd series motorboats were as follows:

- *general dimensions*: practically unaltered, except for a slight increase in mean draft as a result of a modest addition to full load equipment;

6.Engineer Guido Cattaneo of CABI was in the 'Moccagatta' land convoy as captain in the Naval Weapons Corps of the Italian Navy Reserve.

- *pilot cockpit*: while maintaining separate access hatches over each seat, the two 'canopies' were unified in a single structure.
- *inside*: between the two pilot seats, the engine controls were placed on a bridge which effectively divided the cockpit in two; the instruments position was more functional, and made more complete;
- *radio equipment*: these were still Italian Army types, produced by Marelli, Allocchio-Bacchini and Ducati. Despite the installation of an ostentatious folding whip antenna, placed immediately forward of the hood, the performance of these devices always remained inadequate for safe and continuous use;
- *passive defences*: fitting on the centreline at the extreme stern of a spherical buoy (chlorohydrin smoke producer) and of a barrel with chlorohydrin diffusor on the left upper stern;
- *flash-lamp*: development of the 360° manually swivelling installation;
- *small arms*: fixed rack inside the cockpit for two version '38 or '42 Beretta MAB submachine guns with 40-round magazines, two steel mod 31 helmets, twelve grenades (SRCM type or similar).

All the 3rd series units were delivered to the Regia Marina by the spring of 1943. Most operated in the waters of the Sicily Strait aboard the trawler *Cefalo*,

3rd series MTSM on moorings in Sesto Calende in 1944. *(M Spertini collection)*

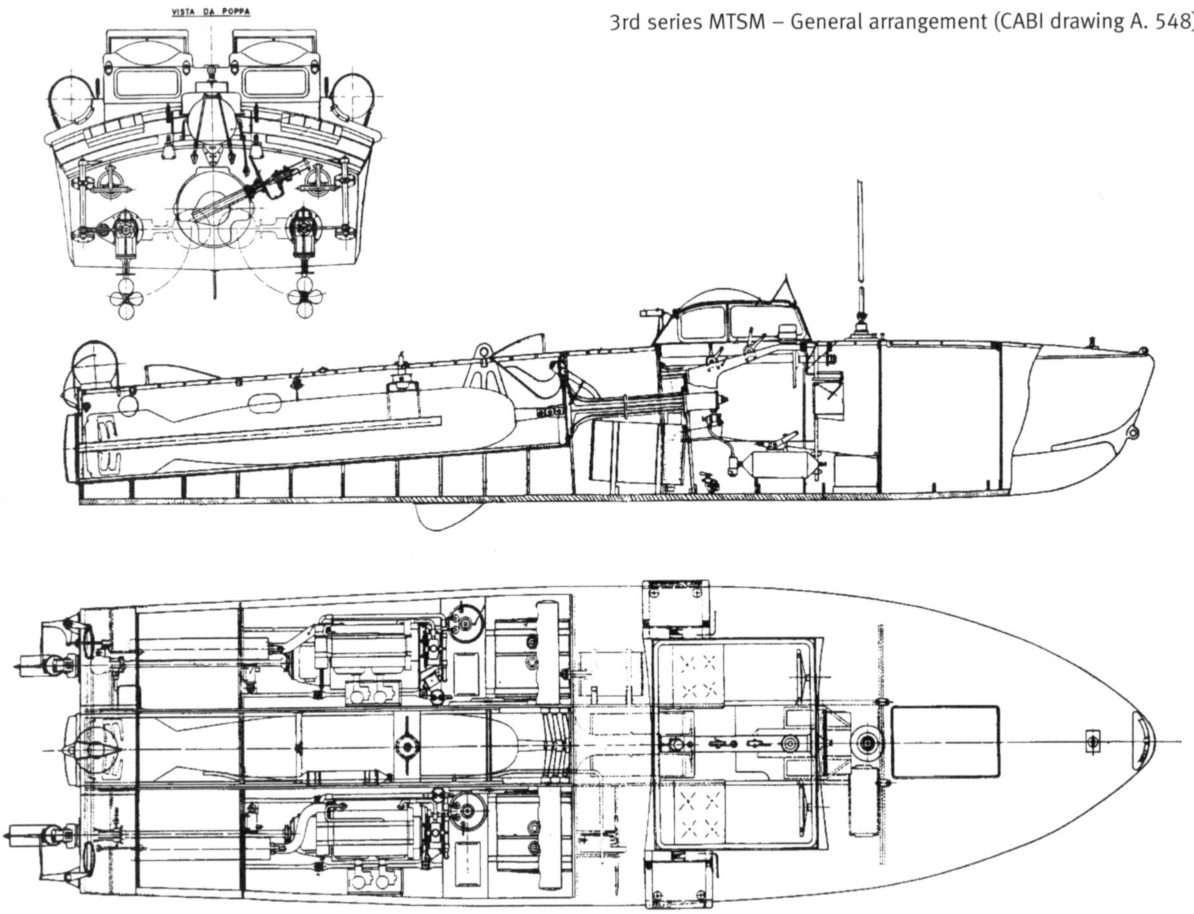

3rd series MTSM – General arrangement (CABI drawing A. 548).

with the 'Giobbe' land convoy in North Africa, or with the Augusta unit.

Of the 34 series built MTSM, less than twenty were still operational by 8 September 1943; following the armistice events about half became part of the Xª Mas of the RSI while the remainder – located in south Italy or Sardinia bases – were passed to Mariassalto. The Xª Mas used some of its 'emme' to train the new pilots at Sesto Calende and others on operational tasks in the Tyrrhenian, where some were lost in action in the course of the cycle of operations conducted in the waters off Anzio/Nettuno in the first months of 1944.

MODIFIED LIGHT MOTOR TORPEDO BOATS (MTSM)

Progressive number	*Order series/month end of deliveries*	*Known numbering*	*Possible numbering*	*Known (or supposed) activity* *Xª = republican X* *(RM) = Mariassalto Regia Marina*
1	1st prototype/ 6.1941–10.1941	–	*200*	–
2	2nd prototype	–	*202*	–
3	1st series (10 units) 10.1941–3.1941	*204*	–	Black Sea 5.42– 3.43; Xª (at works 1.4.1945)
4		*206*	–	Black Sea 5.42–3.43; Xª (sank at Ostia 23.1.44)
5		*208*	–	Black Sea 5.42–3.43;
6		*210*	–	Black Sea 5.42-–3.43; R.M. 1944/45
7		*212*	–	RM 1944/45
8		*214*	–	Augusta spring 1942–March 1943
9		*216*	–	Black Sea 5.42–3.43; Xª (sunk at Anzio 24.2.44)
10		*218*	–	as *214*; RM 1944/45
11		*220*	–	'Giobbe' land convoy; RM 1944/45
12		*222*	–	trawler *Cefalo* 7.42
13	later series	–	*224*	–
14		*226*	–	Xª (sank in Terracina 24.2.44)
15		*228*	–	'Giobbe' land convoy 8.42; (sunk at El Daba 28.8.1942
16		*230*	–	RM 1944/45 and Xª same time. Two different units; on the Xª one (at the Sesto Calende Pilot School) the original number was likely changed to *230*
17		–	*232*	–
18		*234*	–	Xª (at works 1.4.45)
19		*236*	–	Xª (sunk at Fiumicino 24.2.44)
20		–	*238*	–
21		*240*	–	Augusta 11.42
22		–	*242*	–
23		*244*	–	RM 1944/45
24		*246*	–	as *240*
25		*248*	–	Tunisia and Sicily 1943
26		*250*	–	Mariassalto 1944/45
27		–	*252*	–
28		–	*254*	–
29		*256*	–	as *240*; RM 1944/45
30		*258*	–	trawler *Cefalo* 12.42; destroyed by air attack at La Galite (Tunisia) on 14.12.1943
31		*260*	–	as *258*
32		*262*	–	'Giobbe' land convoy 4.43; Sicily 7.43
33		*264*	–	as *258*; Xª (damaged at Santa Marinella 3.1944)
34		*268*	–	'Giobbe' land convoy 4.43; Xª (shown as *263* on some documents)

3rd series MTSM – Engine control details (CABI drawing A. 615).

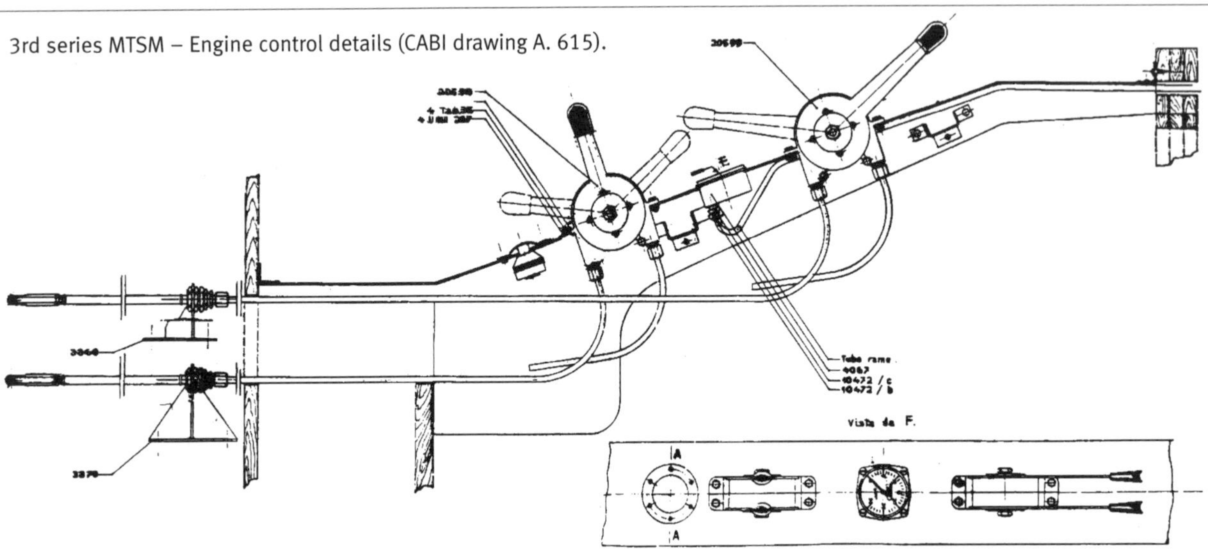

Mariassalto instead employed its few 'emme' both in the southern Adriatic and in the Tyrrhenian, especially for the transport and recovery of agents behind the lines, and in support of underwater assault craft actions against La Spezia and Genoa. Those intended mainly for diver support missions had their launch equipment removed and were fitted with additional seats in the torpedo bay; they also carried a small reel of thin buoyant (or float-fitted) cable used to make it easier for divers to find the craft in the operator recovery phase. By the end of the conflict, the number of 'emme' survivors in operational condition did not exceed four or five units. A few were overhauled and refitted by CABI for the Italian Navy, where they served together with some MTSMA for assault diver transport and recovery up to the early 1950s, with new alphanumeric numbers (*MEB 1518* etc). The last of these craft, which were based in Venice, was lost in November 1951 during aid operations to the local populations on the well-known occasion when the River Po broke its banks.

An old MTSM (or 'SMA?) hull was used from1956/1957 in the construction of the first Radio Guided Motorboat (MRC) target for artillery training of Italian naval units. Normally transported aboard the support ship *Stromboli* and guided from the torpedo boats *Orsa* and *Orione*, it served up to the mid-1960s, until replaced by new construction MRC.

Apparently, no MTSM has been preserved as a memorial.

MTSMA (Widened and Modified Light Motor Torpedo Boat)

At the beginning of 1943, the war experience gained with the 1st and 2nd series, and trial results from the first units of the 3rd series, it was decided to modify

MTSM on exercise on Lake Maggiore in 1944. *(M Spertini collection)*

Refuelling an MTSM in Sesto Calende in 1944. *(M Spertini collection)*

the original design, above all to improve its seaworthiness.

The result was a new type of motor torpedo boat of slightly increased size that was termed MTSMA (or 'SMA for short); in Italian, the 'A' stood for 'Widened' (or, according to some documents, 'Expanded' or 'Stretched').

In practice, the overall length went up from 8.3m to 8.77m (of which 0.576 represented the stern drives protruding from the transom), the breadth from 2.2 to 2.32m and the draught from about 0.6 to about 0.7m. As a result of increases in the dimensions and onboard equipment, the full load displacement reached 3.760 tons:

Complete hull (Baglietto-built)	2400kg
Torpedo and launch devices	520kg
Crew (2 pilots)	160kg
Fuel	350kg
Water and lubricating oil	30kg
Miscellaneous equipment	70kg
Depth charges and smoke generators	180kg
Sundries	50kg

The propulsion system remained almost unchanged from that of the 'emme', but the left engine was arranged vertically instead of inclined by 5° thanks to the availability of more space. Range went from 200 to 250 miles from the bigger fuel capacity: from about 190 litres to almost 500, divided into four tanks (2 x 150 and 2 x 100 litres). Given the higher displacement, with the same power, the maximum speed was reduced from 32 to 29–30 knots.

The general lines of the hull followed those of the MTSM, except for a significantly less convex deck cross-section, and the deletion of the stabilising fin. The deck and cockpit arrangement were significantly different, while the internal partitioning and the general arrangements aboard remained almost unchanged.

The cabin was a unified type as in 3rd series 'emme', but wider, squared and fitted with two side glasses of the same size; the front ones held the wipers in front of each pilot, manually operated by a small lever placed inside. The instrumentation was similar to that of the 'esse', with the addition of a panel (to the bottom right of the dashboard) with switches for the electric bilge pumps and related red warning lights.

The side saddles for the two depth charges (upgraded from 50 to 70kg each) were moved distinctly further aft compared to the 'emme'.

At the extreme stern were the fog generator and the smoke buoy, while the engine mufflers were routed to both sides and exhausted through two silencers placed below the waterline.

Based on the new design prepared by CABI, and Baglietto Shipyards for the hull, the Regia Marina

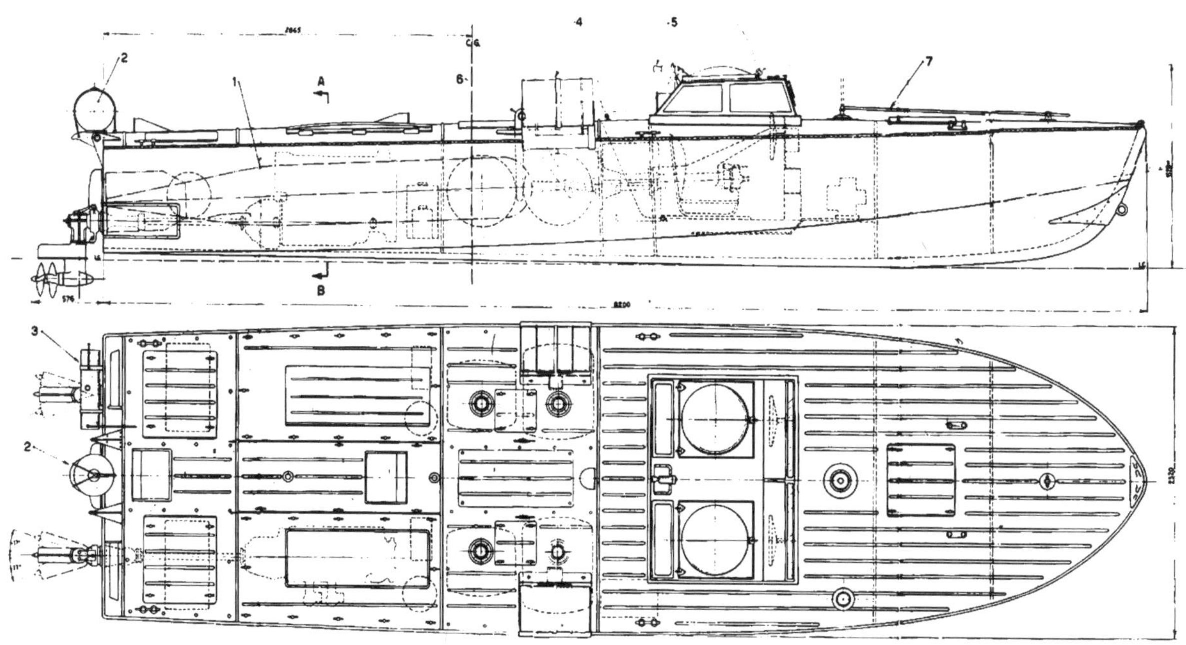

SMA-D (CABI drawing A.730 of 2.3.1944).

'*SMA 325* (or *326*) in 1944.

MTSMA 312 during a 1944 exercise in La Spezia roadstead. *(S Nesi collection)*

ordered a total of 83 MTSMA in various lots before 8 September 1943. Prime contractor was CABI of Milan, but they could use different shipyards (Baglietto in Varazze, SIAI in Sesto Calende, etc) for hull construction. The numbering of these units, using only even numbers as usual, should probably have started with *MTSMA 302*.

By the date of the armistice just three of these SMA[7] had been delivered to the Regia Marina and were being fitted out, while many others were already at an advanced state of construction. Trials of the first units gave satisfactory results for seaworthiness and range, even though these units turned out to be a little slower than the previous model and less manoeuvrable.

After the armistice the SMA was supplied only to the republican X^{a} Mas, which commissioned 23, and to the Kriegsmarine which requisitioned most of those already under construction and later ordered more of its own. Almost all RSI motorboats[8] came from the first 'SMA batch ordered by the Regia Marina ('A' and 'B' versions) and just a few to later series ('C' and 'D' versions) built on behalf of the German Navy, which in 1944 placed orders with CABI for a total of 97 motorboats, 40 of which were actually delivered before the end of the conflict, some with Baglietto hulls and some with hulls by SIAI or some minor shipyards in northern Italy.[9]

Generally speaking, the SIAI's 'SMA differed from those produced by Baglietto in the hull structure, which applied some aeronautical techniques traditional to the Varese company,[10] in the cockpit shape (similar to that of the 3rd series) and for the round or rounded

'*SMA 312* at La Spezia with the wreck of the cruiser *Gorizia* in the background. *(S Nesi collection)*

The same boat as in previous picture at speed in the Gulf of La Spezia in 1944. *(S Nesi collection)*

7. These presumably were *MTSMA 302, 304* and *306* which later operated with the republican X^{a} Mas.

8. The 'SMA commissioned by the republican X^{a} Mas would seem to total 23 of which, by the beginning of April 1945, less than a dozen still survived, the others being war losses. At the end of the same month 7 more 'SMA were found at SIAI of Sesto Calende nearly ready for delivery, probably to the X^{a}: *403, 406, 409, 416, 421, 422* and *423*.

9. According to CABI documents 12 'SMA were delivered to the RSI; adding the three motorboats previously delivered to the Regia Marina, we can deduce that at least ten of the twenty 'SMA in X^{a} service had come from German orders.

10. Construction with 'shell' moulding: for further details, see section on the MTM produced by SIAI.

– rather than square or rectangular – deck hatches shape. Moreover, SIAI hulls had small support strips running outside the planking along each side.

Altogether, the 'SMA commissioned before April 1945 would not exceed seventy units.

At the end of the conflict many 'SMA hulls were at

A SIAI-built MTSMA pictured at CABI in Milan, where its outfitting was completed in early 1945. Note the rounded shape of the hood top, the round deck hatches and the side reinforcing strips. These features, amongst others, differentiated SIAI hulls from those built by Baglietto Shipyards in Varazze.

Wreck of an SIAI-built 'SMA D' pictured in the Venice Shipyards by Aldo Fraccaroli in 1947. Note the support for a light machine gun, above the cockpit.

Stern close-up of the 'SMA in the previous photograph. It had been reclassified as a 'motorbarge' and marked with the identifier *1518* immediately after the war.

WIDENED AND MODIFIED LIGHT MOTOR TORPEDO BOAT (MTSMA or 'SMA) 1943–1945

Units ordered by the Regia Marina

Progressive number	*Known numbering*	*Possible numbering*	*NOTES (RM = Mariassalto; Xª = republican X Mas)*
1	302	–	Xª (sank at Fiumicino 18.1.1944)
2	304	–	Xª (sank at Viareggio 14.6.1944)
3	306	–	Xª
4	308	–	Xª (sank at Fiumicino 14.5.1944)
5	310	–	Xª (scuttled at Fiumicino 22.5.1944)
6	312	–	Xª (scuttled at Imperia 24.4.1945)
7	314	–	Xª (sank at Anzio 13.5.1944 by USS *PC 627*)
8	316	–	Xª (sank at Fiumicino spring 1944)
9	318	–	Xª (sank at Fiumicino 24.5.1944)
10	320	–	Xª (scuttled at Imperia 24.4.1945)
11	–	322	–
12	324	–	Xª (sank at Viareggio 14.6.1944)
13	326	–	Xª (sank at Viareggio 14.6.1944)
14	328	–	Xª (scuttled at Imperia 24.4.1945)
15	–	330	–
16	–	332	–
17	334/2	–	Xª (sank at S Remo 20.10.1944)
18	336/3	–	Xª (sank at S Remo 24.2.1944)
19	338/4	–	Xª
20	–	340/5	–
21	–	342/6	–
22	–	344/7	–
23	–	346/8	–
24	349/9	–	Xª (sank at S Remo 17.9.1944)
25	–	350/10	–
26	–	352/11	–
27	–	354/12	–
28	–	356/13	–
29	358/14	–	Xª (sank at S Remo 24.2.1945)
30	–	360/15	–
31	362/16	–	Xª (sank at S Remo 31.1.1945)
32	–	364/17	Xª (probable)
33	366/18	–	Xª (sank off Bordighera 16.3.1945)
34	–	368/19	–
35	–	370/20	–
36	–	372/21	–

CABI and SIAI in various stages of construction: these were subsequently scrapped or designated to other tasks.[11]

The Italian Navy kept less than a dozen in commission for a few years; some had been found in poor condition at the end of the war, others were completed after May 1945.

All were employed until the early 1950s for trans-

11. In the immediate post-war period the Anglo-Americans requisitioned some of the 'SMA found almost completed at CABI and SIAI and ordered their conversion into communications motorboats with 4 or 6 seats. These craft were ready by the autumn of 1945, and were assigned the following numbers: *1525, 1530, 1531, 1536, 1537* and *1540*. It would seem that *1525* was re-converted for military use and later commissioned by the Italian Navy. At least two unfinished SMA hulls were adapted by the CABI for leisure use towards the end of the 1940s.

Those 'SMA not commissioned by the RSI were probably used by the Germans. In the units with double numbers (*eg MTSMA 334/2*) the first group of digits – omitting odd numbers up to *402*

Progressive number	*Known numbering*	*Possible numbering*	*NOTES (RM = Mariassalto; Xa = republican X Mas)*
37	–	374/22	–
38	–	376/23	–
39	–	378/24	–
40	380/25	–	Xa (sank off Cape S Martin 4.2.1944)
41	–	382/26	–
42	–	384/27	–
43	–	386/28	–
44	–	390/29	–
45	–	392/30	–
46	–	394/31	–
47	–	396/32	–
48	–	398/33	–
49	–	400/34	–
50	–	402/35	–
51	403	–	Found incomplete t Sesto Calende (SIAI) in April 1945
52	404/39	–	Xa (scuttled at S Florent, Corsica 24.4.1945)
53	405/40	–	Xa (as 404/39)
54	406	–	as 403
55	–	407	–
56	–	408	–
57	409	–	as 403
58	–	410	–
59	–	411	–
60	–	412	–
61	–	413	–
62	–	414	–
63	416	–	as 403
64	–	417	–
65	–	418	–
66	–	419	–
67	–	420	–
68	421	–	as 403
69	422	–	as 403
70	423	–	as 403
...	...	...	–
...	501	–	Xa (ceded to the Germans at La Spezia 22.4.1945, later sunk by aircraft)
...	1B 1	–	Xa (ready 1.4.1945)

porting assault divers whose training took place in the upper Adriatic, based in Venice. The craft had been converted for this purpose by eliminating almost all the torpedo equipment.

– refers to the series started by the Regia Marina, while the second is the progressive number assigned by the RSI. In several cases only the second part of the number (*eg 9, 14* etc) was painted on the sides. Some documents show an *MTSMA 325*/(?) commissioned by the RSI which was destroyed at La Spezia in the spring of 1945.

A single SMA survives today, preserved in the Naval Museum of La Spezia.

In the first months of 1945 (M-2/4 drawing of 26.3.45) SIAI developed an interesting 'simplified' model of the SMA. It was a motorboat that followed its general lines, but was faster and cheaper to build as a result of the elimination of the two stern drives, which were replaced by conventional propeller shafts and rudders. The use of stern drives was had been born out of the requirement to overcome defensive obstructions in harbour forcing operations, a task that was no longer expected of this type of craft: in practice, by that time both the Kriegsmarine and the Xª Mas used them almost exclusively as light coastal motor torpedo boat.

Venice-S Andrea, autumn 1950. A group of Italian Navy raiders in training aboard an 'SMA used as 'approacher'.

MTSMA

At 8.65m long overall and 2.4m wide, these 'modified SMA' would probably have been slightly lighter than the previous model. The engine was the same Alfa Romeo model, modified to include a built-in reverse.

The 'bridge' remained in the cockpit, with the throttles probably moved forward to make them easier to use by pilots standing upright with the upper body outside the canopy. Instrumentation was less complex and more compact; reverse controls now consisted of two levers placed next to the seats. An interesting detail was the small metal tripod structure just behind the canopy, probably intended as a mounting for a light machine gun (possibly a 7.62mm MG.42 with saddle drums) for close defence.

No information has been found relating to the

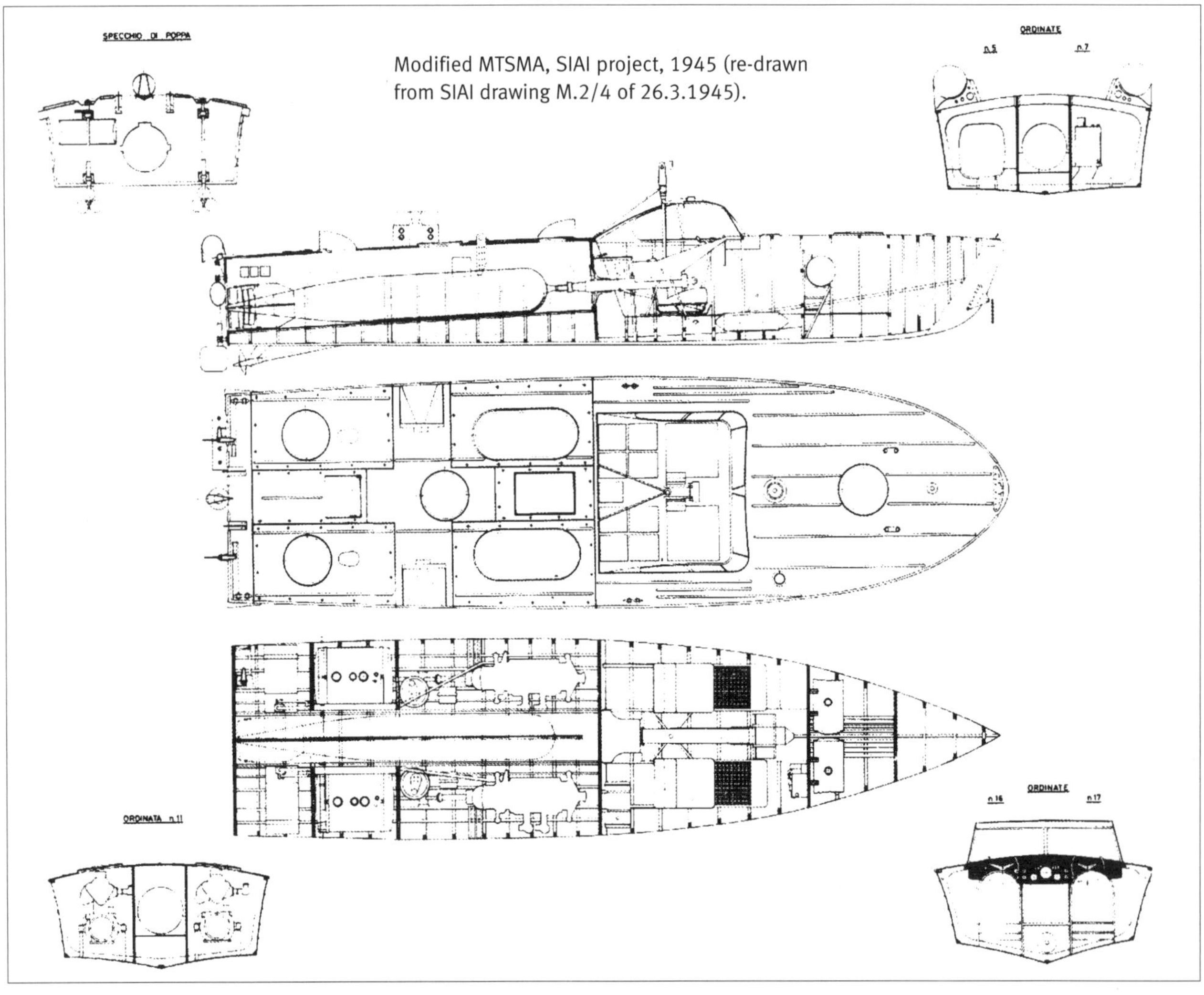

Modified MTSMA, SIAI project, 1945 (re-drawn from SIAI drawing M.2/4 of 26.3.1945).

ordering or actual construction (even a prototype) of this last model of torpedo boat.

PROTOTYPES, EXPERIMENTAL CRAFT AND PROJECTS

'R' (Ramognino) Boats

Despite many positive and encouraging results, from the very first trials of 'Gamma' assault diver operations against naval targets, it was clear that this new speciality was seriously limited by the short range and slow speed of the swimmer, worsened by the need to tow or somehow carry heavy and bulky explosive charges. Therefore, it was necessary to equip the 'Gamma' with an individual means of transport which would allow them to make the final stage of the approach to the target with the utmost discretion, even when they were at a significant distance, perhaps a few miles, from the starting point.

The idea of such a craft came to a Decima 'agent' Antonio Ramognino in 1941. He combined his own youthful experiences as a sports canoeist with the professional skills in aeronautical construction he learned working for the Piaggio Company.[1] Acting on his own initiative and employing a couple of workers who had no idea of the use he intended to make of it, he built a small hull similar to a long and thin sculling boat, initially propelled by a standard paddle. He used readily available material, such as aluminium alloys widely used in aircraft manufacture such as 'Peraluman', 'Alumex', etc. The boat turned out about 5 metres long and just about twenty centimetres wide, to be able to sneak easily between the buoys of any barrage net. Depth was about 50cm and empty weight was around 70kg. Sufficiently stable thanks to side inflatable bags, it had a remarkable resemblance to a seaplane float, although the upper part was very flat, to let the operator lie on top of it.

What its inventor offered to the Regia Marina departments charged with development and use of the assault craft was, ultimately, a means of carrying a 'Gamma' as well as a good explosive load. Overcoming several – particularly bureaucratic – difficulties, Ramognino was authorised in the first months of 1941 to build two prototypes at the Piaggio works, incorporating all the modifications he and Navy technicians had developed in the meantime – principally the adoption of a very quiet propulsion system of sufficient range.

An 'R' boat during construction. *(Courtesy F Harrauer)*

The result was a craft 5m long and just 23cm wide with a total weight of 250kg, whose transverse stability was ensured by two air-filled compartments (inflatable bags). Propulsion was by a 12,000rpm Siemens electric motor driving (with a 1:8 reduction) a three-bladed propeller protruding below the hull. The

1. Antonio Ramognino, the well-known patron of Villa Carmela on the Bay of Algeciras, suggested the use of the old oil tanker *Olterra* interned in Algeciras, on the Spanish side of the bay of Gibraltar, as an advanced underwater craft base within sight of the Rock.

propeller was placed between two vertical metal sheets that constituted a tunnel: at its end was a rectangular steering rudder. Energy came from three batteries whose capacity (300 amps in total) was enough to achieve a maximum speed of 4 knots and an endurance of about 10 hours under way.

The bow area of the hull was particularly well streamlined and was completely sealed. On the deck, at the bow, a hatch gave access to a well which contained two small compressed air tanks; another was immediately aft, closed by butterfly screws, sealing the compartment holding the batteries, which weighed about 170kg. A single deck 'hump' contained a small dashboard with compass, clock, voltmeter, ammeter and air pressure gauge for the tanks. On the right side of the dashboard was a 'throttle' for engine speed adjustment, and at the rear the rudder control handlebar. Another set of main controls was located further aft, so the operator could pilot the boat even while lying in a rearmost position.

The central part of the hull had a 'U' shaped lower section holding the batteries and the electric motor. The stern section supported the propeller, its shaft and the rudder; on the top were three small wells port and starboard, each holding an explosive charge of about 3kg stored vertically. A main charge of about 300kg could be placed over the stern area cover and secured with removable metal straps; its container was similar to that of an aircraft bomb and, once in the water, it had neutral buoyancy and was to be fixed with a magnetic attachment to the hull of a ship.

The craft was intended to proceed awash and to match the weight of the loaded charges, its buoyancy could be adjusted by varying the volume of two thick rubber bags placed alongside and connected to the two compressed air cylinders at the bow.

The boat could be broken down into three sections so as to be shipped in packages that did not arouse too many suspicions (for example, when being sent to the *Olterra* in Algeciras). The various modules were independent and could be connected with special joints.

One of the prototypes was tested, probably in the first half of 1942 at the 'Cottrau' battery in La Spezia, with a favourable outcome, although presumably some modifications were recommended for the first series of 'R' boats, whose building was ordered shortly afterwards.

'R' boat close-up showing the stern (foreground) and bow pilot's arrangements.

Two newly finished 'R' boat prototypes. Note the deck camouflage on the lefthand craft, and the side rubber air bags on the inverted hull.

While the boats were still under construction, their inventor had been sent to Spain to organise a support organisation in the Bay of Algeçiras from which the 'Gamma' could attack British ships using Gibraltar. From this mission was born the 'System' of advanced bases in Villa Carmela and on the *Olterra* from which the SLC and 'Gamma' operated successfully from the summer of 1942.

But the 'Gamma' had no opportunity to use 'R' boats in action, since these never became operational, probably because of delays and technical difficulties that surfaced during the course of series production. It would seem that the 6 boats ordered from Piaggio in 1942 were actually delivered to the X Flottiglia Mas just before the armistice, but no further traces were found.

Afterwards, simple inflatable canoes were designed by tv Eugenio Wolk – 'father' of this speciality – to solve those same 'Gamma' operational transfer problems that had inspired the design of the 'R' boats: and they fulfilled their tasks quite well.

Moreover, in the last part of the conflict another simple 'Gamma' transport craft was created.

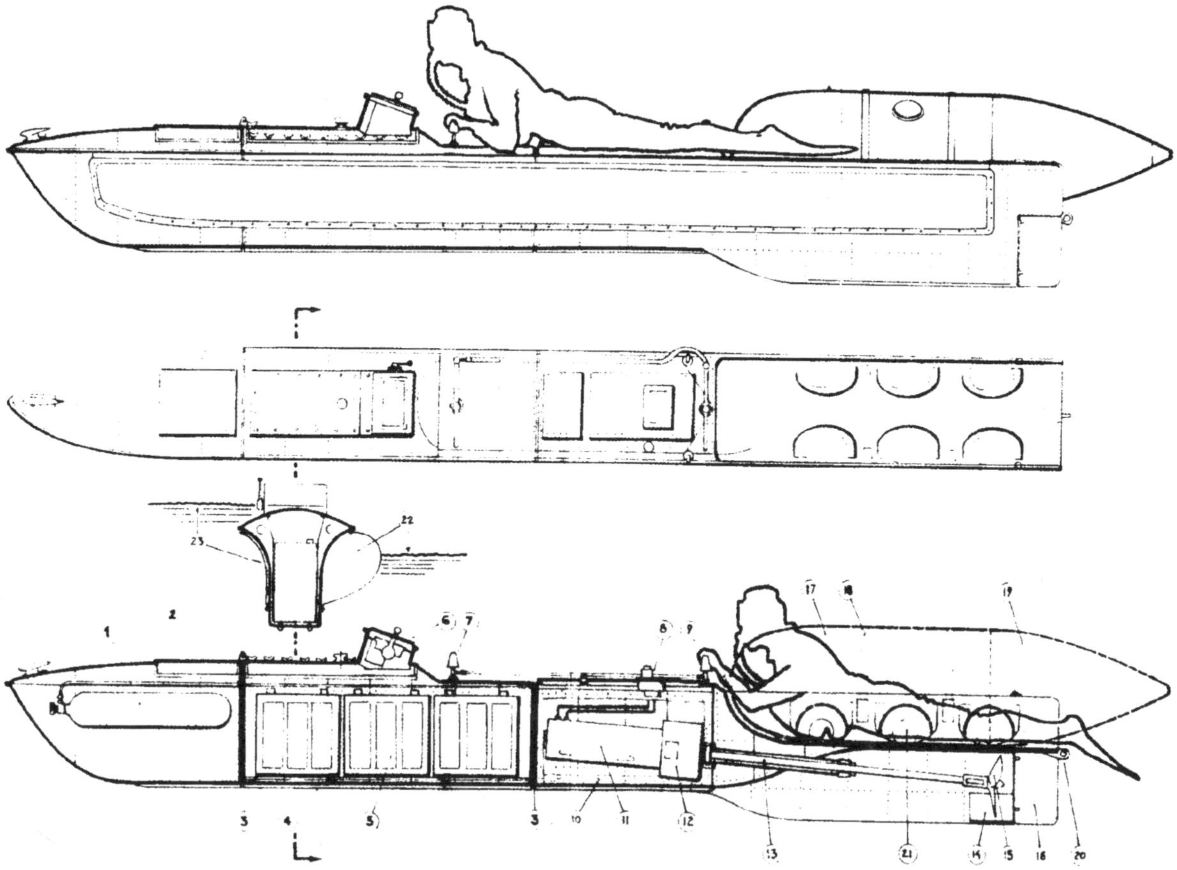

'R' boat, Ramognino self-propelled craft. *(F Harrauer drawing)*

1. Air tank
2. Tank compartment watertight hatch
3. Dismantling joint
4. Protective 'skids'
5. 3 x 8 V in series (24 V) batteries, 300 Amp.
6. Waterproof dashboard with compass and motor controls
7. Rudder control
8. Auxiliary dashboard
9. Auxiliary rudder control
10. Motor compartment, sound-deadening Kapok insulation
11. Siemens 12,000rpm motor
12. 1/8 Epicyclic reduction gear
13. Shaft line
14. Propeller duct
15. Three-blade propeller
16. Rudder
17. SLC type (300kg) neutral buoyancy explosive head
18. Head retaining straps
19. Hydrodynamic fairing
20. Head tow eyebolt
21. Side housings for 6 x 3kg explosive charges
22. Rudder air bag (inflated) and related waterline
23. Rudder air bag (deflated) and related (neutral buoyancy) waterline

Nicknamed 'turkey', it consisted of an inflatable boat – of the type commonly called a 'raft' today – fitted with a small folding screen, also inflatable, at the bow. Besides the usual paddles, it could also be equipped with a small outboard engine (see top picture on page 164).

'Campini-De Bernardi' single-seat semi-submersible

Amongst the projects for new types of assault craft that for varying different reasons did not reach fulfilment, one is particularly interesting for its concept and planned method of use. This was the semi-submersible designed and proposed in February 1942 by engineer Secondo Campini,[2] who also made use of the work of commander Mario De Bernardi.[3]

It was a torpedo-shaped hull with a diameter of about 860mm whose immersion, limited to just a few metres below the surface, was mainly due to the hydrodynamic action of diving planes controlled by an operator located in a small waterproof pilot cockpit fitted with a periscope, located towards the stern.

The propulsion system was to consist of a small internal combustion engine for proceeding surfaced or awash and on a 'closed cycle' turbine (oxygen + oil) for periscope depth navigation at about 20 knots. Planned armament consisted of one or two 450mm torpedoes slung below the hull of the craft that, for its employment against naval formations, would have been carried by seaplanes or specially equipped surface units during the approach phase.

It was certainly a brilliant project, but it could never have been realised, especially given the difficulties that would certainly have arisen in the practical construction of the closed circuit engine which stretched the technology of the time.

'X°' (Tenth) Light Motor Torpedo Boat

CABI drawing no A.664 dated 20.7.1943 and reproduced on page 127 shows an 'Experimental motor-boat' called 'X°' (Tenth). It was a craft of considerable size compared to the light motor torpedo boats previously built, and was probably intended as an attack boat with better seaworthiness and more powerful torpedo armament.

Its main dimensions would have been: 15.400m overall length; 4.300m breadth. Displacement would have reached 13,000kg (almost that of a Mas boat!). The designed propulsion system was two Fiat A.30 engines with a total of 900 hp; planned speed was around 40–41 knots with a corresponding range of around 320 miles.

The design drawing shows other interesting details:

- rounded shape 'hood' with upper edge curved to the outside, in particular towards the bow, for spray deflection;

2. In 1931 the Italian Air Force placed an order with engineer Campini and his VENAR company for a 'jet motorboat' which was successfully tested in Venice the following year. Continuing his experimental work, he built the first Italian 'propellerless' plane, the CC.2 (Caproni-Campini), test-flown by commander De Bernardi on 28 August 1940. It was an experimental aircraft propelled by a conventional double V engine driving a four-stage ducted fan; a rudimentary afterburner was also fitted. It subsequently performed a demonstration flight from Milan to Rome, but was not series-produced.

3. Born in 1893 in Venosa di Puglia, in 1913 De Bernardi was a soldier in the Aviators Battalion of Rome. Promoted corporal, he was chosen for pilot training in Aviano where, without taking a single lesson, he immediately got into a plane, started the engine, took off, flew and landed, risking being sent back to the infantry. The following year he was an instructor; in 1916, by then promoted to sub-lieutenant, he shot down the first of nine enemy aircraft, and would become one of the Great War 'aces'. In 1927 he won the prestigious 'Schneider Trophy' for racing seaplanes in Baltimore. He was discharged as lieutenant colonel in 1930 at just 37, becoming a Caproni test pilot. He was killed in an aircraft accident in 1959.

Projected single-seater 'Campini-De Bernardi' semi-submersible craft. *(Courtesy Navimodel, Bologna)*

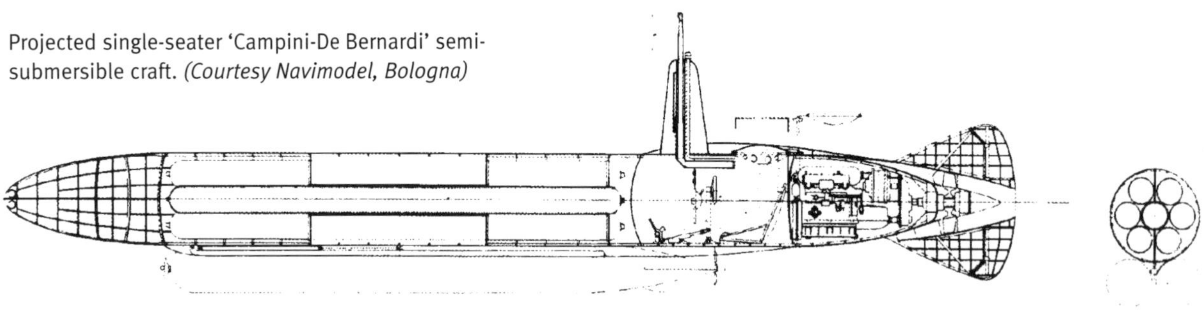

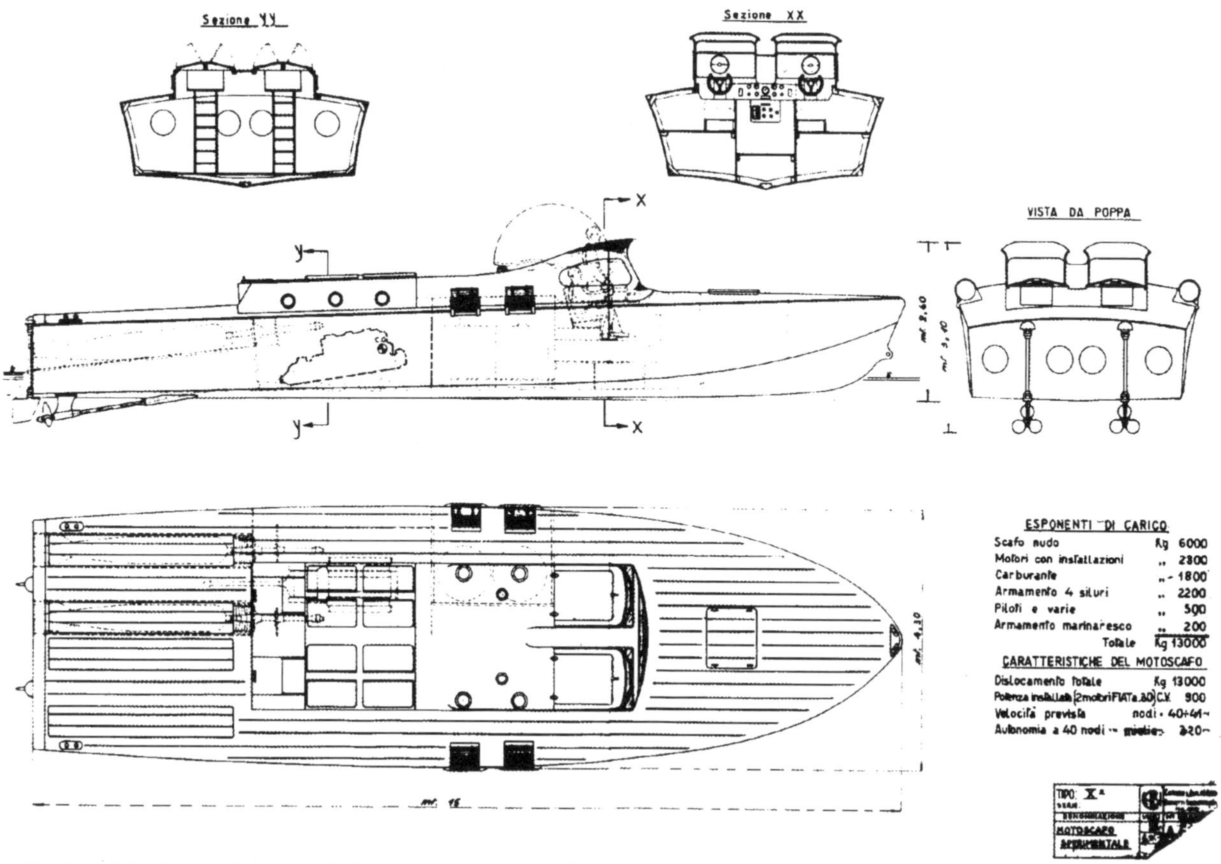

Design of the 'X° - Decimo' type light motor torpedo boat (CABI drawing A.664).

- large three-element glazing (two on the sides and one on the front);
- clear-view screens driven by an electric motor;
- instrumentation reduced to the essentials (still duplicate for each engine), with a more compact transceiver compared to the Italian Army type in torpedo boats;
- pilots' seats placed in an elevated position, with better external visibility;
- 'hood' elongated towards stern with a small sheet-metal deckhouse (about 50cm high) with the rear connected to the engine room skylight, equipped with three doors on each side;
- four short torpedoes embarked, launched through hatches in the transom;
- two three-bladed propellers and two rudders in the traditional arrangement;
- four amidships depth charges on two-by-two side saddles;
- four cylindrical fuel tanks fitted in the centre.

This project, still under study in September 1943, had no practical outcome, but was taken up and modified after the armistice on behalf of the republican X^{a} Mas, giving birth to another study. It was of a smaller unit than the 'X°' type, yet still of remarkable size (see 'provisional' CABI drawing no A.796 probably of November 1943). Overall length would have reached 12.4m and breadth 3m. Displacement was expected to be around 7 tons, and planned armament was two short torpedoes instead of four, and two depth charges. The propulsion system was also downsized, reduced to a single Isotta-Fraschini type 11R engine converted by CABI for marine use, acting on a single three-bladed propeller. With a power of about 700hp speed should have reached 41 knots with a corresponding range of about 230 miles.

Even this last project did not, however, reach practical implementation, although it should perhaps have replaced the SMA, compared to which it carried an extra torpedo and would probably have turned out more seaworthy.

Project for the 'enlarged' SMA light motor torpedo boat (CABI drawing A.796).

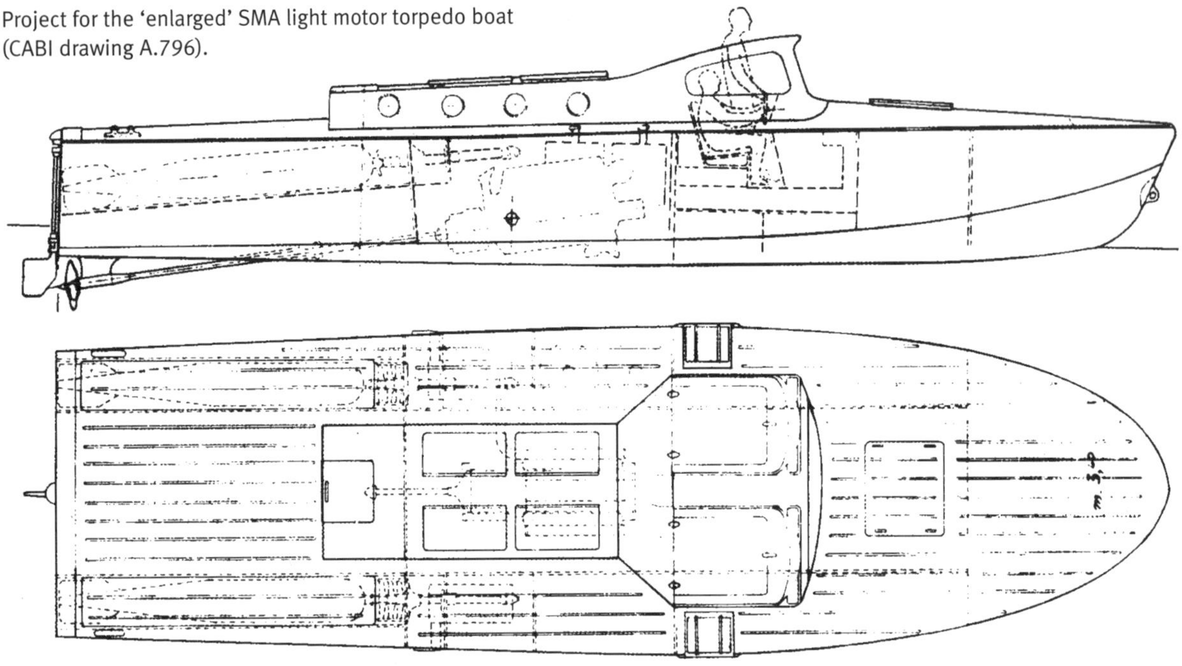

'Rosicarelli' armoured airboat

Amongst the various unbuilt assault craft projects, there is a particularly interesting design for an 'armoured airboat for torpedo attacks' probably drawn in 1943. It was a small hydrofoil with a speed believed to be in the order of 80 knots, piloted by a single operator and armed with two 450mm torpedoes.

About 6.00m long and 1.50m wide, with small side stabilising floats, it would have had a total weight of 4930kg at full load, including about 2180kg of armour with maximum thickness, at the front, of 40mm. Propulsion was by a 700hp Isotta-Fraschini 'Delta' diesel engine driving one marine propeller; expected endurance was 5 hours of full-power, or about 400 miles.

Because of its limited size and weight, it was planned to be deployed in large numbers from medium displacement surface units that would launch many of these craft once within range of enemy ships.

The main limitation of this craft – as engineer Rosicarelli himself noted in a presentation in January 1942 – was that even slightly rough sea conditions would prevent operation at high speeds.

Project for the 'Rosicarelli' armoured airboat. *(Courtesy Navimodel, Bologna)*

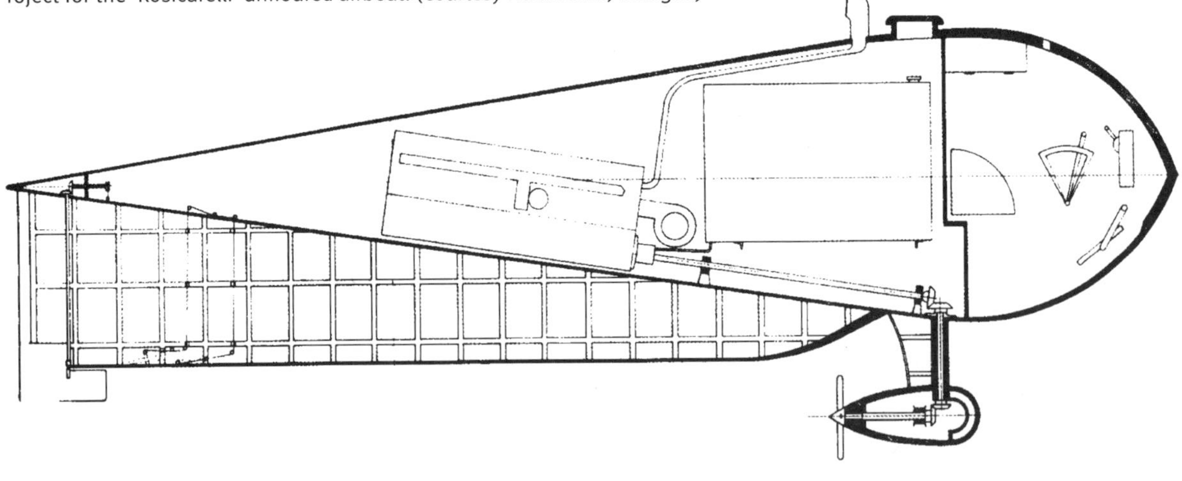

UNDERWATER CRAFT
'Slow-running torpedo' (SLC)

Of all Italian assault craft used in the Second World War, the 'SLC' (*Siluro a Lenta Corsa*) was the most successful.

In terms of its intended role, the development of the SLC might seem like a descendant of the *Mignatta* of 1918,[1] but in fact the new weapon was a very different concept. While the compressed-air craft of Rossetti and Paolucci was designed to move awash, this one could dive, and was propelled by an electric motor powered by batteries.

During 1935, with the 'Ethiopian crisis' in full swing, two captains of the Genio Navale, Teseo Tesei and Elios Toschi (both engineer officers aboard 'H' type submarines of the La Spezia Group), began work on an idea that Tesei had been mulling over since 1927, when he attended the Naval Academy and had not yet graduated in naval and mechanical engineering. It involved converting a 533mm (21in) torpedo to carry, at low speed, two operators equipped with self-contained underwater breathing apparatus – of the type developed for rescuing submariners – and an explosive charge to be attached stealthily to the hull of ships moored in an enemy roadstead or harbour.

1. During the Great War, it seems that engineer Ettore Bussei (an Italian Navy officer responsible for the development of many pieces of fire control equipment) had drafted a project for a device that in many ways prefigured the 'slow running torpedo', but unfortunately no details have been traced.

An outline proposal was submitted and was found to match the immediate needs of the Regia Marina, so was carefully evaluated by the Naval Staff. Their conclusion was favourable and in the first days of October 1935 the San Bartolomeo Torpedo Workshop (La Spezia) was secretly tasked with the construction of a prototype using, as far as possible, materials and equipment that could be found in the La Spezia Shipyard stores or by designing or adapting them for the purpose; everything had to be done without compromising the secrecy that would play such a big part in the future success of the new weapon.

As proof of the interest aroused by the project, while the first prototype (called *Device No 1*) was still under construction, a second unit (*Device No 2*) had already been authorised. To keep the costs down, however, both craft made use of readily available torpedo parts and, for *No 1*, even scrap material.

On 26 October 1935 *Device No 1* performed initial trim tests in one of the shipyard basins in the presence of Admiral Mario Falangola, designated to assist by the Navy ministry, and by 2 November the craft was ready for sea trials: the results were modest, although quite encouraging.

Device No 2, which had shown several shortcomings during trials carried out on 6 January 1936, was modified based on experiences with *No 1* and was ready for new tests on 28 May. However, on 17 April the Naval Staff had already ordered four more 'self-propelled mines' or 'self-propelled Tesei craft', the cover names given to these devices by then. Construction of these

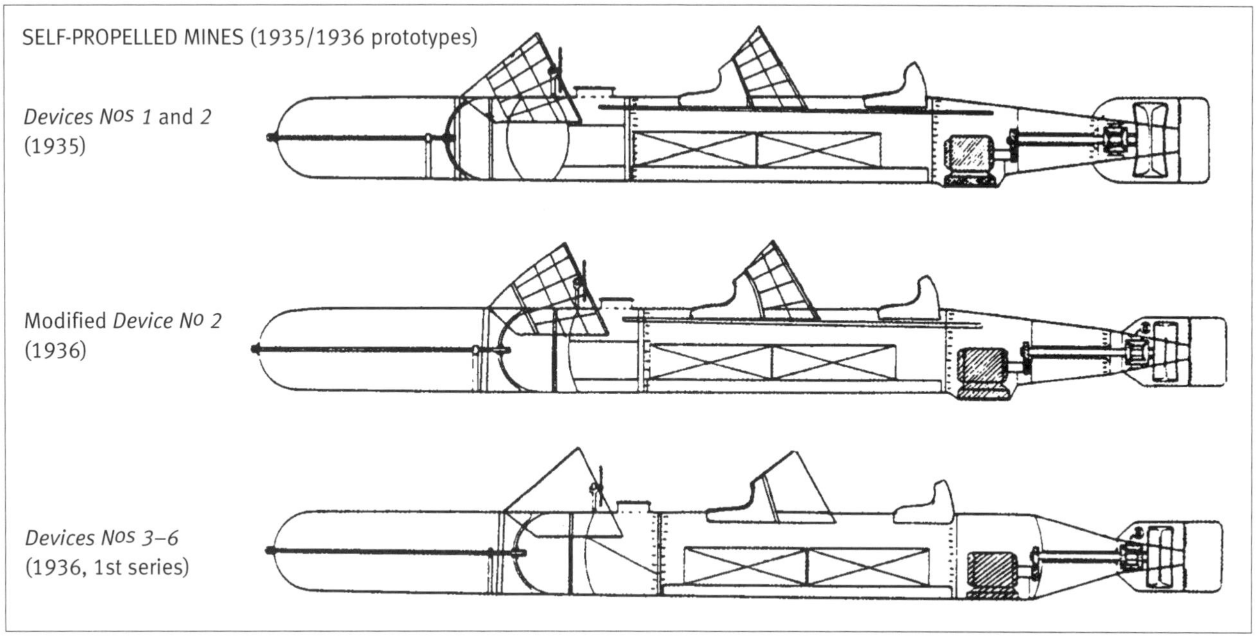

One of the 'self-propelled mine' prototypes, probably *No 2*. (USMM)

four additional craft was again entrusted to the San Bartolomeo Torpedo Workshops, but under supervision by the Headquarters of the Underwater Arms Department in La Spezia.

The Ethiopian campaign ended in May 1936 and with it the prospect faded of a direct confrontation with the Royal Navy on clearly disadvantageous terms; as a result, the Naval Staff's interest in the project waned. Fitting out the craft ordered on 17 April 1936 was halted, and training of personnel chosen for those self-propelled craft, which had been underway for some months, was slowed down until it was suspended the following August. The first operators were therefore reassigned to normal seagoing and shore appointments, although they were sworn to absolute secrecy about their particular training; and the 'devices' themselves were consigned to long-term storage at the San Bartolomeo Torpedo Workshops.

However, the idea of employing underwater assault craft was never completely abandoned and in June 1937 the Plans and Operations Department of the Naval Staff – which had been assigned responsibility for supervising this activity the previous March – was ordered to update the two 'self-propelled Tesei craft' prototypes and at the same time proposed to build at least six more.

These new self-propelled craft actually numbered five, joining those built or begun in 1936, as a 1st Mas Flotilla report dated 18 August 1939[2] notes that a total of eleven underwater 'devices' were available (probably including the two prototypes; see table on page 141), but only *Nos 9* and *10* were ready for service while the others still had significant shortcomings. The same report mentioned modification work to be carried out to *Device No 8* intended to increase its speed and improve trim and buoyancy.

Commander Paolo Aloisi, commanding officer of the First MAS Flotilla, brought in engineer Guido Cattaneo of CABI (Cattaneo Application of Industrial Patents) of Milan – which was already involved in the development of 'explosive boats' – to improve the characteristics of the 'self-propelled Tesei craft'. Under the cover name of 'Project Trespolo [Perch]' CABI revised the original design, making numerous changes.

In particular, the whole 'trim and propulsion' arrangement was redesigned, bringing the overall length of the craft to 7.30m and electric motor power to 1.6hp. The modifications proposed and implemented on *No 8* were successful and were extended to almost all the existing craft in the following months. Now officially named 'Slow Running Torpedoes' (*Siluro a Lenta Corsa*, or SLC), a further series of these craft would be ordered in July 1940 shortly after Italy entered the European conflict. This probably comprised eight craft with improved characteristics (called series '100'), followed by a more numerous series ('200') from the beginning of 1941, incorporating all the lessons of both training and the first war missions.

In particular, it seems that 1st and 2nd series SLC from the original group of eleven were used for attempted or completed actions up to the end of 1940

2. The unit entrusted with the preparation and deployment of the first assault craft since the end of 1938; from February 1939 it had resumed trials and operator training.

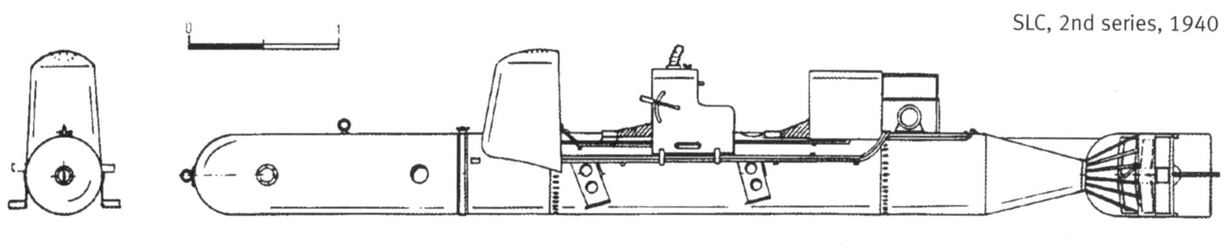

(see table on page 141). For those actions carried out before the autumn of 1941 (Gibraltar in May and Malta in July), '100' series craft were used. One '100' and two '200' series craft took part in the well-known forcing of Alexandria in December 1941. Subsequent actions would instead be carried out with '200' series craft (some with 'double' charge) and possibly with some '100' series survivors modified to the standard of the next series.

As already stated, the first SLC were largely constructed from recycled materials.

The *head*, *main body* and *tail* with its *frame* for propellers and rudders were drawn from the standard 533mm torpedoes as supplied to submarines and surface units, and appropriately modified.

The transmission to the propellers had to be completely redesigned, given the replacement of the wet-heater torpedo machinery with an electric motor, whose power was progressively increased from 1.1 to 1.6hp.[3] The two contra-rotating coaxial propellers, typical of the torpedoes, were initially retained; later, they were replaced a single three- or even four-bladed larger (about 38.5cm) right-handed propeller, more suitable to low craft speeds and less noisy.

The rudders, both horizontal (depth) and vertical (steering) were appropriately oversized for the new, slower craft speeds. Weights and dimensions were:

Total weight: about 1300kg, then about 1400 after the first units;
Overall length: initially 6.70m (of which 1.80 was the detachable charge head), then 7.30m;
Cylindrical body diameter: 0.53m;
Maximum gauge height and width (excluding operators): approximately 1.30m x 0.90m (measured at the so-called 'stirrups' for the pilots' feet).

The two pilots – most commonly called 'operators' – sat in tandem, that is, one behind the other, astride the craft.[4] At first, the operators' legs simply dangled along

3. It would appear that the first prototype of the 'self-propelled Tesei craft' had been fitted with an old elevator motor (direct current).

4. Back-to-back operator seating was also tested, but it was not considered convenient.

Loading an SLC aboard the support barge at the Bocca di Serchio base in late 1941.

A 'pig' during training at Bocca di Serchio in 1942.

Close-up of a '200' series SLC 'instrument box' and controls.

the sides of the self-propelled craft, a position that created considerable fatigue; later, appropriate feet supports ('stirrups') were fitted on the craft sides.

Power was supplied by a 30-element battery of accumulators that delivered about 150 (later 180) amps at 60 volts, allowing a maximum underwater speed of about 3 knots (initially 2.5) and a theoretical range of approximately 15 miles at the economical speed of

The same craft as that pictured on page 131 resting on crutches. Note that a tarpaulin was spread over the barge for secrecy reasons as soon as the SLC were embarked.

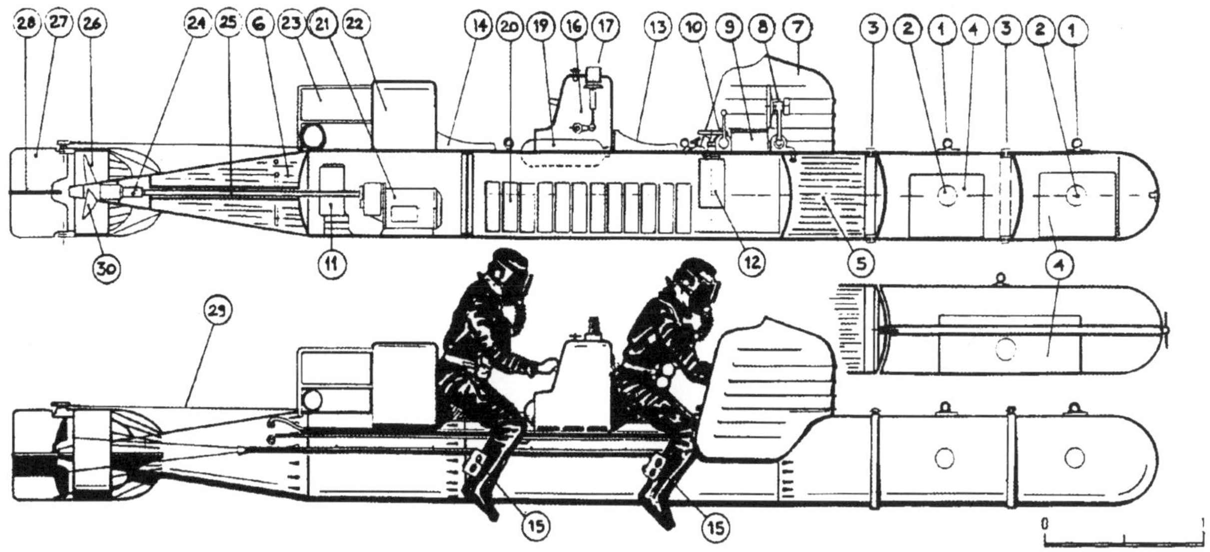

SLC of '100' series (top) and '200' series (below) *(F Harrauer drawing)*

1. Explosive warhead eyebolts
2. Time fuses
3. Head-holding straps
4. Explosive
5. Bow trim tank
6. Stern trim tank
7. Breakwater
8. Steering controls
9. Waterproof dashboard with: compass, pressure gauge (depth), ammeter, voltmeter, spirit level, air pressure gauges
10. Trim tanks controls
11. Electric venting pump
12. Propulsion motor rheostat control
13. 1st operator's seat with craft lifting eyebolt
14. 2nd operator's seat with craft lifting eyebolt
15. Leg pads
16. Rapid dive tank
17. Rapid dive valve
18. Rapid dive control
19. Rapid dive tank venting air cylinders
20. Batteries (30 elements 60 V)
21. 1.6hp electric motor
22. Balsa wood block for motor weight compensation
23. Case or cage for back-up breathing apparatus, shears, pneumatic net raiser, clamps and food tube
24. Motor shaft bearing
25. Motor shaft
26. Propeller guard
27. Steering rudder
28. Dive rudder
29. Rudder control cables
30. Three-bladed propeller

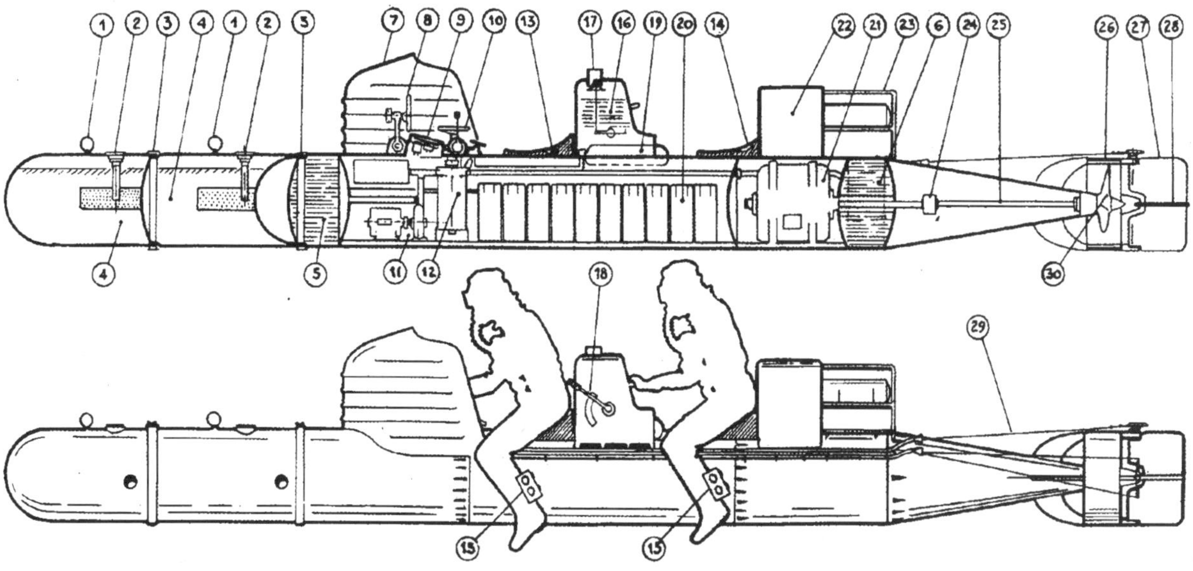

An SLC of series '200' photographed in Venice-S Andrea in summer 1945 during tests performed by Italian and Anglo-American operators. Note that the craft is equipped with a double explosive warhead, whose fixing screw latches and fuse setting access holes are clearly visible. *(Imperial War Museum)*

A 'pig' during training in Bocca di Serchio.

Close-up of the '200' series 'pig' on display at the Venice Naval History Museum. In the foreground is the 'rapid dive' flood control lever.

SLC positioned on the crutches of the support barge at the Bocca di Serchio base. Note that, on the lefthand craft, the reel of white rope called the 'lift' is hanging on the handrail of the 2nd operator's position, on the back of the 'Rapid' tank case.

2.3 knots. Surface or awash speed was not very different, but this type of navigation allowed the operators (or at least the forward one, known as 'first') to save the precious oxygen of the breathing apparatus provided. In fact, on increasing the speed beyond the 'minimum' the craft tended to bring the stern down, and the 'second' operator ended up with his head underwater and was therefore forced to employ the breathing apparatus.

Speed control was through the clockwise rotation of a wheel keyed to a rheostat: with each click – from the 1st to the 4th 'notch' – the number of engine revs increased. In the last SLC models a 5th notch (corresponding to maximum speed) was added. Turning the wheel anti-clockwise beyond the 1st 'notch' reversed the propeller rotation for movement astern.

The craft was fitted with two 'trim tanks' for the dive, one at the bow and the other at the stern, drainable by two small electric pumps, and a ballast tank (called 'rapid') drainable by injecting compressed air at 200 atmospheres (200 kg/cm^2) via a special tap from two cylinders arranged at the base of the same case between the seats of the 1st and 2nd operator.

At the top of the ballast case was a mushroom ('vent') valve which sometimes ended with a short rubber corrugated tube. Controlled by a lever located on the left side of the case itself, opening the 'vent' allowed the air to escape and caused the immediate flooding of the 'rapid'. The immediate loss of buoyancy that followed allowed the complete immersion of the craft in 6/7 seconds.

The first prototype also had a 'compensation tank' placed in the manoeuvring head, which was emptied or flooded to compensate for the considerable negative buoyancy (94kg) of the first type of warhead used, which contained 260kg of explosive and whose empty shell weighed 68kg. From the second prototype onwards, heads with neutral or slightly negative (1–2kg) buoyancy were adopted, and this tank was eliminated.

Starting from the bow, an SLC comprised: the *explosive head* (or *service head*), the *manoeuvring head*, which contained the controls, the cylindrical *central body* with the two operator seats on top, the *tail*, which contained the propulsion system, and the *frame* that carried propellers and rudders.

The service head consisted of a cylinder with a rounded front end detachable from the rest of the craft and containing approximately 229–230kg of high explosive ('tritolite' or 'tritolital') with the related clockwork detonators made up of special mechanical fuses produced by Borletti of Milan. The head containing the charge was fixed to the manoeuvring head with a circular strap. To detach it from the device it was necessary to loosen the strap by acting on the *wing nut* of a special threaded pin. The strap was then abandoned on the sea bottom and the head hooked to the target. In the final models of SLC with a single explosive warhead, the strap was eliminated and replaced by a central pivot screw that crossed the head longitudinally could be locked or unlocked acting on a large *butterfly nut* placed at the front end.

Connection to the target was initially via a rubber adhesion bag, integral with the head itself, which was inflated with compressed air; the positive thrust thus obtained retained the charge under the hull of the target. The self-propelled craft for the first two unfortunate attempts against Alexandria – which ended with the sinking of the 'approacher' submarines *Iride* and *Gondar* – had heads with adhesion bags; subsequently the system was modified to hang the warhead under the hull of the target using a cable connected to the two bilge keels and a *suspension eyebolt* placed above of the centre of gravity of the head itself. The latter was initially single; later the so-called 'multiple' heads were also adopted, made up of two connected cylinders, one ahead of the other, each containing about 125kg of high explosive, considered sufficient to cause serious damage to the (less resistant) structure of merchant ships. The two charges were separable, and each was equipped with independent detonators, its own suspension eyebolt and mobile connection strap.

The manoeuvring head weighed about 160kg and was 1.20m long; it had a rounded front to reduce resistance after the service head, single or multiple, had been detached.

The manoeuvring head, which contained the forward trim tank and propulsion system controls, ended with a concave watertight bulkhead and was connected to the central body by a double nut ring with 32 screws (torpedo type) with a seal in between of hemp braid soaked in tallow.

Next aft was the central body and the operators' seats, protected by a breakwater. At first this consisted of a thick transparent celluloid plate, suitably shaped and reinforced by a wooden frame. However, the transparency of the celluloid rapidly deteriorated through the action of hydrocarbons always present in harbour waters, their deposits on its surface blocking the view; to eliminate this problem, and to make it stronger, the breakwater was built with smooth metal sheet, or with horizontal reinforcement ribs in the last SLC produced.

Close to the breakwater, with non-magnetic characteristics, the steering position was fitted with controls and dashboard. The latter consisted of a panel, also called the *instrument box*, closed by a metal frame with a thick celluloid slab superimposed, with windows at the various quadrants, equipped with a rubber seal and fixed by a series of peripheral screws. For night vision, the panel was initially equipped with electric lighting; later, instruments with 'Radiomir' phosphorescent dials were adopted.[5]

The instruments consisted of: a *depth gauge* (with scale up to 30 metres), a 'Lazzarini' type *magnetic compass*, a *clock*, a *voltmeter* for battery voltage check; two *ampére gauges*, one for the batteries and the other for absorption control of drainage and transfer trim cases pumps, and a *spirit level* for checking the longitudinal trim of the craft.

A handwheel working through metallic cables controlled vertical rudder movements and therefore direction. The wheel was mounted atop a longitudinally movable vertical bar acting like an airplane *joystick* on the horizontal rudders, allowing depth control. Next to the wheel for engine speed adjustment was a 'throttle' (with related vent valve) that commanded a tap with four or more ways to control closing and opening of the pipes connected to service pumps of the trim tanks, which generally ran externally (mostly over or at the sides) of the central body. Between the shaped seat (first in wood, later perforated metal) of the 'first' and that of the 'second' operator was the structure containing the 'rapid' case and its compressed air cylinders, with a horizontal handle fitted to be used as 'handrail' by the 'second'.

Then came the place of the 'second' operator and the joining strap of the central body to the tail, similar to that connecting the warhead. The central body, closed at the front and rear by two vertical watertight bulkheads, contained the batteries and their electrical connections. Behind the second operator seat, over the front of the tail section, was originally arranged a shaped block of balsa wood, whose positive buoyancy partly balanced the weight of the electric propulsion motor underneath. That wood block was subsequently deleted, and does not appears in the later SLC series, replaced, as will be seen in more detail later, by the so-called *small trunk*.

The rear trim tank and its electric pump were placed abaft the electric motor, having a capacity of about 46 litres. The motor shaft, which passed through this box in a watertight cylinder, was connected to differential gearing which, on the early units equipped with two counter-rotating propellers, was made of parts from standard 450mm torpedoes. Later this element was replaced by a purpose-built reduction gear: the related 'coupling' however proved to be very delicate and its break caused the failure of some missions.[6]

Between the reduction gear and propeller (or propellers) was a thrust bearing.

Placed above the tail was the final external feature: known as the *tools bonnet* and about 1.10m in total length, it was a light structure of angle-irons with free circulation intended to contain special equipment ('net risers', 'net cutter', shears, cramps, cables, 'elevator' etc, as well as small watertight containers (including a food container tube) and a back-up breathing apparatus, with reduced endurance compared to the standard ones supplied to the two operators.

In detail, these were:

- the 'net riser' was initially no more than a small tackle, made up from cables and blocks, which was used to lift the 'slack' of the nets, which normally lay on the bottom, enough to let the craft pass underneath. It was later replaced by a more powerful compressed air device projected and built by CABI;
- the 'net cutter' was originally a large hand-operated shear with wooden grips, later replaced by a more powerful compressed air tool, designed and built by CABI;
- the cramps: were large screw clamps to be fixed tightly to the target's bilge keels and to which the warhead suspension cable was connected;
- 'elevator' was the rather picturesque name for a simple cable, initially wound on a wooden board, then on a reel, which was fixed with to the craft and unrolled by one of the operators when leaving the craft and used to easily find it again stopped on the bottom in complete darkness.

5. 'Radiomir' was a trademark of the Panerai Workshops in Florence, and consisted of a lighting mixture containing radioactive material. The night brightness of the instruments was excellent (De La Penne said he had to cover with mud the very visible dashboard of his 'pig' when abandoning it with the head primed under HMS *Valiant* in Alexandria), but also dangerous for the emission of penetrating radiation; so much so that towards the end of the conflict, it was replaced by a completely safe material marketed as 'Luminor'.

6. It would appear that such breakages resulted from the malfunction of two elements of the coupling, one metallic and one fibre; the choice of this last material, which proved unsuitable for the purpose, was an attempt at noise reduction. It seems that Birindelli, when a prisoner, managed to report the fact in a (censored) letter to his mother, pretending to talk about school exams (' ... *same defect of Bruno [Falcomatà] and Gigi [De la Penne] ...*') and that the message was received and understood by the 'X^{a}' Headquarters.

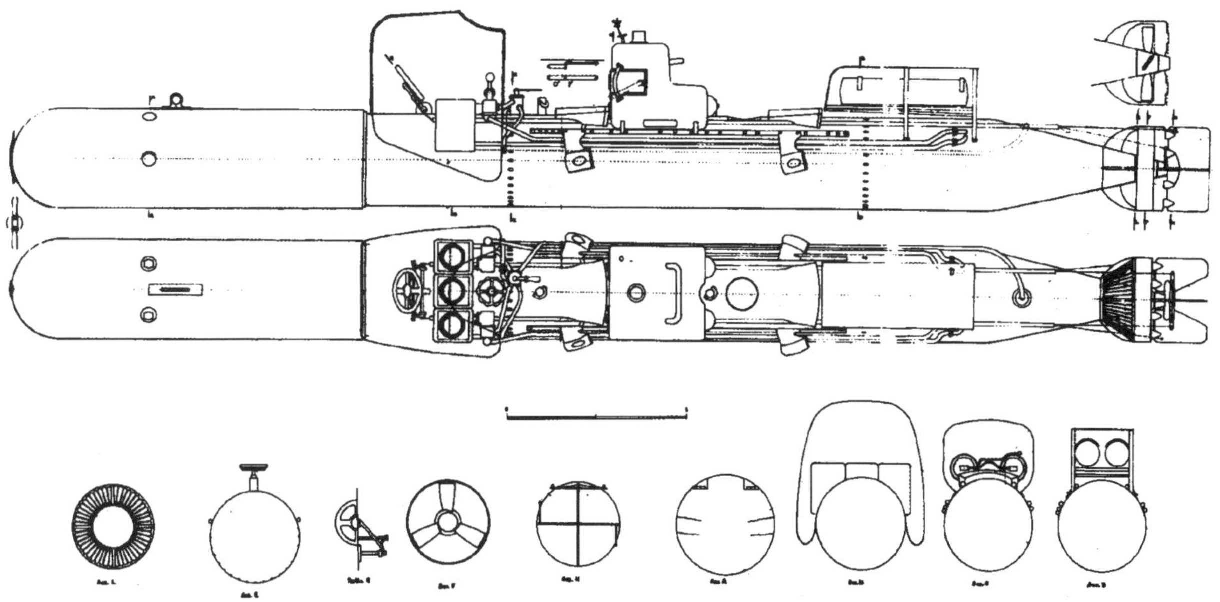

'200' series SLC. *(Drawing of the craft preserved in Venice by courtesy of Navimodel, Bologna)*

At the rear of the tail was the *frame*, which included a kind of conical guard to protect the propeller or propellers (to prevent them from catching in nets or cables), and vertical and horizontal rudders. These were aft of the propeller and were connected to their controls via a pulley system of tiller wires.

For craft lifting operations during launching and recovery, two large eyebolts were welded on the upper part of the central body at approximately the position of the operator seats, which hooked to the shackles of the steel cable sling. Finally, it seems that every craft was equipped with *self-destruct charges* with time fuses, operated by the crew.[7]

The SLC was not a complicated craft, but it was rather 'capricious' (an adjective frequently used by its operators). Apart from the mechanical failures to which they were subject (especially the early units built with cannibalised materials), one of the negative features that all those who used it in war remember most clearly was its depth-keeping instability. Despite the fact that the craft was appropriately trimmed (*ie* balancing the liquid ballast in the bow and stern tanks) before every action, the SLC would often suddenly lose stability and sink to the bottom, diving beyond the safety limits. This may have been due to the incorrect operation of the pumps but the reasons were not always determined with certainty.[8]

In addition to the previously mentioned weakness of the coupling, one other frequent cause of failure was the malfunctioning of the batteries – despite precautions there were even small explosions of the gases which sometimes formed in the battery compartment during the often prolonged period in the watertight containers of 'approacher' submarines during the voyage towards the target. This inconvenience was later partially remedied by the forced ventilation of the 'cylinders' via pipework through the hull which exhausted any dangerous gases into the submarine or into the sea.

Last but not least, the cause of many failed missions by 'pigs' (see note 8) can traced to operators breathing apparatus malfunctions (see Appendix 1-H).

Employment techniques of SLC

Normally the vehicle and the operators were released with the advantage of darkness close to the target to be

7. It seems that these charges (according to information obtained during interviews with some veteran operators) were located in the central area, with a timer to activate them under the 2nd man's seat. These were small amounts of explosives, whose function was to open waterways that provoked the immediate sinking of the craft.

8. It seems that the nickname – initially not so affectionate – of 'pig' (*maiale* in Italian), which later became common usage, was given to it by the inventor himself, Teseo Tesei. On returning from a rather demanding exercise, he is reputed to have shouted to sailors at Bocca del Serchio base, *'... c'mon, moor this pig!'*. The slang was in common use in Tuscany and particularly on the island of Elba, where Tesei came from.

attacked by a surface or underwater 'approacher', unless they could set out directly from an advanced operational base, as in the case of *Olterra* in Algeciras.

Having extracted the craft from the container cylinder (sometimes with the help of reserve operators) if the 'approacher' was a submarine, or having otherwise put the craft into the water from a surface vessel, the operators checked the *trim* and carried out the necessary *compensation* with appropriate movements of liquid ballast, checking the reserve buoyancy of the 'pig' that naturally varied with water temperature and salinity, especially near rivers, etc.

Having completed the operation in absolute silence and as quickly as possible, the final approach to the target began, and was carried out on the surface as long as possible, given the limited endurance of the breathing apparatus.

If a safe surfaced approach was not possible because of lighting conditions (presence and phase of the moon, etc) or phosphorescence of water or active enemy vigilance, navigation was conducted 'at glasses depth' using the self-contained breathing apparatus or 'awash' with only the head of the first operator (and sometimes the top of the breakwater) out of the water. In this case, however, the 2nd operator was necessarily forced to use the breathing apparatus, as he was completely underwater with the craft in a stern-down trim.

For the action to succeed it was essential that the presence of the craft was not detected in any way. Therefore, when approaching the target it was essential that the operators manoeuvred to avoid being sighted by the ever more numerous enemy surveillance units; after the first SLC actions, the defenders had taken to dropping small but dangerous anti-personnel underwater charges blindly into the sea at irregular intervals.

When a few hundred, if not tens of metres from the target to be attacked or from the entrance of the harbour to be forced, the craft was slowly dived by opening the valves of the tanks (with caution to avoid a visible and noisy production of air bubbles). It then began to navigate on a compass bearing taken with a last look by the 1st operator (or the 'first', as he was simply called in the jargon of the assault – not just underwater – craft world).

If the harbour mouth, or the target ship, was protected by a net obstruction that was not easily surmountable on the surface, or by passing between the support floats of the net itself, the 'pig' was dived to the bottom – assuming it was within the depth limits allowed – slowly approaching the net to see if there was a gap big enough to pass under. If not, it was necessary to create one using the 'net riser'. Placing it high on a mesh of the net and fixing the lower hook to the bottom edge, by hauling on the tackle fall the 'diver'[9] almost always managed to lift the obstacle enough to let the craft slide under and move on.

The operation was actually quite simple and quick to carry out, but it had to be performed silently and in total darkness, which certainly did not make its execution easy. After the first successes of Italian underwater craft, to prevent the nets from being raised relatively easily, the British took the precaution laying nets of excessive depth, so that the considerable weight of the 'slack' lying on the bottom made this manoeuvre impossible.

Save some stroke of luck, like the unexpected opening at the opportune moment of the boom defences to allow the transit of naval units, only the shears remained to cut a hole in the net steel cable meshes wide enough for the craft to pass. However, it was necessary to be very careful not to cut any electrical wires attached to alarm systems.

Finally arriving in open waters, the 'pig' faced the last stretch that separated it from the ship to attack. Normally it moved in a dive with a few short ascents to 'glasses depth', to 'go and see', as it was called in the jargon (or by sending the 'second' to the surface using the 'elevator'), monitoring the target bearing and distance with continual checks. Sometimes the operators were also guided by the noise produced by machinery in operation on board.

They aimed for contact with the hull ('at hull') and then with one of the bilge keels which equipped almost all ships.[10] On this ledge the 'second' fixed a cramp, taking a turn with a cable. Restarting the craft to pass underneath the keel, the opposite side bilge keel was reached, to which another cramp and the other end of the cable was attached after tensioning. With engine stopped, by manually pulling on the cable, the operators moved the craft to roughly the centre of the hull. Then the 'second', having tied a rope to the head

9. In SLC jargon the 'second' operators were called 'divers' (*palombaro*, in italian) because they normally came from that specialist category of the Royal Maritime Crew Corps (CREM).

10. Should the target lack bilge keels, it was planned to hang the charge from the propeller shafts, or from the rudder or to any other ledge or foothold that could be found (paravane shoes, etc). In case the hull of the target turned out to be close to the bottom (no more than ten metres), the charge could also be simply abandoned under the ship; this was something which happened more than once during war operations.

eyebolt, connected it to the transverse cable: afterwards, loosening the 'strap' or the 'fixing pin', the craft was separated from the explosive warhead that hung below the ship.

With counter-clockwise movement of a knob, they started the fuses by establishing with the 'notches' the time interval after which the explosion would take place. This interval was calculated with enough safety margin to allow for the craft to move away, or be safely destroyed, or its eventual recovery or return.[11]

This short description represents a typical action, intended only to illustrate in general terms the usual methods of employing the 'pig'. It was obviously impossible to take into account all those variables that required immediate decisions and actions that usually presented during every mission in a completely unpredictable way. Above all, was the need to continuously adapt the methodologies of employment to the increasing defensive vigilance and countermeasures.

It is interesting to note that even before the creation of a permanent organisation to counter Italian assault craft, the Royal Navy resorted to rudimentary and expensive countermeasures, but ones that could be implemented quickly. One of these is remembered by Admiral Andrew B Cunningham: in his famous *A Sailor's Odyssey* the then Commander-in-Chief of the Mediterranean Fleet writes that, on the advice of one of his young officers, after the lucky attack of the 'pigs' in Alexandria in December 1941 it was ordered that during the hours of darkness the major ships at moorings and at anchor kept their engines turning the propellers in slow backwards motion – the current generated under the hull would, if not prevent, at least make the placement of explosive charges by Italian assault craft difficult.

Subsequently, the effectiveness of countermeasures gradually increased through the introduction of an extensive anchorage surveillance service, with dedicated boats continuously patrolling the area and launching anti-personnel depth charges, and with the establishment of special diver units for checking hulls and removing charge, etc. Such countermeasures diverted a large number of men and materials from other services but limited the freedom of movement of Italian underwater assault craft, although failing to completely prevent their actions until the last day of the war, despite the painful losses caused.

Quantities of craft produced

The design, development and use of Italian underwater assault craft were always subject to the greatest secrecy, so that to date it has proved impossible to trace any documents, lists, etc which reliably indicate how many craft were actually built. Using available information, however, we have attempted to reconstruct a tentative general picture (see table on page 141) of the craft produced, from which we believe we can conclude that, between 1935 and the date of the armistice, no more than 45–50 SLC, including prototypes, were completed.

The first eleven (1st and 2nd prototype of 1935–36, a first series of 4 craft ordered in April 1936 and a second series of 5 ordered in 1939) were identified according to a progressive numbering from *1* to *11*. A following series, probably of 8 SLC with improved features, ordered in summer 1940, appears characterised by numbers belonging to the '100' series: therefore the 12th to 19th units would be identified by numbers *120, 130, 140* etc, that is with a zero added after the sequential number. The other SLC built after the beginning of 1941 seem to have been assigned a number in the '200' series, or by preceding the progressive construction number (from the 20th unit on) with a '2': *220, 221* etc.

The highest number known for certain is *236* (December 1942), which probably corresponds to the 36th unit readied out of a total of just under fifty, esti-

Lieutenant Wolk (right) and a Royal Navy officer aboard an SLC in Venice in the summer of 1945. The operators are not wearing breathing apparatus, as this is a surface navigation test inside the former S Andrea seaplane base basin. *(Imperial War Museum)*

11. Only the operations against Gibraltar planned for the return of SLC to the advanced base (the *Olterra* moored in Algeciras harbour, in Spanish territory). Normally, the craft should have been destroyed by the operators, who would then try to save themselves. In a single case in Italian assault craft history (the 19 April 1945 attack on *Aquila* in Genoa harbour) a craft returned to its 'approacher' following the action. In this case, it was a British-built craft (a Chariot Mk I) piloted by Mariassalto operators.

Souvenir snapshot of some divers aboard a 'pig' raised from the bottom of Venice Lagoon in 1945.

mating that between the autumn of 1942 (the time of probable delivery for *236*) and September 1943 about fifteen more craft may have been prepared. However, *SLC 210*, employed and lost off Gibraltar in September 1941, is an exception to this rationale. It should not be the 21st built (which more probably was called *221*) but it may have been a '100' series (or even earlier) device, modernised and brought to the technical standard of the '200' series, thus requiring the number change.

The operational losses of SLC from June 1940 to 8 September 1943 turn out to be 25 units in total, to which we must probably add some seriously damaged craft (for example, those raised after the sinking of the submarine *Iride* in August 1940), besides some amongst the first built that were worn out by intensive operator training, and certainly scrapped or 'cannibalised' in favour of others.

Therefore, on the date of the armistice, including the 3 or 4 SLC based on the *Olterra* in Algeciras, the craft ready for use on Italian territory had to be about ten, concentrated in the facilities of the Bocca del Serchio School and the San Bartolomeo Torpedo Workshops in La Spezia. Their capabilities were now clearly exceeded by those of the more modern SSB ('Siluro San Bartolomeo'), whose first units were being readied, and these few SLC remained under the control of X^{a} Flottiglia Mas operating with the RSI, but it seems they were never used in war actions. It is documented instead that some SLC were transferred to carry out training in various locations, including Sesto Calende, Arona, Portorož and Venice. At least one was scuttled in April 1945 in this last location, and then recovered immediately after the war.

Currently there are at least 5 SLC (divided between originals and replicas) preserved in the Naval Museums of Venice and La Spezia, at the Shrine of the Flags under the Altar of the Homeland in Rome, at the Science and Technology Museum in Milan, at the Assault Divers Headquarters of the Italian Navy ('Comsubin') at the Forte del Varignano in La Spezia, and the Aragonese Castle of Taranto.

*From the published photos and drawings of SLC it can be seen that there were numerous differences in fitting-out details (*eg *configuration of the 'stern tools bonnet', shape and size of the breakwater, configuration of the aft guard, etc) even amongst craft belonging to the same series.*

An SLC on display in Turin in 1961. The 'Z' on the side of the breakwater is not an operational marking, but some kind of identification applied post-war for underwater filming. Also note one of the side floats fitted to increase the buoyancy of the craft and make it more visble in the waters of the pool. *(G Arra)*

SLOW-RUNNING TORPEDOES (SLC) – POSSIBLE INDIVIDUAL CRAFT NUMBERING (1935–1943)

Progressive number	*Series/ building year*	*Known numbering*	*Possible numbering*	*Known operations*
1	1st prototype/1935	*1*	–	–
2	2nd prototype/1936	*2*	–	–
3	1st series/1936	*3*	–	–
4		*4*	–	–
5		*5*	–	–
6		*6*	–	–
7	2nd series/1939	*7*	–	–
8		*8*	–	–
9		*9*	–	–
10		*10*	–	–
11		*11*	–	–
12	Series '100'/1940	*120**	–	BG 3
13		*130**	–	BG 3
14		*140**	–	BG 4
15		–	*150*	–
16		*160**	–	BG 3
17		–	*170*	–
18		–	*180*	–
19		–	*190*	–
20	Series '200'/ 1941 on[1]	*220**	–	BG 4
21		*221**	–	GA 3
22		*222**	–	GA 3
23		*223**	–	GA 3
24		–	*224*	–
25		–	*225*	–
26		–	*226*	–
27		*227*	–	–
28		*228 (*)*	–	BG 5
29		*229 (*)*	–	BG 5
30		–	*230*	–
31		–	*231*	–
32		–	*232*	–
33		–	*233*	–
34		–	*234*	–
35		–	*235*	–
36		*236 (*)*	–	BG 5
37		–	*237*	–
38		–	*238*	–
39		–	*239*	–
40		–	*240*	–
41		–	*241*	–
42		–	*242*	–
43–50(?)		–	*243–250(?)*	–

Notes

1 Amongst the known numbers there is a *210* (lost at Gibraltar on 20.9.1941 during Operation BG 4). Most likely this is not the 21st unit built, but a series '100' craft updated to series '200' standard.

* Craft definitely lost.

(*) Two out of three of these craft lost during Operation BG 5 from *Olterra*.

'San Bartolomeo torpedo' (SSB)

The employment of SLC in both training and in war actions had highlighted distinct limitations of this craft. Even with the use of new materials and more recent technology developed since the first underwater self-propelled craft were designed, a complete re-think rather than improving the original project was considered necessary.

The studies were entrusted to engineer Major Mario Masciulli, with the collaboration of Captain Travaglini (also on the *Olterra* as manager of the secret workshop) and with the advice of engineer Guido Cattaneo of CABI of Milan, based on specifications provided by the X Flotilla Mas Headquarters. Under the supervision of the Underwater Weapons Command of the La Spezia Dockyard, the completion of the prototype of the new underwater self-propelled craft was handled by the San Bartolomeo Torpedo Workshop, which provided the official designation of the new device: 'Siluro San Bartolomeo' (SSB), called *'Delta' type assault craft* in the records of the Caproni company which, as prime contractor, was responsible for its series production.

The construction of the SSB prototype was allegedly undertaken at the beginning of 1943 and the first sea trials took place in late spring of the same year. Results were positive but they did show up the need to make some minor changes. The new device followed the general rationale of the SLC, but although of almost equal length the SSB was decidedly more bulky, derived essentially from the adoption of a wider diameter body (about 780mm against 533mm) and a large upper fairing inside which was the cockpit for the two operators, who sat on tandem seats inside the central section instead of riding astride.

This more protected arrangement was designed to better shelter the operators from the increased water resistance at the higher speed of the craft (4 knots instead of 2.5) and to allow longer surface passages

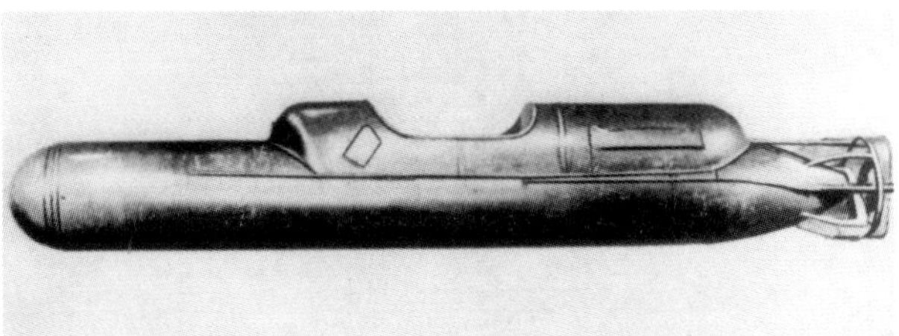

Retouched photo of one of the former republican X Mas SSB found by the Allies in Venice-S Andrea in May 1945 *(Imperial War Museum).*

A Caproni-built SSB on the former Venice-S Andrea seaplane base ramp in the summer of 1945. This craft has a double explosive head. *(Imperial War Museum)*

even in rough seas. The SSB, whose prototype reached a total weight of about 1860kg, had a standard war load in the order of 400kg.

Engine power and battery capacity – split into two groups, one forward and one aft of the pilot seats – were significantly increased, giving higher speed and better range.

The main dimensions of the SSB, especially length and depth, did not vary significantly from those of the SLC as it was intended to transport them in the watertight cylinders of the 'approacher' submarines already in service. As on the 'self-propelled Tesei craft' prototypes, two counter-rotating three-bladed propellers were adopted for the 'San Bartolomeo'[1]; another peculiarity was the installation of two small foldable horizontal fins with depth stabilising function, placed at the front of the craft.

It is likely that after the first favourable tests at sea of the prototype, two more pre-production SSB were ordered, almost certainly at the same San Bartolomeo Torpedo Workshop, with modifications and improvements subsequently added based on the continuation of the trials.

It is impossible to accurately determine how many series SSB were ordered before September 1943. However, craft of this type had been laid down in the summer of 1943 at the Taliedo (Milan) factory of the Caproni Aircraft Company of Milan, which used the Gianazza Bros Company of Legnano, specialists in steel processing, for the construction of the hulls

1. Subsequently, to reduce the noise, at least one experimental SSB was fitted with a single three-bladed propeller, modifying and properly sizing the rudders and probably also varying the engine/shaft reduction ratio.

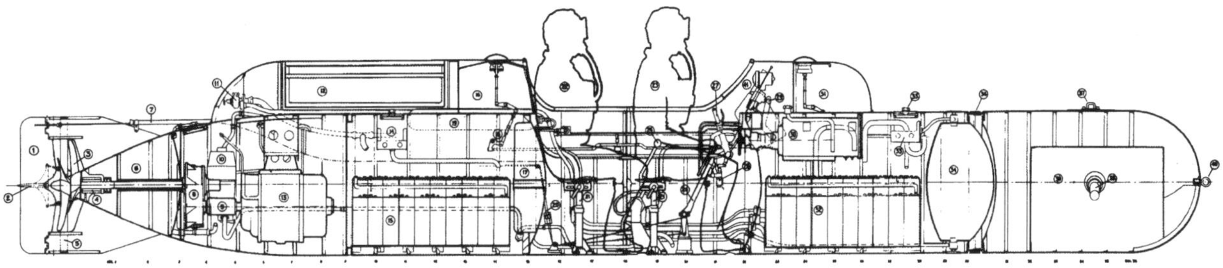

'San Bartolomeo torpedo' (SSB), 1943

1. Steering rudder
2. Diving planes
3. Co-axial, contra-rotating propellers
4. Rubber bushing and gland sealing
5. Propeller guard
6. Stern trim tank
7. Steering rudder rods
8. Reduction gear
9. Elastic coupling
10. Trim tanks electric pump
11. Battery ventilation tubing valve
12. Net raiser and back-up breathing apparatus case
13. Propulsion electric motor
14. Battery charge socket
15. Stern battery
16. Rear surfacing tank
17. Centre trim tank
18. Tank venting valve control transmission
19. Two compressed air tanks
20. Rudder control cables
21. Adjustable seats
22. Second operator
23. First pilot
24. Pump control lever
25. Pump control
26. Control yoke and wheel
27. Air vent valve control
28. Push-valve for tank 16 and 31 venting
29. Folding trim fins control
30. Controller
31. Bow surfacing tank
32. Bow battery
33. Bow battery charge socket
34. Bow trim tank
35. Autoclave hatch
36. Explosive head fixing strap
37. Explosive head suspension eyebolt
38. Explosive charge
39. Fuse socket
40. Towing eye
41. Dashboard

(Re-drawn from original blueprints by F Harrauer)

(8 units built),[2] and the 'Vulcano' Company of Brescia for the warheads.

It still seems certain that by the date of the armistice just 3 SSB were available. These were probably the prototype and the first two pre-production units, all built in La Spezia. One of these was already earmarked to be disassembled and soon shipped secretly to Spain, to the *Olterra*, to take part in the action against

2. From a 1992 publication commemorating the centenary of its foundation, it appears that the same company also built some of the watertight steel cylinders used for the transport of assault craft aboard the last 'approacher' submarines built.

The same craft as seen in the previous picture being put into the water at the former Venice-S Andrea seaplane base. *(Imperial War Museum)*

An SSB at maximum surface speed in Venice-S Andrea in summer 1945. *(Imperial War Museum)*

Venice-S Andrea, summer 1945. Some of the Italian operators recruited by ANES (Allied Navies Experimental Station) in front of one of the SSB used in tests. *(STORIA militare archives)*

Gibraltar, scheduled for 2 October, to be performed in coordination with 4 MTR type explosive boats that should have been transported to Algeciras harbour aboard the submarine *Murena*.

The SSB was a craft with characteristics and performance clearly superior to the SLC: it had higher speed, range, manoeuvrability and war load, but above all it was a craft of more modern conception, safer overall efficiency and less subject to mechanical and electrical failures. For its description we make use of a technical data sheet compiled at the time (probably in 1943) by the Caproni Company which is reproduced here:

Caproni-built 'DELTA' type assault craft

General characteristics

Length overall	6.766m
Maximum width	0.790m
Maximum depth	1.080m
Total weight of the war-ready craft	2200kg
Explosive warhead weight:	
standard head	400kg
medium head	300kg
double head	180kg each

Close-up of the pilot's cockpit in a Caproni-built SSB in a 1945 picture.

The torpedo-shaped hull has an overlaid superstructure with fully streamlined external profile. In the middle there is a free circulation cockpit for two operators.

The craft consists of the following main parts:

1st element = warhead;

2nd element = front trim tank, forward accumulator compartment, cockpit and control systems;

3rd element = rear accumulator compartment and trim tank;

4th element = propulsion motor compartment, trim pumps, rear trim tank, transmission, propellers, rudders.

In future constructions it is planned, having been successfully tested by Caproni, to arrange the trim pumps under the operator seats in the cockpit.

This arrangement allows, besides saving on pipes, easy inspection even with the system mounted.

Armament

Standard head: under normal conditions of war use, the craft is equipped with a semi-spherical element attached by a strap and containing a charge of about 400kg of explosive. Two triggers are fitted in radial positions, provided with a time fuse.

For drills there is a training head with identical characteristics to the warhead, but without explosives and appropriately ballasted.

Medium head: it is a cylindrical section to be inserted between the standard head and the second element in situations where the device can be used with no length limits. [*ie* not transported in the cylinders of 'approacher' submarines]

Contains an explosive charge of approximately 300kg and two triggers equipped with time fuses.

Short heads: in case operational needs suggest its use, a short head with the same overall dimensions to the standard head is available, but divisible into two elements, each containing a charge of approximately 180kg of explosives and each with two triggers, equipped with time fuses.

Each element described above has a slightly negative buoyancy (1-2kg) in water and an almost horizontal trim.

Propulsion system

The propulsion system consists of a 7.5hp DC motor which, through a gearbox-inverter transmits the motion to two coaxial propellers rotating in opposite directions (for possible [series] construction it is planned to use a patented motor that eliminates the reduction gearing). The contra-rotating propeller was adopted in order to improve propulsive efficiency, neutralise propeller torque and increase course stability with modest sized steering and depth rudders.

The motor, as silent as possible, is powered by a battery of electric accumulators divided into two sub-batteries arranged in two separate internal compartments. A special slip ring contained in a watertight case and made of non-magnetic material is placed in the second element and operated from the cockpit with a special wheel, providing the necessary motor controls, to get four forward speeds and one reverse.

Main features of the electrical system

Motor (elastically suspended):
Shaft power 7.5hp = 5.51 kW
Maximum supply voltage: 120 V
Current absorption at full load: 70 A
Speed without load (V = 120) 1000rpm
Weight 165kg
Propeller transmission ratio 2:1
Batteries (two compartments):
Number of elements
(divided into 2 sub-batteries): 60
Capacity of each sub-battery: 190 A/h
Voltage of each bank: 60 V
Weight of each bank: 350kg

The systems for charging and ventilation of the battery compartments are accessible through special hatches, allowing operation with the craft assembled.

Trim tank operation

Main circuit: two tanks are fitted for this purpose, one in the forward compartment with a capacity of 90 litres, the other in the rear compartment with a

One of the SSB requisitioned by the US Navy in 1945. *(US Navy)*

Close-up of the same craft as in the previous picture. Note the double warhead, and the folded bow dive planes on the breakwater. *(US Navy)*

capacity of 58 litres. The two tanks are served by two gear pumps, each driven by an electric motor.

The pumps are operated with special levers located on both sides of the pilot.

On the right side there is the control for the pump that serves the two stern and bow trim tanks, and on the left side the one for the central trim tank pump.

For flooding: trimming water is sucked from the strainer by the left pump.

For venting: the water circuit is identical, but moved in the opposite direction.

For trimming water transfer from bow to stern or vice versa, the starboard pump is operated.

Backup circuit: in the case of failure of one of the pumps, there is a backup circuit which connects to the distribution valve and allows the possibility of using the other pump for the service of the two trim tanks.

The operations to carry out are as follows:

1. *In case of starboard pump failure for the service of the stern and bow tanks:* lifting the left valve, water can be transferred from bow to central tank, and from central to bow.
2. *In case of left pump failure for the sea to central tank or central tank to sea service:* lifting the right valve, water can be transferred from sea to stern, or from stern to sea.

Surfacing system

The rapid surfacing and diving system is operated by two 'rapid tanks' equipped with flooding and air vent valves; a dedicated high pressure air circuit, with an air reserve of 10 litres at 200 atmospheres, allows the execution of over 15 venting manoeuvres.

A 'Delta' type SSB during construction at the Caproni factory in Milan. *(A Rastelli collection)*

The two tanks are arranged, respectively, one forward and the other aft of the operators' cockpit and their operation, both in flooding and venting phase, is synchronous, commanded by a single operating lever.

Cockpit and steering gear

The cockpit is located at the centre of the device, has free seawater circulation, and all the piloting and control gears and instruments are grouped in it. The perforated sheet-metal seats can be easily moved both longitudinally and vertically to better suit different operators; the operators have foot boards and adjustable and quickly foldable knee pads to keep them in the seats.

All controls and instruments are easily accessible to the first operator. The depth and steering rudders are operated by a steel cable continuous transmission moved by a single wheel yoke placed between the pilot's legs. Two levers are arranged on the sides of the dashboard; their simple movement deploys the front fins. On both sides of the pilot are the pump control levers; further forward, to the left, is the control lever of the rapid trim tanks. The propulsion system command wheel is at the front, immediately below the dashboard.

The following instruments are mounted on a single dashboard made of non-magnetic material:

Compass: watertight, spherical, front-reading;
Inclinometer: also front-reading, for control of the craft's longitudinal trim;
Pressure gauge: depth, with scale up to 30m of sea water (produced by SACMA, Milan);
Ammeter: for direct current, with scale from –20 to +140 Amperes, showing the current absorbed by the propulsion motor;
Voltmeter: for direct current, with scale from –20 to +140 Volts, indicating the motor supply voltage;
Ammeter: for direct current, with scale from 0 up to 70 Ampères, showing the total current absorbed by the electric pumps;
Pressure gauge: showing the air pressure in the rapid surfacing tanks;
Water meter: graduated in litres, showing the variation of the trimming water.
All instruments are equipped with luminous hands and dials.

In a dedicated hood, placed on the extension of the stern rapid trim tank, and fitted with easily-opened locks, the following accessories can be found:

Two more 'Delta' type SSB during construction. *(A Rastelli collection)*

- a net riser, a net cutter and a cable-cutting shear (all with pneumatic operation), each with a series of spare air cylinders;
- N ° 4 incendiary bombs;
- N ° 2 spare breathing apparatuses;
- other service accessories.

At the aft end of the bonnet, in a completely closed compartment with a screwed hatch outside, are the battery control valves.

Battery charging, with the help of a gas extraction system, is performed with the craft completely assembled.

The craft is equipped with a timed self-destruct device.

This document shows that the total weight of the craft had risen from the 1860kg of the prototype to the 2200 listed. This is probably the total weight of the self-propelled craft fully equipped, without the *standard head*, or even the *medium head*. In this case the overall length would have been around 8 metres, and therefore no longer transportable in standard watertight cylinders of 'approacher' submarines.

After the armistice, the construction of the self-propelled 'Delta' type craft was restarted by Caproni on orders from the republican X^{a} Mas, which already had the 3 SSB available in La Spezia on 9 September 1943. The order was to complete 3 already partially fitted-out craft and prepare another 8 with hulls already manufactured by 'Fratelli Gianazza' of Legnano, all belonging to previous Regia Marina orders.

In August 1944 the German authorities also ordered from Caproni 16 'Delta' type devices to be built both in the Taliedo and Rovereto factories, with deliveries within November/December of the same year. These delivery terms could not be met because of production problems and difficulties in procuring the necessary materials – this, at least, was the official response of the Company. The number or delivery dates of 'Delta' craft possibly supplied to the Germans are unknown,[3] while of those for the X^{a} Mas the first four were not delivered until March 1945, followed on 10 April, by four more. All or almost all the 'Delta' had defects, due perhaps to sabotage, but also to careless workmanship by some small artisan firms which operated as subcontractors. From a report by engineer Goeta (the Caproni manager for this order), we learn that the total cost of production start-up and delivered craft was around 36.5 million lire of the time, and that none of the self-propelled craft delivered was immediately ready for use.

It is believed that a good proportion of these craft were deployed to Venice, and perhaps also in Pola, where they were surprised by the end of the conflict shortly thereafter, without ever being employed in war missions.

The only SSB actually used were those of 'San Bartolomeo' construction, of which two appear to have remained in La Spezia, and one sent to Venice, where it was found in working order at the end of the war.

The two La Spezia craft were assigned to the X^{a} Mas 'Operational Group' based at the Castagna battery, on the western side of the roadstead. Under the orders of Lieutenant Augusto Jacobacci (first operator of the SSB already chosen for the action against Gibraltar planned for 2 October 1943), crew training took place in the gulf of La Spezia using as targets for simulated attacks initially the hull of the former heavy cruiser *Bolzano* and later the hull of the similar cruiser *Gorizia*. *Bolzano* had been badly damaged in the summer of 1942, not repaired and by then largely dismantled, but moored within a net enclosure in the roadstead (where it was sunk in June 1944 by a British

3. From some documents of German origin it appears that at least one action had been planned with 'underwater self-propelled craft' in the Adriatic to be carried out from Pola with three devices operated by Italian operators and three by German operators, 'approached' by German torpedo boats and from *MS 75* of X^{a} Mas. The target would have been Bari harbour but, from the date of the plan of operations (GKDS N° 2809 of 29.9.44) issued by the *Kommando der K-Verbände* it seems unlikely that the craft to be used were 'SSB/Delta'; it is much more likely they were SLC found in La Spezia at the time of the armistice. Planned for October 1944, the operation was never carried out, although some SLC were transferred to the Adriatic where they were almost all scuttled at the end of the conflict and partly recovered later.

An SSB, built by Silurificio San Bartolomeo, preserved at Comsubin Museum in La Spezia. Raised post-war and designated 'A' type, it remained in commission until the end of the 1950s.

Detail of the tail of the SSB in the previous picture.

Chariot Mk I). *Gorizia* was also abandoned, before being half-scuttled by the Germans.

With the two devices available – transported and 'approached' by *MTL 476* and with the support of *SMA 501* – an attempt to force Livorno harbour was carried out on the night of 7 November 1944; however, it had to be called off because of the mechanical breakdown of the MTL. The operation should have been retried in the following January with the same devices, transported by *MTL 571* with the support of *SMA 501* and *312* but, due to difficulties in the supply of spare parts for the craft to be used, it was repeatedly postponed until March, when it was definitively cancelled, as the advanced season no longer provided periods of darkness long enough.

On 22 April, the Castagna base was abandoned, but the two SSB were hidden in an inlet of the Palmaria island, whence their crews (Jacobacci, Pucciarini and their 'seconds') were to have attacked enemy ships which once the front had collapsed were expected to try to enter the harbour as soon as this was cleared of mines. But the war ended only a few days later with the roadstead still deserted and full of wrecks. It seems that the two SSB were taken offshore and sunk near the outer breakwater after starting the self-destruction fuses.

The SSB found in Venice at the end of the conflict were requisitioned by the Allies; others, concentrated at Caproni Taliedo in various stages of construction (4 at 80%, 4 at 50% and 4 at 40%) came into Italian Navy ownership in the second half of the 1940s.

Nowadays four copies of 'SSB/Delta' still exist: one is showcased at the Imperial War Museum in London (Delta N° 3 device, tested on 20.02.1945); one kept at the Groton (Connecticut) Submarine Museum in the USA; one, recently restored, at the Submarine Museum at Gosport in Great Britain; and another is part of the memorabilia collection of the Comando Raggruppamento Subacquei e Incursori (Comsubin) of the Italian Navy in Varignano (La Spezia).

The unit preserved at Comsubin remained in commission until the 1960s, and was used as a model for the development of similar craft made after 1950. Being of 'San Bartolomeo' construction, it might be one of the first three 1943 SSB, recovered after the war.

The 'Modified San Bartolomeo' project (SBM)

During the co-belligerency with the Allies, the Royal Navy decided to work on an improved model of the SSB to be implemented with US Navy collaboration, which had shown a particular interest in the initiative.

The head of Mariassalto technical Services at the San Vito di Taranto base, Captain engineer Sebastiano Battaglia, was put in charge of this project. Starting from a copy of the 'Siluro San Bartolomeo' drawings, engineer Battaglia began his work around mid-1944, making use of the invaluable experience of captured SLC operators who had been released at Regia Marina request, and pressed into Mariassalto service.

The new design was known as SBM (Modified San Bartolomeo) and introduced numerous innovations that 'Decima' veterans assessed as much improving craft efficiency and effectiveness. In particular, with other dimensions unchanged, the overall length of the SBM was increased to 8.30 metres, compared to 6.76 of the SSB, which accommodated a battery bank of almost tripled capacity, resulting in better range.

Another significant innovation was the cover – a robust wooden sliding hatch – over the 'cabin' that housed the two operators to better protect them from

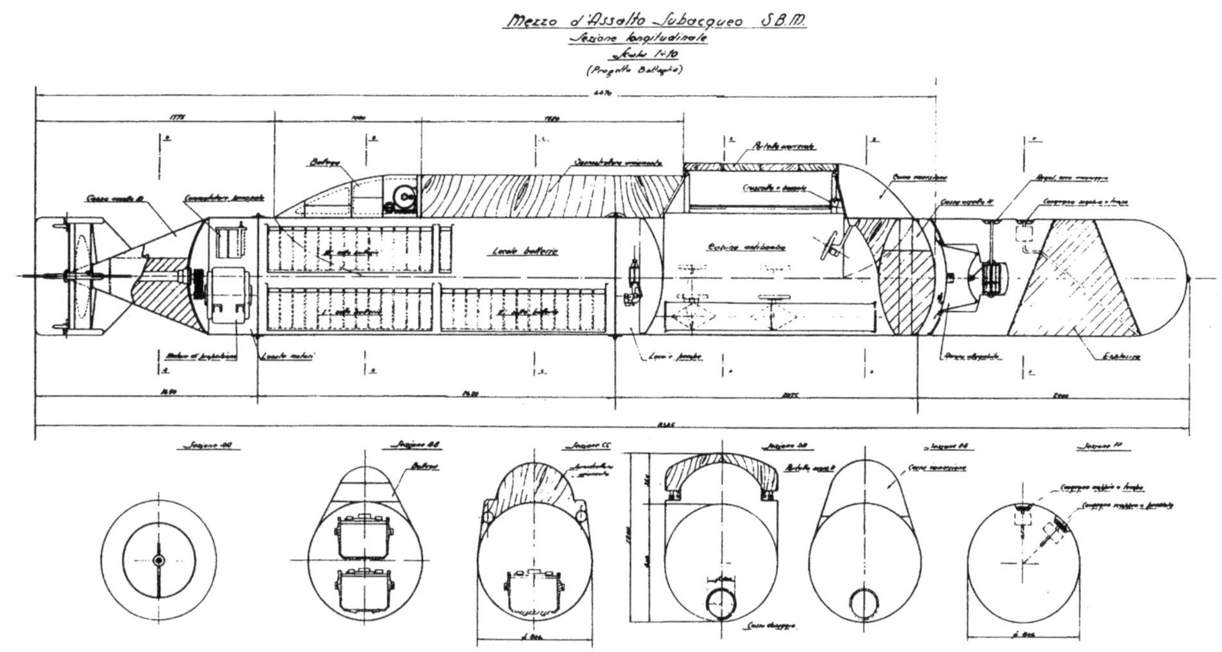

Project SBM (Modified San Bartolomeo) – Longitudinal and cross-sections. *(Courtesy of S Battaglia)*

the effect of underwater anti-personnel charges used by anchorage patrol boats. The steering position – now called the 'anti-bomb cabin' – was not watertight, and self-contained breathing apparatuses were still used; the operators, though, were less exposed.

The weight of the charge had been raised to 300–350kg of high explosive, and the detachable head that contained it was to have had a slight positive buoyancy; thus, equipping it with an anchor and an adjustable length steel mooring cable, it would have been possible to fix it under or as close as possible to the target, without necessarily having to attach it to its hull, an operation that had proven very long and difficult.

Artist's impression of an SBM: longitudinal section, and illustration of the detached explosive head, with its slight positive buoyancy. *(F Harrauer drawing)*

SSB copy made by the Argentinian Navy towards the end of the 1950s with Eugenio Wolk's assistance.

The final plans for the new self-propelled craft were completed in April 1945. It was believed that the prototype was to be built in the United States, but with the almost simultaneous end of the conflict in Europe support for the SBM fell way, and the project was shelved. On the other hand, the Allies had come into possession of a few 'SSB/Delta' craft formerly belonging to the republican Xª Mas, captured at San Andrea di Venezia. These craft, after a series of comparative tests with an SLC conducted with mixed Italian and Anglo-American personnel, were sent to Great Britain and United States, briefly accompanied by some Italian operators to train the Allies in their use.

As for the SBM project, according to engineer Battaglia, it was probably used as reference for the development of similar Italian craft after the end of the war.

CA type assault submarines

The first two CA, designed and built by Caproni in Milan-Taliedo, were delivered to the Regia Marina in April 1938. Classified as 'submarine ambush motorboats' they took the names *CA 1* and *CA 2* ('Caproni type A'), but were not added to the Navy List because their construction was to be kept absolutely secret. It was originally intended to employ a relevant number to constitute defensive barriers in certain coastal areas (outside the harbours of the gulfs of Genoa and Naples, in the Tuscan and Dodecanese archipelagos, etc) or in channels that opposing naval forces would have to pass, and possibly also for forcing enemy bases.

They displaced about 13 tons surfaced, had a two-man crew and carried two 450mm torpedoes; thanks to their modest size (maximum length 10 metres) they could be transported by railway like their type 'A' and 'B' forerunners of the First world War. The two prototypes carried out a long series of trials first in Venice, then in La Spezia from 1938 to 1940. While showing no serious deficiencies, these small submarines proved extremely delicate and barely manoeuvrable underwater, and a new design with significant changes to the original – including the addition of a third crewman – had already been put in train by 1939.

This project was followed by another with considerable changes and improvements, which led to the construction of the famous CB type 'pocket' submarines of greater displacement and superior performance. However, during the conflict in Mediterranean they produced only very modest results; on the other hand in the Black Sea – where,

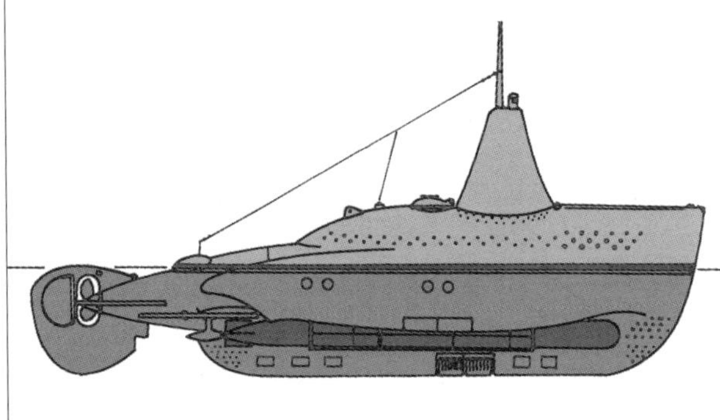

Caproni type 'A' mini-submarine (CA) – Original version

MAIN CHARACTERISTICS OF CA TYPE SUBMARINES

Series /year	*Displacement tons*	*Dimension metres*	*Propulsion system power hp*	*Speed kts*	*Armament mm*	*Range miles/kts*	*Notes*
1st series/1938							Torpedo version
CA 1	13.5	10x1.9x1.6	1x 60 hp MAN Diesel	6.2	2x450 torp	700/4	
CA 2	16.4		1x 25hp Marelli elec	5	(on racks)	57/3	
	(with torpedoes)						Dive depth 55m
1941–1941 Modification							
CA 1	12	as above	1x 21 Kw Marelli	7		70/2	'Gamma'
CA 2	14			6			transport
					8x100kg		modified version
					charges		Assault
					20 'bug' charges		submarines
2nd series/1943							Assault
CA 3	12.8	10.4x1.9x1.8	as above	as above	as above	as above	submarines
CA 4	14						Developed from
							the 1st series
							Dive depth 70m

Design and construction: Caproni, Taliedo (first unit delivered in April 1938, last in 1943).

Crew: 2 men in the Torpedo version, 3 in the Assault version.
CA 2 was further modified in Bordeaux after 1942.

NB The top figures refer to the surfaced characteristics; below the line to the submerged characteristics.

during the siege of the Russian naval base in Sevastopol, they found operational conditions ideal for their characteristics – the results were more significant.

After the completion of the CB, in 1940 the two CA ceased all activity, having fulfilled their task as experimental units. The two small craft were hauled out on the La Spezia submarine quay and were almost abandoned for a long time.

After the first successes of the assault craft, the defences of British Mediterranean bases were noticeably enhanced, with patrol boats continuously under way at the entrances, dropping anti-personnel depth charges at frequent intervals and constantly illuminating with searchlights the areas around boom and net defences. The underwater charges proved fatal to several SLC operators, but even when their craft were not damaged, they were subjected to remarkable physical strain that, when added to the discomfort of using breathing apparatus, sometimes made them unable to react promptly and cope with those significant difficulties inherent in the kind of missions they were meant to perform.

Although the use of 'Gamma' divers was promising, their chances were still limited both because of the small power of the charges they could carry, their absolute vulnerability to the action of defence depth charges, and limited range of action.

Commander Angelo Belloni, the ingenious inventor of many improvements to underwater equipment, in collaboration with Lieutenant Eugenio Wolk, creator and leader of the 'Gamma' diver unit of the 'Decima', proposed the idea of an underwater craft big enough to accommodate a number of 'Gamma' with their charges, yet smaller than a standard submarine, so able to escape modern underwater surveillance systems and penetrate a harbour with relative ease. The craft would have sheltered the operators from depth charge blast and if necessary also be able to tow them underwater holding on to special handles.

In point of fact, the underwater operators involved with this particular type of 'approacher' differed from the 'Gamma', as they were expected to operate mainly underwater whereas the latter were only equipped with a lighter and short-range self-contained breathing apparatus, so worked mainly on the surface, diving only if forced by enemy vigilance, or to place the charges in contact with the target hull. In particular, divers transported by the 'mini-submarine' imagined by commander Belloni, would first of all have assisted the craft to overcome the defensive barriers, then when it lay on the bottom near the targets, the divers would attack using the big charges it transported, possibly making several submarine-to-target journeys, and moving within the harbour towed by the craft, if the distances from ship to ship were too great. At the end of the action, they would again assist the craft in passing the barriers, finally escaping from the target harbour with the craft itself.

The size of this craft had necessarily to be very limited, which would have certainly restricted the range and seaworthiness. Given the considerable distance between the Italian bases and the harbours to be attacked, this craft needed its own 'approacher', that is another, larger, craft with better range and seaworthiness, capable of transporting it close to the bases to be penetrated, and then left free to act and wait for its return. These assumptions meant that the 'approacher' could not be a surface ship, but had to be another suitably equipped submarine.

To refine this mini-submarine assault divers model, Decima's attention was first directed at the small 36/45-ton CB type 'pocket' subs, armed with torpedoes. The first experiments, intended to demonstrate the theory that a man in a diver's outfit could be towed underwater without excessive discomfort up to a speed around 8 knots, were in fact completely unofficial, due to agreements between Lieutenant Wolk of the 'Decima' and Sub-Lieutenant Eugenio Massano of the CB Squadron in La Spezia.

The official request to let the 'Xª Mas' have a CB for a series of trials to be performed off La Spezia was rejected: they were instead assigned the two decommissioned CA in September 1941. The two small submarines, worn out by two years of tests and one out of commission, were ordered to be restored and suitably modified once more for experimental service. It was expected that if the tests ended satisfactorily, it would then be possible to define the methods of employment and the characteristics of the new craft to be built specifically for this particular 'diver-carrier' function.

As a result, the two CA were transferred by rail to Caproni of Milano-Taliedo to be overhauled and suitably modified for the new job. In November 1941 *CA 2* completed the initial modification work, which included: taking out the surface propulsion diesel engine, removing the periscope, elimination of the conning tower, and replacement of the torpedoes with 8 removable depth charges of 10kg each. A new electric motor with increased capacity batteries combined with significantly reduced drag resulting from the elimination of superstructure and periscope, produced substantial increases in both range and underwater speed.

Towards the end of the same month the *CA 2* was transferred to Lake Iseo where, in a small base established at the 'Caproni Aeronautica Bergamasca' (CAB) factory in Montecollino, it was to perform the trials and begin crew training. The tests took place between November 1941 and February 1942 with satisfactory results despite the particularly intense winter weather

The modified *CA 2* under way on Lake Iseo; and lifted on a chain hoist at the local workshop on 27 December 1942.

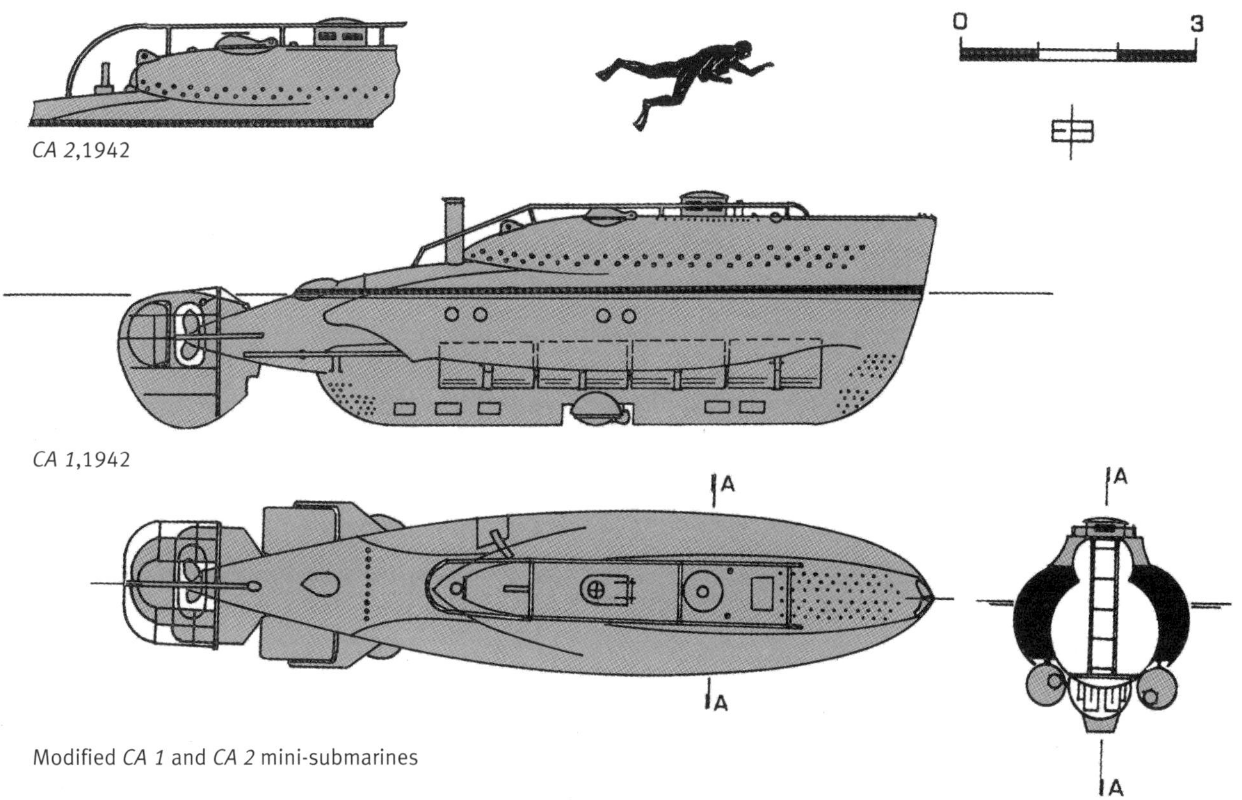

Modified *CA 1* and *CA 2* mini-submarines

in that area. During the tests a dive depth of 47 metres was reached, and data was collected on performance and shortcomings (unfortunately still noteworthy) of the craft as modified for the new task. The boat was therefore returned to Milan for some further alteration work and fitting a diver's lock-out chamber of the original, simpler 'Belloni tub' design which, for various reasons, did not meet the purpose.

At the same time, *CA 1* was transferred from Milan to the Lake Iseo base where some works were completed, and the boat prepared for testing. During this work a failure in the water distribution tank, under maintenance at the time, sank the craft near the battery charging barge in 4 metres of water. Promptly raised, it was put back into service but, due to the delay cause by the accident, the tests in the lake lasted until early summer 1942; at that point the sub was transferred to the La Spezia headquarters of the X^{a} Flottiglia Mas.

The long testing period prompted a belief that the two craft, while generally meeting to the purpose for which they had been adapted, had not achieved the high performance required, being still too complicated and difficult to manoeuvre. Depth keeping forced the crew to expend a considerable amount of energy (mainly due to lack of bow diving planes) and, at low speeds, to continuous manoeuvring of the trim tanks. Moreover, the electric pumps were too noisy, and their replacement with hand-operated ones was recommended. This replacement was then carried out on *CA 2* during the last changes at Bordeaux in 1942–1943.

Finally, the arrangement of the charges under the double bottoms had proved to be impractical, making it difficult for the divers to unhook them from the submarine when it was resting on the bottom, which was necessary due to the excessive difficulty of keeping the craft stationary at a constant depth.

These defects, and a study of the modifications required, prompted a project for a second series of boats (*CA 3* and *CA 4*). Ordered from Caproni, development began after experiments with a 'carrier' submarine and *CA 2* in Bordeaux towards the end of 1942.

Given the particular characteristics of the CA, it was decided not to employ them immediately in the Mediterranean, where the effective harbour defences would have easily stopped these still imperfect craft in their first actions, and where there was a sufficient availability of SLC. Instead, the chosen theatre of operations was the Atlantic, where no attack by assault craft had yet been carried out. In fact, by the summer of 1942 the defences of the Mediterranean naval bases had reached an efficiency that only proven craft could face. The CA could only operate in the Mediterranean

Iseo Lake, 1942: Commander Borghese aboard *CA 2*. The conversion of the CA to 'Gamma' diver carriers was an original and especially interesting project for Decima Mas that, moreover, would lead to remarkable developments after the war.

CA 2 converted to assault craft during tests on Lake Iseo in 1942.

CA 2 aboard the oceangoing submarine *Leonardo da Vinci* moored at Bordeaux in September 1942.

after testing in seas where they could prove themselves without excessive risks.

Furthermore, the CA was a 'multiple shot' weapon, and even a single craft, with its numerous charges, had the capacity to devastate an enemy base; this was something for which several SLC would have been necessary, while in 1942 the 'approacher' submarines could not carry more than three.

At that time, one or two actions with *CA 1* and *CA 2* in the Atlantic would have cast a long shadow, with psychological and strategic effects of considerable importance. The Atlantic harbours would no longer have been considered safe, with the Allies forced to organise defences against assault craft almost from scratch. This would have required remarkable effort with significant repercussions, given that it would absorb huge quantities of men and resources, distracting them from other important tasks.

According to the original plans, there would have been two operations: the first with a CA, carried by an Italian ocean-going submarine, and the next with the other craft 'approached' by a German U-boat, probably of Type IX.

However, the idea was not enthusiastically received by the German Navy Command whom the Italian Navy first addressed to obtain the assignment of a submarine, and the necessary information on the Atlantic, African and United States harbours in order to study possible operations in detail. The Germans replied that they could not assign any submarine of theirs to this activity, all units being very busy in the oceanic convoy war, and Admiral Dönitz would not accept any diversions from this fundamental task. It was therefore decided to postpone the second operation and operate with only one CA using an Italian submarine for its transport. The mission with the second unit would have been carried out later, again with Italian craft. However, the Germans agreed to share all their information about enemy Atlantic harbours.

As already mentioned, the CA would have to be transported by another submarine up to the vicinity of the target harbour and would then wait for its recovery after the action, an important aspect of the operational rationale. It was therefore a matter of experimenting with the unusual task of transporting a submarine, however small, by another submarine, in order to establish the limits and procedures.

Since the first theatre of CA action would have been the Atlantic, for the trials it was decided to use one of the Italian ocean-going submarines based in Bordeaux (Betasom), whence the planned operations was to have begun. This would avoid the passage of the Straits of Gibraltar, which had been carried out several times by all Italian Atlantic submarines involved, but always involved very high risk – further increased by the foreseeable manoeuvrability limitations of the submarine with a CA on the deck.

Therefore, at the beginning of July 1942 the *CA 2* with the 'Decima' staff destined to to service it was sent by rail to Bordeaux. One of the submarines available at that time in Betasom was chosen as an 'approacher' for the experiments, since it was due a normal schedule of works. On 20 July the submarine *Leonardo Da Vinci* – favoured over the *Archimede* both for structural reasons and better seaworthiness, higher speed, longer range and higher reserve of buoyancy – began conversion work at the local Submarine Workshop directed by Major Giulio Fenu. Suitably modified, the *Da Vinci* (see 'Approacher' submarines on page 183) with the *CA 2* on deck left Bordeaux in the afternoon of 9 September heading for Le Verdon, from where it put to sea the following morning under German escort to carry out the first offshore experiments.

After the planned dive for trim adjustment, the *Da Vinci*, under command of Lieutenant Gianfranco Gazzana Priaroggia, dived again to release the special craft commanded by Sub-Lieutenant Eugenio Massano. After the release, the submarine surfaced and returned to Bordeaux that same evening, with the CA in tow. During this first test, on its release underwater the craft had collided with the *Da Vinci*'s conning tower, producing various dents at the height of the radio direction finder; the CA however, had not suffered serious damage.

After the necessary repairs the *Da Vinci* left Bordeaux again on the morning of the 13th, still with the special craft aboard, for a new 'release' trial. This second experiment gave unsatisfactory results again due to a strong current in the area, and the *Da Vinci* reported slight damage to the left handrail in collision with the CA.

That same evening the submarine returned to Bordeaux with the craft under tow, putting to sea again on the morning of the 15th for more trials with the *CA 2*. During the morning a trouble-free 'release' was achieved, and in the early afternoon recovery of the craft at sea was also attempted, again successfully. In the evening the submarine returned to Bordeaux, with the *CA 2* aboard this time.

More trials were carried out in the following days to test submarine manoeuvrability in a dive with the CA on deck. During these tests however the *CA 2* sustained some damage from rough seas off La Pallice. On the 23rd the submarine returned to Bordeaux, the CA and related materials were landed, and the *Da Vinci* reverted to operational conditions to resume its normal activity in the Atlantic.

The series of tests was considered completed with

CA 2 found by the Allies in Bordeaux at the end of the war. The charge housings had been moved over the side dive tanks during the most recent modifications at Betasom in 1943.

sufficiently satisfactory outcome. The 'release' and recovery experiments with the craft were carried out according to procedures that had been gradually refined. The submarine, after the trim set up dive with the CA on board, surfaced again; the securing was then removed, so the special craft was held back by the 'clamps' only. The submarine then went into a stationary dive to about 12 metres and heaved-to. The holding clamps were then loosened from inside the submarine and the CA 'took off' towards the surface.

The 'approacher' submarine – immediately nicknamed the 'kangaroo' because the CA nestled in a pocket similar to a pouch – emerged in turn nearby and, in the first trials, took the special craft in tow to return to harbour. To recover the craft, the 'kangaroo' was brought to periscope depth and the engines stopped; the CA manoeuvred on the surface to get in line with its lodging ahead of the tower casing, and then the submarine, slowly venting its tanks, began to rise horizontally towards the surface under the craft, which fitted snugly into its 'pouch', being drained by its complete emergence as the submarine surfaced.

The 'release' tests were carried out with the craft crew on board; equipped with underwater breathing apparatus, they first removed the securings with the *Da Vinci* half-surfaced, and entered the CA from the upper hatch awash. It was planned to subsequently carry out all these operations not with the submarine awash, but completely submerged at appropriate depth.

The positive outcome of the tests confirmed the hopes X^a^ Mas harboured about the actual action possibilities of these craft. The *Da Vinci*, while manoeuvring under water with certain difficulties due to the *CA 2* lashed down on the deck, proved to be suitable for transport and to be able to perform it without too many risks. However, the damage suffered by the *CA 2* because of the rough sea showed once again how delicate these craft were; furthermore, some mechanical failures that occurred during sea trials revealed that the small subs were not yet perfectly tuned and therefore, for the moment, they were unfit to undertake risky missions whose outcome, based essentially on the surprise factor, would have been compromised by a failure of the assault craft.

Given that by September 1942 collecting intelligence on Atlantic harbours was still in its early stages, it was decided to delay the planned missions until the two new improved type CA (ordered from Caproni in the meantime) were ready for use, or when *CA 1* and *CA 2* reached such a level of operational safety as to offer a good chance of success.

After the experiments with the *Da Vinci*, the *CA 2* in Bordeaux and the *CA 1* in La Spezia continued the trials and crew training sessions. In the late 1942 to early 1943 timeframe *CA 2* was subjected to further modification work in Bordeaux including, amongst other things, the arrangement of the charges above double bottoms like the second series units. In that circumstance it would seem that the charges were reduced to four of 200kg each instead of eight of 100kg.

Meanwhile the building of *CA 3* and *CA 4* at Caproni in Milan proceeded slowly because of changes that were continuously made to the project, based on experience gained with the first two 'pocket' subs. The second series showed remarkable improvements compared to the first, such as: greater structural strength to allow a deeper operating depth and to reduce the risk of sea damage during transportation; increased rudder surface area and the arrangement of two bow planes for better manoeuvrability; better hydrodynamics of the hull, stretched about 40cm. The two boats were delivered to the Navy in January 1943 and were transferred to La Spezia shortly thereafter for sea trials and to start training.

While the craft were being prepared, X^a^ Mas worked out plans for future operations with the CA, based on intelligence received from the German and Italian information services and from the German Submarine Command. Assuming that the most complete surprise would be achieved, hopes were high for a major success.

One of these missions was a scheme to penetrate New York harbour: the 'kangaroo' (the *Da Vinci* had unfortunately been lost meanwhile and another submarine would have been chosen) would carry the CA up to the mouth of the Hudson, where it would release the craft that would run submerged up the river to the harbour. The return to the 'kangaroo' after the attack would have been very problematic indeed, and the loss of the mini-submarine, which still had to scuttle itself in case of difficulty, appeared almost certain.

Preservation of the secrets of its characteristics and operating methods was therefore of utmost importance, so as not to prejudice subsequent actions by the other CA. The psychological effect on the Americans – who had no direct experience of the war at home – would have produced enormous consequences in the strategic and logistic field. The establishment of extensive surveillance services and the increase in the laying of nets, booms, etc would have imposed a heavy

CA 3 and *CA 4*, 1943

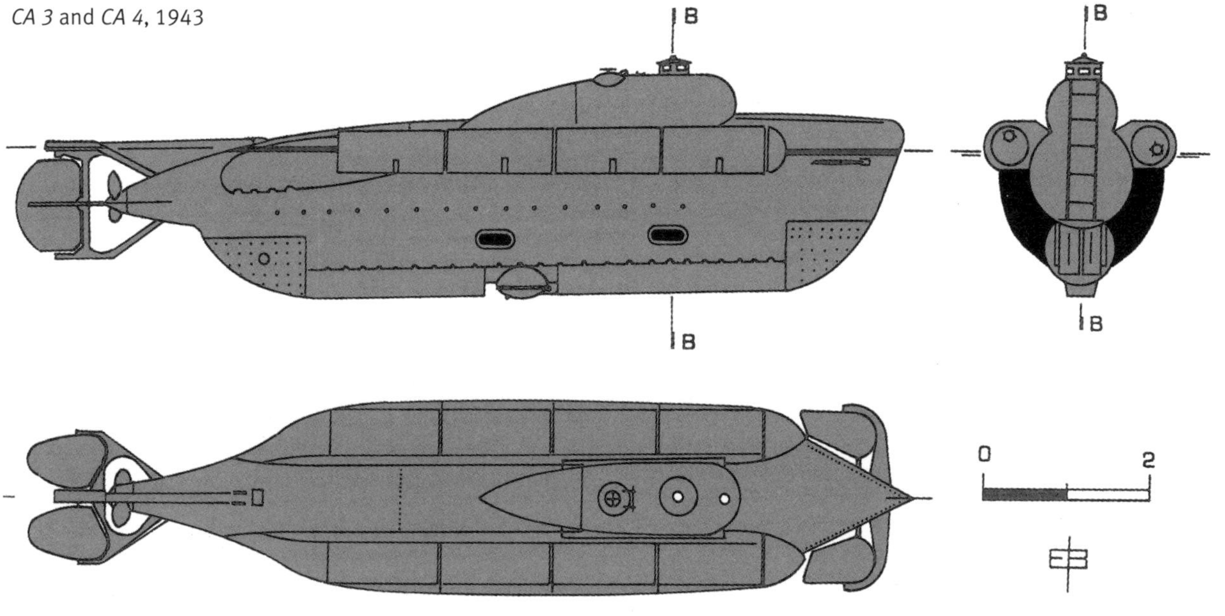

burden – certainly of much greater significance than any tactical success like the sinking or serious damaging of a few laden merchant ships, or even new warships under construction in the Brooklyn Navy Yard.

A second CA foray was planned against the important naval base at Freetown on the West African coast where many warships and merchantmen were constantly present. It would appear that the action against New York was to have been the first and was slated for December 1943; however, given the accumulation of delays in the preparation of the craft and training, it is unlikely that this date could have been achieved. The proclamation of the armistice on 8 September 1943 blocked all CA activities; with the occupation of the Italian bases in Northern Italy and in Betasom by the Germans, the four craft under preparation (*CA 1*, *CA 3* and *CA 4* in La Spezia, *CA 2* in Bordeaux) fell into their hands. It would seem that, of the three boats in La Spezia, one was transported to Germany, perhaps to attempt one of the planned actions with German resources, or simply to study the capabilities of the craft. However, nothing came of it, and only the republican X[a] Mas, on the initiative of commander Belloni himself, undertook a modest training programme with the units present in La Spezia. The two CA remaining in Italy were lost from unknown causes (perhaps sunk at the end of the conflict, or destroyed by air raid). One unit (*CA 2*) was found unserviceable in Bordeaux at the seizure of that base by the Allies, and scrapped afterwards.

It had been planned to prepare a mobile base for the CA through the conversion of the pontoon *GM 225* (ex-*Apuano*) that had been towed from Rome, where it was anchored on the Tiber river under Italian Fascist Youth Academy control, to La Spezia in April 1942. The pontoon, transformed into a floating dock, could accommodate two of the craft and had been equipped with air and battery charging stations and equipment for minor repairs. Work on *GM 225* was unfinished at the armistice and the pontoon was captured by the Germans who assigned it to a different task.

The course of the war prevented the CA from seeing action, but the idea of a small assault submarine for transporting 'Gamma' divers was undoubtedly one of the best developments – alongside the SLC – in the field of Italian underwater assault craft. The concept was actually revived and developed by many navies in post-war years. Moreover, the British 'X-craft', although developed independently, were craft of quite similar characteristics that operated with success in 1944–1945.

PROTOTYPES, EXPERIMENTAL CRAFT AND PROJECTS

'Minisini-Ferretti' type assault mini-submarines

The development of the small *SA 1* 'pocket' submarine began at the end of 1940 and was designed and built by Lieutenant General of Naval Weapons Corps Eugenio Minisini. At that time he was director of the Baia (Pozzuoli) Torpedo Workshop and well-known for having created, amongst other inventions, the ingenious 'lateral impulse' torpedo launcher that bore his name and was used on all Mas built after the 1930s and later on motor torpedo boats up to and well beyond the end of the Second World War.

It was a small unit with a displacement of 13 tons, characterised by a unique 350hp four-stroke Isotta-Fraschini Asso engine modified to be fuelled by oxygen – stored in cylinders – and alcohol. This power source had been devised in 1936 by Professor Pericle Ferretti as a step towards further developments of much greater power, which in the end proved unattainable, even though that first, small 'closed cycle' engine prototype had passed the bench tests.[1]

SA 1, completed by the end of 1941 and followed the following year by the similar *SA 2*, was able to develop an underwater speed of 15 knots for two hours.

Characterised by two tractor, coaxial contra-rotating bow propellers, and armed with two 450mm torpedoes at the stern, the 'Minisini-Ferretti' (so defined in a Supermarina note to the Prime Minister on 12 March 1942) would have been transported on the stern of a destroyer and launched into open water to make a high-speed submerged attack on an enemy naval fleet.

Subjected to numerous trials, the two small boats naturally required continuous modifications. Finally, at the beginning of 1943 they were superseded by a different and more evolved project: the *SA 3*, this time of conventional layout, equipped with a 'single engine' (as ever, designed by Ferretti) of a different type, and capable of propelling the submarine at 20 knots.

At the time of the armistice *SA 1* and *SA 2*, now abandoned, were destroyed. Their wrecks, however, were recovered by the Americans, and immediately transferred to the US for study purposes, together with

Rare picture of an SA type mini-submarine. *(Courtesy of E Cernuschi)*

Another image of the same craft in previous picture. *(Courtesy of E Cernuschi)*

their inventor. However, the *SA 3*, which was still very far from completion, was broken up instead. After the conflict the development of its single engine continued under a joint Italian-American programme aimed at producing a 30-ton mini-submarine; it was finally abandoned in 1957.

'Sassaroli' (fast) assault submarine

This was an experimental craft whose construction took place in 1944–1945. Designed by engineer Licio Sassaroli[2], the prototype was laid down at SIAI-Marchetti of Sesto Calende (Varese) in the spring of 1944 on behalf of X^{a} Mas. At the end of the conflict the hull was almost complete, while the engine was still on the test bench. The bare hull was subsequently transported to La Spezia, but its outfitting does not appear to have continued.

The 'Sassaroli' was a small and fast midget submarine, capable of operating up to a maximum depth of about 30 metres. The one-man crew was equipped with an oxygen breathing apparatus, since he had to work in a cramped environment in the presence of carbon dioxide. The attack would be made using a 450mm reduced torpedo hanging under the keel, with the tower just breaking the surface occasionally for

1. There have been many attempts throughout the world since the beginning of the 1940s to develop a single source of power that could propel submarines both on the surface and submerged, but 'closed cycle' propulsion has only been successfully adopted relatively recently in conventional submarines.
2. Licio Sassaroli was aboard Italian cruiser *Pola* sunk in 1941 at Cape Matapan and was taken prisoner; nevertheless he was allowed to return to Italy from India in 1943 for health reasons.

Longitudinal section of 'Sassaroli' mini-submarine project.

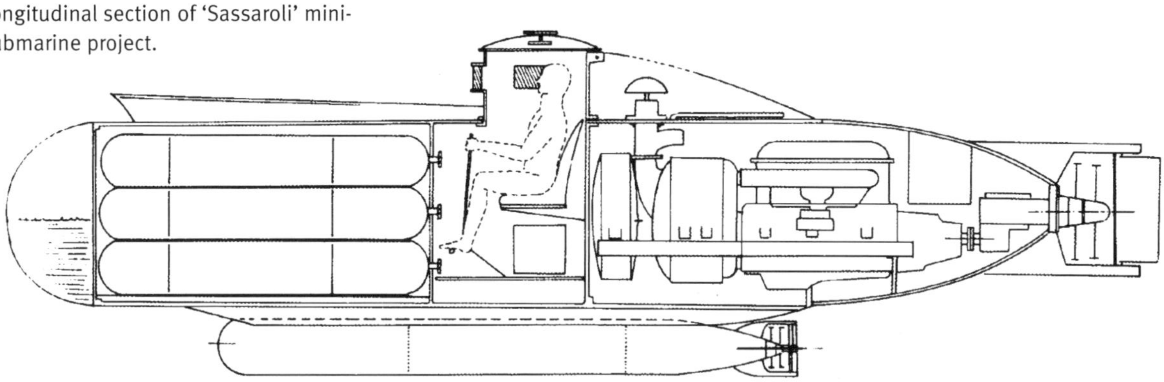

aiming purposes (a manoeuvre called 'porpoising'). After the launch, it planned to escape submerged at high speed. On the surface this small submarine should have been able to move at 18–20 knots, while awash or dived it was expected that the speed could reach 28–30 knots with a 'close cycle' operating endurance of a couple of hours.

The project was proposed to commanders Borghese and Arillo, and clearance to proceed was obtained. The following technical description is based on documents and a drawing copied from a sketch that engineer Sassaroli himself provided. The prototype was laid down in Sesto Calende and with the collaboration of engineer Gorla and some SIAI technicians, the main features were defined as reported below:

Hull

Cylindrical shape with rounded ends: 1.30m diameter, length overall about 8m. Maximum working depth: 30m. Monocoque construction in four layers of aeronautical plywood, thickness 13-15mm, formed on a series of wooden ring frames. Adhesive used: black Kaurit. No nails or screws. A sturdy external sheathing tightened the whole hull, that resulted in a particularly robust and solid structure that resounded like a bell. The external keel was in cast iron, divided into three sections; it represented the stabilising ballast and its weight was calculated to ensure a residual positive buoyancy at full load of about 200kg.

The hull was completed:

- at the bow, by a hemispherical tank to compensate for the progressive lightening due to the consumption of petrol and oxygen, and a pair of horizontal semi-fixed planes operated from the control cabin with a wheel;
- at the stern, by a steel body that carried the propulsion system with two contra-rotating propellers, and the rear controls with one steering and two depth rudders;
- at the pilot's cockpit, placed about centrally, there was a tower (with upper access hatch) equipped with three 15x20cm windows, one on the front and two on the sides. The turret was streamlined at the bow by a fairing that served as a breakwater when surfaced, and towards the stern by a second that contained the air intake and the exhaust of the propulsion system during surface operations.

Propulsion system

- Alfa Romeo 1001-B petrol engine rated 200 HP at 1500rpm;
- oxygen mixer on the intake manifold during closed circuit operation;
- heat exchanger for exhaust gas cooling;
- collection of condensation from exhaust gases and expulsion to the sea by mechanical pump;
- compressor group for venting outside the operating fluid of the engine compartment, so as to preserve the atmospheric pressure inside. The discharge to the sea occurred through a perforated tube placed on the back of the craft. Given that after a few minutes of closed circuit running the atmosphere in the cabin consisted essentially of CO_2, the gases were diluted in water, very quickly rendering the trail visible from the surface negligible;
- fuel tank of about 300 litres capacity which ensured an endurance of approximately 10 hours of movement.

The engine drew directly from the engine room. The exhaust gases were sent to the heat exchanger which lowered the temperature to about 25–30 degrees and at the same time freed them from condensation.

The engine compartment was in communication with the outside through a small valve with mushroom closure, placed inside the rear fairing of the tower.

The exhaust gas exchanger was connected to a diverter device at the output that communicated with the outside through a valve similar to the suction one, or with the engine compartment.

In surface navigation the two valves were open and then the engine aspirated and discharged to the outside.

The transition to diving operation occurred by closing the two small valves, deflecting the drain in the engine compartment and injecting oxygen into the special mixer placed on the intake manifold. Being a fuel-injection engine, mixture dosage was independent of density of the working fluid that passed through suction, but depended exclusively on the position of the throttle to adjust the engine speed.

Oxygen reserve

The fuel reserve was contained in seven cylinders placed in the bow compartment.

The oxygen capacity allowed closed-cycle operation for about two hours at full speed.

As already mentioned, by the end of the conflict only the hull was finished: its wooden structures were then easily destroyed.

ASSAULT DIVERS (FROGMEN AND 'GAMMA')

This speciality of X Flotilla Mas underwater operators originated from the experiments conducted within the 1st Submarines Group in La Spezia in 1935, for the exit from 'H' class submarines of divers equipped with self-contained breathing apparatus, and the training of bottom-walkers (see page 24) that carried a charge (then called a bomb) on their shoulders, to be applied to the hull of anchored enemy units.

'ARO mod. 49/bis' closed-circuit oxygen rebreather.

Diver Giuseppe Guglielmo ready for a training dive in the small San Leopoldo harbour in the Naval Academy complex, where the Diver School was located.

Such experiments, conducted by divers equipped with 'autonomous diving suits' ('Belloni hood', 'Davis' or 'Dräger' rebreathers), were part of a larger programme that involved the small and manoeuvrable 'H' submarines in precision underwater passages inside harbours covering long distances slithering on the bottom as quietly as possible.

The divers were also intended to lead and assist the submarine in approaching and overcoming possible obstructions; to this purpose, underwater navigation tests had been carried out in shallow waters with a diver in the tower, or placed on a seat at the bow and connected by telephone with the manoeuvring room.[1] Once close to the target (a few tens of metres) the submarine had to rest on the bottom and start exit

1. In the course of the conflict a similar technique was used more than once employing a diver or a 'Gamma' as 'relay' to guide movements of 'approaching' submarines within enemy bases (Algiers roadstead etc).

A group of divers in training.

operations of the 'autonomous divers' (*ie* equipped with self-contained breathing apparatus not connected to the boat or surface). These were to carry out the actual attack on enemy ships at anchor with suitable clockwork fused explosive charges after approaching the targets by 'walking' on the bottom.

The results of the experiments were deemed valid and encouraging as regards the submarine approach manoeuvres;[2] but not for the divers, whose progress on the bottom turned out to be very tiring, slow (about 500 metres in an hour) and inaccurate – the first portable underwater compasses with which they were equipped were unreliable, and visibility of the compass itself was strongly limited by clouding of the water as the bottom mud was churned up; and finally, the performance of the breathing apparatus then in use was very limiting. For these reasons, and because of the decline in international tension following the conclusion of the Ethiopian campaign, the idea of 'autonomous divers' and 'walkers' was abandoned.

When the experimental activity around the assault craft prototypes was resumed in 1938, underwater training was mainly oriented to the formation of 'self-propelled' craft operators, and continued so until the outbreak of war. But with the creation of the 'Decima' diver school, installed at the Naval Academy in the summer of 1940, the idea of the 'walkers' was revived and developed on the initiative of its director, first commander Giulio Belloni, then Lieutenant Eugenio Wolk.

Meanwhile the technical means (self-contained breathing apparatus, clothing and other diving technology) had greatly improved and shortly afterwards a happy inspiration by commander Wolk produced a new speciality. They were known as 'Guastatori' (military engineers, although 'sappers' might be the best English equivalent), from which derived the identification letter 'G', or 'Gamma' in the Greek-based phonetic alphabet of the time.

They were no longer operators that had to approach by walking on the bottom with weighted boots – or moving in 'heavy' trim as Belloni had imagined them – but were swimmers that moved in a 'light' trim, mainly on the surface, using special 'flippers' on the feet[3] and

2. The experimental techniques tried out in those years began with the use of heavy chain pendants dragging on the bottom during the approach phase with the submarine in light bow-down trim brushing against the seabed. These techniques formed the basis of those used by 'approacher' submarines in many missions conducted during the Second World War.

3. The 'flippers' were already available on the diving equipment market at that time. As early as January 1941 the famous German magazine *Signal* published an extensive report showing their use by sport divers in the Caribbean.

A 'Gamma' fixing the charge to the target's bilge keel in a drawing by Eugenio Wolk.

An assault diver returning from an exercise.

'Gamma' operators in training.

Underwater operator with Pirelli 'G 50' rebreather and heavy cloth 'Belloni suit'.

able to dive to place the charges they were equipped with. Explosive devices made for this purpose (called 'bedbugs', 'small trunks' etc) were specially designed for use against merchant ships.

The first action conducted by 'Gamma' (12 operators) was an attack against merchant shipping at anchor in the bay of Gibraltar on 14 July 1942, operating from the secret base of Villa Carmela, that resulted in four heavily damaged steamships.

After that the activity of the 'Gamma' had no restrictions and their techniques and their equipment gradually improved. Particular care was taken in recruitment and training, choosing subjects of outstanding physical strength, possibly already expert competitive swimmers, and subjecting them to a strict selection. The divers in general, after passing a thorough medical examination for the assessment of essential physical characteristics, were first trained in the use of self-contained breathing apparatus, then to the execution of underwater work on a course known as 'accelerated'. Only a few, the best, continued training to be dedicated assault divers with a specific course lasting about 10 months.

Of those 'Gamma' trained in Livorno, only fifty were ever used in action, sinking or heavily damaging a dozen merchant ships of over 30,000 register tons. Not all operations were fortunate and sometimes men,

Diver at wreck recovery work in the early post-war period.

despite having been chosen with the greatest care, succumbed to the effort – often at superhuman levels – and to the tension inherent in an individual action that could only be overcome with exceptional strength of character.

From the middle of 1942 the 'Gamma' were recruited not only amongst Regia Marina personnel, but also from those of proven ability from other services. The most skilled and fortunate of these was Milmart (the coastal artillery of the Voluntary Militia for National Security: MVSN) Lieutenant Luigi Ferraro who was awarded the Gold Medal of Military Valour for his individual actions successfully conducted in the harbours of Iskenderun and Mersin in July–August 1943.

For their operations, the 'Gamma' used different types of 'approachers': from the submarine to the specially adapted MTSM, and finally small specifically designed 'MT – Gamma' motorboats. The essential simplicity of their equipment and the considerable operational flexibility that distinguished the 'Gamma' allowed their use also from advanced bases that did not have any specialist technical equipment. Distance from the targets – which had to be as short as possible – was especially important, as was absolute secrecy (for example, Villa Carmela on the Spanish side of the Gibraltar harbour).

Republican Xa Mas diver in training.

A diver at underwater work in the early post-war period.

Two pictures of the motorised raft for 'Gamma' tactical transport; conceived by Eugenio Wolk and nicknamed 'turkey', it was built in a few examples for the republican X Mas.

The limitation represented by the impossibility of making long sorties fairly quickly carrying large explosive charges[4] was to have been overcome by the use of craft like the 'R' light motorboats (although these did not become operational) or other similar means for the tactical transport of the 'Gamma' on short and medium distances. At the request of the assault craft headquarters, CABI designed a special 'diver towing' raft equipped with accumulator batteries which fed a 0.25hp electric motor.

Although the tests conducted were encouraging, this small craft did not become operational before the end of the conflict. Similarly, an inflatable boat (similar to later 'rafts') equipped with a small, also inflatable screen, designed by commander Wolk for the 'Gamma' had only limited use. Nicknamed the 'turkey', it could carry two or three operators and, in addition to the normal paddles, also had a small and silent outboard motor for propulsion. Moreover, another initiative which ran out of time before the war ended was the operational use of the small CA type assault submarines that in practice were 'approachers' for the 'Gamma', who were assigned the unusual role of assisting the midget submarine in overcoming the defences and to help connect its large charges to the targets.

It must be remembered that, until the spring of 1942, at the Livorno Divers School the 'N' (Swimmers) operators of the eponymous Battalion belonging to the 'San Marco' Regiment of the Regia Marina were trained together with the 'Gamma'. Their training was similar, although that of the 'N' was more focused on sabotage and coastal incursion activities. Later, the 'N' operators merged with 'P' (Paratroopers) operators giving birth to the 'NP' unit of the 'San Marco' and were trained at the parachuting school of the Regia Aeronautica in Tarquinia.

Republican X Mas assault divers towed by an electric self-propelled raft during training. *(A Molinari collection)*

Like the X^{a} Flotilla Mas the 'NP' units came under the orders of Mas Headquarters (Generalmas), up to the armistice. Subsequently the 'NP' units reconstituted in the South continued to be part of the 'San Marco' Regiment; in the North, the 'NP' became part of X^{a} Mas.

The current Italian Navy 'Intruders' trace their origins above all to this particular speciality, and that of the 'Divers' is largely derived from the 'Gamma'.

4. Special watertight rubber containers (known as a 'coop') were produced in the last period of the conflict: they had neutral buoyancy, and could be towed by the operators easily enough. Their capacity was about 50kg, and they could be employed in addition to that of 'small trunks', 'bedbugs' etc that the 'Gamma' generally carried hanging from the belt.

'APPROACHER' CRAFT

Assault craft of any kind, either surface or underwater, shared the common weakness of short range. This required that they be transported somehow to the immediate vicinity of the target to be attacked. Hence the birth of the so-called *avvicinatori*, translating as 'approachers', which could be one or more different types, acting in succession, depending on the circumstances, distance to cover and type of craft to be carried.[1] These were both existing craft suitably converted or adapted each time (surface ships, submarines, trucks, etc) and also specially designed and manufactured craft like the MTL, etc.

Sometimes standard naval units were used, generally of light displacement such as torpedo boats and Mas, which did not require special modification to provide towing, support and assistance to the assault craft right up to the vicinity the target.

CONVERTED SHIPS

Warships adapted for use

In the Great War, for the first operations of Italian assault craft ('jumping' boats and the *Mignatta* self-propelled torpedo), standard coastal torpedo boats and Mas with electric motors for silent motion were used as 'approachers'. Generally, the torpedo boats towed the Mas, which in turn towed the assault craft for most of the route from starting point to target area. Then the Mas took the assault craft for the last phase of the 'approach', to the immediate vicinity of the external boom defences of the enemy base to be penetrated (which in the actions carried out in 1918 was always Pola). The torpedo boats belonged to the 'PN' and 'OS' types of about 150 tons, and the Mas to the 'Orlando 12 tons' – 1st series type (*Mas 95* and *96*).

Throughout the many actions conducted by Italian assault craft between 1940 and 1945, the conventional surface units used for their approach were destroyers, the scout *Diana* and some Mas.

1. A typical example of a 'chain' of approacher craft was represented by the CA type mini-submarines that had to be transported close to the target harbour by a suitably converted standard submarine and then, in turn, acted as 'approachers' for the 'Gamma' embarked, while at the same time carrying the related offensive charges close to the targets.

Destroyers *Quintino Sella* and *Francesco Crispi*

Members of the *Sella* class (4 units of about 1480 tons commissioned in 1926–1927), in early 1941 they were equipped with davits and crutches for the transportation and launching of 6 MT light explosive motor boats each. These fittings were placed amidships, three per side, which prevented the use of the two torpedo launchers carried.[2] Thus adapted, the *Sella* and *Crispi* sailed from Astypalea in the Dodecanese to Suda Bay (Crete) carrying the 6 MT that carried out the first Italian surface assault craft action on 25/26 March 1941, a successful attack on the cruiser *York*.

Scout *Diana*

Designed as a yacht for the Prime Minister, the ship had a normal displacement of 1568 tons and was launched in Rijeka (then Fiume, in Italy) in 1939.

2. A report by commander Moccagatta notes that on these units 'after adequate training, an MT was put into the water in 35 seconds, and three in 7 minutes with a single davit.'

Destroyers *Francesco Crispi* (foreground) and *Quintino Sella* moored in Alimia (Dodecanese) in June 1940.

Scout *Diana* in summer 1941. *(Aldo Fraccaroli collection)*

Officially classified as a 'fast scout', it was equipped with special crutches and davits to handle MT type boats in the spring of 1941. Towing an MTL (with two SLC aboard), it transported the 9 explosive motorboats that took part in the unfortunate action against Valletta harbour on 25/26 July 1941 from Augusta to Malta.[3]

Destroyer *Grecale*

Belonging to the *Maestrale* class (4 units of 2200 tons, built in 1931–1934), it was converted for the transportation of explosive and light motor torpedo boats in January 1944, deleting one of its 533mm triple torpedo tubes. The planned loads were 2 MTSM and 3 MTM that were to attack Suda (Crete), a base occupied by the Germans. The *Grecale* was deployed to Tobruk with the craft aboard, waiting to begin the mission: however, persistent bad weather conditions in the area at that time delayed the operation, and it was later cancelled.

In June 1944, embarking two MTSM and a group of four 'Gamma', *Grecale* transported the craft (used as 'Gamma approachers') from Bastia, in Corsica close to La Spezia on the evening of 21st. The operation also involved *MS 74* with two British Chariots on board, whose attack led to the sinking of the abandoned hull of the cruiser *Bolzano*.

Destroyer *Legionario*

Belonging to the 'Soldati' class, 2nd series (7 units of 2550 tons, of which only 5 were completed, in 1942), it was adapted as an MTSM transport in the spring of 1945.

Arriving off Genoa from Livorno on the evening of 18 April 1945, the destroyer had acted as 'approacher' for *MTSM 230* and *232* that were to assist two Chariots Mk I with Mariassalto operators, transported by *MS 74*. Their goal was the sinking of the unfinished aircraft carrier *Aquila* (former liner *Roma*) to prevent its use by the Germans to block the harbour. Due to a whole set of circumstances, the big hull, while mined by one of the Chariots, was found still afloat at the liberation of the Ligurian capital in the first days of May.

Mas (Anti-Submarine Motorboats)

Without undergoing particular conversion work, some Mas were used for assault craft towing and assistance during the unfortunate 'Malta 1' and 'Malta 2' opera-

3. At first, instead of *Diana* the minelayer *Fasana* had been chosen for the Malta action: it was deployed to Augusta where it would have been converted for the purpose.

Destroyer *Grecale* awaiting work at La Spezia on 24 July 1947. *(Aldo Fraccaroli)*

Destroyer *Legionario* moored in Taranto in August 1946. *(Aldo Fraccaroli).*

tions. On the first, on 28 June 1941, which was interrupted by various factors that delayed target approach, *MAS 451, 452, 509, 556* and *562* participated with 8 MT and an MTS under tow.

Only *MAS 451* (Lieutenant Giorgio Sciolette) and *452* (Lieutnant G Battista Parodi) took part in the second. Both units were lost during the retreat after the assault craft action: *MAS 451* sunk by aircraft and *452*, damaged and abandoned, was captured by the British and towed to Malta.

MAS 509 belonged to the 1st class '500' series (24 tons, 17m length, 42 knots speed); while *MAS 556* and *562* belonged to the 3rd series of the same class (29.4 tons, 18.7m length, 43 knots speed). *MAS 451* and *452*, were two 'one-off' units (24.5 tons, 18m length, 42 knots speed). All had been built in 1941, except *509* which dated back to 1936.

In addition to the above, which actively participated in assault craft operations, some other warships were made available to the X Flotilla Mas for short periods:

- Destroyers *Dardo, Strale* and *Freccia* (*Freccia* class; 2100 tons; 36 knots); torpedo boats *Pallade* and *Partenope* (*Spica* class; 1054 tons; 32 knots). Planned to be used as 'approachers' for MT explosive motorboats during late 1940/early 1941, they were then replaced by the two above-mentioned *Sella* class destroyers.
- *MAS 567, 563* and *564*. In October 1941 the first was located in Genoa and the others in Mazara del Vallo in Sicily. *MAS 567* was probably used for training while *563* and *564* were assigned to support tasks to torpedo boats that operated in the Sicilian Channel and in Maltese waters. They all belonged to class '500' (3rd and 4th series) and *567* operated in the Black Sea from summer 1942.

MAS 451 on trials off Varazze, where it was built, on 1 February 1941. *(Courtesy of Baglietto Shipyards).*

MAS 452 moored at Malta following its capture at the end of the July 1941 action. *(NWM Association, Malta via R J Caruana)*

Converted merchant ships

These were a few motorsailers and steam-powered trawlers which, from the beginning of 1942, were initially adapted purely as transports and later, in the summer of 1942, also as support craft for MTSM light motor torpedo boats (normally three) or MTM explosive motorboats (up to four). Their task was to establish mobile operational bases for the X Flottiglia Mas light boats, and provide their transfer between the mainland and advanced bases in North Africa.

Motorsailer *Costanza* (former *Costa D'Oro*, former *San Nazario*, former *Riviera*, former *Rive d'Or*, former *Maricel*)

In June 1940, when it was requisitioned by the Regia Marina, it belonged to Soc Anonima Pignone in Florence and was registered in the Maritime Compartment of La Spezia (serial 51). Built in the United Kingdom in 1906 (Hawthorns & Co Ltd, of Leith in Scotland), it was equipped with a 188hp reciprocating steam engine turning a single propeller, and had a maximum speed of about 8 knots. Its main dimensions were: 136.70grt; 33.85m length, 6.30m breadth and 3.04m maximum draught.

After being employed for some missions to monitor possible enemy shipping movements in the Western Mediterranean with the codename of 'correspondent Beta', in March 1942 the *Costanza* was designated to be converted for the transport of surface assault craft.[4] The necessary work (fitting of crutches and securing points on deck, etc) was done at Naples and in July of 1942 it moved to Tobruk with 3 MTSM aboard.

4. Initially, instead of *Costanza* the motorsailer *Maria SS Ausiliatrice* (formerly codenamed 'Gamma correspondent') had been chosen; it was however assigned to another role (anti-aircraft gunnery school).

Motorsailer *Costanza*. (USMM)

Shortly thereafter its light motor torpedo boats were designated to form the 'Giobbe land convoy', and *Costanza* returned to Italy in early September. It was still used occasionally for some 'Decima' craft and material transfers in Italian waters up to the armistice, which found it in La Spezia, where it was scuttled on 9 September 1943. Refloated subsequently on behalf of the Kriegsmarine, it was sunk again, as always in La Spezia, in April 1945. After the war it was raised once more and scrapped soon afterwards.

Steam fishing trawler *Sogliola*

Owned by Soc Anon Pesca Atlantica and registered in the Maritime Compartment of Trieste (serial 402), it was requisitioned by the Regia Marina on 24 May 1940 and, with the designation *F 111*, assigned to the pilotage service. Built in Germany (Schiffs und Dockbauwerft AG Flender Shipyard of Lübeck) in 1924, it had one 452hp triple expansion steam engine. Fitted with a single propeller, it could reach a maximum speed of 9.5 knots. Its main dimensions were: 306.82grt; 44.99m length; 7.43m breadth and 3.73m draught.

In early 1942 it was assigned to X^{a} Mas and converted for the transport of surface assault craft (3 MTSM or 4 MTM) at the La Spezia Dockyards. In July 1941 with 4 explosive motorboats on board, the vessel reached Tobruk from La Spezia almost at the same time as *Costanza*. Shortly afterwards, the MTM were landed and joined the 'Giobbe land convoy'. *Sogliola* left north Africa and returned to Italy the following September.

On 2 May 1943, while it was heading towards the northern area of Sardinia after having transported some MTSM assault craft to Carloforte, *Sogliola* was attacked and sunk with gunfire by the British submarine *Safari* off Asinara.

Steam fishing trawler *Cefalo*

Owned by Lucio Ercole and registered in the Maritime Compartment of Naples (serial 406), it was requisitioned by the Regia Marina in La Spezia on 10 July 1942 to be converted as a transport for surface assault craft. A few days later, on the 14th, after embarking *MTSM 220* and *230* and their crews, it headed for the sea area between the Balearics and the Iberian peninsula. With the two light motor torpedo boats hidden under nets and other fishing gear, it sailed in those waters – where aircraft carriers launching aircraft to reinforce Malta's defences were believed to be operating – until the end of July when, without having seen any warships, it returned to Italy. The mission was repeated from 5 to 18 August, again with no results.

The following October, on the 21st it left La Spezia with 3 MTSM aboard, reaching Pantelleria where it remained as a support ship for these boats that carried out night offensive surveillance along the Malta access routes. This activity lasted until November, when *Cefalo* was deployed to Bizerte with the same functions as support for light motor torpedo boats tasked to counteract enemy naval activity along the Tunisian and Algerian coasts.

On 14 December 1942 the vessel was in an anchorage of the La Galite islet to support the MTSM which, under the command of Lieutenant Commander Salvatore Todaro, had attempted to force Annaba harbour – occupied by Anglo-American forces – that was interrupted by equipment failures and adverse weather conditions. The boats had recently returned onboard when the *Cefalo* was attacked by two fighter-bombers. Strafing killed commander Todaro and others and, due to the effect of some flooding, *Cefalo* had to be run aground to prevent its sinking. Refloated by the work of 'Gamma' and 'Giobbe land convoy' operatives, it reached Bizerte a few days later (on 29 December), where it was hastily repaired, and later returned to Italy.

On 22 August 1943, while it was heading for Livorno, it ran aground between the Vegliaia shoal and the coast due to a navigational error. Refloated on 25 August, it was transferred to La Spezia for the necessary repairs. Here it was surprised by the armistice and, unable to move, was scuttled on 9 September, resting on the muddy bottom near the San Bartolomeo quay with most of the hull above water.

Recovered by X^{a} Mas personnel, the vessel was put back into service, making several sorties (mostly towards Genoa and the Riviera) under the republican navy flag.

It was sunk in Genoa by aerial bombardment on 4 October 1944 while moored at Giano quay. Recovered and scrapped in the post-war period.

Steam fishing trawler *Pegaso*

Owned by Soc Anon Pesca e Reti Italiane (SAPRI) of Rome, it was requisitioned by the Regia Marina on 18 May 1940 and, with the designation *F 66*, intended for pilotage service. Built in Germany in 1924 (Deutsche Werke AG Shipyards of Rüstrilen), it had an iron hull and a 450hp reciprocating steam engine. Its main dimensions were: 295.54grt; 44.85m length, 7.69m breadth and 3.64m draught. It was assigned to 'Decima' in summer 1943, to replace the *Sogliola*, sunk by a submarine.

After 8 September it was armed by republican navy personnel and in February 1944 it was operating with the 'Antisom' group of Genoa. On 18 September 1944, it was sunk during a bombardment of Genoa harbour by B-17s of the US Army Air Force.

Some supply missions to the advanced bases of Augusta and Carloforte were also performed by the requisitioned motor trawler *Salvatore M* in 1943.

SPECIAL CRAFT

MTL (Motoscafo Trasporto Lento – Slow Transport Motorboat)

Conceived as an 'approacher' for the SLC, twelve units were built in three successive series, with hull numbers between 400 and 600.

The first MTL, based on a design by Colonel Eng Mizzau, began to enter service from the late spring of 1941. The 1st series (CABI drawing n^{o} A.429 of 16.2.41) probably comprised two units, of which one took part in the unfortunate Malta action on 26 July 1941 at the end of which it went missing.

The hull was wooden, with the following main dimensions: length 8.50m and max breadth 2.90m; the considerable (1.5m) depth ensured good seaworthiness especially with a head sea, and allowed two SLC to be carried in an inclined position next to the cockpit, although they protruded above it. The hull form had a rather pronounced 'V' at the bow; continuing sternwards the angle decreased, until it disappeared at about 1.30m from the transom.

The front compartment that constituted the 'cockpit' was open, and wide enough to accommodate two people, one (the 'master', in nautical jargon) on the left, at the steering wheel and compass (raised in a faired binnacle). To the right was a dashboard with engine instruments, and a seat for the mission leader. Immediately aft was a wide compartment (1.60 x 1.00m) closed with a removable hatch, with the motor power supply batteries on the bottom. Further aft another compartment contained the wooden slat seats for the operators of the 'pigs' being transported.

The motor, to be used for the stealthy approach phase, was placed immediately behind the operators' compartment. It was electric, with just 8hp and a range of 10 miles at 4 knots, connected with a short shaft to the propeller-rudder unit (notice the accentuated curvature of the 'flap' of the unit, sized to increase the manoeuvrability of the craft).

Since the MTL was an 'approacher' intended to

proceed under its own power only in the final phase of the attack, it required neither range nor high speed. The craft was normally towed by larger units until close to the target, lifting the stern drive by tilting to starboard, to reduce towing resistance as much as possible. The two crew compartments were protected by small wave guards.

A peculiar feature of this craft were the two large side recesses (6.80 x 0.60m), each intended for an SLC that could be gravity-launched, taking advantage of the slope of about twenty degrees of the support saddles, consisting of seven double frustoconical rollers. The transom openings of the SLC compartments could be closed with removable panels.

At the bottom of the hull were four bilge water pumps, exhausting through the hull, and two strong perforated metal plates with long brackets bolted inside the central bulkheads, which allowed the connection of MTL lifting cables.

The hulls were built by Baglietto Shipyards in Varazze (Savona) and fitted out with equipment, motors and instruments by CABI. No drawings or technical data have been found for II series MTL, but they must have been very similar to the previous ones.

However, units of the III series (CABI drawing n° A.440 dated 21.1.42) showed considerable differences. The hull dimensions were almost unchanged (8.50 x 2.85 x 1.45m), but the role of the crew compartments was reversed: the 'pig' operators were at the bow, while 'master' and mate were in the after one, where the steering wheel was still on the left, while the compass had been moved to the centreline, probably to make it more visible to both operators. The side compartments for the SLC remained the same size, but the rollers (though still seven) were moved sternwards, so that the rearmost protruded from the transom, clearly to ease the launching of the devices that were secured with cables from the warhead suspension ring to deck eyebolts, as in the previous type. Again, to ease the sliding of the 'pigs', three side rollers were placed on inner bulkheads. The SLC were also secured by two collars each, folding outwards and lockable with screw handles.

There were significant changes in propulsion: a new system consisting of an internal combustion engine connected to an electric one powered by batteries driving through a reduction gear with integrated reverse (CABI drawing n° A.424 of 2.3.42). These were connected to the propeller-rudder unit by a short half-shaft. Indicated power was 22hp for the petrol engine and 8 for the electric motor, with maximum speeds in the order of 5.5 and 4 knots respectively. Range was 60 miles at 5 knots. The indicated powers referred to 3200rpm on the petrol engine (730 at the propeller) and 2500 (570) for the electric motor, which could be regulated with reduced rpm (1500 for a corresponding power of 3hp) to allow greater flexibility in the final approach phase. Reduction ratios were 1.56 for the transmission and 2.85 for the reducer, with a resulting total of 4.41. The petrol engine was two-cylinder, seawater-cooled, with front radiator and a small muffler, arranged transversely above the engine with the exhaust manifold tube to starboard.

On the left, the clutch control lever allowed the shaft to engage that of the electric motor (which was then

MTL wrecks awaiting scrapping in Venice in 1949. *(Aldo Fraccaroli)*

1st series MTL 'Slow Transport Motorboat'
(re-drawn from CABI A. 429).

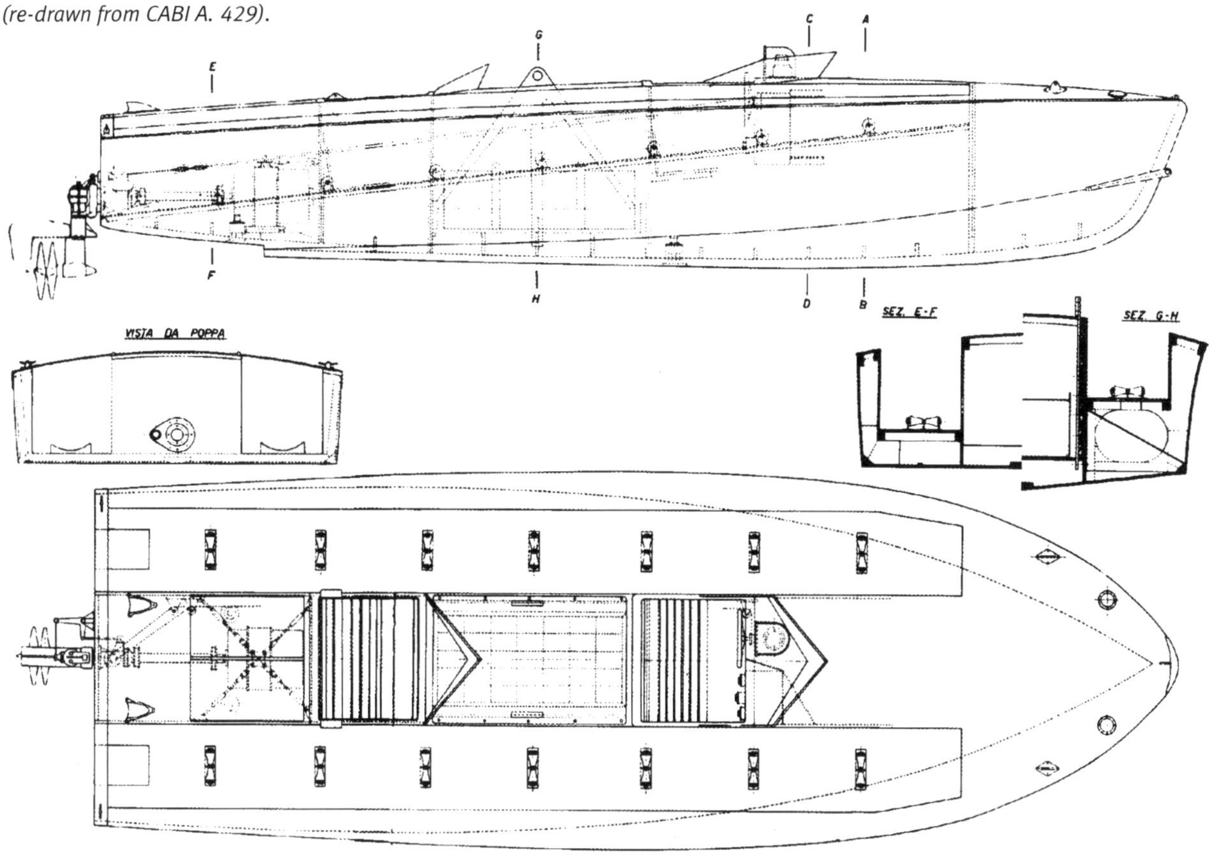

3rd series MTL (CABI drawing A. 440 of 24.9.1942).

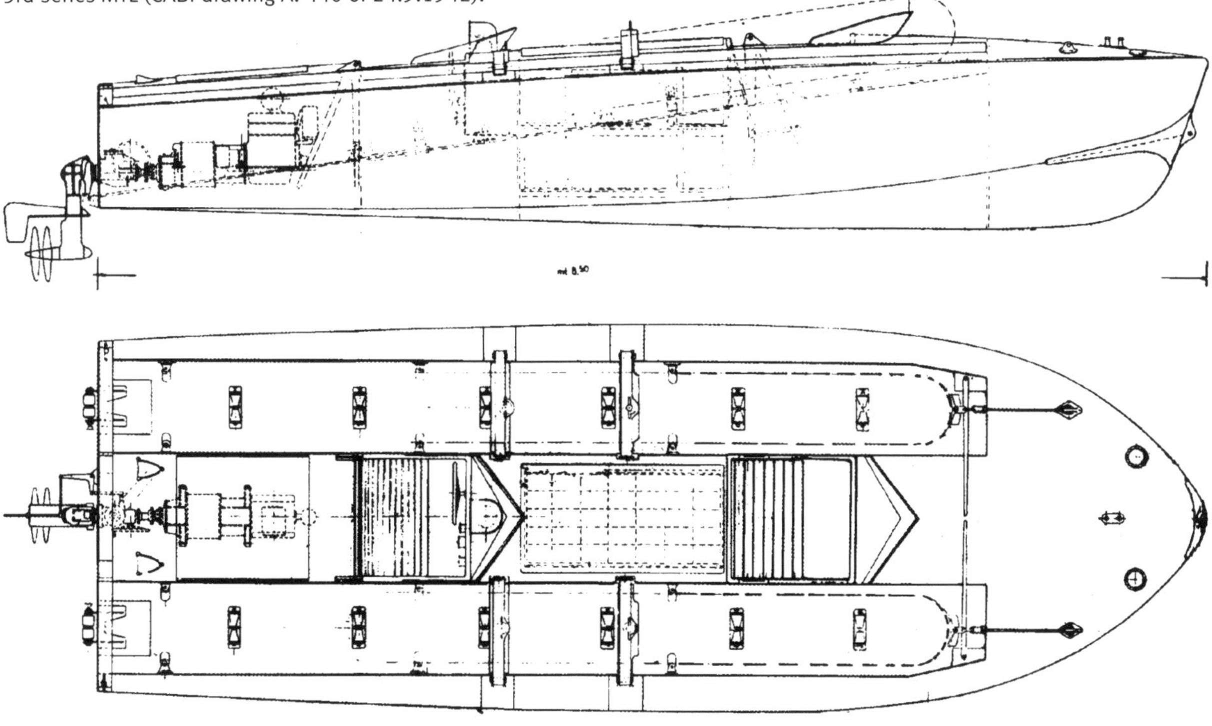

dragged) or to be disconnected during the stealth run; this was carried out using the electric motor alone, driven by power supplied by FAH (Hensemberger Accumulator Factory) batteries.

For easier accessibility, and to allow normal maintenance or repair operations, the propulsion machinery was placed in a well with removable cover. The propeller-rudder could be lifted to starboard. The maximum rudder angle was 20° on either side.

There were four lifting points on III series MTL, arranged in pairs alongside the crew compartments, to allow them to assist during coupling and uncoupling operations. Total weight of the craft at full load was around 7300kg.

In CABI records there is reference to an MTL of greater length (10.72m) but same breadth (2.85) and weight; speed 5 knots (one electric motor) and payload of 2600kg. It can be assumed that this craft had been designed in 1942 for transportation of the new SSB intended to replace the SLC but never built.

As already mentioned, between the beginning of 1941 and 8 September1943 the Regia Marina ordered the construction of a total of 12 MTL from CABI, with hulls produced by Baglietto Shipyards. Six of these were delivered before the armistice, two were delivered later to the republican Xª Mas, and two to the Caproni Company in Milan, probably after 1943 for some modification work.

Venice Shipyards, September 1949. Close-up of an MTL awaiting scrapping. This, and the previous picture are the only known photos of the 'Slow Transport Motorboat'. *(Aldo Fraccaroli)*

From a statement of craft assigned to the X Flottiglia Mas dated 20 October 1942, there were 5 MTL in service and 6 under construction. Reflecting the small number of MTL built, there are only a few known incidents from their careers:

a) One (whose hull number is unknown) participated in the Malta action. Its 'master' was Leading Seaman Tindaro Paratore, who brought the SLC of Tesei and of Costa as close as possible to the targets. When retiring towards *Diana* (after the raiders had been discovered by the British) it was attacked, hit and immobilised by aircraft. To avoid capture, the 'master' decided to scuttle the craft with the special valve placed at the bow.
b) An MTL (unknown number) was assigned as a training craft with various support tasks to the Pilot School of the republican Xª Mas in Sesto Calende in 1943–1945.
c) *MTL 476*: piloted by Lieutenant Uras, it took part in the attempted 'Xª' mission against Livorno with SSB on 7 November 1944. Besides the crew, *476* embarked: 2 self-propelled craft, each with two 150kg heads, 5x 50kg 'coops', 10 x 10kg 'small trunks' and 5 x 5kg incendiary bombs. The mission had to be aborted due to the half-shaft overheating, possibly from excessive load.
d) *MTL 571*: was at La Spezia in shipyard hands at the beginning of 1945. It was blown up on 22 April 1945, when the 'Xª' staff abandoned La Spezia.
e) *MTL 442*: on 10 April 1945 it was being overhauled for the republican Xª Mas.

MTV (Motoscafo Trasporte Veloce – Fast Transport Motorboat)

At the end of 1943, following a request by the Xª Flotilla Mas Headquarters, CABI designed a new type of approach motorboat with greater speed than the MTL: the 'Fast Transport Motorboat'(MTV). The project probably underwent a number of iterations (from I to III) culminating in the MTV type IV, the only one of which any documentation was found (CABI drawing A.617 of 23.3.1943).

This was a craft generally similar to the MTL, but with much more powerful propulsion, provided by a petrol engine and an electric motor with batteries (arranged in a special stern compartment), geared to a standard shaft line with a three-bladed propeller. The hard-chined, unstepped wooden hull was 11.15m long

Type IV MTV (re-drawn from CABI A. 617 of 23.3.1943).

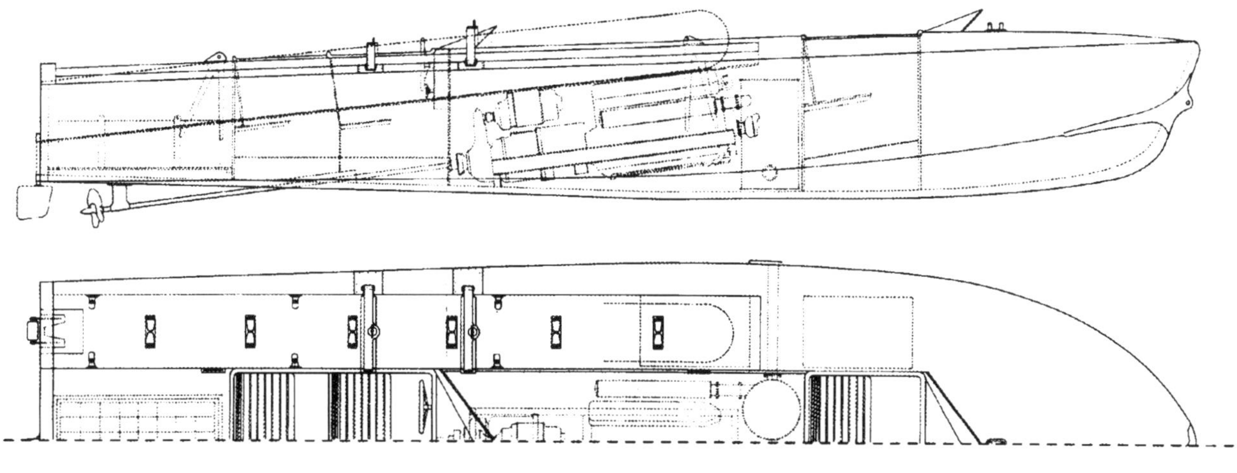

overall and 3.30m in breadth. Besides the two pilots, it could carry two SLC or two 'SSB/Delta', placed in angled side recesses fitted with sliding rollers, and four operators arranged on bow and stern seats.

No boats of this type appear to have been built before the end of the conflict; only later was the concept resurrected giving birth to some MTV models (actually rather different) which were in service for a few years with the Italian Navy Comando Subacquei e Incursori.

'MT GAMMA' or 'MT g' (Motoscafo Transporto 'Gamma' – 'Gamma' Transport Motorboat)

Some special transport and approach craft called 'Gamma' Transport Motorboats (MT g or simply 'emmetigamma') were built after 1943 for those needs arising from the rapid development of the use of 'assault divers – raiders' ('Gamma').

It was probably a design by CABI of Milan on Baglietto or SIAI hulls but since no drawings of this craft have been found, its description here is mainly based on descriptions by operators who employed them, and on some photos taken at Venice in 1944. The drawing illustrating the probable arrangement of the 'MT Gamma' was prepared from these photos. It appears to be a variant of the III series MTL used for training Kriegsmarine assault swimmers (*Kampfschwimmer*) of Special Assault Squadron 700 at their Venice base.[1]

1. The German 'Gamma', all carefully selected volunteers, were drawn from many different specialities within the Kriegsmarine, and were trained as divers in Valdagno (Vicenza) at the divers school of Xª Mas; after this first phase of their preparation, training continued at the Venice unit base.

The pilot and another operator were seated in the cockpit at the centre of the hull, while the two side loading compartments – with a capacity of three 'Gamma' each – were no longer raked aft but arranged almost horizontally, which made accommodation of both men and their equipment (explosive charges) easier. When the amount of explosives was substantial, as it usually was for Italian divers, it was placed in heavy-duty waterproof canvas 'coops' sealed with synthetic rubber, easier to tow by the divers, once they were put into the water in the operations zone.

The most obvious peculiarity of the 'MT Gamma' was a sprocket (with crank, but probably also motorised) at the extreme stern, used to unwind a guide cable – with small floats interspersed, as in fishing nets – that would float for a long stretch behind the craft to facilitate recovery of the operators. Preserving the lives of the operators at the end of certain types of operation became an ever-increasing priority for both the Italians and Germans, to avoid the

A photo of MT 'Gamma' *002* in Venice in 1944 with German military personnel aboard.

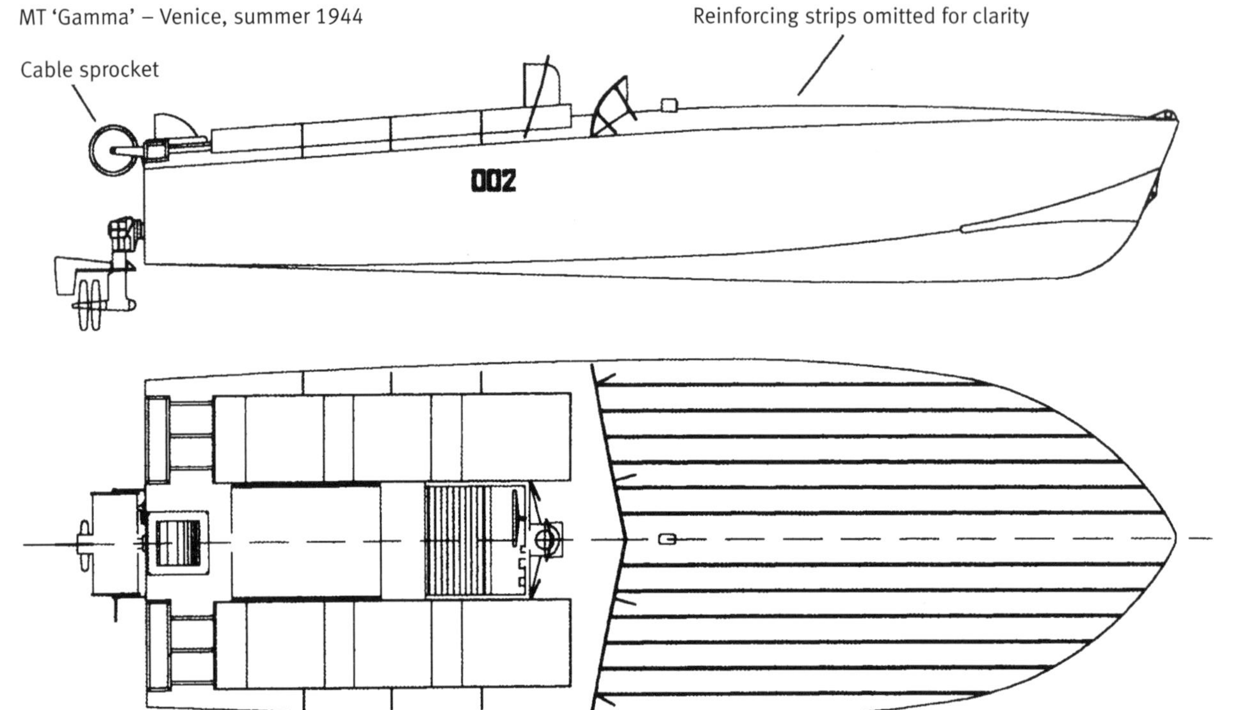

Drawing by L Carretta

capture of highly trained personnel that could be profitably used in more actions.

It would seem that Kriegsmarine had least two 'MT Gamma' available, which were finally destroyed to avoid capture at the end of the war. Craft of this type were never available for Xª Mas use; the Italian 'Gamma' (and, if necessary, agents and/or saboteurs) were transported by standard MTL, or light motor torpedo boats where the short torpedo had been landed and the central compartment – with its hatch eliminated – was equipped with narrow makeshift passenger seats, and sometimes a sprocket for winding the so-called guide cable.

MOTOR TORPEDO BOATS

At the end of 1942, two of the 18 'CRDA 60-ton – 2nd series' motor torpedo boats under construction in Monfalcone were modified for use as 'approachers' for assault craft. These units derived from the German 'S 2' *schnellboote*, a few of which had been built in Germany for the Yugoslav Navy in 1937–1938 and acquired by the Regia Marina in April 1941.

One of the units captured during the Dalmatian invasion was transferred to Monfalcone, where the Cantieri Riuniti Dell'Adriatico (CRDA shipyards) replicated the design, with a few changes, in a first series of 18 motor torpedo boats (*MS 11–16; 21–26*

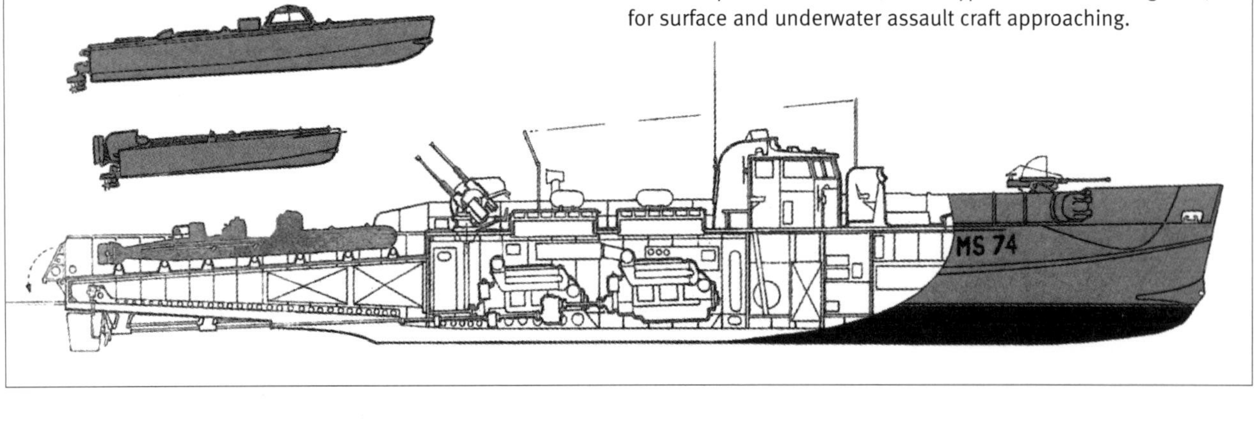

Motor Torpedo Boat *MS 74*, of the type nicknamed 'kangaroo', for surface and underwater assault craft approaching.

Republican X Mas *MS 75* with a German 'Linse' type explosive motorboat and other materials on board.

and *31–36*), which were delivered to the Regia Marina in spring/summer 1942, at the same time as an order for a second series of almost identical units was placed.

They had wooden hulls with metal reinforcing elements, conventional hull lines with round-bilge section, flattened towards the stern; the displacement was about 63 tons, increasing to 68 in the second series following some changes to the armament. The overall length was 28m, with a breadth of 4.3m. Powered by three Isotta-Fraschini 'ASM 183' petrol engines, their maximum speed was 32 knots with an economic range of about 900 miles on one engine at 12 knots. The armament of 2nd series units consisted of two steel 533mm (21in) torpedo tubes with cap, two 450mm torpedo side launchers, one or two Breda 20/65mm machine guns, two Breda 6.5mm submachine guns and two stern rails for eight 100 kg depth charges.

The two units chosen for conversion to 'assault craft transport and support units' for X Flotilla Mas were *MS 74* and *75*, delivered by the shipyards to the Regia Marina on 30 June 1943 with the official (cover) classification of 'minelayer motor torpedo boats'. Nicknamed 'kangaroos' in contemporary usage, the main modification was the creation of a large roller-equipped rear slide starting approximately from the engine room skylights, and ending at the extreme stern, where the above-water hull had been significantly widened and equipped with a lowering flap. This accommodation allowed the transportation and launch of almost all types of assault craft in service: that is, either two SLC or SSB, an MTSM or an SMA, an MTM or two MTR.

However, the shipboard equipment did not allow the recovery of the craft after launch at sea, as the boats were not equipped with winches, and loading relied on the lifting facilities of a naval base or a major warship.

MS 74 during a Mariassalto exercise in the Gulf of Taranto.

The vast space obtained in the stern area also allowed the transport of 'Gamma' or saboteurs groups with all their weapons and equipment (charges, boats, etc), besides the laying of various types of mine.

As a result of the changes undertaken for this special employment, the remaining armament consisted of the two 533mm torpedo tubes and the 20/65 bow gun, to which a quadruple German 20/65 mounting (*Flak Vierling*) was added amidships. The full-load displacement should have been about 70 tons, with a corresponding maximum speed around 30–31 knots.

At the date of the armistice, the two units were in Venice, completing crew training. The first operation, a short-notice mission transporting 4 MTR, was planned for Sicilian waters now occupied by Anglo-American forces. The next day *MS 74*, under the command of Lieutenant Piero Carminati, headed for a southern Italian harbour while *MS 75*, which was undergoing dockyard work and unable to move, remained in Venice. On 12 September the latter was captured by the Germans, who later ceded it to the republican X^{a} Mas.

MS 74 reached Bari on the morning of 1 September.[2] Joining the 1st Flotilla Mas, it reached the Termoli operating base on 18 October and, on 2 November following, it passed into the control of the newly-established Assault Craft Command (Mariassalto), relocating to Taranto.

After a training period in that base, on 16 May 1944 the boat moved back to Termoli whence, between 17 and 29 May, it carried out six special missions close in

2. Pilots of the Decima surface craft for the planned mission with 4 MTR in Sicily (Lieutenant Corrado Garutti and petty officers Papurello, Tonissi, Guercio and Sguanci), who had boarded *74* in Venice, asked his commander, Lieutenant Piero Carminati, to land them in Manfredonia whence, with a good deal of luck, they reached the X^{a} Mas Headquarters in La Spezia on 19 September.

MS 75 alongside in Venice in 1944.

to the Albanian coast, transporting an MTSM tasked with carrying out hydrographic surveys and landing agents.[3] Later transferred to the Tyrrhenian Sea and operating from Bastia, on the night of 21 June 1944, during the forcing of La Spezia harbour by Mariassalto in collaboration with Allied forces, it carried two British Chariots to within 300m the outer harbour boom. The action culminated in the attack by one of them on the now abandoned hull of the cruiser *Bolzano,* which sank, settling on the bottom of the roadstead. The following night the unit returned to La Spezia waters carrying an MTSM for the intended recovery of the operators, but none of them was found at the rendezvous.

Once back in Taranto, *MS 74* moved to the Adriatic where it operated from Brindisi, performing a cycle of missions between Porto Palermo and Sarandë on the Albanian coast in support of British sappers between 22 and 29 September. Transferred back to the Tyrrhenian Sea, at 14.15 on 18 April 1945, *MS 74* (still commanded by Lieutenant Carminati) left Livorno harbour with two Chariots and their Italian crews on board. Arriving off the eastern entrance of Genoa harbour, at 21.12 the boat launched the two craft, which continued escorted by an MTSM. One of them succeeded in reaching the mooring of the unfinished aircraft carrier *Aquila* and, leaving its charge, regained open water and met the MTSM off the entrance. The *Aquila* did not sink, however.

After the war *MS 74* was initially used as a patrol boat (*MV 619*), then it was made available to the 'Raggruppamento Subacquei ed Incursori' (Comsubin) remaining located mainly in La Spezia with the new identity of *MS 475*. In early March 1962, while under tow by the support ship *Cavezzale*, it was surprised in mid-Tyrrhenian by a violent storm that quickly caused the towing cable to break and the engines to fail. The boat was driven by wind and sea onto the coast near Civitavecchia and was seriously damaged. Following the damage caused by running aground, it was decommissioned on 31 December 1963.

MS 75, commanded by Lieutenant Giovanni Santagata, operated in the Adriatic with the X^{a} Mas from the Pola and Venice bases until April 1945. On 22 August 1944, it carried out a torpedo attack against enemy ships anchored in Ancona harbour, and in the following September completed a mining operation in waters off Rimini. Finally, in January 1945, it participated in the landing of a saboteur on the Yugoslav island of Mljet. On 2 May 1945 *MS 75* – which was moored in San Nicolò di Lido – was surrendered to the Regia Marina by its crew.

Operational again from October 1945, after being employed for some time on anti-smuggling duties in Adriatic, the boat went into reserve. Decommissioned on 18 May 1949, on 6 July following it was handed over to the Soviet Union in Odessa harbour in the Black Sea, in execution of a provision of the 1947 Peace Treaty.

3.Lieutenant Edoardo Longobardi, Sub-Lieutenants Carlo Coda and Andrea De Angelis and Leading Seaman Luigi Gattorno alternated on the MTSM.

SUBMARINES

The submarine was initially judged 'a not very suitable craft' for an 'approacher'. However, because of its particular characteristics – the ability to sail stealthily up to the target harbours – it soon turned out to be the most suitable carrier for underwater assault craft (SLC) engaged in operations a long way from national bases and colonies, and as such was intensively employed for the whole duration of the conflict.

Towards the end of 1942 the X Flotilla Mas began to use the submarine also as an 'approacher' for assault divers ('Gamma') and finally, in 1943, it was also tasked to transport explosive motorboats (MTR). After the armistice, during operations conducted in the North and South by Italian assault craft, the submarine was no longer employed because the reduced distances between operational bases and targets allowed the more economical use of surface 'approachers' of reduced size.

The small and outdated 'Holland' type (364/441 tons 'H' class of 1916–1918) had been used in the earlier experiments with divers, but were considered unsuitable as 'approachers' because they could carry only two SLC, the transportation arrangements on deck significantly reduced the submarine's stability and, because the deck of the 'H' class had so little free-board, the devices would be too exposed to wave action. The choice therefore fell on bigger units, and in particular on the excellent and modern medium range (also called 'coastal') units of the various series of the numerous '600' class.

Later, from the beginning of 1940, the following submarines were specifically converted – or designated to be converted – as assault craft transports:

- *Ametista* ('600' class, *Sirena* series): at the beginning of 1940, for tests with SLC at La Spezia;
- *Iride* ('600' class, *Perla* series): from July, 1940 to her sinking on 21 August 1940;
- *Gondar* ('600' class, *Adua* series): from August 1940 to her sinking on 30 September 1940;
- *Sciré* ('600' class, *Adua* series): from August 1940 to her sinking on 10 August 1942;
- *Ambra* ('600' class, *Perla* series): from October 1941 to her scuttling on 9 September 1943;
- *da Vinci* (*Marconi* class): summer 1942 for tests with mini-submarine *CA 2* in Bordeaux;
- *Murena* (*Flutto* class): new construction unit, ready for use on 9 September 1943 (scuttled);
- *Sparide* (*Flutto* class): new construction unit, undergoing tests on 9 September 1943 (scuttled);
- *Grongo* (*Flutto* class): new construction unit, building on 9 September 1943 (sabotaged and captured by the Germans);
- *Aradam* ('600' class, *Adua* series): undergoing work on 9 September 1943 (scuttled, then raised and lost at Genoa in an air raid on 4 September 1944 while completing the rebuild).

In detail, the only submarines which carried out actual assault craft transport missions were *Iride, Gondar, Sciré* and *Ambra*; *Ametista* and *Da Vinci* were confined exclusively to trials; the last four were lost during the armistice chaos, before becoming operational. One further submarine that X^{a} Mas possibly intended to allocate to assault craft transport was *Beilul* ('600' class, *Adua* series), captured by the Germans at Monfalcone, where it was undergoing work on 9 September 1943; ceded to RSI, which had already assembled its crew, it was sunk during an air raid in May 1944 shortly before commissioning.

Ametista

This was the first submarine converted for SLC transport: three devices mounted on deck saddles placed on board by the La Spezia Shipyards in the first months

Submarine *Ametista* in a 1934–1935 picture.

Submarine *Iride* towards the end of the 1930s.

Submarine *Sciré*, with SLC transport cylinders, leaving La Spezia for trials, probably on 19 October 1940. *(Aldo Fraccaroli collection)*

of 1940.[1] Under the command of (then) Lieutenant Junio Valerio Borghese, it was used for the first SLC transportation and release experiments in the waters of the Ligurian base. During the final exercise, three 'self-propelled' craft transported close to the boom defences by *Ametista* attempted an attack on the hull of the old decommissioned cruiser *Quarto*, moored to one of the roadstead buoys for the purpose. Only one of the devices managed to reach the target and fit its training head under the hull.

Trials completed, the saddles were disembarked from the submarine, which was returned to its operational condition. The outcome of the tests conducted with *Ametista* was generally encouraging, even though '... the accommodation of SLC on deck saddles did not seem ideal, considering that the submarine would have faced a long passage before reaching the enemy base to attack, while being confined to a depth of just 30 metres (maximum diving depth for the 'self-propelled' craft) and would expose the devices to the sea to an excessive extent, enough to cause serious damage to the devices transported.'

Ametista was to be lost by scuttling off Numana (Ancona) as a result of the armistice events on 12 September 1943, after completing 27 war missions.

Iride

Despite the negative evaluation of the SLC transport arrangements tested aboard *Ametista*, *Iride* was converted – to meet an urgent requirement – at La Spezia Shipyards in July 1940 to transport four such devices on simple deck saddles.

Under the command of Lieutenant Francesco Brunetti, *Iride* was lost to an aerial torpedo attack in the gulf of Bomba in Cyrenaica on 21 August 1940 during a short test cruise carrying the SLC designated to force Alexandria harbour (Operation GA 1). This was the first action attempted by Italian assault craft, whose operators did their best during the 24 hours after the sinking to save crew members trapped inside the hull lying on the bottom, at a depth of about twenty metres. The four SLC, although probably damaged, were recovered.

Gondar

Converted at the La Spezia Shipyards from the end of

Submarine *Gondar* (left) moored in La Spezia Shipyards in the first half of September 1940. The work of fitting the three watertight cylinders for SLC transport has just been completed.

1. Previous experiments had been carried out with SLC lashed down on the deck of 'H' type submarines.

August 1940 to replace *Iride*. Unlike the latter, this entailed landing the gun and its ammunition, two reserve torpedoes, three chain shackles, a kedge anchor, a towing cable and other non-essential equipment, and it was fitted with three watertight metal cylinders placed on the deck, one forward and two abaft the conning tower, for the transportation of three SLC.

Carrying the devices in cylinders which could withstand the maximum submarine operating depth (90 metres) overcame the most severe limitation of the *Iride*, which was restricted to the 30-metre diving depth of the self-propelled craft. These cylinders, weighing 2.8 tons, were manufactured by Odero-Terni-Orlando (OTO) in Muggiano (La Spezia), had a capacity of 21.75 tons in sea water and a buoyancy when empty of 23.3 tons.

They were equipped with a hemispherical watertight hatch, which could be opened with a side hinge to insert and extract the SLC. Valves and pipes for flooding and venting could be controlled from inside the submarine, and a ventilation and recharge system for the SLCs' batteries could be operated while cruising towards the target.

Tests carried out in the waters of the Ligurian base had pinpointed two main operating procedures for operators to leave the submarine and extract (or 'launch') the SLC from their cylinders:

- *with the submarine resting on the bottom* (8-15m depth). The operators came out of the lock-out chamber wearing breathing apparatus, opened the doors of the cylinders (which had been previously flooded), extracted the devices and then locked the cylinders, which could then be vented so as not to compromise the submarine's stability and buoyancy;
- *with the submarine awash* (hove-to, with just the upper part of the conning tower emerging). The operators exited the tower upper hatch and descended to the deck, where they opened the hatches of the already flooded cylinders and extracted the appliances, then closed the hatches.

In both procedures, 'reserve' operators helped, returning inside the submarine as soon as the SLC were on their way.

Gondar left La Spezia on 21 September 1940 with three SLC on board under the command of

Close-up of the bow watertight cylinder aboard *Gondar*. Unlike the two stern cylinders on the same boat, and those aboard other Italian 'approacher' submarines, this one is missing the typical reinforcing 'ribs'.

Lieutenant Brunetti, a survivor of the *Iride* sinking the previous month. Reaching Messina on the 23rd, the boat left the following morning after embarking the operators and headed towards Alexandria harbour (Operation GA 2) where the self-propelled craft were to penetrate and attack ships at anchor. Since the British fleet had meanwhile gone out to sea, the submarine received a radio order to divert to Tobruk and wait for new orders. Thence it left again when the enemy ships had returned to Alexandria.

On the evening of 29 September, while approaching the target, it was forced to dive after being spotted at close range by an enemy destroyer. It was then subjected to a long hunt lasting over 14 hours, during which the submarine tried in vain to escape the depth charge attacks by destroyer HMAS *Stuart* joined by other units and a four-engine Sunderland flying boat. The damage inflicted forced *Gondar* to surface in full daylight which was then scuttled.

The crew and SLC operators were all taken prisoner. First-hand observation and pictures of the submarine before it disappeared beneath the surface clearly revealed the container cylinders, while the unusual presence of so many 'diver' specialists amongst the survivors gave the Royal Navy its first indications of the probable use of special underwater craft by the Regia Marina.

Sciré

This unit is considered the archetypal 'approacher' submarine with a long and glorious involvement with assault craft, for which its flag was decorated with the Gold Medal of Military Valour.

It was converted similarly to *Gondar* in the La Spezia Shipyards in August–September 1940. Subsequently the boat underwent further changes – as did almost all Italian submarines built before the conflict – involving, amongst other things, the lowering of periscopes standards and reducing the size of conning towers. The original dark iron grey colour was modified several times, adopting various camouflage patterns: notably, the *Sciré*, on the initiative of its commander, sported the dark outline of a small trawler painted for a short period on the tower sides; later, a 'standard' (small light brown triangles on light ash grey background) colour scheme was adopted.

In total, the *Sciré* – under the command of Lieutenant Commander J V Borghese (later promoted

La Spezia, September 1940. Close-up of watertight hatches of the stern SLC transport cylinders on the submarine *Sciré*.

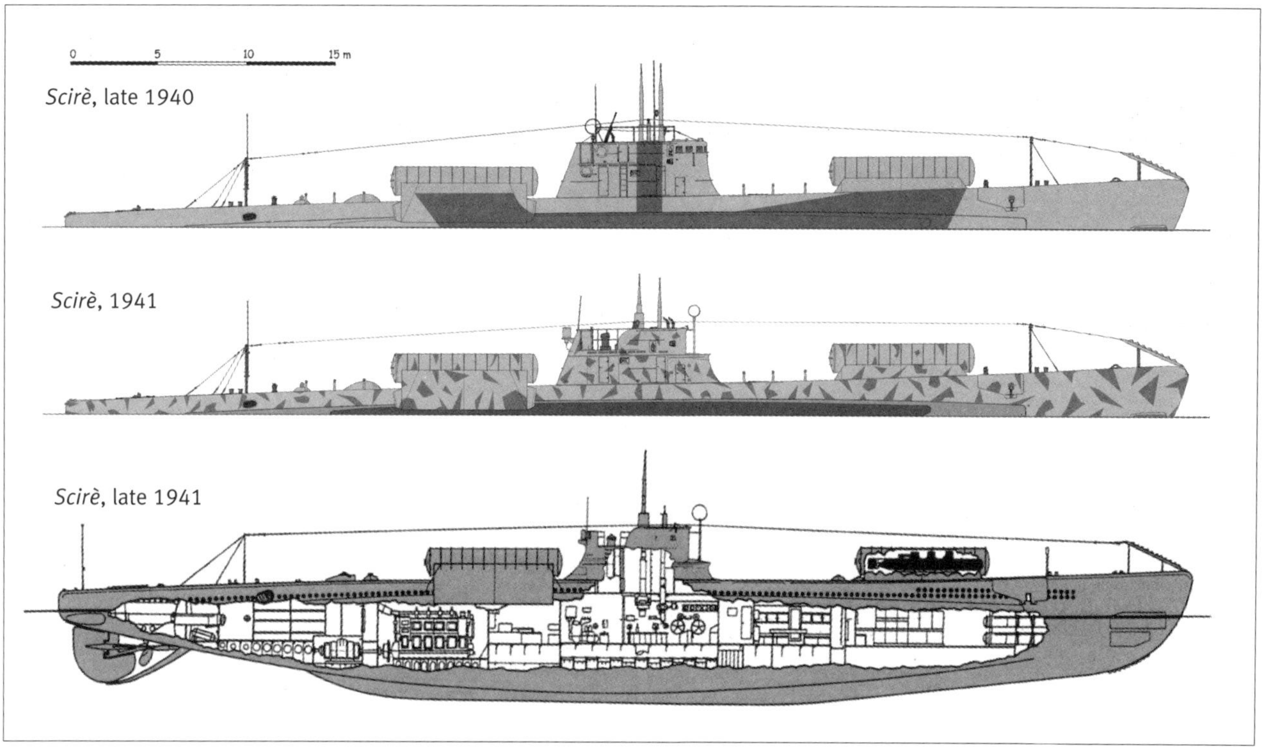

to Commander) and later Bruno Zelich of equal rank – carried out four assault craft transport operations, penetrating heavily defended enemy bases such as Gibraltar and Alexandria, until lost during its final mission in waters off Haifa.

These are the missions accomplished by *Sciré* as assault craft carrier:

- *Operation BG 1*: target Gibraltar with 3 SLC (LtCdr Borghese).
  Started 24.9.1940 and called off 50 miles from target by Supermarina order as the British fleet was out at sea.
- *Operation BG 2*: target Gibraltar with 3 SLC (LtCdr Borghese).
  Craft released 3 miles from the target at 02.19 on 10.10.1940. Because of mechanical breakdowns and failures of the operators' breathing apparatus, the three SLC failed to penetrate the military harbour.
- *Operation BG 3*: target Gibraltar with 3 SLC (LC Borghese).
  After embarking the operators in Cadiz from alongside Italian tanker *Fulgor*, at 23.58 on 26 May 1941, it released the craft on the bottom of the huge Algeciras roadstead. The mission failed again due to SLC failures and breathing gear malfunctions.
- *Operation BG 4*: target Gibraltar with 3 SLC (LtCdr Borghese).
  Craft release at 01.07 on 20 September 1941 in the Algeciras roadstead. First success of the underwater craft with the sinking of two tankers and a motor vessel.
- *Operation GA 3*: target Alexandria with 3 SLC (LtCdr Borghese).
  Craft release at 20.47 on 18 December 1941 1.5 miles from the coast and 4.5 miles from the harbour entrance. The three craft reached their respective targets, sinking or heavily damaging two battleships (*Valiant* and *Queen Elizabeth*), a tanker and a destroyer. This is the most successful single mission by Italian assault craft.
- *Operation SL 1*: target Haifa with 10 'Gamma' operators (LtCdr Zelich).
  The submarine was sunk by trawler HMS *Islay* and coastal batteries near the mouth of Haifa harbour, with the loss of the entire crew and all Decima operators on board.

Over the years, some parts of the *Sciré* hull have been raised from the bottom and are preserved as memorabilia in various Italian Naval Museums and Navy Headquarters.

Recently a new Italian submarine was baptised *Sciré*, a name that has become legendary in the Italian Navy.

Ambra

After some reconnaissance-attack missions (during one of which, while commanded by Lieutenant Mario Arillo, it had sunk the cruiser HMS *Bonaventure* south of Crete), *Ambra* was chosen for assault craft carrier conversion in October 1941. It was transformed by La Spezia Shipyards during a work programme which included removing the gun and installing three watertight cylinders similar to those of the *Sciré*. The conning tower was also modified and reduced in size to decrease its visibility on the surface. The submarine was ready by the early months of 1942, and assigned to the operational control of X Flotilla Mas to start training for the new role.

Ambra moored at Lakki (Dodecanese) in May 1942.

Ambra was first commanded by Lieutenant (later Lieutenant Commander) Arillo and then Lieutenant Commander Renato Ferrini, and carried out three assault craft transport missions:

- *Operation GA 4*: target Alexandria with 3 SLC (Lt Arillo).
  Craft release at 20.30 on 14 May 1942 near the target. Because of problems encountered during the approach, the three SLC could not find the harbour entrance and were scuttled.
- *Operation NA 1*: target Algiers with 3 SLC and 10 'Gamma' (LtCdr Arillo).
  Exit of the operators and craft release in Algiers roadstead was at 22.24 on 11 November 1942, after the last approach stretch sliding along the seabed, guided by an operator (Lt Augusto Jacobacci) on the surface. The action by the SLC and 'Gamma' caused the sinking of 4 merchant ships totalling 20,266grt.
- *Operation against Syracuse harbour* (occupied by Anglo-American forces) with 3 MTR (LtCdr Ferrini).
  The submarine embarked surface assault craft (MTR type reduced explosive motorboats) for the first time, loaded inside the cylinders. At 03.00 on 18 July 1943 the submarine was spotted by an aircraft and attacked with bombs off the coast of Syracuse, while heading towards the craft release point. Badly damaged, it managed to retire and then reach Naples under tow. Hastily repaired, it headed for La Spezia where it was to be repaired at the shipyard. At the armistice, *Ambra* was still undergoing work in La Spezia and, unable to move, it was

Close-up of the stern watertight cylinders aboard *Ambra*.

scuttled. Salvaged, it was again sunk in La Spezia by air attack in 1944. Raised and scrapped after the war.

Leonardo da Vinci

This was the only 'oceanic' type submarine (1190 tons surfaced and 1489 submerged) to operate with assault craft; all the others belonged in the 'coastal' (or 'medium cruise') category and had displacements between 690 and 900 tons surfaced and 870 to 1070 underwater.

The need for a large submarine with considerable range (10,500 miles at 8 knots, on the surface) was dictated by the particular type of employment intended: to serve as 'approacher' for a CA type mini-submarine of 12/14 tons, modified to carry 8 big charges and some 'Gamma' divers, operating from Bordeaux in France to act against Atlantic and US harbours (planned objectives: Freetown in Sierra Leone, Capetown in South Africa and New York).

In the summer of 1942 *Da Vinci*, which was refitting at the Betasom workshops[2] following a normal war mission in the Atlantic, was converted to carry out a series of transport, release and recovery experiments with the *CA 2*, which had been transferred from Italy by rail. In detail, a cradle about 10 metres long had taken the place of the 100/47 mm gun ahead of the conning tower. It had side coamings, keel blocks and two retaining clamps manoeuvrable from inside the submarine to cradle the 'midget' sub.

A pipeline connected the CA on the blocks with the compressed air circuit of the carrier submarine (nicknamed 'kangaroo'); appropriate electrical connections also allowed the batteries of the craft to be recharged at sea. The weight of the CA was offset by the landing of the gun and ammunition, besides about 8 tons of lead from the submarine ballast. Overall, the *Da Vinci* conversion work turned out to be minimal, affecting the pressure hull at just two points, and was performed in less than a month.

Close-up of the *CA 2* transport arrangements aboard *Da Vinci* in 1942.

In September 1942 some tests were carried out, with encouraging results, where the *Da Vinci*, under the command of Lieutenant Gianfranco Gazzana-Priaroggia and the *CA 2*, piloted by Lieutenant Eugenio Massano, successfully carried out craft release and recovery experiments, besides submerged 'kangaroo' manoeuvrability tests with the 'midget sub' on board.

At the end of the trials programme the *Da Vinci* was returned to operational condition for missions against merchant ships in the Atlantic. Resuming its normal activity, the boat was sunk on 25 May 1943 off the coast of Spain by British anti-submarine vessels.

The *Da Vinci*, with 16 merchant ships sunk (116,000grt in total), was the top-scoring Italian submarine in terms of tonnage destroyed during the Second World War.

Murena, Sparide and *Grongo*

These three boats of the *Flutto* class were built under war programmes at OTO in Muggiano (La Spezia), where they were launched respectively on 11 April,

2. The base of Italian Atlantic submarines, created in Bordeaux, in the Gironde estuary, in September 1940.

Leonardo da Vinci and *CA 2*, summer 1942

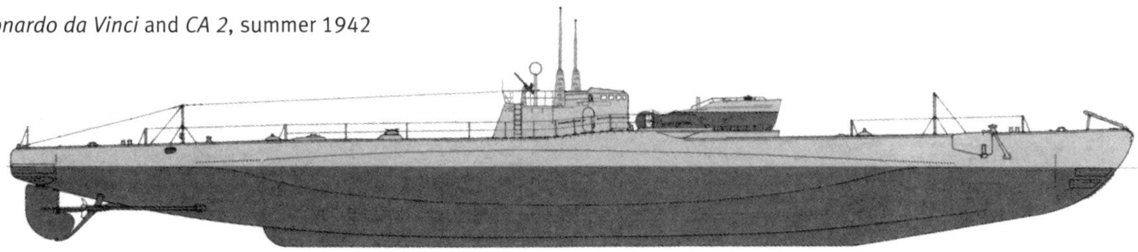

La Spezia, 11 April 1943. The launch of the submarine *Murena* at the OTO Shipyards in Muggiano. Note the side arrangement of the watertight cylinders for assault craft transport.

21 February and 6 May 1943. *Sparide* and *Grongo* were assigned to Xª Mas for assault craft transport during outfitting, while *Murena* was already fitted with watertight cylinders at launch.

This type had four cylinders compared to three on the previous conversions, placed above the ballast tanks at the sides of the conning tower, instead of forward and aft it.

Murena should have carried out its first war mission in early October 1943 against Gibraltar under the command of Lieutenant Commander Luigi Longanesi-Cattani, transporting four MTR explosive motorboats in its cylinders. At the armistice the unit was ready in La Spezia, but inaccurate information about its status (operationally, the submarine was controlled by Decima Mas) prompted the local Navy Department Headquarters to order its scuttling, which was carried out together with that of *Sparide*, at that time unable to move under its own power. The *Grongo*, still under construction, was sabotaged and later captured by the Germans.

Murena and *Sparide* were refloated and, together with *Grongo*, were respectively named *U.It. 16*, *U.It. 15* and *U.It. 20* by the Germans. Towed to Genoa to be outfitted again, they were finally lost to aerial bombardment in September 1944.

It was envisaged that at the end of restoration work at least one of these submariness (probably *Murena*) would have been entrusted to the republican Xª Mas for assault craft transport.

Aradam

Like *Sciré* and *Gondar*, this boat belonged to the so-called 'African' series of the '600' class. At the armistice date it was in Genoa for a programme of work at the end of which it was expected to operate as an assault craft transport. Unable to move,[3] the submarine was scuttled by its crew before abandonment.

Aradam in drydock in Genoa in 1944.

Recovered a few months later, it was assigned by the Germans to the Marina Nazionale Repubblicana, which intended to restore it as an 'approacher' submarine.

For this purpose, it was equipped with two deck watertight cylinders, a bow and a stern one.

While work was being completed, with the Italian crew already on board, it was forcibly seized by the Germans on 18 August 1944, one of a number of aggressive actions taken in that delicate period of their always difficult relations with the RSI Navy (in contrast to Borghese's Xª Mas, whose relations with the Germans were marked by greater mutual trust). This sensitive issue had not yet been completely resolved when the former *Aradam* was destroyed on 4 September 1944, again in an air raid at Genoa.

PROTOTYPES, EXPERIMENTAL CRAFT AND PROJECTS

'Moschini-Viola' type 'approacher' mini-submarines

When the first prototypes of the 'Tesei self-propelled

3. It would seem that the *Aradam* had been refloated shortly before, following accidental sinking in the harbour, where it was found with a lot of partially dismantled equipment for work in progress.

craft' – the future SLC – were being completed, the problem of how to 'approach' the target was raised at the same time. Given the restricted endurance (estimated at the time to be less than one hour) and the physiological limitations on working for a long time with breathing apparatus, in September 1935 it was decided to resurrect the old suggestion of Angelo Belloni for a 'harbour forcing submarine', by properly converting modest-size standard units. A long cycle of difficult experiments carried out with *H 6* in La Spezia in 1936–1937 eventually produced a positive outcome – at least, enough to induce the Naval Staff to request a project for a small conventional 100-ton submarine to use for this purpose, transporting two SLC on deck. It was drawn up in 1937 by Lieutenant Commander Giuseppe Moschini and Captain (Eng) Alfredo Viola. The idea was to secretly build four such units and train six crews which would be ready to attack Malta and Toulon at a moment's notice, with at least one or two units per objective.

In the same time period, however, improvements to the 'underwater self-propelled craft' and an increase in the range of breathing apparatus showed that the divers could operate for more than two hours with no problems, and the whole scheme was revised, giving up the construction of new, small 'Moschini' type submarines. The idea of operators exiting larger vessels and launching their craft near, but outside, the enemy bases to be attacked, prevailed. Therefore, the development of 'approacher' submarines then turned to standard boats with 'self-propelled' craft initially mounted on deck saddles (*eg Ametista* and *Iride*), and then stored in safer watertight cylinders (*Gondar, Sciré, Ambra, Murena*, etc).

AIRCRAFT

Experiments were carried out in the Orbetello lagoon in spring–summer 1936 for the transportation of the first 'explosive motorboats' models by twin-hulled Savoia-Marchetti S.55 flying boats. This approach was, however, almost immediately abandoned, and it seems that no aircraft was used as assault craft 'approacher' during the Second World War.

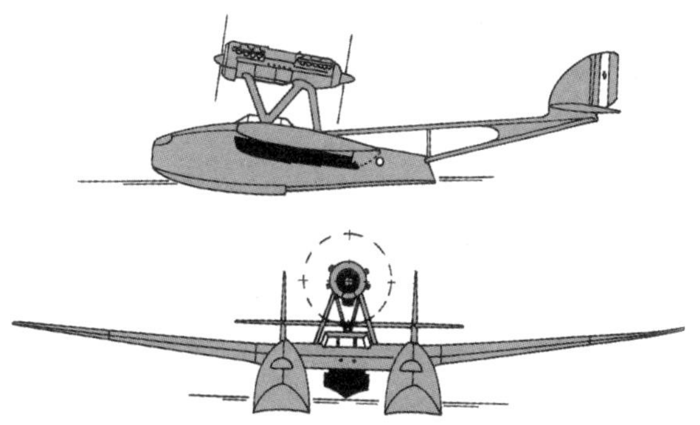

Housing of the MA/MAT explosive motorboat between the hulls of the S.55 flying boat.

The possibility of using Cant Z.506 seaplanes for SLC transport and final approach to the target area (in the Persian Gulf) was studied in 1940. One craft would have been transported by each aircraft, probably suspended under the fuselage between the two floats, but the idea was abandoned shortly after many technical difficulties and operational limitations had emerged as early as the study phase.

Among other things, the charge (or charges) of the 'pigs' would have been excessive for use against the ships operating in that area. It was then thought to use these seaplanes for 'approaching' groups of assault divers ('Gamma') equipped with inflatable boats with outboard engines, but soon this project was also set aside. The same was true for a series of actions planned against Atlantic harbours in the US and in Africa, to be accomplished by transporting SLC and/or 'Gamma' groups using the new, large four-engine Cant Z.511A seaplane. A passenger aircraft destined for transatlantic routes, it was designed by eng. Zappata in 1937 but which, for various reasons, did not make its first flight until 1943. It was a monoplane with twin floats, a wingspan of 43.5 metres and a length over 30, equipped with 4 Piaggio P.XII RC.35 engines, a total weight over 30 tons, with a

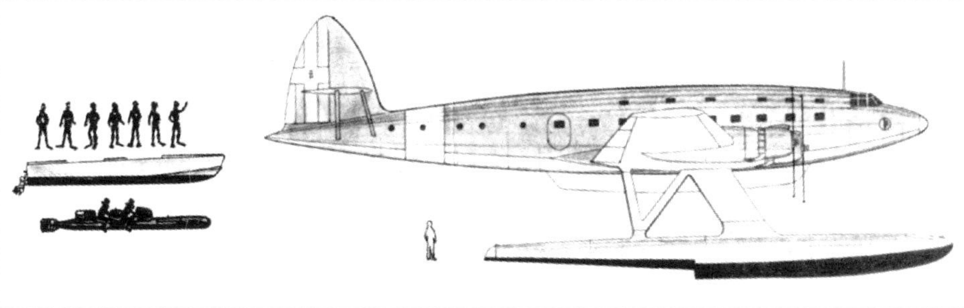

The four-engined Cant Z.511 seaplane could transport an SLC or a motorboat with seven 'Gamma'. *(drawing by F. Harrauer)*

cruising speed around 400 km/h and a range over 4500km.

Construction of two prototypes was started in 1938–1939, but only the first was completed. First flown in late 1940, at the armistice date it was undergoing tests in Vigna di Valle (Bracciano lake), and was scuttled to prevent its capture, and later scrapped. It could have carried at least two SLC, or a single 'pig' and 7 'Gamma' with their 'approacher' craft modified from a MTSM deprived of its superstructure and the torpedo launch gear.

LAND CONVOYS

During the Second World War the X Flotilla Mas created a very special kind of 'approacher': the land convoy, intended as a combination of land vehicles suitably adapted not only for assault craft transport over long distances, but also as a mobile operational and logistics base.

Generally speaking, the main vehicles were selected from those already in Regia Marina and Regio Esercito (Army) service, comprising the following models:

- *trucks:* Fiat 666 NM and Lancia 3-RO M (heavy); Fiat 626 NLM (medium)
- *tractors:* 4x4 S.PA. and O.M. od types T.L. or T.P. 34 or 37 (light and heavy)
- *trailers:* normally 2-axle Viberti for various materials and 2 front axles and 2+2 rear coupled axles with low floor, for boat transport.

The first land convoy was organised at La Spezia ('Cottrau' battery) in April 1942 for transfer to the Black Sea in support of 101st Special Craft Squadron motorboats (LtCdr Aldo Lenzi and, later, LtCdr Salvatore Todaro and Lt Roberto Romano) employed by the specially constituted IV Flotilla Mas (Cdr Francesco Mimbelli).

It was called the 'Moccagatta Land Convoy' in memory of the Decima leader killed in the action against Malta of July 1941 and included a total of 31 vehicles able to carry all the equipment and personnel[1]:

- 5 trucks with an MTM each;
- 5 special trailers for the same number of MTSM[2];

Genoa, spring 1944. Tractors and trailers with surface assault craft on the last stretch of the 'camionale' (truck road) linking the Ligurian capital to the Po river valley.

- 3 tractors;
- 5 Fiat 666 heavy trucks (commonly called the 'sixty-six');
- 2 torpedo trailers;
- 1 12,000-litre tanker;
- 3 tank trailers (water, lubricating oil, etc);
- 1 mobile workshop;
- 1 flatbed trailer with crane for heavy work;
- 1 crane truck (for boat lifting);
- 1 accommodation/command bus with 8-12 foldable bunks (Fiat 621) number plate: RM 26 104;[3]
- 1 radio/secretary car;
- 1 Fiat 1100 car – colonial version;
- 1 Fiat 1100 tarpaulin van.

Besides clothing and personal weapons, the loads included field kitchens, motor compressors, power generators in addition to supplies, equipment and spare parts for engines and more.

Leaving La Spezia on 5 May 1942, the 'Moccagatta' land convoy loaded the assault craft (which had arrived by rail) in Verona. Then it moved to Austria via the Brenner Pass, whence it continued the transfer in stages, by rail and by ordinary road, up to Foros in the Crimea, arriving on the 23rd. Here the craft were unloaded and launched, and a base with slipways was set up, etc.

Between June 1942 and February 1943, the 'Moccagatta' craft carried out many operations against

1. Fifty-seven in total, of which 41 formed the headquarters and support services, and 16 the operational group for piloting the craft.
2. These were *MTSM 204, 206, 208, 210* and *216*.

3. The Regia Marina land vehicle plates (small and rectangular on front, bigger and square at rear) had the 'RM' letters in red, and black numbers on white background. In the RSI period the 'Decima' land vehicles had a red 'X^{a}'.

Maintenance work on an MTM engine in the makeshift Taormina base built for the defence and later evacuation of Sicily in summer 1943.

Soviet ships, especially during the final phase of the siege of the Soviet base in Sevastopol (June 1942). After a few failed launches against enemy war units by *MTSM 216* and *210*, on the night of 12/13 June *MTSM 210* (SBLT Aldo Massarini) hit a big Soviet motorship off Cape Chersonesus with a torpedo, immobilising it. Taken in tow by its own escort – which the motorboats had managed to evade – the ship was sunk the next day by German aircraft.

The land convoy should have been transferred to Simferopol in view of its intended use in the Caspian Sea but, as a consequence of the Soviet counter-offensive of February–March 1943, it returned to Italy with all craft except *MTM 80*, which had been used in a diversionary action against the enemy coast in the Balaklava area of Crimea on 28 June 1942.

The second land convoy organised by X Mas was called 'Comandante Giobbe', in memory of the leading officer of the Flotilla's Surface Craft Department, also killed off Malta in 1941. It was formed in North Africa in summer 1942 with the task of operating along the coast against the enemy naval formations that often carried out bombardment operations close to the front – around El Alamein in those months. The assault craft assigned were those originally embarked aboard the motorsailer *Costanza* (3 MTSM) which found it increasingly difficult to hide from active enemy reconnaissance for any length of time, with easily predictable consequences given the growing Anglo-American air supremacy in that area.

Because of the urgency behind its establishment, and the distance from Italian bases, the convoy was formed using only vehicles readily available in the area, not excluding war prizes. The equipment (compressors, generators, kitchens, etc) was provided by the Regia Marina Headquarters in Libya, which collected elements from everywhere it could under the pressing demands of the Decima leader, Commander Forza, temporarily moved to Africa for the mission. The naval vessels of the land convoy were initially the three aforementioned MTSM from *Costanza*, equipped with 5 torpedoes, 300 litres of petrol and 6 depth charges. Personnel amounted to 19, joined by about 50 'San Marco' regiment sailors for defence and surveillance duties.

The 'Giobbe' left Derna on 21 August 1942 heading for Ras el Dab'a area in Egyptian territory. There, in the following days, an operational base for the craft was established on the shores of a small inlet in El Garut, about 50km west of El Alamein.

The opportunity to act came almost immediately. On the night of 29 August *MTSM 228* (Lieutenant Piero Carminati and Leading Seamen Cesare Sani), putting to sea at short notice, torpedoed the escort destroyer HMS *Eridge* (a 'Hunt' Type II of 1050 tons). It was part of a squadron of four similar units engaged in the bombardment of shore installations, conducted at about 4000m from the coast. The 450mm short torpedo exploded under the 102mm (4in) after gun mounting and, tearing the entire stern section away, immobilised the ship. The *Eridge* was taken in tow by another British destroyer and managed to reach Alexandria harbour but because of the scale of the damage the ship was written off as a Constructive Total Loss and was scrapped in the early post-war period. *MTSM 228* managed to escape the British response but was mistakenly destroyed shortly thereafter by two German aircraft. The two 'pilots' of the craft, however, survived the action, and were decorated with the Silver Medal for Military Valour. After the price paid at Ras el Dab'a, the British ships became more wary, and in

Transport of an MTSM on a trailer towed by a SPA TP 37 tractor.

the following months the 'Giobbe' MTSM could not get an opportunity to launch.

They had been subsequently joined by the 4 MTM formerly embarked aboard the trawler *Sogliola* (pilots: Garrone, Grilli, Raffa and Rossi), arriving from Italy with their transport trucks. However, they were sent back to Derna shortly afterwards, as there was little chance for profitable employment in that area.

With the failure of the Italian–German offensive, which had begun in the last days of August 1942, against the British positions in El Alamein, and the newly acquired RAF air superiority in the area which resulted in continuous bombing and strafing, towards the end of September it was decided to withdraw the 'Giobbe' from El Dab'a and move it to Ras Hilal (30 miles west of Derna). With the front falling back as a result of the great British offensive started in El Alamein at the turn of October and November 1942, the 'Giobbe' land convoy[4] retreated along with the Italian-German forces, reached Bizerte (Tunisia) on 15 December 1942 after a brief stop in Tripoli. At this point it comprised 4 MTSM and 6 MTM, 5 trucks with trailer, 2 tractors with trailer, a pickup truck, one motorcycle, a crane truck with compressor and two tanker trucks. Shortly afterwards, the explosive boats were returned to Italy while the 'Giobbe' light motor torpedo boats later operated in Tunisia, together with those of the *Cefalo*, up to end of the struggle on the African front. Somehow the survivors returned to Italy, and were assigned to surface assault craft units operating from Augusta and in Sardinia waters.

A 7 July 1943 notice from the Mas Headquarters (Generalmas) shows that, in the period immediately preceding the Anglo-American landings in Sicily (launched on 10 July), X Flotmas was organising two more land convoys for the defence of the island. One, designed to operate in the Mazara del Vallo area and provide support to 4 MTM located on the south coast of Favignana in the Aegadian islands, was to have been ready by 25 July, with 4 MTSM. The other, with 4 MTSM and 4 MTM was in preparation for 15 July in Falconara Sicula in the area of Gela.

It was also expected that during August a further land convoy (as always, based on 4 light motor torpedo boats, and the same number of explosive boats) would be established in Catania to operate in the eastern sector of Sicily. The craft returning from Tunisia and Lampedusa would have gone to Melilli (home of the Ist Decimadist of Augusta) for overhaul and repair: this centre would have then supplied the boats to the aforementioned bases, as their refits were completed.

The rapid advance of the Anglo-American forces after the landings prevented the completion of these land convoys. Some of their craft reached the mainland, but the rest were destroyed by their own crews or enemy action.

INFRASTRUCTURE
COMMANDS AND MAIN BASES

What would become an autonomous department in charge of develpment and use of Regia Marina assault craft was born in September 1935 as a section of the 1st Submarine Group (Cdr Catalano Gonzaga di Cirella) and was based in the same offices, overlooking the first basin of the La Spezia Shipyards. It was given the cover name X Flottiglia Mas in March 1941.

In September 1938 the I Flottiglia Mas (Cdr Paolo Aloisi) was established, again in La Spezia. It brought together the three Mas squadrons already active at the same base, and its headquarters was tasked with continuing the training and preparation of the assault craft and their personnel; for technical matters, it looked to the Permanent Commission for experiments in war material (Mariperman) based in La Spezia-San Bartolomeo. Known as the 'Aloisi core', the original group of personnel assigned to the assault craft consisted of thirty people, divided between officers and petty officers, many of whom would become protagonists of the first operations after the Italians joined the war in June 1940. By then, however, the command of I Flottiglia Mas and assault craft department had passed to Commander Mario Giorgini.

When the latter was captured in September 1940 following the loss of submarine *Gondar* in the second unfortunate attack attempt with SLC against Alexandria harbour, the command of the I Flottiglia Mas passed to Cdr Vittorio Moccagatta.

On 15 March following, the department which at the time was temporarily known as the 'Special Mas Flotilla' was separated from the I Flottiglia Mas and assumed the definitive denomination of 'X Flottiglia Mas' (X Flotmas); it remained under the command of Cdr Moccagatta.

Meanwhile, the unit organisation had been defined, and was slightly modified and enlarged (see the March 1941 organisational chart). The headquarters offices remained in the same La Spezia Shipyards building which housed the Mas Flotilla; the surface department moved to the 'Cottrau' battery buildings near the

4. Under the orders of LtCdr Todaro and, later, of Lt Giuseppe Cosulich.

Barracks of the former 'Fiastri' seaplane base in Muggiano, headquarters of Xa Flottiglia Mas, in a photograph from the 1980s.

western end of the Gulf of La Spezia, while the underwater department was split between the Bocca di Serchio training base and the Divers School established in Livorno, relying on accommodation in the Naval Academy. A detachment of the diver department was also established shortly afterwards aboard the *San Marco*, an old cruiser transformed into a radio-controlled target ship, and the minelayer *Fasana*, both based in La Spezia.

After the disastrous July 1941 action against Malta, where the leading officers of the flotilla (Cdr Moccagatta) and surface department (LtCdr Giorgio Giobbe) were killed, Lieutenant Commander Junio Valerio Borghese (then commander of the underwater department, and of the 'approacher' submarine *Sciré*) temporarily assumed the flotilla command, and Lieutenant Commander Salvatore Todaro replaced LtCdr Giobbe. Shortly afterwards, Commander Ernesto Forza – fresh from receiving the Gold Medal of Valour earned on the Mas in the Sicilian Narrows – assumed command of the 'Decima', which he retained until 1 May 1943, when he was replaced by Borghese, in the meantime promoted Commander for his achievements in the war. The organisation of the unit was further expanded (see the September 1941 organisational chart) but without losing those features of simplicity and flexibility that had been the basis of its creation. As reported in the often-cited notes by Admiral Forza, although there were many 'assignments' the number of officers in charge did not exceed a dozen; and many of them were operators, too.

In the second half of 1941 the underwater department was upgraded with the addition of a new speciality represented by the first nucleus of assault divers (conventionally referred to as 'Gamma') and a 'special ships' section responsible, amongst other things, for the development of new craft including the CA mini-submarines transformed into assault/ 'Gamma' approacher submarines.

On 3 September 1942 the flotilla headquarters and those of the dependant departments and services were transferred to Muggiano, on the outskirts of the city on the eastern side of the Gulf of La Spezia, occupying the buildings (barracks, hangars, etc) of the 'G Fiastri' seaplane base which had been abandoned by the Regia Aeronautica some months before. It was situated close to the San Bartolomeo torpedo works, where the underwater assault craft were assembled, between the buildings and barracks of the CREM schools and the then shipyards of Odero Terni Orlando (OTO); with its large ramp into the sea, the 'marine railway', the lifting cranes and the big aircraft hangar, the old seaplane base became the main home for Decima Flottiglia Mas men and craft. The Livorno Divers School and the SLC training in Bocca di Serchio, however, remained in use; furthermore, secondary bases in other anchorages (Brindisi, Augusta, Leros, Foros in the Black Sea, Taormina, Carloforte, Amalfi, etc) were activated as required.

From its establishment until 6 February 1942 the organisation created for the development and employment of assault craft was directly controlled by the

Naval Staff; from the latter date it passed to the auspices of the newly constituted General Inspectorate of the Mas (Generalmas), governed by Vice Admiral Aimone di Savoia, duke of Aosta, created specifically for supervising and coordinating the activities of the assault craft and 'S Marco' Regiment. Generalmas, with an almost non-existent staff, was first located in Livorno and then, from spring 1942, in Lerici (La Spezia). The name of this command was initially chosen with the intention of disguising its real tasks, while trying to imply that it had responsibility for the inspection of Mas and motorboats flotillas. This was actually undertaken by the various Coastal Commands, and it was only in April 1943 that Generalmas also assumed this inspection function – even then, Mas and motor torpedo boats still received orders for their employment from the commands to which the various flotillas and squadrons were assigned.

Except for the replacement of Commander Forza with Commander Borghese at the top of X Flotilla Mas, which took place on 1 May 1943, the organisation of the 'Decima' remained almost unchanged until September 1943, when, due to the armistice, it was essentially split in two.

In the South, Regia Marina reorganised a nucleus with the few craft remaining to them that took the name of 'Assault Craft Command' (Mariassalto), again headed by Forza, now promoted Captain. Mariassalto had its main base in Taranto, in the San Vito area on the Mar Grande, and operational or secondary bases in Brindisi, and later Livorno. Its organisation reflected the existing one but in reduced form, with a preponderance of the surface department over the underwater one; in fact, although the Regia Marina surface craft had been reduced to a few MTSM and MTM, the underwater craft were almost entirely non-existent so, to maintain the level of training for the few SLC operators, Mariassalto had to resort to the use of some Mk I Chariots made temporarily available by the Royal Navy.

In the North, on the other hand, the organisation of the assault craft retained the Xª Flottiglia Mas identity and, under the command of Commander Borghese joined the Armed Forces of the Italian Social Republic. The main base remained in the Muggiano complex of buildings in La Spezia but the Headquarters, Operational Office (LtCdr Uxa) and the Technical Office ended up being transferred to Milan, as the 'Xª' maritime activities were progressively joined by the formation and employment of large Navy Infantry units and 'NP' (Parachute Swimmers) departments, whose story is outside the subject of this work. In the naval field the Flottiglia organisation gradually changed, extending its field of action to the use of conventional vessels such as Mas, motor torpedo boats and CB type mini-submarines.

As for the genuine assault craft sector, the organisa-

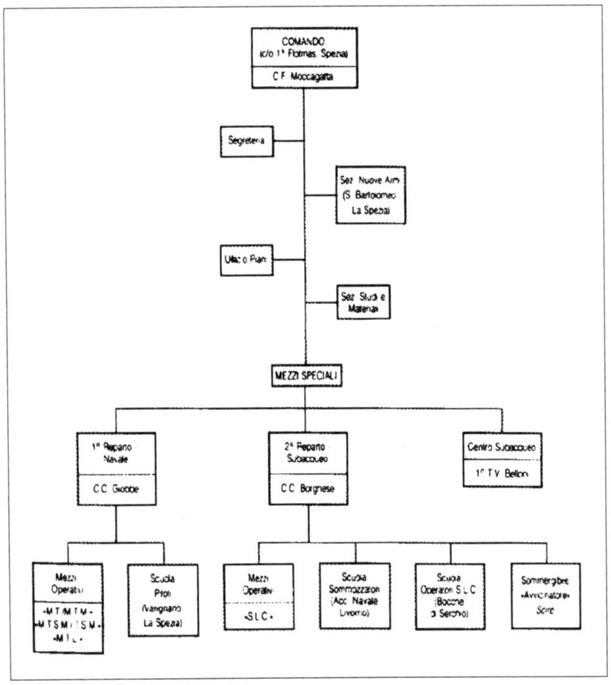

X Flottiglia Mas (Organisational chart, March 1941)

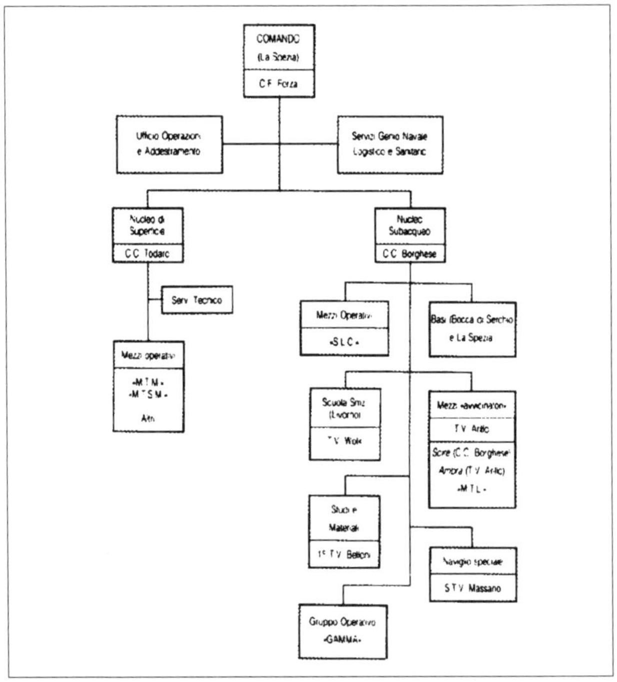

X Flottiglia Mas (Organisational chart, September 1941)

MTM explosive motorboats on exercise in the basin off the 'Cottrau' range at La Spezia in 1942.

tion remained split into two departments, surface and underwater, with related services. The first had two subordinate operational commands (Assault Craft Command – Adriatic, LtCdr Aldo Lenzi in Trieste; Assault Craft Command – Tyrrhenian, LtCdr Mario Arillo in Genoa), besides the Sesto Calende (Varese) Pilots School, various stores (La Spezia, Albissola Marina etc) and short-lived operational bases that were established and then abandoned as the front retreated ('South' Base, Fiumicino; 'West', Villefranche and San Remo; 'East', Brijuni Island in Istria; La Spezia, etc).

The underwater department was formed of the Experimental Centre (1st Lt Belloni, La Spezia), the Valdagno Diver School (Vicenza), the 'Approacher' Craft Group (*MS 75*, MTL, submarines being refitted, etc), in addition to personnel and craft located at the various operational bases: Portorož in Istria and Venice (SLC); Venice, La Spezia and Punta Castagna (SSB); Portofino, La Spezia, Venice and Portorož ('Gamma'); Tarquinia (Viterbo), La Spezia, Venice and Iesolo (NP), etc.

SCHOOLS AND TRAINING CENTRES

The preparation of the operators, together with the continuous improvement of the characteristics and performance of the craft, was considered one of the most important aspects of assault craft warfare from the very beginning. The search for locations, with features and buildings suitable for carrying out discreet and realistic training, began at the same time as the development of the craft themselves.

For surface craft, training of the first explosive-boat pilots occurred in the waters off the 'Cottrau' battery, almost at the western end of the Gulf of La Spezia, close to Palmaria and Tino islets. It was an expanse of water little frequented by tourists, some distance from coastal roads, and sufficiently sheltered from wind and sea for the pilots to practice the 'jump' (the abandonment of the craft once launched towards its target), as well as the night-time overcoming of boom defences which were specially installed for training purposes. This activity began in the autumn of 1938 with the MT, then continued also with light motor torpedo boats, and progressively extending out to the adjacent areas of Punta della Castagna and Seno del Varignano, where during the war the Base Seaward Defence command and the Antisom School were based as well.

The first actual launch of an explosive boat against a ship took place on 13 November 1940 in La Spezia. One of the two prototype 'MA/MAT' was sent, with reduced charge, against the old scout *Quarto* (decommissioned in 1939) moored to a buoy near the breakwater. The motorboat was completely destroyed, but the extent of any damage to the hull of *Quarto* is unknown. It could not have been serious, however, as the ship did not sink, and was transferred to Livorno the following year, still at the disposal of the assault craft organisation. Until September 1942 the 'Cottrau' battery was also the main base for the 'Decima' surface department, that later moved to the former 'Fiastri' seaplane base in Muggiano, where many of the craft ready for use were also concentrated.

During the conflict, temporary sites for motorboat training were also established in Brindisi, Leros and Augusta. After the armistice, training for the few surface craft remaining in the possession of Mariassalto in the South was developed mainly in Taranto, based at San Vito, a small town on the eastern side of Mar Grande. In the North, however, soon after the armistice the republican 'X^a^ Mas' formed a Pilot School for the training of explosive and light motor torpedo boat crews at the former 'Sant'Anna' seaplane base in Sesto Calende on Lake Maggiore. It was close to the SIAI-Marchetti factory which, together with CABI-Cattaneo in Milan and Baglietto Shipyards in Varazze, built MTM and MTSMA type motorboats. The Sesto Calende Assault Pilots School, named 'Gold Medal Commander Salvatore Todaro', enrolled over 120 cadets between December 1943 and February 1945; these were volunteers of all ranks, drawn from many forces besides the Republican National Navy. At the Sesto Calende School courses also included many Kriegsmarine cadets, destined to use MTM explosive boats and SMA light motor torpedo boats built in Italy to German orders.

An explosive boat tactic developed by 'X^a^ Mas', especially after the armistice, was the attack against moving ships; to train pilots in calculating the 'Beta'

Bocca di Serchio, 1941. River mouth and surrounding environment.

The Bocca di Serchio farmhouse, the first accommodation for SLC operators, in a 1941 picture.

(angle between target bearing and course) and target speed – indispensable for making a successful attack – some small lake motor vessels were used, including the biggest *Monfalcone* (81 tons; 30.4m) and its twin *Racconigi*.

Training for the first operators of 'self-propelled' craft (SLC) began in October 1935 with one series of aptitude courses lasting a few days each, initially held in Porto Santo Stefano, where the Regia Marina had commandeered and fenced off a stretch of quay. Generally, personnel of various specialities that had already attended diver schools were assigned to these induction courses; nonetheless, there were very few cadets declared suitable.

Given the proximity of the village to the harbour, training could be undertaken in Porto Santo Stefano with only limited privacy, so in April–May 1936 one of the induction courses was carried out in La Spezia while the search for a more suitable site was going on.

After discounting some areas of Elba, in the summer of that same year a location was chosen at the mouth of Serchio river, a secluded area bordering the San Rossore royal estate. It was a small portion of the estate of Marquises Salviati in Fornacino, including some rural buildings and easy access to the sea through the last stretch of the river. A first induction course was carried out here from 22 July to 15 August 1936, but then the training activity was suspended after the relaxation of international tension that followed the conclusion of the Ethiopia campaign. This activity was resumed only at the end of 1938, and from then until the September 1943 armistice the training base in Bocca di Serchio remained in constant activity, becoming the home-from-home for the crews of the 'pigs'.

It turned out to be an excellent choice, providing both the necessary confidentiality, as it was in a remote area but under constant surveillance (near the Viareggio range and the royal estate), and also safe conditions for the use of 'capricious' underwater craft. The almost constant river flow, with low current speed and a sandy bottom gently declining towards the open sea, were optimal conditions for training exercises which were inherently demanding and –

Another view of the same farmhouse in a picture from the 1990s. To the left of the entrance door there is a marble plaque commemorating the endeavours of assault craft operators during the Second World War. *(G Pitacco)*

Bocca di Serchio, 1941. A 'pig' lifted on tackles, and the support boat used for towing the SLC to and from the open sea.

especially at the beginning – marred by frequent breakdowns of the SLCs, that often involved their sinking to the bottom followed by the need to recover them as easily as possible.

Besides accommodation (initially rather spartan) for the base staff and operators, Bocca di Serchio's facilities included shelters for the self-propelled craft, with rails and carts for moving them to the water, and others with compressors for battery recharge equipment. A small workshop was also organised for minor repairs. Another, better equipped, workshop was subsequently installed at Migliarina. Some powered craft (diesel-driven and motor-launches of types used by Regia Marina) and a couple of small but well-equipped pontoons were used to support the SLC during the trials and exercises. Communication with the nearby La Spezia base was both overland, using trucks, and by sea with self-propelled barges for local support from the shipyards and the services of the Naval Base.

For the training on hull operations, the SLC crews relied on the detachment stationed aboard the old cruiser *San Marco*, long since transformed into a radio-controlled target ship and moored from the beginning of the war at the Scali quay of Duca degli Abruzzi basin in La Spezia. Other exercises, tests and equipment transfers took place with the support of the minelayer *Fasana* also deployed at the La Spezia base.

After the armistice it seems that the Bocca di Serchio equipment was not used by the republican 'X^{a} Mas', which organised its own diver training instead. The Diver School in Livorno was born and developed almost together with the Bocca di Serchio base, commencing its activity on 1 September 1940 and operating within the Accademia navale complex. Under the command of Lieutenant Eugenio Wolk, with the support of LtCdr Belloni, the school initially received personnel already experienced in swimming and diving so most of the training was in the use of self-contained breathing apparatus supplied to the crews of the 'pigs'. Later, the courses became more challenging, and the 30 cadets and 10 instructors of 1940 reached a total of 230 people at the beginning of 1943.

Entrance of one of the barracks built in Bocca di Serchio in 1942. Note the training centre name and motto.

The new officer accommodation block.

The new Bocca di Serchio officers mess hall during a visit by duke Aimone d'Aosta, seen at the head of the table with Commander Forza next to him.

The choice of the Naval Academy as school headquarters was born from reasons of both privacy and convenience, since it was a well-guarded military installation and already provided with a large pool that could be used for training. School organisation and equipment were quickly improved and strengthened; in the summer of 1941 the hulls of two old decommissioned naval units were placed at its disposal: these were submarine *Galvani* and scout *Quarto*, which were towed from La Spezia to Livorno and moored in the harbour for training cadets in operations against the hulls of targets.

The school gradually expanded its field of action: the initial training of SLC operators was joined by that of divers for underwater work, assault divers (frogmen or 'Gamma'), and 'N' operators (Swimmers), a particular speciality of saboteurs of the 'San Marco' Regiment of the Regia Marina. At the beginning of 1942 the training of these latter specialists, together with that of 'P' operators (Paratroopers, always of 'San Marco'), was transferred to the Regia Aeronautica Parachute School in Tarquinia (Viterbo); only the training of divers, 'Gamma', and underwater assault craft operators remained in Livorno.

After the armistice, Mariassalto found itself practically devoid of underwater assault craft, and had to resort to Mk I Chariots made available by the Royal Navy for training and for completing its only harbour forcing action (Genoa, April 1945). Furthermore, 'Gamma' training was quite limited, and carried out at the San Vito base in Taranto with what little underwater materials were available.

At the republican 'X^{a} Mas', diver training took place mainly in Valdagno (Vicenza) where, after a brief time spent in La Spezia and Portofino (Genoa), the Diver School had moved from Livorno. In Valdagno, the school used the swimming pool of the Marzotto woollen mill recreational club for training, and the logistic arrangements were organised under the cover name 'Rehabilitation Centre for injured'. After a period of initiation, selection and basic training, the 'Gamma' were sent to Venice and housed in an old convent on the islet of San Giorgio dell'Alga; they practised in the waters of the lagoon using as targets the hulls of the old tanker *Tampico* and other ships out of service (motor tanker *Illiria*, etc). There was no proper school for SLC and SSB operators: their training was directly carried out at the craft operational bases – Portorož, in Istria, Venice (former Sant'Andrea seaplane base) and La Spezia (Punta Castagna).

ADVANCED BASES AND SUPPORT UNITS

Throughout the conflict, X Flottiglia Mas organised several advanced bases as part of various projected or planned operations. In chronological order, the surface craft depended on advanced bases set up in Brindisi (MT and MTS, spring 1941); Leros (MT, February–March 1941); Augusta (MT, MTS, MTL and SLC, spring–summer 1941); Villa Carmela in the bay of Gibraltar ('Gamma', spring 1942 to September 1943); Foros on the Black Sea (MTSM and MTM of the 'Moccagatta' land convoy, May 1942 to March 1943); El Dab'a in Egypt, Bizerte in Tunisia, etc (MTSM and MTM of the 'Giobbe' land convoy, and trawlers *Cefalo*, *Sogliola* and *Costanza*, summer 1942 to spring 1943); I Decimadist Augusta (MTSM and MTM, June 1942–July 1943); II Decimadist Carloforte (MTM, MTSM and 'Gamma', March–September 1943);[1] Taormina and Amalfi (MTSM and MTM drawn from I Decimadist of Augusta, August–September 1943).

Following the armistice, Mariassalto established small advanced bases in various Tyrrhenian and Adriatic harbours, that were gradually made operational as the the front line advanced. In contrast, the

1. The first nucleus of II Decimadist was established in Carloforte, Sardinia, on San Pietro island on 24 March 1943 with 3 MTM transported by the *Sogliola*. Between May and the following July craft numbers were increased to 11 MTM and 5 MTSM divided amongst various Sardinian anchorages: Cala Domestica on the coast, 10 miles north of Carloforte (4 MTM and a MTSM); at the mouth of Temo river, 17 miles south of Alghero (4 MTM and an MTSM); Cala Reale, on Asinara island (3 MTM and an MTSM); and Carloforte (2 MTSM). In April 1943 a group of 'Gamma' operators and an 'N' department (Assault swimmers of the 'San Marco') were also sent to Sardinia.

Tanker *Fulgor* while moored in Cadiz.

republican 'Xª Mas' instead established operational bases in Fiumicino (Base 'South'), Villefranche and San Remo (Base 'West'), in Brijuni in Istria ('East' Base), as well as support points in Portorož, Istria; Poula and Venice.

Other advanced bases, whose existence and activity were considered secret, were:

Tanker *Fulgor*

Owned by 'La Columbia' company of Genoa, it was a tanker built in 1922 (6504grt, 8000 tons capacity; 122m x 17m x10m; 3 oil-fired boilers and quadruple expansion engine; 10 knots). From June 1940, Gibraltar was a primary objective of Decima Mas and therefore many SLC operations had been aimed there, with the submarine *Sciré* under the command of Lieutenant Commander Borghese as 'carrier'.[2]

Italy's declaration of war had surprised *Fulgor* in the port of Cadiz, where she was interned. The ship was moored along the Guadalete river, at some distance from the sea: to reach it, one had to go upstream for a stretch of the waterway. Nevertheless, it was to become an important reference point for the secret organisation set up in Spanish territory by the Regia Marina.

In the first actions against the Rock, the operators boarded the *Sciré* in La Spezia, therefore the long days at sea, mostly underwater, was detrimental to their physical condition, which had to be always at the highest level of efficiency. To avoid this, it was decided to use the *Fulgor*, where the operators were concentrated while waiting for the *Sciré* to sail up the river at night – manoeuvring silently on electric motors – to embark them quickly, together with some supplies. More than once, the operators were sent to Spain by air or by other means, subsequently reaching Cadiz by car or in small groups hidden in the load of a truck, finally boarding the tanker mixed with members of its civilian crew returning from shore leave.[3] Also via *Fulgor* came a stream of spare parts and fresh food for the submariners, sent under the name of the shipping company as routine supplies.

The secretly-cut opening in the hull of the tanker *Olterra* moored in Algeciras. It was used for exit and entry of the SLC using this ship as their operational base for attacks on shipping at anchor in the Gibraltar roadstead, or inside the harbour of the 'Rock'.

Tanker *Olterra*

The prolonged use as an advanced operational base of this old merchant ship moored in view of the Gibraltar Rock was a tour de force of Italian secret services and a brilliant achievement of the Decima organisation.

2. Junio Valerio Borghese had defined his submarine as 'almost a liner used to transport the "pigs" between La Spezia and Gibraltar'. Besides being very skilled in underwater navigation, the famous commanding officer of the *Sciré* was considered particularly lucky, a gift not to be underestimated in an environment always inclined to superstition like that of sailors. Furthermore, it seems that he also had the ability to transmit his luck to others via a unique ritual: all the operators 'given a ride' in his submarine, just before leaving the *Sciré* for action bent over and were sent on their way with a propitiatory kick in the backside!

3. Decima operators heading for both *Fulgor* and *Olterra* from Italy employed some curious gimmicks. On one occasion a group of operators reached Spain as members of the civilian crew of the merchant ship *Mauro Croce*, but as soon as the ship docked at Barcelona they deserted and were transferred by Italian agents to the *Olterra*. On another occasion, three 'Gamma' were taken from a group of seven previously arrested by the Carabineiros, and with the connivance of the local authorities swapped with the same number of 'regular' *Fulgor* sailors. This might appear surprising, but it reflected the delicate Spanish position: favourable to the Axis powers, but subjected to continuous British pressure, and thus needing to seem neutral.

In early 1940s the fleet of the Genoese shipowner Andrea Zanchi included numerous ships (*Augusta*, *Bonzo*, *Cervino*, *Mar Bianco*, *Norge*, etc), which were partly oil tankers and partly refrigerated or for dry cargoes. Amongst the Zanchi ships was the steam tanker *Olterra*, a medium-sized ship (4995grt, 7600 tons capacity, 126m long, 16m broad with a draught of 7.5m) built back in 1913. The single propeller was driven by a quadruple expansion steam engine powered by two boilers, and the maximum speed was about 9 knots.

Since the beginning of the war the ship, under the command of Captain Amoretti from Imperia, had been interned in the Spanish harbour of Algeciras, which is in sight of Gibraltar, whose military harbour is about 6 miles to the East. The tanker was moored alongside the outer mole (with the Lauro company *Lavoro*, also interned). It had been towed there after being raised from the bottom, where it had rested for about a month following its scuttling by the crew opening the Kingston valves on the announcement of Italy's entry into the war on 10 June 1940.

'Pig' assembly and tuning workshop, secretly set up inside the *Olterra*'s forward hold.

A report on the opportunities offered by the use of this ship had come from a Decima Mas 'agent', Antonio Ramognino. He had rented a house (Villa Carmela, near the Spanish town of La Linea) to use as an observation point, that would eventually become, as will be seen, a 'Gamma' base. An agreement was struck with the shipowner, but he was unaware of the particular use that would be made of his vessel.

Under the cover of 'restoration' work, the ship was secretly equipped to serve as an advanced base for a group of SLC intended to attack both the military harbour of Gibraltar and the large merchant ships at anchor in the roadstead. The craft would no longer have had to be transported aboard submarines all the way from Italy but, with undeniable savings in time and risk, operate directly from the *Olterra* where they would return at the end of the mission.

Using the excuse of routine changes, the original crew was gradually replaced by pseudo-sailors who were actually 'X Mas' members, and some specialised workers directed by Captain Eng Travaglini. Eventually, the only members of the original civilian crew left were Captain Amoretti and chief engineer officer De Nigris.

Citing hull cleaning requirements, the stern double bottoms were flooded, thus bringing the bow out of the water, at the same time heeling the ship to starboard. A tarpaulin nominally laid out to protect men from the sun allowed an opening of 1.20 x 2.00 metres to be secretly cut at the bottom of the port side. With the ship back in normal trim, the compartment inboard was open to 'free circulation' of the sea, ready to be used to trim the craft, that then exited and returned through the said opening.

Together with pipes (officially for boilers), metal sheets, pumps and other machinery, in the crates arriving from Italy were SLC parts and accessories, which were then assembled in the well-equipped workshop clandestinely created aboard the ship.

To get to the 'secret part' of the vessel, one had to face a winding path through corridors, steps, false bulkheads and bolted manholes, which made it practically impossible for those who were not insiders to reach the heart of the Decima men's activity.

That movement of men and materials to the *Olterra* was given a certain justification by spreading a rumour of refitting and repair work, to be carried out on the oil tanker in view of its hypothetical sale to another shipowner. A picket of Carabineros was permanently aboard the tanker with the task of monitoring compliance with the international rules on neutrality; not to mention that the mooring place was practically under the windows of the Vittoria Hotel, office of the local British consulate.

The summer of 1942 was entirely spent preparing the ship as a secret base for attacks on Gibraltar with the 'pigs'. The command of the advanced base aboard the *Olterra* was entrusted to Lieutenant Visintini and, after his death in action, to Lieutenant Commander Notari. X Flottiglia Mas carried out three actions from the *Olterra*: 'BG 5' of 7 December 1942; 'BG 6' of 7 May 1943 and 'BG 7' of 3 August 1943.

It was only after 8 September 1943 that the British – to their great surprise – found out about the activity aboard the *Olterra* that had taken place almost under their noses. At the end of hostilities, *Olterra* resumed sailing until, finally decommissioned, it arrived in the

Tanker *Olterra* photographed in Genoa, post-war.

Vado roadstead (Savona) in the first months of 1961 to be scrapped. The La Spezia Naval Museum has on display some old metal sheets that once formed part of the stern moulding, on which can be read, in large

Olterra in Vado Ligure in 1961 at the start of the breaking up process. The two visible hull openings are not related to the wartime activities of this ship, but were cut by shipyard workers to get on board more easily. *(L Venturino)*

white letters on a black background: '*Olterra* - Genova'. In the same museum a life preserver with the name of the ship, the steering wheel, the binnacle of the magnetic compass and the bell are kept as memorabilia.

Steamer *Gaeta*

This single-screw vessel (4457grt, launched in 1927, 122m long, 16m wide with a draught of 8m) was owned by the 'Nivosa' Shipping Company of Naples. Its three coal-fired boilers powered the triple expansion steam engine to give the ship a maximum speed of less than 10 knots. It was commanded by Captain Michele Coccorullo.

At the outbreak of the war the *Gaeta* was in the Spanish harbour of Huelva, on the southern Atlantic coast, just beyond Gibraltar, almost on the border with Portugal. It was interned, and remained in that anchorage while Allied shipping increased steadily, principally loading iron and copper minerals from the Rio Tinto mining area. Therefore, its strategic position could not escape the attention of Decima Mas.

With the support of Commander Pierleoni, Italian Consul in Barcelona, and in the face of British counter-espionage, operations began to make *Gaeta* an advanced 'Gamma' base. Posing as replacement crew, two assault divers arrived on the ship in spring 1943. The operation, codenamed 'GOG', took place between May and June 1943. Although details of the circumstances are unknown, the operators Salvatore Nizzi and Carlo Vianello managed to fit explosive charges to the hulls of some merchant ships. However, these were discovered and removed by British divers of the 'UWWP' (Under Water Warfare Patrol) during an unexpected stopover at Gibraltar. The merchant ships involved were the 9700grt *Ladovich*, the *Willowdale* and the *Imber*.

Villa Carmela

This was undoubtedly the most peculiar advanced base amongst those organised by X^{a} Flotilla Mas during the Second World War. It was a modest cottage located near Puenta Maiorga, at the end of the Bay of Algeciras in Spanish territory, within sight of the Rock of Gibraltar. It was only a few dozen metres from the sea, along the beach running from the mouth of the Guadarranque river to the Spanish town of La Linea. An easy and discreet connection with the sea was provided by the almost always dry bed of a small stream that passed near the house and reached the sea making a wide curve, and passing under a bridge. The entire Gibraltar harbour was visible from the house, and the freighters normally anchored there were 500 to 2000 metres from the beach front.

It was chosen by Antonio Ramognino, a Regia Marina agent, formerly a Piaggio technician who designed the 'R' boats for 'Gamma' target approaching. He had noticed it during a reconnaissance of the area carried out secretly in the spring of 1942, with a view to installing an observation post and a secret base for Decima operators. In the first months of 1942 the assault craft command considered the use of SLC approached by submarines as too expensive and risky for attacks on merchant ships anchored in the Gibraltar roadstead, outside the boom defences of the base. By contrast, almost all operators who had participated in the previous actions against Gibraltar had found the return to Spanish territory relatively easy, which boded well for the establishment of a base from where 'Gamma' teams could make relatively short round trips – without too much risk – to attack anchored merchantmen. To facilitate these operations, it was planned to use 'R' boats, then under construction, which would have allowed them to carry big charges and save the divers from a long, strenuous and slow swim to the targets.

Having married a Spanish citizen, Ramognino was able to rent the house without arousing the suspicion of the Spanish authorities, claiming that his convalescent wife needed a rest period in a warm climate like that of southern Spain.

As soon as he settled in Villa Carmela, Ramognino had a small parrot cage built outside the house, on the side facing the sea, which concealed an opening through which, unseen, he constantly kept ships' movements in the harbour under observation. At the same time, he suggested the idea of using the tanker

Villa Carmela, first building on the right, and the dry stream bed used by 'Gamma' to reach the waters of Gibraltar roadstead, passing under the bridge this picture was taken from. Far right is Mrs Concita Ramognino.

The Gibraltar roadstead, with many anchored ships, seen from the bridge in the picture opposite.

Portrait of Antonio Ramognino in Regia Marina chief petty officer 3rd class uniform with his wife, and two souvenir pictures taken in the vicinity of Villa Carmela. *(Courtesy of the Ramognino Family)*

Olterra, interned and moored in Algeciras harbour, as an advanced base for the SLC designated to operate against Gibraltar.

Although the 'R' boats were not yet available, X Mas decided to carry out its first 'Gamma' action against steamers in the harbour (Operation GG 1) on the night of 13/14 July 1942, operating from Villa Carmela. Twelve operators who had arrived on the *Olterra* from Italy moved to Villa Carmela, from where they attacked the targets the following night, heavily damaging four steamers (*Meta, Shumma, Empire Snipe* and *Baron Douglas*). All the 'Gamma' returned from the action, some to Villa Carmela and some to other points of the harbour where they were arrested by the Spaniards; but, thanks to the intervention of Italian diplomatic authorities, they too were subsequently repatriated.

A second, similar operation (GG 2) with three 'Gamma' also setting out from Villa Carmela in the evening of 14 September following, led to the sinking of one steamer (*Rovens Point*). Two of the operators managed to return to Villa Carmela and later to the *Olterra*; the third was intercepted by the Spanish police, but no indication about the existence of the two advanced bases of the Decima in Gibraltar was leaked.

Minelayer *Fasana* moored in Augusta in summer 1941. *(N Siracusano collection)*

Villa Carmela proved to be an ideal base for the two operations conducted by the 'Gamma', who reached the beach completely equipped along the dry bed of the stream next to the house and then entered the water silently, without attracting the attention of the Spanish Carabineros patrolling the beach. The return to Villa Carmela took place along the same path, and an old artesian well dug nearby was used to make empty tanks and other useless, compromising materials disappear.

The movements from and to the *Olterra* were in small groups, walking along country lanes and unfrequented roads in the dark. Like the *Olterra*, Villa Carmela also unveiled its secrets only after the end of the conflict.

'Gamma' had proved to be Decima's most flexible offensive tool, but the armistice of September 1943 blocked plans to create new advanced bases in the neutral harbours of Barcelona and Malaga in Spain, and Lisbon and Porto in Portugal.

Other naval and merchant vessels were used by X Flottiglia Mas fleet for logistic and/or training purposes:

Minelayer *Fasana* (normal displacement 530 tons; 66.3m x 10m x 2.01m; 10 knots) one of a class of four built in 1923–27. It was used mainly in the La Spezia area as a training and support unit in 1941–1942.

Target ship *San Marco* (normal displacement 8600 tons; 140.9m x 21m x 6.7m). Formerly a *San Giorgio* class armoured cruiser launched in 1908 and converted in the second half of the 1930s to a radio-controlled target for gunnery exercises. At the beginning of the war it was placed in reserve and moored at the Scali Quay of the 'Duca degli Abruzzi' Basin. From the beginning of 1941, the 'X Mas' underwater department began to use the ship as a logistics base for a detachment of the Bocca del Serchio Group, and for the training of SLC operators in under-hull operations. It would be sunk at La Spezia in 1944 by air attack.

Ex-scout *Quarto*. Built in 1909–1913 (normal displacement 3442 tons; 131.6m x12.8m x 4.1m), it had been decommissioned in 1939, and in 1940 it was in La Spezia waiting to be scrapped. In November 1940 it was employed as a target for a live trial of an explosive boat with reduced charge in La Spezia harbour. In the summer of 1941 it was towed to Livorno, where it used as a pontoon for under-hull operations training at the local X Flotilla Mas Diver

Radio-control target ship *San Marco* moored at La Spezia in the late 1930s.

Light cruiser (former scout) *Quarto* in a 1930s picture.

School. It was just a hulk with all the superstructure removed, but its internal arrangement provided temporary housing for a small number of operators, and a reduced crew.

Ex-submarine *Galvani*. Commissioned in 1918 this submarine (842/1244 tons) had been decommissioned in the 1930s and subsequently employed as a pontoon in La Spezia. In the summer of 1941 it was towed to Livorno, where it was used for similar purposes as those of *Quarto*.

Tanker *Tampico*. Property of the Società Navigazione e Commercio of Genoa, with a gross tonnage of 4958 and a capacity of 7250 tons; 177m in length, it had an reciprocating steam engine that gave a maximum speed of 10 knots. In the last phase of the war, it was laid up at the island of San Giorgio in Venice, with its bow beached in the sand, but the stern afloat. It was an ideal target for the training of assault divers, and was employed as such by the Gamma Group 'Licio Visintini' of the republican 'Xª Mas' and equivalent Kriegsmarine operators.

Old steam tanker *Tampico* in Venice in 1944.

APPENDICES

1. SYSTEMS, MATERIALS AND SPECIAL EQUIPMENT

A) Propulsion systems of surface assault craft

Engine. In the explosive and light motor torpedo boats it consisted of a gasoline engine using aircraft-specification fuel with high tetraethyl lead content, produced by Alfa-Romeo in Milan. It was broadly similar to the Mas '500' auxiliary power unit. Developed from the 'AR-6 b 2500 M' and designated '6 c 2500 M', it had a maximum power output of 85.77hp at 3300rpm, 72mm bore, 100mm stroke, 2473cm^3 capacity and 320–334kg weight. The engine was progressively developed into the higher-powered 2500/1 (88.7hp) and 2500/2 (93.6hp) versions used aboard MTM; while the two upgraded 2500/4 engines mounted on MTMS and MTSMA type torpedo boats reached a total 187hp output.

The engine essentially retained the good basic features that had determined its initial success. Designed for automotive roles, it was modified for naval purposes directly by Alfa-Romeo for Mas, and by CABI for assault craft. It employed four-stroke internal combustion, 6-cylinder with 1-3-2-6-5-4 (bow to stern) firing order and left-hand rotation. Lubrication was forced, with a gear pump and a 20–22kg cylindrical reservoir (vertically mounted and painted blue) linked to the engine by two (supply and return) flexible rubber hoses covered with steel mesh and headed by threaded copper pipettes atop the reservoir and on the engine block.

Depending on the series (and sometimes on individual craft within a series) the reservoir, and battery, was variously placed: it usually was in the front, right-side engine bay corner, but could be found in the rear, facing the bow but still on the right.

The cooling system had two circuits:

Fresh water: front radiator fitted to the engine block, and upper screw cap. To avoid the formation of air bubbles, refilling was via a hand pump with wooden lever, placed low to the right of the frame. The same pump could also serve for transfer between the two side tanks, and bilge water venting (if the dedicated pump connected to the engine could not be used, for example with the engine stopped). This obviously only applied to craft with this detail: for example, late series SIAI craft were no longer provided with a bilge pump, given the better hull waterproofing thanks to the particular construction system adopted.

Sea water: in the engine block cavity, taken dynamically from a hull inlet (strum) and therefore effective only while moving.

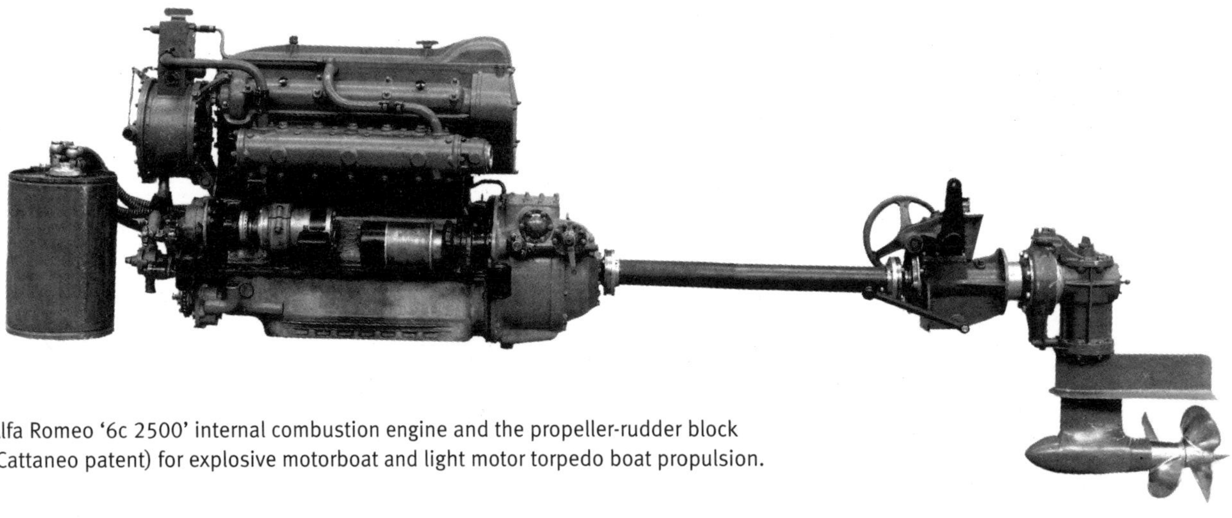

Alfa Romeo '6c 2500' internal combustion engine and the propeller-rudder block (Cattaneo patent) for explosive motorboat and light motor torpedo boat propulsion.

End of the swinging stern drive on an MTM explosive motorboat.

'CABI – Cattaneo' of Milan logo.

On the MTM there were two fuel tanks (coloured in fern green and about 50 litres each), arranged along the keel, one on each side of the engine. They had a large screw cap with peripheral knurling and a small vent hole on top.

The battery (Marelli 12 V at 32 W - 64 A/h) was similar to automotive types, protected from possible water splashing by a wooden cover, fixed with two wing nuts to two threaded steel rods locked on the wooden base, firmly holding the battery itself. The electrical system aboard MTSM and SMA was appropriately shielded to avoid interference and disturbance to any radio transceiver.

At the top, the engine had the classic covers of the 'overhead valves' (blue-grey in colour), over the intake (right) and exhaust camshafts. The rest of the head, like the block and the base, was painted in matt black. Also black were the electric wire sheathings (those of the spark-plugs were sometimes red), the ignition coil body (brown shell) and the starter motor.

The two carburettors (normally 'Weber' brand), fed three cylinders each, and were overhanging to the right, with an underlying drip tray. On the fuel supply circuit, just upstream of the carburettors, was a small thick glass bowl, as a filter to help eliminate the remaining impurities in the petrol (although when refuelling the fuel was passed through deer skin placed in the funnel filter). Some craft had a fuel level indicator on the dashboard; however, it was subject to frequent breakdowns, which were compensated by manually measuring the level with a rod.

When it was adopted on assault craft, the Alfa Romeo 2500 engine was already well known by a great part of the Regia Marina engine specialists, with a consequent considerable economy in the training.

This engine was equipped with:

Inverter (reversing gear)

Integral with the back of the engine, it consisted of a steel cast structure, closed at the top by a bolted plate. Inside, a series of oil-bathed steel discs received the rotary motion from the end of the crankshaft, transmitting it to the half-shaft connected with the propeller-rudder unit. Depending on the selection made by the pilot in the cockpit with a special lever, different discs clutched against each other, constituting a transmission that was at the same time flexible and reliable, allowing the choice of forward - neutral - reverse.

Because the connection was made by clutch discs, the propeller shaft responses were not immediate, but gradual. Especially in the case of emergency manoeuvres, before the boat *felt* the command, some fractions of second passed while the disks slipped before 'getting a grip'.

The control levers of the inverter were arranged:

- on the MTM in the hood, on the right side of the bulkhead with the front engine compartment.
- on MTSM and SMA in the cockpit on the so-called 'bridge' (engine control support) which was on the centreline and served as a divider between the pilots' seats.

The inverter gear was very reliable; enclosed in a single casing, it did not normally require maintenance. A copper pipe connected to the dashboard in the cockpit led to a special pressure gauge, which indicated oil pressure in the hydraulic circuit (normally about 15kg/cm^2).

Drive shaft

This emerged from the rear of the inverter and was connected to the stern drive; it consisted of a hollow steel shaft fixed, at each end, through flanges secured by bolts and nuts. Generally known as the 'transmission shaft' both on the explosive and torpedo boats, it was about 60cm long (on the MTM it passed between the pilot's legs, while on MTS and on SMA it was in a well at the extreme stern with a lockable inspection hatch with wing nuts or bolts).

Stern drive

In Italian it was known by terms that translate as 'stern foot' and 'boot', but most commonly it was referred to simply as the 'group'. Though today this type of 'Z-drive' is fairly common in motorboats, then it constituted an absolute novelty. Defined by CABI as a 'swinging inboard-outboard', it was born to better exploit the advantages of traditional outboard engines, combining them with the benefits typical of internal engines, while at the same time minimising the shortcomings of each.

For the specific purposes of assault craft, this was the ideal solution, being capable of swinging laterally out of the water, both for overcoming obstructions and significantly reducing drag whenever the craft had to be towed close to the area of operation. The rotary motion of the engine was no longer transmitted to the propeller via the traditional shaft, with the consequent need for gland, collars, suspension arms or rods, but directly to the 'group'. Here rotation was converted from horizontal to vertical through a complex conical gear system, then down to the lower part of the drive, where more similar gears turned it back to horizontal.

Two hollow shafts (coaxial and rotating one inside the other) finally transmitted motion to two contra-rotating propellers, giving the craft good directional stability.

The bronze propellers were respectively: two-bladed forward (left-hand), and three-bladed aft (right-hand), suitably sized to balance the torque (240mm diameter).

The 'group' was composed of different parts forming a single complex. The main and most striking element was the stem, a single die-cast vertical piece, of cylindrical-ovoid section, with external strengthening ribs and internal cavities for shafts and gears. Just above the propellers in the single cast piece was a flat, downward-facing surface intended to direct the water stream generated by propeller rotation. This surface (called the 'sole') joined the upper stem with a thick vertical rib like a rudder to enhance the steering function of the 'group' itself.

To further reduce drag, the lower part of the stem was shaped like a 'bulb' with a lower skeg which – besides further improving the steering – was primarily

The Alfa Romeo '6c 2500' engine of an MTM explosive motorboat commissioned by the Germans and captured by USS *Gleaves* off Provence in 1944.

Life-raft arrangement aboard an MTM on display in Turin in 1961. After somewhat approximate restoration work, this craft is missing the engine exhaust – clearly visible in the picture to the right taken in Sesto Calende in 1944.

intended to prevent propeller damage in shallow waters. The propellers were keyed on the short coaxial half-shafts, and fixed by an ogival screwed bronze cone which allowed their easy disassembly and replacement. The reduction ratio between the engine rpm and propellers was 0.64.

The 'block' came out of the transom, connected with the inside through a waterproof ball joint, designed to allow it to swing on the horizontal plane and lift vertically, to switch between 'work' and 'clear' positions. Lifting, depending on the various types of explosive boats, could be either to starboard or to the left. On the light motor torpedo boats, which were equipped with two engines and therefore two drives, lifting was always inwards, towards the centreline, so the left drive rotated to the right, while the starboard consequently lifted towards the left.

To facilitate this manoeuvre, an articulated steel rod pivoted on a cantilevered shelf on the transom, acting simultaneously as a terminal for the set of steel cables with tensioner, return wheels and friction bearings of the tiller wire rope system.

On the right side of the part of the 'block' inside the hull, there was a vertical steel spoked wheel that when rotated lifted the drive sideways. The return of the 'block' to 'working' position was by gravity. In SIAI-built MTM (1944), things were simplified, since the procedure was no longer manual, but through a gear keyed to the engine.

On the explosive boats at the level of the seat, between the legs of the pilot, was a large screw, initially with a circular knob but subsequently star-shaped with rounded tips to improve the grip of the operator's fingers. Familiarly known as the 'big screw', it was intended to fix the stern drive rigidly on the centreline after aiming the boat against the target.

Steering of the boat was through a sector wheel (it was not a full steering wheel) inside the cockpit in front of the pilot. Transmission of the heading direction was through a gear keyed on its column, which transmitted the rudder angle to the stern drive. With the traditional rudder blade of normal boats, moving it either side creates drag and eddies, with consequent speed loss; with the 'block', instead, all thrust is oriented to the intended direction, nearly eliminating all such drags, at the same time getting better turning characteristics. The maximum rudder angle was between 18° and 20° each side.

B) Life-raft for explosive boats

From the very first experiments with prototypes, amongst the designers' major concerns was the safety and survival of the operator. Initially there was no provision for a 'life-raft', which only came into general use later. There was not even the 'Belloni suit', but the pilot (or 'helmsman' as he was then called) wore a rudimentary 'life-bag': a bulky neck-to-feet complete suit, with rather thick (10-15cm) 'kapok' (vegetable fibre) padding. Such clothing did provide sufficient buoyancy, sometimes increased by adding a standard life jacket (again filled with 'kapok') of the type supplied to ships. Thus protected, at the moment of

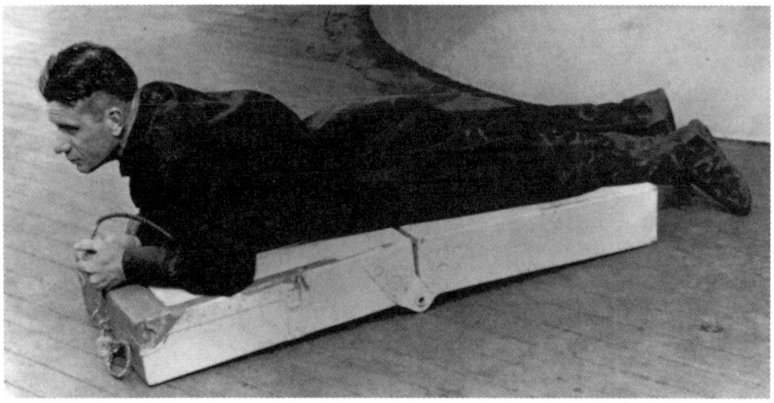

Pilot's position on the life-raft, to be assumed after the 'jump' at sea.

Close-up of an MTM life-raft.

Experimental self-propelled raft made for X Mas in 1944. *(A Molinari collection)*

Republican X Mas operators training with the experimental self-propelled raft. *(A Molinari collection)*

charge explosion and consequent underwater concussion the operator was supposed to lie flat on the sea surface (not in a standing position), with feet if possible facing towards the burst point.

The raft definitively adopted up to the final MTM series consisted of two parallelepipeds (each of 0.70m x 0.55m x 0.15m) with cellular interiors formed of hardwood strips, externally covered with beech plywood panels interlayered with waterproof canvas. A flat sheet metal hinge in anti-corrosion metal, placed at the top on each side, held the two parts joined in a folded position. The life-raft formed the aft closure of the cockpit, and at the same time the pilot's seat back-rest. It was fixed to the canopy edges with brass ring latches, to be inserted in the appropriate seats, held by a hook or pawl. When launching, lifting the red burst lever – besides activating the various devices – broke the life-raft restraints, causing it to fall into the water, along with the pilot who was leaning against it. The action of 4-5 sturdy elastic cables opened the two raft sections, forming a single support base.

When the craft were at a mooring (or when the life-rafts had to be stored in a warehouse), the rafts were held open, to maintain cable elasticity. A small line for faster recovery of the life-raft by the operator (especially at night and in rough seas) was tied to a metal ring on the far side of one of the parts. Then he had to climb on it (belly down, arms and legs raised out of the water) in the few seconds available before the boat charge burst against the target, or at the end of the run.

On early MT, however, the raft was held in place by a sailcloth or canvas strip. At Suda, then sergeant Emilio Barberi lost it while overcoming one of the defensive barriers and the life-raft ended up in the sea (although immediately recovered). Clearly, the raft-burst device link functioned in a different way.

When the folded raft was placed on its stern support, the craft's distinctive number was in the centre of its flat back surface, initially in black, later in yellow-gold paint which stood out against the uniform grey-blue colour of the rest of the hull.

An attempt to motorise the life-raft was made in Sesto Calende in early 1944, giving birth to the *Self-propelled Life-raft.* A small two-blade ducted propeller with a small stabilising fin underneath was fitted on the top of the after outer face. In the bulb the propeller was attached to was a 0.25hp electric motor powered by a battery placed inside the raft body.

The fore and aft lower edges were no longer sharp but rounded to improve seaworthiness. The size of each section was about 105cm x 55cm x 20cm, and the hinge between the two parts was no longer on top, but at the bottom. At front, on the upper 'deck', two simple metal handles provided secure hand-holds, while a square black rubber 'patch' hid a button – initially to be pushed with the chin – which controlled the propeller drive. Also on the upper 'deck', two circular lids gave access to wells intended to hold reserve food or water, and some tools deemed indispensable. The already modest freeboard of the 'standard' type was further reduced, as the additional weights decreased buoyancy. This was already evident on the calm lake waters where it was tested, and with even the slightest swell the inconvenience would certainly have been more serious at sea. For these reasons the 'electric raft' never got beyond the experimental phase, which also included trying to tow a group of operators. Individual initiative took over, however: someone 'invented' paddles similar to those used for table tennis, that would have eased the movements of pilot waiting for recovery after launch. Thus most pilots hung these on the belt of the 'Belloni' suit, together with other tools, even though they were commonly known as 'signalling discs'.

C) Torpedoes and launching equipment

The types employed by Italian surface assault craft should more correctly be called 'short torpedoes', being smaller than standard. Their calibre was 450mm (17.7-inch), the same used on minor Regia Marina torpedo units (motor torpedo boats, Mas, etc) and sometimes even on submarines that generally had 533mm tubes by using special 'reduction cages'.

On the first light motor torpedo boats (MTS type) a different type of weapon was initially used. These were special small torpedoes built in San Bartolomeo and specifically modified by CABI of Milan: 450mm calibre, length 3.18m, charge weight 150kg, cold air-powered turbine engine, a single distance adjustment with a run of 1000 metres at a speed of about 12 knots. These 'short torpedoes', with a total weight of about 300kg, were abandoned shortly after their commissioning due to their low speed and short range; they were replaced on all light motor torpedo boats with the more valid SB and W hot air types:

SB 120/450 x 3.18

SB stands for 'San Bartolomeo' (headquarters of the Underwater Weapons Workshop in La Spezia), that is the manufacturer of the weapon;

120 indicates the weight of the charge in kg (TNT, then Tritolital);

450 represents the calibre in mm;

3.18 is the total length in metres.

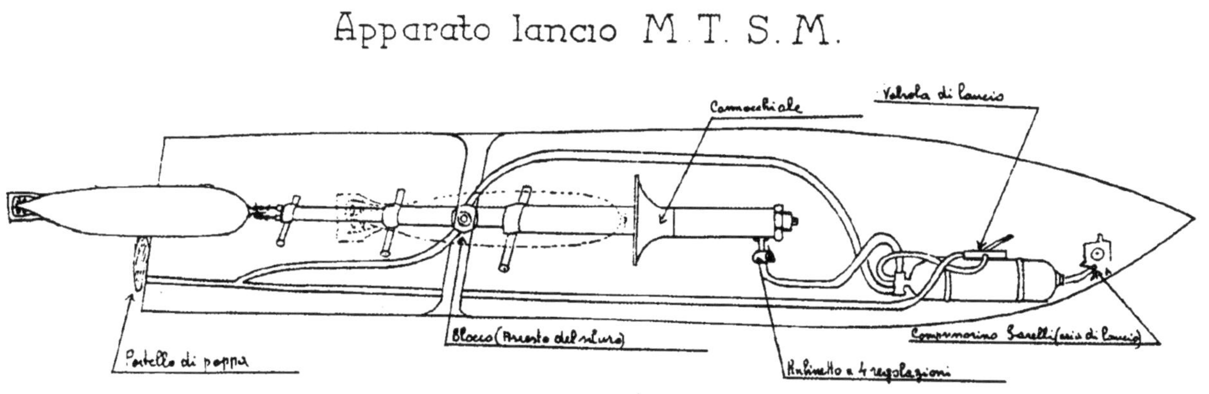

Launch system for short torpedoes aboard MTSM light motor torpedo boats

W 150/450 x 3.30 (reduced for MTSM)

W was short for 'Whitehead', used indiscriminately to indicate the Fiume factory or its (then) branch in Livorno (later 'Moto Fides').

While the design and production origins of the SB model probably date back to the end of the 1930s, the 'W' model began to be manufactured from 1941. In both cases these were standard torpedoes with shortened head and tank sections.

Warheads of 115, 150, 180 and 200kg were also planned for the SB. The average total weight was around 400kg, and speed ranged from 28 knots at maximum range (2000m) to 33 on the shortest setting (1000m). Although at the beginning the run could be adjusted, in practice it was considered fixed and only 2000 metres was used. The engine was reciprocating (4 radial cylinders at 90°, for 113hp) powered by air heated by burning oil in a closed tank with a capacity of 51 litres at a pressure of 200kg/cm^2.

The 'W' model also weighed about 400kg and had an engine of similar characteristics. Speed was 24–25 knots, and the weapon had a single setting for a run of 2000 metres.

All the warheads employed were equipped with contact pistols (called 'inertia universals') that armed automatically after a run of about 60m, when weapon depth and speed should have stabilised.

After the armistice, the republican 'X^a Mas' entrusted the making of short torpedoes for its MTSM and SMA to other companies such as, for example, RUMI with a factory on Lake Iseo which acted as chief contractor, also assembling parts produced by various small precision machining workshops in northern Italy. These weapons were mostly replicas of the SB model, still with radial engine and a fixed speed of 21 knots.

The torpedo was loaded with the head towards the bow of light motor torpedo boats, and launching was effected by pushing the weapon tail-first into the water from the stern, by means of a compressed air telescopic ejector. As soon as it entered water, the action of its propellers started the run, and so the launching craft had to turn away sharply.

Aboard MTSM and SMA the *launch system* consisted of:

- the *torpedo compartment*, with square section, located on the centreline of the hull, inclined about 15° towards the stern and closed at the rear by a circular hatch that could be opened outwards with a pneumatic control;
- a *suspension pin* (above the torpedo compartment) with a pneumatic control for locking the weapon in the rest position and unlock it at the moment of launch;
- a *telescopic push system* (commonly called the 'telescope') acting through a compressed air piston against the torpedo head to push it into water;
- a *regulating valve* ('4-way tap') to control the thrust applied to the torpedo through the 'telescope';
- a *tank* of air compressed to about 18-20kg/cm^2, placed low between the two pilot seats;
- a small *compressor* driven by a petrol engine ('Garelli' of about 30cm^3 initially, later increased in the following 'Lds' model, still by 'Garelli'). These were small air-cooled two-stroke engines of aeronautical origin (where they were used for aircraft starting, services, etc), hence their official name of 'avi-compressors'. The 'Garelli', as commonly defined in the Navy, was equipped with an oil-petrol mixture tank and was placed atop a shelf to starboard of the cockpit, first towards the bow under the dashboard, later towards the stern. The exhaust was through a short tubing ending in a 'mushroom' cover to prevent the entry of water.
- a *launch valve* with lever control and related piping for connection with the various components. The red lever was placed within the pilot's reach, on the blue coloured compressed air tank.

The launch system was complete with a remote control, consisting of a crank placed in the cockpit and a 'Teleflex' cable which moved a gear in contact with the regulator atop the torpedo. It was thus possible to adjust weapon running depth while at sea. This was normally set at 3 metres: three crank turns to the right corresponded to an extra metre; to the left, to one less.

For the execution of the launch, the light motor torpedo boats were equipped with a very simplified aiming system, consisting of a graduated semi-circular plate equipped with a mobile *index arm*, which was fixed to the hood roof in front of the pilot's position. Against stationary targets, for example inside an anchorage, aiming did not present much of a problem: attacking a moving ship was different. It was first of all necessary to estimate the direction of the target's course (*Beta* angle) and its speed. The launch angle value (or 'aim'), based on these two estimates, was obtained from a pre-calculated table related to a specific weapon speed; then it was introduced into the instrument.

Aligning the two front sights on the *index arm* with the target, through appropriate rudder action, the pilot 'aimed' the motorboat – and consequently the torpedo – ahead of the target with the same deflection as the calculated 'target angle'. He then launched the weapon, that would proceed on the same heading as followed by the boat at that moment.

The limited distance of the light motor torpedo boat's cockpit from the sea did not offer a wide and extended vision of the horizon and, especially in poor visibility and rough seas, gross errors in the estimation of target motion elements, aiming etc were inevitable, which impacted negatively on the chances of an accurate torpedo run, thus missing the target. To make up for all this, it was therefore necessary to get as close as possible to the target, so that such errors could be largely offset by its greater angular size, and the shorter weapon run. On the other hand, the reduced size of these motorboats had been specifically researched just to be able to perform sudden attacks, trusting its effectiveness to the limited chances of sighting such a small craft, especially if it was not forced to move at high speed.

There was no possibility of 'angled firings', performed by acting on the torpedo guide, as instead occurred on almost all larger torpedo units.

D) Depth charges (BTG: Bomba Torpedine da Getto)

Depth or anti-submarine charges were the only active defence system employed by light motor torpedo boats. They were dropped from the craft with the intent to damage, or at least keep deter, any chasing unit. It was certainly not a new tactic: Luigi Rizzo at Premuda on 10 June 1918, after torpedoing the battleship *Szent Istvan*, did the same with his *MAS 15*, when closely followed by an Austro-Hungarian torpedo boat.

Two of these cylindrical weapons or Depth Charges were placed on the deck of MTSM and of SMA on side saddles just aft of the pilot's canopy. The charges were secured by a steel cable bight, with an eye at the terminal top part. This was secured to a hook that could be opened by a rope after removing the 'safety pin' of the weapon.

The BTG were of two types: commonly used standard anti-submarine charges (BTG Mod 50/1927 IA and Mod 30/1941), and specially designed anti-ship charges (BAN). The 50/1927 were automatically triggered weapons with a 4-setting fuse (25, 50, 75 and 100 metres deep) and a 50kg charge of TNT. Before any mission they were set (normally to 25m depth) by torpedo specialists by rotating a bronze ferrule placed on the flat upper part of the cylindrical body. At the pre-set depth, the corresponding pressure against the 'hydrostatic plate' triggered a spring-loaded cock, whose action through the so-called 'pyrotechnical chain' caused the charge to burst.

The 30/1941 were charges for dissuasive employment with a 30kg charge that exploded at a fixed depth of 25m. Because of its limited power, however, its use was short-lived.

BAN had an explosive weight of 40kg, even though the outer casing was the same size as the 50kg types; they had a slight positive buoyancy that tended to make them float. A 10kg lead weight was attached to the trigger device that, around 20m deep, broke off due to the dissolution of the retaining pins consisting of compressed salts soluble with sea water. Thereafter the lightened charge began to rise, and about 7–8m from the surface the 'hydrostatic plate' caused its explosion. The whole cycle took place within 3–4 seconds, thus allowing the craft making the drop to move away to relative safety. Launching was recommended with engines at a minimum speed of 3000rpm: this would

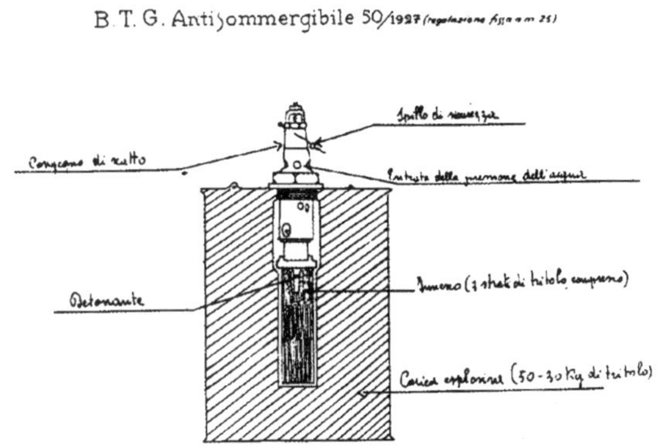

Anti-submarine depth charge

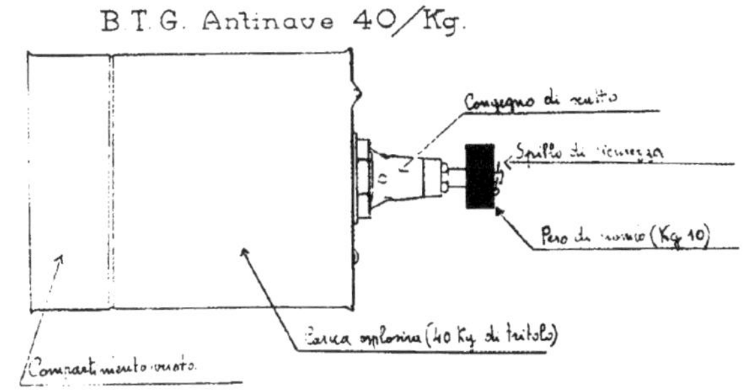

Anti-ship depth charge

correspond to a speed of 7.5 m/s (15 knots), meaning the boat would be at a distance of over 30 metres at the burst. For the latest models of SMA it was planned to adopt depth charge of this type with 70kg charges.

The so-called drifting depth charge was under development towards the end of the conflict. Loaded with 40kg of TNT, it went 8–10 metres deep and then rose up to explode 1–2m beneath the surface causing, amongst other things, an impressive foam column.

E) Passive defences and concealment

Although protected by their small size and good speed, the light motor torpedo boats made use of some simple equipment to ease concealment from enemy units that might be hunting them, or to facilitate the approach manoeuvres. The devices used for this purpose were essentially the fog 'trunk' and the smoke buoy.

Small Fog 'trunk'

On MTSM, and later on SMA this was fixed at the extreme stern, on the left. It was a welded steel sheet container (length 65cm, height about 25cm) with oval section with convex ends. A screw cap was placed on the top for filling, while near the outside edge was a cylindrical tube with the 'diffuser', consisting of five tubes arranged in a fan.

It was filled with 'chlorohydrin', a liquid compound based on chlorine, which reacted on contact with the atmosphere producing dense white vapours that, by use of the wind or appropriate manoeuvres, created artificial fog curtains that hid the craft from enemy view. This generally simple and effective system was operated from the cockpit.

Smoke buoy

Again fitted at the stern, on a cantilevered circular wooden base placed above the door for closing the torpedo bay, this spherical sheet-metal buoy (about 50cm diameter) was surmounted by a brass nozzle, and held in place by a double elastic rope ending with an eye, fixed to a moveable retaining hook. It was also loaded with chlorhydrin. In case of need, when pulling a knob on the dashboard a metal cable triggered the hook, letting the buoy fall into the wake. The buoy initially sank, but resurfaced after a few seconds, and the white smokescreen began to spread from the nozzle.

F) Compasses

The compasses installed were different models, depending on the various types of craft.

For 'Slow-Running Torpedoes' (SLC = Siluro a Lenta Corsa or 'pig')

The choice of the most reliable compass was very laborious, because the 'first man' – low in the water, and with the mask glass exposed to wave splashes – had a very limited view. Therefore, he had to rely mainly on the instruments. The final choice was a magnetic compass built by the Italian Navy Hydrographic Institute in Genoa, to a design by commander Lazzarini (20.2.1936); it was card in a metallic case, self-contained lighting with batteries and magnifying glass. Through further changes and improvements, the 'Lazzarini' was finally adopted, after giving up the idea of using a small gyro-compass, which 'San Giorgio' of Genoa-Sestri Ponente had been working on.

The 'Lazzarini' was sufficiently corrected for deviations produced by the induced magnetism of the metals constituting the craft, breathing apparatus and other equipment of a'pig', but it was very sensitive to influences from buoys, chains, anchors, nets, etc that the craft had to pass close.

Another type of compass fitted on the dashboard of some SLC models was produced by Officine Panerai of Florence.

For explosive and torpedo motorboats

After several attempts with different models, they were all fitted with a single type of magnetic compass, of aeronautical origin, probably deriving from an earlier model used on Italian aircraft ('Pezzani' type). It was Mod A, produced by OMI (Ottico Meccanica Italiana) of Rome. Its User Manual, published by Regia Aeronautica (Direz Gen le Costruzioni ed Approvvigionamenti) has the CA number 237 of 18.2.1936-XIV. On MTM it was placed in a special binnacle at the centre of the wash strake, in front of the pilot, while on light motor torpedo boats it was placed on the centreline between the two pilots, almost touching the cockpit windscreen.

It was a non-periodic, fluid-filled compass: that is, with remarkable damping of the oscillation time that normally occurs after rather large and rapid manoeuvres. Sufficiently compact (about 15cm high including the base, with a diameter of 12.5cm base excluded) and contained weight (2.7kg), its size was ideal for the limited space available aboard the craft it was intended for.

The main part of the body supported: a thick glass bowl called the 'mortar' filled with liquid, intended to float the 'magnetic equipment' (in practice two parallel prismatic magnets); and the related card, a black-painted cylindrical band, on which were highlighted the letters corresponding to the cardinal points (N-E-S-W), abbreviated Arabic figures every 30°, and dashes corresponding to further 5° subdivisions. The lower part of the support mortar was fixed, and had another (reference) card, similar to that of the magnetic equipment but with the single degrees marked.

On the outside of the support base there was a further card called 'route circle', which could be rotated using a knurled front knob. All letters, figures, notches, etc, were rendered phosphorescent with 'radiomir' paint for night-time reading. The unfreezeable suspension and damping liquid was 'cherosina', obtained through a special form of oil refining. Two small screws with knurled edges for compass compensation could be accessed through a slit in the base.

In the last part of the war the 'X^a Mas' MTM pilots were also provided with a wrist compass on a synthetic leather strap, for use after the 'launch'. Rather simple, it was of German origin, made in transparent material (plexiglas), and offered sufficient indication of direction.

Wrist compass

The SLC operators, 'Gamma' divers etc, were equipped with various models of fluid-filled wrist compasses, depending on the period.

Generally representative of other types, these are the features of the model produced by 'Panerai' of Florence. It was a portable instrument, applicable to the wrist and usable both on the ground and underwater, day and night, in total absence of external lighting. It consisted essentially of two parts:

1. The non-magnetic stainless steel base, which was watertight and fitted with a sturdy one-piece transparent plexiglas dome. The self-luminous lubberline was traced along the dome diameter. A leather bracelet was applied to the metal base, with a stainless steel buckle.
2. The magnetic equipment was immersed in a flotation and damping liquid, and consisted of a quadrant with self-illuminated indications in relief.

G) Overalls and waterproof suits

'Belloni' waterproof suit

This 'suit' – also called the 'costume' or 'waterproof coverall' – was a complementary but not insignificant accessory in the operational framework of explosive boats. However, it was also used (slightly modified and reinforced, especially at the seams) by SLC operators.

Panerai waterproof wrist compass.

It was named for its creator, Lieutenant Commander Angelo Belloni[1], and in practice, personnel referred to it as 'the Belloni' for short. It was a protective garment against the rigours of the cold during the approach navigation or, following launch, of the low water temperature, giving the pilot an effective guarantee of survival. Thanks to its sufficient reserve of buoyancy, it also ensured easy floatation. It had replaced the original kapok-filled 'life-bag', which was somewhat rudimentary and uncomfortable. Personnel did not require expert swimming skills and training: it was enough to know the most elementary expedients

1. Born in Pavia in 1882 and becoming a Sub-Lieutenant in the Royal Italian Navy Reserve in 1909, over the Great War years Angelo Belloni was interested in submarines, and was long assigned to the Muggiano Shipyards in La Spezia to monitor, on behalf of the Regia Marina, the construction, testing and preliminary training of various Italian and foreign-destined submarines. Highly imaginative and very gifted in the brilliant resolution of technical problems, he was responsible for numerous inventions, especially in the diving sector: from the rescue equipment for the crews of incapacitated submarines, to the self-contained breathing apparatus, suits for divers and assault craft operators, their main equipment etc.

Angelo Belloni had a long career as sailor and inventor, working on his projects up to well over 70 years of age. In 1957, an elderly gentleman was crossing a wide avenue in Genoa when he was run over by a tram and badly injured. Only after being transported to hospital, where he could not be saved, did it became known that he was commander Belloni, and his profound deafness – contracted as a result of his professional activities, and which had plagued him for years – was blamed for the fact that he had not noticed the arrival of the rattling vehicle. But maybe this was not the problem: it is very possible that he was absorbed in who-knows-what new projects, as he was heading to the scuba diver equipment manufacturing company of his friend and pupil Luigi Ferraro, Gold Medal of the 'Gamma'.

to keep afloat, using arms and legs. A long journey wearing it, however, was not practical.

The 'Belloni' consisted of two separate parts:

- the *inside* was a thin black rubber film, like a lining, enclosing the whole body, donned through a large tubular opening at the level of the abdomen, while at the neck it extended in cylindrical shape into a hood which, without pressing on the skin, like a rather soft scarf, prevented water infiltration. This part of the dress was called the 'fur' (from its lining), while the abdominal section took the name of 'kangaroo', by analogy with that animal's pouch.
- *outside* of the thin layer was a robust waterproof rubberised canvas coat, covering the body from neck to legs, including feet.

The various component parts (torso and extremities) were joined by sturdy stitching, with reinforcements of the same canvas glued over, to avoid water penetration as much as possible. Therefore the seams were the points of greatest rubbing that sometimes caused painful irritations in prolonged use. The naked hands came out of tight cuffs of thick black rubber like those of divers' dress. Therefore, it was good practice to abundantly soap forearms before wearing the suit.

Heavy cloth 'Belloni' drysuit for MTM pilots in a 1944 picture.

Pulling up the sleeves towards the elbows, the cuffs became quite tight even though they tended to slip again towards the wrists with the passing of time and the wearer's movements. Thus the operation had to be periodically repeated: in particular, immediately before the 'jump' by explosive boat pilots.

To don the suit, the operator put one of his legs into the 'kangaroo', then the other (like pulling on a pair of trousers); he bent forward – possibly helped by others – and the upper part was passed over his head, then putting the arms into the sleeves and bringing the head out of the 'fur'.

The broad membrane of the 'kangaroo' that hung down in front was then fixed and closed carefully. The thin rubber edges were stretched and levelled off around a thick circular wooden disc which had a groove all around. The disc ('caster' in the jargon) was pierced by three or four holes: inserting the fingers into them allowed, through a slight rotation, the alignment of the rubber edges. Fixing took place by peripherally rolling a thin line with an eye at one end, tightened with a series of knots (half-hitches). The resulting bundle was best stuck in the front panel for external cladding.

This opening was originally closed (with changes as experience was acquired) with buttons and buttonholes, then with cord eyes crossed by wooden pegs (toggle fastening like in duffel coats), and finally with metal clips with variable opening similar to those used on cloth slippers in those days. The procedure was complicated but functional, even if with that bulk between diaphragm and abdomen, the wearer remained somewhat hindered. If there was time and opportunity (instead of performing a series of energetic push ups on knees) it was good practice to dive or gradually plunge into the water to vent excess air from the 'Belloni', simply by spreading the 'fur' on the neck with two fingers.

To maintain an ideal body temperature, a thick white knitted wool suit was worn on the skin. A single outfit down to the ankles was closed on the chest by a series of buttonholes. These suits were generally referred to as 'wools' and derived from the traditional ones used by the divers.

Underneath the 'Belloni', sailors wore the regular khaki cloth (summer) uniform, with stars or – for the republican 'X^a Mas' – the gladius on the collar, besides any rank or speciality badge. Officers and petty officers, on the other hand, preferred standard blue or grey work overalls with rank insignia. It proved very easy to lacerate the outer casing during short walks so 'calzerotti' (a form of coarse hemp ankle boots) should always have been used, as no shoes were worn.

Initially, hard caps with neck cover were planned, if necessary padded with fur.

When the explosive boats were employed, especially on open seas rather than in harbour forcing operations, those who wanted to wore a handgun with belt and holster under the 'Belloni'. At the waist any leather belt was used, also helping to tighten the cumbersome suit, from which everyone hung whatever his fantasies suggested might be useful: a knife, the 'signalling discs', a flashlight or, whoever possessed one, a diver dagger.

Amongst many others, a dramatic problem was urination. Helmet divers used a thick, standard wine bottle with the bottom removed, usually capped at the mouth, which was placed in a strategic location near the groin. However, the 'emme' pilots struggled: it was completely unthinkable during a mission to wrestle with buckles, 'wheel' and 'kangaroo'; instead, they tried to direct the superfluous liquid into one of the legs. Under the foot of the other, they usually kept their identity documents.

Diving suits

In the early days, on top of the 'wools' SLC operators wore the 'Belloni suit' with some variations compared that of MTM pilots. Later, however, another model was adopted, complete with a thin rubber hood that better prevented water infiltration from the neck area due to poor watertightness of the 'fur'. They wore ballasted boots on their feet, as the particular attack procedure did not generally include long swimming stretches.

The 'N' (Swimmers) and 'Gamma' (Sappers) wore suits of thin matt black (anti-glare) rubber, allowing better freedom of movement, always over 'wools' of varying thickness, depending on the particular employment. To form a better seal, the constituent parts were not sewn, but glued with synthetic resinous glues. The suits could be with or without hood and were generally split into two parts: the upper part, which covered the trunk and arms – excluding hands – starting from the neck and long enough to cover the abdomen, overlapping the lower part that effectively served as trousers, from waist to ankle. Light boots of a slightly thicker rubber were adopted for the feet, each with three pairs of eyelets to pass the closing laces; the flippers were worn over these. Thin black rubber half-gloves were supplied for the hands: they had a membrane between fingers, designed to help the swimming action.

An SLC underwater assault craft operator in a picture taken probably in 1941.

The flashlight, knife/dagger etc were hang from the waist belt, along with ballast weights. A metal snap-hook was used to hang the flippers when they were not necessary (sections on foot, especially in shallows, or other peculiar situations).

On the head, above the possible cap was the 'small net', which had a useful camouflage function. It looked like a pile of algae, and so a surfaced operator could be easily mistaken for the kind of flotsam that is commonly seen, especially in harbour basins. The natural whiteness of face and hands was concealed by spreading a layer of black or greenish cream on the skin.

The adherence of the suit to the body, guaranteed by the natural elasticity of rubber, was not enough – especially with increasing dive depths – to prevent seawater from infiltrating inside, soaking the 'wools'. However,

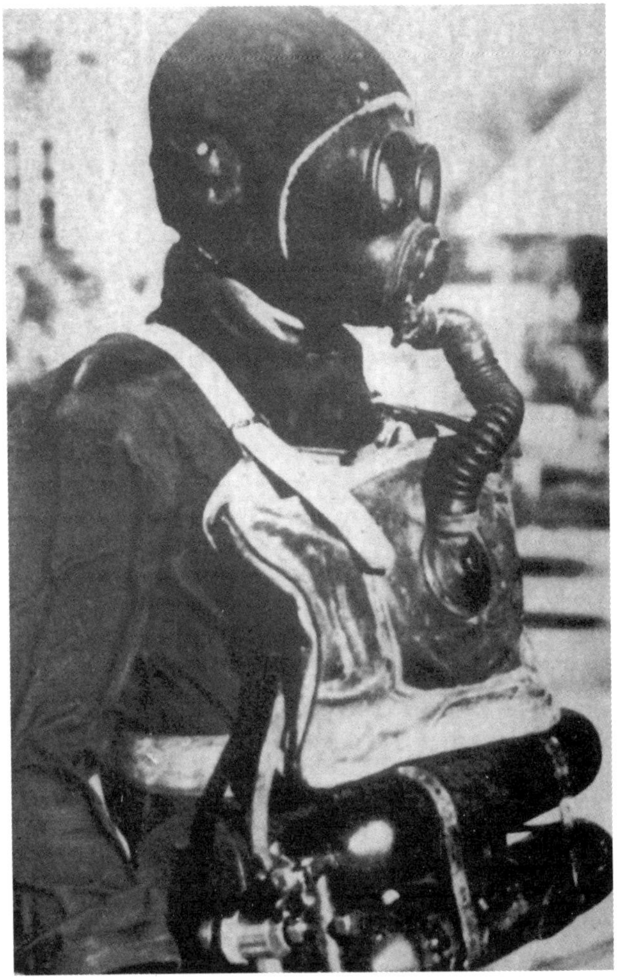

Detail of the diving suit and rebreather (ARO 49/bis long-endurance type) of an operator also wearing the original fur-lined hood.

body heat was enough to warm it without creating excessive discomfort.

This type of suit was called 'free water circulation', but there were also drysuits. In the latter, the high trousers reached almost beneath the armpits, with the excess rolled down. The same applied for the upper part that went down to the thighs, with the surplus then rolled upwards: this barrier against the leaks that formed over the abdomen was made even more watertight by overlapping a large belly fixing band.

To prevent tears, breaks or lacerations in the thin rubber sheath – especially from friction against the encrusted hulls of targetted ships – over this suit was worn a second, protective, sturdy waterproof canvas suit, derived from the standard 'Belloni'.

It should, however, be noted that the equipment supplied to 'Gamma' (wetsuits, breathing apparatus, etc) did not allow easy movement while submerged, preventing lengthy underwater swimming as is now normal for divers. In practice, they turned out too heavy or too light, so that long passages were made on the surface and those of more limited distance by 'walking' on the bottom, in heavy trim.

H) Self-contained breathing apparatus

Like all autonomous underwater rebreathers employed during the Second World War, those adopted by Italian assault craft operators and 'Gamma' divers derived from the well-known British 'Davis' made in the 1920s for personnel emergency escape operations from damaged submarines. This oxygen breathing apparatus was certainly the most widespread, but other quite similar models were developed in the 1930s, like the German 'Dräger', the US Navy 'Mommsen' etc.

These devices had a small oxygen tank equipped with valves, a rubber expansion bag called the 'lung', to which a flexible rubber pipe was connected, ending with a 'mouthpiece' that was held tight between the teeth and lips. There were neither mask nor goggles, but a single, simple spring-loaded nose clip. Their operating principle came from the combination of oxygen with soda lime, contained in a watertight capsule, that absorbed the carbon dioxide generated by breathing. The use of oxygen allowed safe dives down to about 12 metres; deeper prolonged dives produced a dangerous phenomenon called hyperoxia, that produced a kind of operator drunkenness with potentially serious consequences.

This was the state of the art when (then) Lieutenant Angelo Belloni began to actively work on 'rebreathers'. He planned to modify an apparatus for performing underwater work at shallow depths by surface-supplied divers, so they could move freely without the burden of heavy diving suits and the constraint of compressed air supply pipes, typical of traditional divers.

To make his diver movements independent and fairly free, Belloni thought of combining the 'Davis' with a special light rubber *hood* of his own invention that, working on the principle of the diving bell, would have dispensed with the nuisance of the mouthpiece. Successfully tested in Portovenere in spring 1930,[2] the 'Belloni hood', equipped with two single glasses and a 'Davis' breathing apparatus with increased range, was the equipment used in the first experiments conducted in the early 1930s by the Submarine Group of La Spezia, for the exit of divers from small, manoeuvrable

2. One exceptional 'Belloni hood' tester was his daughter Paola, aged nine!

Type 49/bis underwater closed-circuit oxygen rebreather produced by IAC, a Pirelli subsidiary. The apparatus shown here has a single tank, like those normally used by 'Gamma'.

'H' type submarines, that at that time were training to penetrate enemy harbours under water.

However, these tests had shown that none of the experimental breathing apparatus models – supplied by the very few firms specialising in this sector then operating in Italy – was perfectly suited to the purpose, and all presented several drawbacks. Therefore in January 1935 a commission was appointed (composed of Commanders Catalano Gonzaga di Cirella and Moschini, as well as Major (Medical Corps) Dorello) and tasked with studying the modifications to be made to the equipment.

Meanwhile, the first experiments with the 'Tesei self-propelled craft' gave glimpses of much more effective results than those obtainable with the so-called 'bottom walkers' with explosive charges carried on the shoulders imagined by Belloni. These were divers in 'heavy trim', appropriately ballasted and wearing diver boots, who would move stealthily along the bottom, guided by their own compasses, for a few thousand metres to reach the targets to which they had been 'approached' by the 'H' type submarines.[3]

After numerous experiences in pools and at sea, the aforementioned commission proposed replacing the hood with a soft rubber mask equipped with internal mouthpiece, closely fitting the diver's face. Many types were tested and finally, in June 1935, the commission produced a list of changes to be made to a breathing apparatus model produced by IAC (Società per l'Industria Caoutchouc) of Tivoli (Rome), a subsidiary of Pirelli. The first modified specimens were presented in November 1935 but it took about eight months of continuous trials, especially with the taps and automatic oxygen dispenser, before the device could be perfected.

Known as Model 49, thirty specimens of this breathing apparatus were ordered, and delivered to the Regia Marina presumably in the first half of 1936. Intensive training of the first SLC operators began with these devices, while continuing tests suggested further changes to improve performance. In July 1936, just as the end of the Ethiopian crisis was reducing interest in the first assault craft, the definitive long-range diver breathing apparatus model was finally approved, and designated IAC 49/bis.

It was made up of the following main parts:

1. IAC anatomical, semi-rigid rubber mask, with separate flat glasses, adjustable elastic straps with neck pad, mouthpiece and multi-way tap (bag-diver, diver-atmosphere);
2. Rectangular shaped lung bag with central socket for corrugated tube connection with the mask, and overpressure valve located on one side;
3. Rectangular, double column filter capsule with central socket and separate watertight top fill for each section, easily removable from the bag through the central front opening, given the good rubber elasticity;
4. Set of two cylinders connected to each other and arranged horizontally under the bag, at waist height, with constant flow oxygen regulator and manually-operated bypass button.
5. Fastening system with adjustable straps.

The IAC mod 49/bis was the standard apparatus of X Flottiglia Mas underwater operators well into the conflict, until replaced by rebreathers of gradually improved features and performance, more suitable for many uses and also produced by other companies (Pirelli, Salvas etc). Some versions of the 49/bis, but

3. These divers were the forerunners of those which, by happy intuition of Lieutenant Eugenio Wolk, in 1941 became assault divers and then 'Gamma'. Moving in 'light trim', swimming mainly on the surface, these towed small explosive charges, and dived only to attach them to the targets, or to conceal themselves. Similarly, to replace the role of the obsolete 'H' submarines, Belloni imagined the use of small 'CA' type assault subs, in turn 'approached' by oceanic submarines.

Operators equipped with long-endurance rebreathers (two tanks) on board former scout *Quarto* in Livorno in 1941, before a training dive. *(Courtesy of A B Duga)*

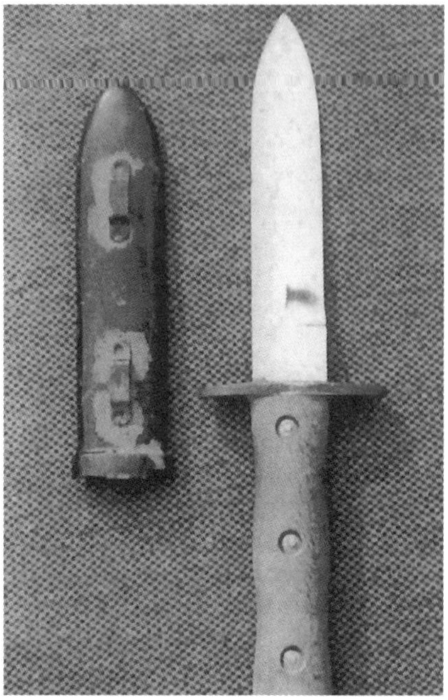

Knife-dagger and sheath. *(M Spertini collection)*

especially of the main later model (G 50), were produced with single-glass masks, with weight and endurance reduced for use as backup rebreathers aboard underwater SLC, and then SSB, self-propelled craft.

The endurance of oxygen rebreathers ranged from approximately one hour for the 'Gamma' version (one cylinder) to about four hours in the version for self-propelled craft operators (two cylinders). The use of oxygen, even with its operational limitations in terms of diving depth as already mentioned, did not require decompression stops during the ascent, and was completely stealthy, releasing no bubbles in water.

I) Diving accessories

Knife-dagger

It was a weapon with a total length of about 20cm, quite well balanced, but not buoyant. The steel blade was pointed, had a thick back and the cutting edge in the lower side with a longitudinal groove in the upper third. The handle consisted of two wooden grips held together with screws or pins. A guard, consisting of a flat cross-shaped steel sheet separated the blade from the handle. The blade, to avoid rust and corrosion caused by saltiness, was normally covered with a thick layer of grease.

A brass sheath, generally covered with matt black or deep blue paint, allowed it to be fastened to the belt, by a suspension ring and a snap-hook, or using one of the two belt loops the sheath was equipped with. Finally, using special straps connected to the two loops, it was possible to tie the sheath to the leg, generally at calf or thigh height.

Underwater flashlight ('Panerai' type with automatic pressure compensation)

A major characteristic of this flashlight was the system preventing the accidental switching on or off at any diving depth. To get this feature, the switch internal assembly was made with a special pressure balancing system. The external metallic parts in stainless steel or brass were thickly chrome plated, covered with a salt- and oil-resistant rubber casing, closed at the front by a watertight unbreakable transparent screen.

The flashlight was equipped with a button for switch control (which also allowed flashing) and a knurled knob for locking this button in the 'on' or 'off' positions. A tie secured the torch to the wrist during use, and a metal ring was used for hooking.

Depth gauge ('Panerai' type)

Portable wrist instrument whose main parts were:

1. The non-magnetic stainless steel metal base on which was fitted, with a ferrule and locking screws, the single-piece plexiglas shell which constituted the upper part of the instrument. A leather strap with stainless steel buckle was attached to the metal base.
2. The high precision pressure-sensing element, strong enough to withstand the inevitable mechanical stresses during normal conditions of use.
3. The luminous dial with depth expressed in metres.

Close-up of the SLC on display at the Venice Naval History Museum showing what is left of the original paintwork. *(G Garello)*

Instruments and controls of the SLC preserved at the Venice Naval Museum.

Net-cutter of the submarine *Sciré* raised from the wreck and displayed at the La Spezia Naval Technical Museum.

One of the watertight cylinders used for SLC transport aboard 'approacher' submarines – labelled as belonging to *Sciré* – on display in the La Spezia Naval Museum.

MTSMA light motor torpedo boat preserved in a gallery of the La Spezia Naval Museum. *(M Brescia)*

Stern of the SMA preserved at the La Spezia Naval Museum. In the foreground are the propellers and rudders of its short torpedo. *(M Brescia)*

Two cockpit close-ups of the SMA displayed in La Spezia. *(M Brescia)*

A watertight cylinder for SLC transport and a replica of the 'pig' itself on display at the Venice Naval History Museum. *(G Garello)*

A well-preserved MTM explosive motorboat on display in a gallery of the Venice Naval Museum. *(G Garello)*

Part of the bow of the 'jumping' boat *Grillo* preserved at the Venice Naval Museum *(G Garello)*

Close-up of the pilot's cockpit of the MTM explosive motorboat on display at the Museum of Science and Technology in Milan.

A dummy on display at the Venice Naval Museum wearing the SLC operators' diving suit and oxygen rebreather. *(G Garello)*

An SSB piloted torpedo on display in the main hall of the Imperial War Museum in London. This is Caproni-built device 'Delta nº 3' with double warhead. Found in Venice-S Andrea in spring 1945, it was shipped to the UK after an initial series of tests in the Venice Lagoon.

An SSB preserved at the Submarine Museum in Groton, Connecticut, USA.

Close-up of the pilot's cockpit of the SSB preserved in London. The picture was taken before the cockpit was protected with the transparent cover seen in the picture opposite, for better preservation.

Stern detail of the SLC previously taken into action by Teseo Tesei in 1940, today preserved at the Comando Subacquei e Incursori (COMSUBIN) of the Italian Navy in La Spezia. *(M Brescia)*

Explosive motorboat on display at the Sant Elmo's National War Museun in Valletta, Malta. It is painted matt black like the MT which attacked Grand Harbour in July 1941; nevertheless, it is an MTM acquired later and approximately restored. *(M Brescia)*

MTM explosive motorboat on display at the Tel Aviv War Museum. It is one of the craft acquired in Italy by the Israelis and employed during the 1948–1949 War, and possibly later. *(M Grossman)*

The 'pig' preserved in the COMSUBIN memorial at Varignano Fort in La Spezia. It is the SLC used in the Gibraltar attack of October 1940 by the Tesei-Pedretti team and then recovered by the Spaniards and tested over a long period. It was finally given back to the Italian Navy in 1974. *(M Brescia)*

An SSB preserved in the small COMSUBIN Museum in La Spezia. It is one of the first three craft of this type built in 1943; raised post-war and restored, it remained commissioned up to the late 1960s listed as *A 3*. *(M Brescia)*

Detail of the same SSB showing the trim fins in folded position. *(M Brescia)*

Close-up of the pilot's cockpit of the COMSUBIN SSB. *(M Brescia)*

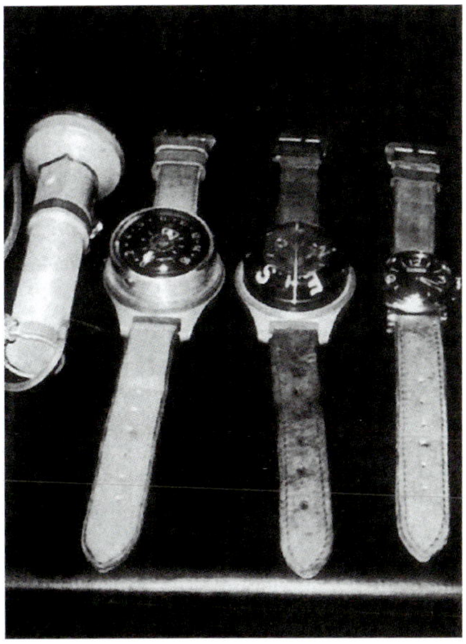

Left to right. Waterproof flashlight, depth meter, wrist compass, waterproof wristwatch.

Wristwatch ('Panerai' type)

Amongst the accessories supplied to assault vehicle operators, both surface and underwater, a tool of the utmost importance was the watch with which men regulated their action (distance, execution times, ascent times, etc). It had to be particularly strong, provide clearly legible readings, and have maximum reliability, features from which the necessary factors for a successful mission largely derived.

The stainless steel case was very strong and of considerable thickness. Almost square in shape (57 x 54mm), it gradually joined the top, where the circular dial was set. The case back consisted of a thick cover hermetically screwed with a fine thread on to a circular seal ring. The cover edge, however, was octagonal for final tightening by means of a special key.

The matt black dial showed the big 3 - 6 - 9 - 12 o'clock numbers in relief; the intermediate ones were replaced by pronounced notches. The hands were simple and clearly visible. One variant had another small dial, usually placed on the left, with a timer hand; the missing numbers were replaced by small more or less marked notches. As for the compasses, numbers, hands and notches were covered with a thick layer of 'Radiomir' paint (based on radium) for visibility at night or at depth, which gave off a yellow-greenish light. It was soon noted that 'Radiomir' emitted significant radiation, so it was replaced by 'Luminor', characterised by a lower radioactive intensity. However, phosphorescence remained unchanged and rather intense, so much so that it was often judged excessive by operators.

The crown, for mainspring winding and adjustment of the hands, was protected by a knurled friction cap that was tightly screwed to ensure absolute watertightness. Calibrated for about 200m depth it can certainly be considered amongst the most successful forerunners of those waterproof watches very widespread today, but which at the time constituted an almost absolute novelty reserved for the few.

The crown was usually on the right side, but on some examples it was on the left. Subsequently (for divers) the hermetic system of screw cap closure was modified, adopting a mobile snap lever, exerting more

Top to bottom. Radiomir and Luminor waterproof wristwatches produced by Panerai of Florence.

An SLC in action, in a famous painting by Rudolf Claudus.

pressure on the crown. The whole was enclosed in a curved profile support, to avoid awkward shapes that might get caught in some obstacle.

The movement had 15 jewels and was produced by one of the most famous Swiss manufacturers: assembly, distribution and periodic maintenance were entrusted to 'Officine Panerai' of Florence, which also employed mechanisms of other provenance in some models. The protective glass was high quality: domed, unbreakable and of remarkable transparency. The watch was accompanied by a thick grey leather strap, closed by a sturdy stainless steel buckle. If a criticism had to be made of this excellent instrument, it would only refer to the case and buckle that being unburnished could generate glare.

Initially, another type of battery-lit wristwatch had been tested (denoted CP), but it was soon abandoned for some deficiencies emerged in practical use.

L) Explosive charges for 'Gamma' assault divers

These offensive devices were used by divers as additional charges aboard SLC but, primarily, as the main weapon for 'Gamma' attack on ships.

'Bedbugs'('Cimici') - 'Limpets' ('Patelle) - 'Leeches'('Mignatte')

Small charges, usually with 4-4.5kg of high explosive enclosed in an ovoid section metal case. A simple clockwork (spring) fuse allowed setting the explosion with an adjustable interval between one and six hours.

Their names came from the system used to make them stick to the hull of the attacked ship: initially they were enclosed in a rubberised canvas wrap that, inflated by a can of compressed air with a break-off neck, assumed a cushion shape, whose positive thrust allowed some insecure positioning under the hull. Later the use of a rubber membrane proved more practical: pushing the weapon against the surface it was intended to stick to, drove out the air and produced a sufficient suction effect. For this reason, they were also called 'adhesion mines'. To make the charge adhere better to the target, the use of proper magnets was also considered; but this system did not reach the operational stage before 1945.

All the charges had almost no buoyancy, which corresponded roughly when immersed to their weight, and the assault divers carried 4 or 5 attached to the belt with rings.

The 'toolbox' of SLC (and later SSB), besides the normal range of accessories and tools, sometimes included 'bugs'. If there was time or opportunity after setting the main charge, these could be used against secondary targets.

'Incendiary bombs' of about 2kg were also conceived for use by SLC operators: they were to have been used in an attempt to ignite any bunker oil eventually spilled from ships hit with the main charges, especially if they were tankers. They were simple containers of calcium sulphide, the same substance used for torpedo exercise heads, which reacted in contact with seawater, producing a flare that should have set the oil layer on the surface of the sea on fire. In practice, bunker oil always turned out to be too thick to be ignited by this type of device.

'Small Explosive trunk' ('Bauletto esplosivo')

This was a charge consisting of a cylindrical body with almost hemispherical ends, containing a greater quantity (12kg) of an explosive ('Nepulit') more powerful than that used in 'bedbugs'. The fuse was not provided with time setting, but was activated by the movement of the target ship.

The 'small trunk' was usually fixed to one of the bilge keels with a pair of clamps or 'sergeants', with the requirement that it faced towards the bow of the target since, as soon as the ship was out at sea and reached a speed of at least 5 knots, it unlocked a small propeller on the front of the weapon, which began to turn in the flow of water caused by the ship's motion. After a pre-calculated number of revolutions, the propeller released a retaining spring which triggered the firing pin, causing the charge to explode. This yielded two important results: the probable loss of the ship in deep waters and the possibility that the sinking might be attributed to other causes (mine, submarine torpedo, etc).

At the same time, the sinking could not be directly connected to the origin of the voyage, or the ship's last port of call. After the alarms caused by the first attacks at Gibraltar, the British took the precaution of subjecting the hulls to frequent inspections, especially those of merchant ships from neutral countries. The inspections were conducted directly by divers, or with steel cables run along the hull.

As a countermeasure, 'Decima' men tried to mislead the check cables by applying a curved metal support around the 'small trunk' profile, over which the inquiring cable would have slipped without raising suspicion.

Against the divers looking for charges, a more drastic solution was adopted. In case of attempts to remove the weapon, an 'anti-tamper system' would have caused the immediate explosion.

Stern view of *MTM 98* used as training craft in Sesto Calende in 1944. Notice the individual number painted on the right corner of the transom. *(M Spertini collection)*

Finally, it was planned to place two 'small trunks' on bigger targets, on the same side, one a short distance from the other, to cause a wider breach, with a greater chance of causing the total loss of the ship.

2. ASSAULT CRAFT COLOURS AND DISTINCTIVE NUMBERS

Surface craft

At the time of the first experiments that led to the introduction of explosive motorboats, the prototype hulls were painted red – the typical colour of Italian racing speedboats – for reasons of secrecy. Later, the MT hulls were in natural mahogany wood colour, opaque and rather dark. This natural colouring was also initially adopted by the MTL.

It would seem that only after the Suda action were the MT painted in matt black, and in this colouring they participated in the attack on Malta.[1] Later it became clear that black is not always the best colour for night use, so both the explosive and light motor torpedo boats and the surface 'approachers' adopted the traditional Italian warship light ash grey colouring, with black boot topping and black or dark blue bottom.

The hull inner surfaces were natural wood colour, the metal ones in cockpits sometimes blue, while the stern drives were often painted black or dark blue like the waterline.

No evidence of the adoption of multi-colour camouflage schemes has been found, and even after the armistice colouring remained unchanged in both the North and South.

Each craft was assigned an alphanumerical 'characteristic' (equivalent of 'marking' in the naval bureaucratic jargon) composed of letters (*eg* MT, MTSM, etc) and a number in Arabic figures. The latter constituted the so-called 'service number' which was painted on the craft so also served as a visual identifier.

This numbering was generally painted on the sides at around midships, with digits no higher than a few centimetres, also repeated on the stern: on MTM on the side of the folded life-raft that remained visible from aft, and sometimes also in the upper right corner of the transom; on MTSM and SMA the number was also repeated on the upper part of the hatch closing the short torpedo compartment.[2]

The assignment of 'service numbers' followed different criteria depending on the time and unit type. The prototypes and boats of the first experimental series (MA/MAT, MT and MTS) were sequentially numbered, with one or two figures for each model (*eg MTS 1–5* etc). Subsequently, with the planned mass production of a greater quantity of craft, it was decided to assign numbering according to some general criteria that included different number series for each type of unit, and often excluding odd numbers, probably for reasons of superstition.

These series of numbers were allocated:

From 1 to 199:	MTM
from 200 to 299:	MTSM
from 300 to 399:	MTSMA
from 400 to 499:	MTL and MTSMA
from 500 to 599:	MTM and MTSMA

1. The explosive boat exhibited at the Malta War Museum is still painted in matt black. However, this craft certainly did not belong to the MT group which attacked Valletta in July 1941, but is an MTM recovered later – perhaps in Sicily – partially (and badly) restored and repainted.

2. Apart from the numbering (which in any case was not always shown on the hull), the presence of other distinctive or personal markings was rather limited. One of the few exceptions was that of the six MTM of the 'Bogani' Squadron (unofficial denomination) operating from the 'X^a^' West Base 'Mataluno' in 1944–1945. According to one of its members, Marco Spertini, these craft carried on their sides a small black spot inside which was the profile, in negative, of Benito Mussolini's head. This was applied with an airbrush and an aluminium stencil taken from a picture casually found amongst the ruins of a bombed house in San Remo.

(craft with SIAI hulls built for Germany after 8.8.1943, some of which were ceded to X^{a} Mas) from 01 to 024 or 026: MTR.

Amongst the MTM commissioned by the republican X^{a} Mas, some carried a number from the first hundred, also including odd numbers, but followed by the letter 'b' (normally lower case). It is likely that these units had reused numbers – at least for the even numbers – taking the identity of a previously destroyed boat, or used to designate new construction units (that is, not ex-Regia Marina).

After the conflict, those few MTSM and SMA which served for a few years with the Italian Navy, mainly as raider carriers, had four-figure designators, being classified – for security reasons – as 'motor barges', because the Peace Treaty originally prohibited the Italian Navy from using any type of offensive weapon.

Underwater craft

The 'Slow Running Torpedoes' were generally painted very dark grey-green or sometimes matt black overall.

The SLC were assigned a particular distinctive numbering (see table on page 141) which the author has partly reconstructed, as follows:

N° *1* and *2*: prototypes of 1935–1936;
from *3* to *11*: devices (9) of the 1st (1936) and 2nd (1939) series;
from *120* to *190*: devices (8) of series '100' (1940);
from *220* to *250*: devices (about 30) of series '200' (from 1941 to 1943).

The examination of available photos and the recollections of the operators seem to confirm that SLC generally did not sport individual numbers visible from a distance; on a few self-propelled craft the number was shown on the shield (see page 75) or in the upper part of the rear side of the 'tool bonnet' (when present) with numbers no taller than a few centimetres painted in some colour (perhaps grey) a little lighter than the background.[3]

British Chariots – craft derived from Italian 'pigs' that were used by 'Mariassalto' operators for training in Taranto and forcing Genoa harbour in April 1945 – were painted in dark green. Their identification number (which was in 'Roman' numerals) was not visible from a distance.

SLC 227 hoisted aboard the support barge at the Bocca di Serchio base in 1942. This is one of the very few pictures of a 'pig' clearly showing the craft number.

From the few existing photos of operational SSB (Siluro San Bartolomeo) they seem to be painted externally in very light blue-grey, in some cases tending to very light green.[4]

Finally, the CA, again from colour interpretation from black and white pictures and memories of their operators, were painted externally in a rather dark grey tending to blue.

3. ASSAULT CRAFT AND RELATED MEMORABILIA PRESERVED IN ITALIAN AND FOREIGN MUSEUMS AND SITES

In Italy there has not always been much care taken to preserve historical military material (ships, aircraft,

3. The large numbers or letters, often in light colours, shown in many Italian or foreign movies are pure fantasy, probably intended to allow the audience to identify the 'pigs' of different protagonists in underwater or night scenes, or simply for visual impact. Equally imaginary are the large 'letters' (like *Z*, for example) on the breakwaters of some SLC or replicas preserved in some museums.

4. From pictures taken after the end of the war showing devices belonging to the series built by Caproni for the republican X^{a} Mas.

armoured vehicles, etc). However, assault craft and related memorabilia are on display in a number of naval museums, and also in some important Navy command locations. Not every type of surface and underwater assault craft built has been preserved and, unfortunately, some of those that have been are in a less than ideal state, whereas others appear well restored.

The reasons why assault craft are fairly well represented amongst museum relics are related both to the fame of their actions and the consequent public interest, and to their limited size, allowing a relatively easy display in the always insufficient space allowed to museums. There are also some replicas, especially of the famous SLC type, in Italian Navy facilities: not all, however, meet the highest standards.

Some Italian assault craft are also present in foreign museums, such as the Imperial War Museum in London; the Royal Navy Submarine Museum in Gosport, also in Great Britain; the Groton Submarine Museum, in the United States, the War Museum of Malta and the War Museum in Tel Aviv, Israel.

In particular, the following types of surface and underwater craft are preserved in:

MTM = La Spezia, Venice, Milan, Trieste, Malta and Tel Aviv;
MTSMA = La Spezia;
SLC = La Spezia (two originals), Venice (an original and a replica), Milan (an original), Rome and Taranto (both replicas). Not all the original craft are completely restored; as for replicas, only a few are acceptable quality; others are less accurate, especially in the details;
SSB = London and Gosport (Great Britain); Groton (USA) and La Spezia (Comando Subacquei e Incursori: Comsubin).

On the other hand, there are no original examples or replicas of: CA assault submarines; MT, MTR and MTRM type explosive motorboats; MTS and MTSM light motor torpedo boats; MTL and similar transport motorboats.

Museo Tecnico Navale, La Spezia
- MTM type explosive motorboat;
- MTSMA type light motor torpedo boat: an 'SMA with Baglietto-built hull, probably of the republican X^a Mas, that remained commissioned even after the war with the Italian Navy, classified as a 'motor barge' (*MB 1029*).
- Slow-running torpedo (SLC);
- Self-propelled torpedo type 'Mignatta' (*S 1* unit);
- Parts of the hull of 'jumping' boat *Grillo*;
- Various types of breathing apparatus;
- Diving suits and clothing for SLC operators;
- Diving accessories for 'Gamma' divers and SLC operators (net shears, compasses, etc);
- Significant parts of the hull of submarine *Sciré* (including one of the watertight cylinders for assault craft transport;
- Parts of the hull of tanker *Olterra*; steering wheel, magnetic compass with its binnacle, bell and a lifebuoy;
- Models of the *Mignatta*, thc *Sciré* and *Olterra* (with details of the secret arrangements for the SLC), etc.

Museo Storico Navale, Venice
- MTM type explosive motorboat: a craft transferred by the Navy to the Air Force around 1950 and used for some years as an air-sea rescue motorboat for the Venice-Lido airport. Finally laid up, it remained abandoned until it was recovered and restored by the Museum;
- Slow-running torpedoes (SLC): an original in good condition, and a replica with one of the watertight cylinders for its transport aboard 'approacher' submarines;
- Fragments of the hull of 'jumping' boat *Grillo*;
- Parts of the hull of submarine *Scirè*;
- Suits and self-contained breathing apparatus for assault operators.

Museo della Scienza e della Tecnologia 'Leonardo da Vinci', Milan
- MTM type explosive boat: an original in good preserved condition;
- Slow-running torpedo (SLC): an original in good condition;
- Fragments of the hull of 'jumping' boat *Grillo*.

Museo navale del Ponente Ligure, Imperia
- Wool overalls for 'Belloni suit';
- Combat clothing for republican X^a Mas surface craft operators;
- Diving suit for 'Gamma' divers with camouflage net;
- Diving suit for SLC operators;
- Diving accessories for 'Gamma' (fins, masks, ballast belts, etc);
- Various types of breathing apparatus;
- Clamps for fitting SLC heads and 'small explosive trunks' to the targets;

- Small parts of the hull of submarine *Sciré* (a ladder, a hatch, etc).

'De Henriquez' Museum, Trieste

Hull of an MTM: with no engine etc and in very poor general conditions after so many years outdoors. This is unit *548* of MTM-D type of 1944 of Baglietto-CABI construction, commissioned by the Germans and captured intact in Trieste in May 1945 by a New Zealand unit that renamed it *Vino* (*Wine*) and used it briefly for sport racing together with some other similar boats later abandoned.

Imperial War Museum, London

- Siluro San Bartolomeo (SSB): device found in Venice-S Andrea at the end of the conflict carrying the identification plate: 'DELTA n ° 3. Tested in Milan (Caproni) on 20.2.1945'. In good state of preservation.

Royal Navy Submarine Museum, HMS *Dolphin*, Gosport, Portsmouth, Hampshire

- Siluro San Bartolomeo (SSB): recovered at the end of the conflict in Venice-S Andrea and recently restored.

Submarine Museum, Groton (Connecticut), USA

- Siluro San Bartolomeo (SSB), originating from The Mariner's Museum, Newport News (Virginia): part of a group of craft that included two SSB and one SLC, transferred to the United States in the late summer of 1945 to carry out evaluation tests in which Italian operators also took part.

Traces of the other SSB and the SLC have been lost.

Saint Elmo's National War Museum, La Valletta (Malta)

- MTM type explosive boat: a craft probably found damaged in Sicily by the Allies in summer 1943. Approximately restored and painted matt black to represent the MT which carried out the action against Malta in July 1941; the stern drive is missing, and the rebuilding of original missing areas (part of the deck and centre stern area) is only approximate.

Tel Aviv War Museum (Israel)

- MTM type explosive boat: craft in excellent state of preservation, belonging to the half dozen units purchased in Italy in 1948, which took part in the Israeli Independence War of 1948–1949, and possibly also in 1956 operations.

Comando Raggruppamento Subacquei e Incursori (COMSUBIN) 'Teseo Tesei', Forte del Varignano, Le Grazie, Portovenere, La Spezia

- Slow-running torpedo (SLC, *Siluro a Lenta Corsa*, or 'pig'): craft belonging to one of the first series built and employed by its inventor, Teseo Tesei, at Gibraltar in October 1940 (Operation BG 2). Abandoned while in motion and pointed towards deep water, it grounded near the town of La Linea after the failure of the self-destruction system; recovered by the Spaniards, it was used for a long time for tests and experiments, and only returned to the Italian Navy in 1974;
- Siluro San Bartolomeo (SSB), designated type 'A': very probably one of the first three units built in La Spezia in 1943; employed for some years in the post-war era, first in Bacoli (Naples), then in La Spezia; served as a model for the development of some subsequent Italian underwater assault craft;
- Engine of an MTM type explosive boat;
- memorabilia of Gold Medal Luigi Ferraro: compass, watch, nose clip;
- memorabilia of submarine *Sciré*: standard magnetic compass and part of a periscope;
- 'Gamma' equipment recovered from the *Sciré* wreck: a rebreather, flippers, diving suit ,etc.

Altare della Patria, Rome

- Slow-running torpedo (SLC): a replica displayed in the 'Shrine of Flags' next to Luigi Rizzo's *MAS 15* which sank the battleship *Szent Istvan* on 10 June 1918.

Comando Flottiglia Sommergibili (COMFLOTSOM) – Scuola sommergibili, Taranto

- Parts of the hull of submarine *Sciré* (a propeller, terminal of a periscope, radio direction finder antenna, etc) recovered in the waters off Haifa.

BIBLIOGRAPHY

Books

Joseph Attard, *The Battle of Malta,* Hamlyn Paperback, Feltham, 1974.

Erminio Bagnasco, *I sommergibili della seconda guerra mondiale,* Ermanno Albertelli Editore, Parma,1972; English edition, Naval Institute Press Annapolis, MD, 1977; Seaforth Publishing, Barnsley, 2018.

——————, *In guerra sul mare. Navi e marinai italiani nella seconda guerra mondiale,* Albertelli, Parma 2005 and *STORIA militare - DOSSIER* N°s 1–4, 2012.

——————, *Le armi delle navi italiane della seconda guerra mondiale,* Albertelli, Parma, 1978.

——————, *Aldo Fraccaroli fotografo navale, 1933–1993: sessant'anni di storia della Marina italiana attraverso le immagini,* Albertelli, Parma, 1996.

Erminio Bagnasco & Marco Spertini, *I mezzi d'assalto della X^a^ Flottiglia Mas 1940–1945,* Albertelli, Parma, 1991.

Caius Bekker, *Les Hommes-Grénouilles,* Presses de la Cité, Paris, 1955.

Angelo Belloni (edited by A Rastelli), *Cinquant'anni in mare,* Mursia, Milan, 2008.

Michael Bertrand, *Commandos de la mer, Sous-marins de poche, Torpille humaines, Hommes-grénouilles* (1940–45), Editions Maritimes et d'Outre-Mer, Paris,1985.

Gianni Bianchi, *Bocca di Serchio. Album fotografico,* Massa Carrara, Sarasota, 2011.

Gino Birindelli, *Vita di marinaio,* Vito Bianco Editore, Rome, 1991.

Junio Valerio Borghese, *Decima Flottiglia MAS. Dalle origini all'armistizio,* Garzanti Editore, Milan in various editions since 1950; *AES-STORIA militare,* Palma, 2005, and later editions.

Armando Boscolo, *Il comandante Salvatore Todaro,* Giovanni Volpe Editore, Rome, 1970.

Gerhard Bracke, *Die einzel-Kämpfer der Kriegsmarine,* Motorbuch Verlag, Hanover, 1981.

Ettore Bravetta, *Sottomarini, sommergibili* e *torpedini,* F.lli Treves Editori, Milan, 1920.

Arnaldo Cappellini, *Torpedini umane contro la flotta inglese,* Edizioni Europa, Milan, 1947.

Joseph Caruana, *The Battle of Grand Harbour, July 26,1941,* Bieb Publications, Malta, 2004.

Richard Compton-Hall, *Submarine Warfare – Monsters and Midgets,* Blandford Press, Poole, 1985.

Graeme Cook, *Small Boat Raiders,* Hart-Davis McGibbon Ltd, London, 1977.

Giorgio D'Ilario, *100 anni di esperienza della Fratelli Gianazza,* Fratelli Gianazza, Legnano, 1992.

Harold Fock, *Marine: Klein-Kampf-Mittel,* J F Lehmanns Verlag, Munich, 1968.

Giorgio Giorgerini, *Attacco dal mare,* Mondadori, Milan, 2007.

A Cecil Hampshire, *The Secret Navies,* Part Three, Sphere Books Ltd, London, 1980.

Robert W Hobson, *Chariots of War,* Ulric Publishing, Church Stretton, 2004.

Michael Jung, *Sabotage unter Wasser. Die deutschen Kampfschwimmer im Zweiten Weltkrieg,* E S Mittler, Hamburg, 2004.

Paul J Kemp, *Midget Submarines of the Second World War,* Arms & Armour Press, London, 1990 and Caxton Editions, 2003.

——————, *Underwater Warrior,* Arms & Armour Press, London, 1996.

Lino Mancini, *Malta 2, 25/26 luglio 1941,* Edit. Lupo, Vicchio (Florence), 2011.

Sergio Nesi, *Decima Flottiglia nostra ... I mezzi d'assalto della Marina italiana al sud e al nord dopo l'armistizio,* Mursia, Milan, 2nd ed 1987; reprinted Scarabeo, Bologna, 2008.

——————, *Sciré. Storia di un sommergibile e degli uomini che lo resero famoso,* Scarabeo, Bologna, 2006.

Beppe Pegolotti, *Uomini contro navi,* Vallecchi Editore, Florence, 1967.

Giorgio Pisanò *et al, Storia delle Forze Armate della R.S.I.,* Edizioni F.P.E., Milan, 1967.

Bruna Pompei, *Eugenio Wolk 'Lupo',* Ritter, Milan, 2008.

Achille Rastelli, *Caproni e il mare,* Giorgio Apostolo Editore, Milan, 2007.

Raffaele Rossetti, *Contro la Viribus Unitis,* Libreria Politica Moderna, Rome, 1925.

Virgilio Spigai, *Cento uomini contro due flotte,* Società Editrice Tirrena, Livorno,1959.

T J Waldron & J Gleeson, *Uomini-rana*, Baldini & Castoldi, Milan, no date.

Marina Militare Historical Office

Series *La Marina italiana nella seconda guerra mondiale*:

Vol XII, Filippo Lupinacci, *Attività della Marina in Mar Nero* e *sul Lago Ladoga*, Rome, 1967;

Vol XIV, Carlo De Risio, *I mezzi d'assalto*, Rome, 1964.

Vol XXI, Giuseppe Fioravanzo, *L'organizzazione della Marina durante il conflitto - Tomo II*, Rome, 1975.

Series *Le navi d'Italia*:

Various authors, *Sommergibili e mezzi d'assalto subacquei italiani*, Rome, 2010.

Erminio Bagnasco, *I MAS* e *le motosiluranti italiane*, Parte V: *I mezzi d'assalto di superficie*, Rome, 2nd ed, 1967.

————————, *I MAS e i mezzi d'assalto di superficie italiani*, Rome, 1995.

Documents and Articles

Appunti dell'ammiraglio Ernesto Forza, già comandante della X Flottiglia Mas nel 1941–1943 e di Mariassalto dal 1943 al 1945 [From the notes of Admiral Ernesto Forza ..., by courtesy of Antonio Fulvi, now in the author's archive].

Office of Strategic Services, *The 'Mezzi d'assalto' Group, I. Navy, San Vito Bay-Taranto*, report 1944–1945, downloaded from the Internet.

Operazione 'G.A. 3', report, internal edition for military use, by Istituto Idrografico MMI, Genoa, 1985.

MTM 'Barchino', brochure (included with a 1/35 plastic kit) published by Italeri SpaA, Calderara di Reno, Bologna, 2007.

Erminio Bagnasco, 'I sommergibili 'tascabili' tipo C.A', in *Rivista Marittima*, September 1962.

————————, 'Mariassalto (1943-1945)', in *STORIA militare* nº 20, May 1995.

————————, 'Canoe contro navi a Lero', in *STORIA militare* nº 107, August 2002.

————————, 'Gli inglesi sapevano ...', in *STORIA militare* nº 120, September 2003.

————————, 'Testimonianze: il miraggio di Alessandria', in *STORIA militare* nº 141, June 2005.

————————, 'Documenti: mezzi d'assalto a Taormina', in *STORIA militare* nº 233, February 2012.

Erminio Bagnasco & Achille Rastelli, 'The 'sinking' of Italian aircraft-carrier *Aquila*. A controversial question', in *Warship International* nº 1/1990.

————————, 'L''affondamento' della portaerei *Aquila* a Genova nel 1945', in *Bollettino d'archivio dell'Ufficio Storico della Marina Militare*, June 1992.

Stefano Bagnasco, 'Nel solco della Decima', in *STORIA militare* nº 340-341, January-February 2022.

Luigi Carretta & Giorgio Martini, 'L' 'M.T. GAMMA', in *STORIA militare* nº 140, May 2005.

Joseph Caruana, 'Malta 26 luglio 1941. Una nuova ipotesi sulla morte di Teseo Tesei', in *STORIA militare* nº 6, March 1994.

Enrico Cernuschi, 'I sommergibili forzatori di porti', in *STORIA militare*, nº 42, March 1997.

————————, 'Nascita di una Marina', in *STORIA militare* nº 148, January 2006.

————————, 'Il Regio Sottomarino *Sandokan*', in *Rivista Marittima*, August-September 2002.

Cristina Freghieri, 'Eugenio Wolk e il recupero del *Bombarda*', in *STORIA militare* nº 124, January 2004.

Marco Gemignani, 'L'operazione G.A.', in *STORIA militare* nº 113, February 2003.

Mark Grossman, 'The Allied Assault on *Aquila*, Operation Toast', in *Warship International* nº 2/1990.

Sergio Nesi, ' "Chiaro di luna" ad Anzio', in *STORIA militare* nº 142, July 2005.

Giorgio Pitacco, 'La X Mas ad Alegesiras e i mezzi R', in *STORIA militare* nº 31, April 1996.

Achille Rastelli, 'Il sogno impossibile. Ipotesi di rinascita della Marina RSI', in *STORIA militare* nº 113–115, February–April 2003.

Decio Romano, 'L'ultimo assalto della Xa Flottiglia Mas', in *STORIA militare* nº 8, May 1994.

Antonio Scialdone, 'L'incursione ieri, oggi e domani', in *RID*, November 1983.

Alberto Santoni, L'intelligence e la 'Decima' in *STORIA militare* nº 120, September 2003.

————————, ' "Chariots" a Palermo', in *STORIA militare* nº 106, July 2002.

Tiberio F Moro, 'Crabb e i subacquei della Marina italiana', in *Diana-Armi*, 1986.

Marco Spertini, 'La distruzione del "Mercato dei Fiori" a San Remo del 20.10.1944', in *RID* nº 3/1990.

INDEX

Page numbers in *italics* refer to illustrations. All ships are Italian unless otherwise specified.